AF695076

Emotions and Values in Equity Crowdfunding Investment Choices 2

Emotions and Values in Equity Crowdfunding Investment Choices 2

Modeling and Empirical Study

Christian Goglin

ISTE

WILEY

First published 2021 in Great Britain and the United States by ISTE Ltd and John Wiley & Sons, Inc.

Apart from any fair dealing for the purposes of research or private study, or criticism or review, as permitted under the Copyright, Designs and Patents Act 1988, this publication may only be reproduced, stored or transmitted, in any form or by any means, with the prior permission in writing of the publishers, or in the case of reprographic reproduction in accordance with the terms and licenses issued by the CLA. Enquiries concerning reproduction outside these terms should be sent to the publishers at the undermentioned address:

ISTE Ltd
27-37 St George's Road
London SW19 4EU
UK

www.iste.co.uk

John Wiley & Sons, Inc.
111 River Street
Hoboken, NJ 07030
USA

www.wiley.com

© ISTE Ltd 2021
The rights of Christian Goglin to be identified as the author of this work have been asserted by him in accordance with the Copyright, Designs and Patents Act 1988.

Library of Congress Control Number: 2020943265

British Library Cataloguing-in-Publication Data
A CIP record for this book is available from the British Library
ISBN 978-1-78630-634-0

FSC
www.fsc.org
MIX
Paper from
responsible sources
FSC® C013604

Contents

Introduction

The first volume of this work[1] made it possible to discover a recent industry: equity crowdfunding. After having justified our interest in the investors' decision and more precisely in the understanding and explanation of their choice of projects, we began a literature review in the field of entrepreneurial finance. The latter revealed a rational investor seeking to reduce information asymmetry by identifying the quality signals of analyzed projects. This cognitive approach seemed insufficient to us to explain the empirical data in our possession – data collected on a platform and constituting a corpus of testimonies from investors justifying their choice of project. It was indeed evident that other affective factors were of significant importance. Consequently, we have extended our state of the art to other disciplines of social science, in particular to marketing and HRM, but also psychology by focusing on theories that appeal to the affect for the understanding of analogous situations. In so doing, we have developed an original theoretical framework for interpreting the phenomenon studied, allowing us to confront reality.

The purpose of this second volume is in fact to continue this effort of conceptualization and modeling by making interdependent hypotheses that constitute an integrated model. We also introduce an original theory called "affective matching", explaining the choice of investors by the attraction of analyzed projects, what with the strength of this attraction being proportional to the coherence of the project's characteristics with the affective and axiological profile of the investor. Data, collected via a laboratory experiment, allowed us to go beyond the hypothesis stage and largely confirms the two proposed models. Finally, this second volume concludes with research perspectives and the managerial implications induced by this work.

---

1 Goglin, C. (2020). *Emotions and Values in Equity Crowdfunding Investment Choices 1*. ISTE Ltd, London, and John Wiley & Sons, New York.

1

Modeling: The Explanatory Model and the Individual Predictive Model

This first chapter begins by making preliminary assumptions (section 1.1) of the modeling, first, of an explanatory model (section 1.2) and second, of an individual predictive model that derives from it (section 1.3).

1.1. Preliminary assumptions

In this section, three assumptions are made: the first relating to the nature of uncertainty, the second to the nature of consequences and the last to the nature of investor rationality.

1.1.1. *Nature of uncertainty*

The central question of our problem concerns the determinants of the choice of projects by individual investors. However, a choice between several alternatives is a decision; therefore, this research is indeed centered on a "decision". The consequences of this decision are not deterministic; they are uncertain and depend on hazards. The question that arises from this observation is that of the nature of the uncertainty at stake, a question analogous to that posed by the theory of individual decision that, according to Kast (2002), aims to "propose a framework for studying rational behavior in the face of uncertainty by distinguishing different types of uncertainties".

Uncertainty taken in the common sense that concerns us, "the unforeseeable nature of the result of an action"[1], is specified by scientific literature, in particular,

---

Abbreviations within figures, tables and equations remain in the original French.

1 Source: http://www.cnrtl.fr/definition/incertitude.

by the oft-repeated distinction, made by Knight (1921), between risk and uncertainty. For the economist, risk characterizes decisions for which the consequences are probabilizable, either by *a priori* calculation or on the basis of statistics. Conversely, uncertainty characterizes decisions that are not probabilizable, due to the uniqueness of the situation.

According to Le Heron (2012), uncertainty is not probabilizable in the social sciences, because human decisions do not come under the law of large numbers. Moreover, the decisions taken change the state of the world so that their repetition is not possible.

In the social sciences, in the field of entrepreneurial finance, in the venture capital sphere, the question of selecting projects financed by the venture capitalist (screening) is not far from our problem. Differences are due, on the one hand, to the sophistication of the venture capitalist – a true financing professional – and, on the other hand, to the stage of development, after the start-up, of the company awaiting funds.

However, Dubocage (2006) noted the extent of the uncertainty that venture capitalists face. The latter can base neither their evaluation nor their selection on objective probabilities. In fact, the business plan offers a limited quantified vision of the future to understand it and analog methods run up against the singularity of the evaluated companies, which are generally carriers of disruptive innovation. The author also decided to use the uncertainty framework proposed by Knight in order to theoretically clarify the mode of judgment of venture capitalists.

This approach corresponds to that of Keynes (1936) according to whom decisions relating to distant future horizons cannot, in most cases, be based on mathematical calculations, due to the lack of data, which can be scarce or even non-existent. Decision-makers then make the choice they can: "[…] choosing between the alternatives as best we are able, calculating where we can, but often falling back for our motive on whim or sentiment or chance".

For these reasons, Keynes developed the concept of state of trust, that is to say, a subjective evaluation of the probability of occurrence of a future event that constitutes, according to him, a more realistic basis of appreciation than that of mathematical calculation to describe the method of determining the actions of entrepreneurs.

We can compare Keynes's concept of state of trust with the successive works of Ramsey, De Finetti and Savage, all three of whom were critics of frequentist probability and who developed the concept of subjective probability. These represent a judgment on the trust placed in the realization of an uncertain future event (Kast 2002).

We choose to place ourselves in the uncertain; there are indeed no objective probabilities associated with the consequences of investment choices. However, subjective probabilities could be associated with them. But what consequences are we talking about? The next point clarifies our view on this subject.

1.1.2. *Consequentialism*

It is important to clarify that in our approach, *decision-making investors are not exclusively or even necessarily consequentialist, that is to say that while the consequences can be taken into account in their choice, it can also rest on the intrinsic value granted to the actions (investments, in our case) themselves, independent of their consequences*, which amounts to saying that the rationality of investors is located between two areas of rationality: instrumental rationality and axiological rationality. As for the consequences to be considered, we consider that they are multifold because they depend on the objectives of the individual. Box 1.1 sheds light on the nature of these consequences.

First, in accordance with the recommendation of Kast (2002), it is essential to form hypotheses about the objectives that the decision-maker wishes to achieve:

> Economic theory is built on the description of the behavior of agents (consumers, producers); management models must make hypotheses about the representation of the objectives to be achieved.

In the description of the issue in the first chapter of Volume 1, we indicated that the first-order choice was determined by investors' objectives, which are themselves associated with the investors' motivations, whether financial and/or not financial and also that we make hypotheses of financial and/or non-financial objectives quite naturally.

Second, it seems natural to us to assess the consequences of decisions in the light of these objectives. As for uncertainty, it relates to future events that determine the consequences of decisions.

For the sake of clarity, let us illustrate this point. Let us consider an equity crowdfunding investor who is firstly motivated by an altruistic impulse and secondarily by an enrichment motivation. Above all, they want to help a cause that is important to them and ideally hopes to get a financial benefit without it being their primary investment motive.

We have:

Motivation 1 = altruism

Motivation 2 = enrichment

To these two motivations, we associate two objectives, respectively:

Objective 1 = defend a cause via the funded project

Objective 2 = improve the profitability of their portfolio of financial assets

The pair of objectives (Objectives 1 and 2) has already determined the choice of investment in equity crowdfunding rather than in any other asset class (first-order choice).

After choosing one project rather than another on a platform (second-order choice), the investor will assess the consequences of their choice with regard to the objectives (Objectives 1 and 2). In other words, the evaluation of the choice relates to *the consequences that matter to the investor*; it consists of answering the following questions:

– will the financed company allow for *progress for the supported cause*?

– will the profitability obtained be satisfactory?

Thus, there are a multitude of possible combinations of objectives, and therefore of consequences, for each investor, the latter being moved by specific motivations.

Box 1.1. *Consequences that matter*

1.1.3. *Rationality of the equity crowdfunding investor: a triptych of rationality*

According to Buttard and Gadreau (2008), in the standard paradigm:

> Instrumental rationality characterizes agents guided in their choices by the selfish search for personal utility. It makes reason a tool for selecting actions that generate utility, the individual a determined, normalized, and selfish being, and the organization (firm, market, or a hybrid) an entity that can be reduced to the agents that make it up.

Thus, the agent endowed with an instrumental rationality maximizes its utility. While this behavioral postulate is simplified to an extreme, it has the advantage of making it possible to model decisions. Our approach deviates from this paradigm, but we keep the idea of an agent in search of an optimum. However, as we will define below, the (local) optimum of our individual predictive model does not relate to selfish utility and is not necessarily determined by reason.

Furthermore, we can contrast economic science and its model of the *homo economicus*, giving a single teleological explanation of behavior, with other social sciences, such as psychology or sociology, which are interested in the multiple causes of behavior (Viviani 1994). Our approach is intermediate, as with economists; the individual has motivations oriented toward objectives or goals, but these are not the only factors explaining their investment choices. The preferences of the individual, as well as the unique situational context of the choice, also determine the formation of antecedent psychological variables of the choice. In other words, the teleological explanation is part of a more general explanation integrating other causes.

Besides this, the theory of rational choice that defines an instrumental rationality oriented toward a goal of maximizing a selfish utility seems to us too restrictive to explain, by itself, the behavior of equity crowdfunding investors. The rationality of the latter seems more complex and requires the integration of other dimensions, all of which make up a more general rationality.

Specifically, Allais (1953) gave a general definition of rationality: "[...] a person is deemed rational when (a) he pursues ends consistent with themselves, (b) he uses means appropriate to the ends pursued". This definition can be supplemented by the postulate of rationality of methodological individualism of Boudon (2004), according to which individuals adopt behaviors because they have strong reasons to do so, with these reasons not necessarily being linked to individuals' interests or a cost–benefit calculation.

If we adhere to these definitions, it seems useful to specify our thinking. To do this, we borrow from Weber, whose book aimed to broaden the scope of classical economics to understand the springs of human behavior (Cuin 2001).

In his book published in 1921, Weber (2003) defined rational actions as those for which an individual deliberately mobilizes means to achieve an end. These rational actions can be in relation to the goals. The actions are rational in the end; this is the instrumental form of rationality (it is also the ethics of responsibility). Actions can also be so in relation to values; when the means are chosen according to their intrinsic value, it is the axiological form of rationality (this time, it is the ethics of conviction).

Boudon (1999) recalled that axiological rationality is indeed a form of rationality complementary to instrumental rationality; individuals do not simply conform to inexplicable values but adhere to one of prescriptive or normative beliefs because they have strong reasons for believing in them. Yet these reasons may or may not be of an instrumental nature. In this case, the ends are based on a system of representations and beliefs. Let us note that Boudon associates axiological rationality and emotions, in particular, in the example already mentioned, of the employee enjoying a minor advantage (office placed closer to the window) within an egalitarian society (a kibbutz), their colleagues' reaction is then determined by a violation of the principle of equality; in other words, the reason being axiological more than instrumental:

> Feelings of justice or injustice well deserve the name "feelings" because they have an essential affective dimension: nothing is more difficult to endure than injustice. But they are at the same time founded on systems of reasons. And the "affective" reaction is all the stronger when the reasons appear more sound to the social subject.

As Cuin (2001) pointed out, instrumental rationality and axiological rationality are ideal, as real individuals act, more or less, according to the goals they set for themselves but also to the values they carry.

These two complementary forms of rationality are, however, not sufficient to explain all the actions of individuals because, as Boudon (1999) stated, the causes of the latter are not always attributable to the meaning given to them by their author. Thus, Weber added the "affectual"[2] or affective actions, that is to say, those carried out under the effect of strong emotions or feelings.

However, unlike Weber, for whom "affectual" actions are not rational, we choose to speak of "affective rationality". While at first glance these two words seem to give rise to an oxymoron, we believe that the developments presented above in the psychology of emotions, as in neuroscience, justify this choice.

Of course, affective reactions are not intentional and do not result from conscious deliberation, as is the case with rational actions. Nevertheless, theories of cognitive assessment, as their name suggests, are based on the idea that subjective emotion is the product of cognition. Moreover, as we have already mentioned, Sander and Scherer (2014) considered that it was reasonable to consider the emotional system as a cognitive system in its own right if we accept that multilevel processing, including non-conscious automatic processes, qualified as cognitive.

In addition, theories of cognitive assessment make goals the main assessment variable, considering an emotion as being triggered only on condition that the event affects one of the goals of the individual. In the Lazarus (2001) model, the so-called

2 As well as the traditional actions, routine and conducted in accordance with a custom or a tradition, we do not develop this modality of action, which does not seem relevant to us to account for the behavior of investors in equity crowdfunding.

"evaluation of the implications" criterion assesses the consequences of the generating event on the subject's goals.

This means, on the one hand, that the system of generation of affective reactions is consequentialist, and, on the other hand, that the bond with axiological rationality is close if one considers values as desirable goals, as Schwartz does. This link, which we have already mentioned with Boudon's (1999) example of the favored employee of a kibbutz, is consistent with the first characteristic of Schwartz's (2006) values, who described values as beliefs closely associated with affects.

However, not only does the affective reaction depend on the consequences of the event on the individual's goals, but, in addition, its role is to prepare the action for the realization of the individual's interests, as explained by the theory "of realization of interests" of Frijda (1988, 2006) that we use. This time, it seems clear to us that with this theoretical framework, the affective reaction is the unconscious instrument of the individual's ends, which makes it a form of instrumental rationality.

In addition, if we consider that the work on somatic markers by Damasio (2006) gives a neuroscientific basis for the idea that emotion is part of rationality by being necessary for it, then it seems reasonable, to us, to propose the concept of affective rationality. It is undoubtedly this type of observation that made Pfister and Böhm (2008) say: "If our emotional appraisals are appropriate, that is, if we fear what objectively is to be feared, and if we hopefully anticipate what will actually make us happy, then these emotions might be called rational".

In addition, let us note that Boudon (2011) could clearly accept the label of "affective rationality":

> As for affective actions, they are not necessarily devoid of a rational dimension. I feel a strong emotion at the sight of an old lady aggressed by a vigorous young man. I immediately understand that my reaction is a reaction of indignation and not, for example, of fear. I conceptualize it immediately. On the other hand, *I could easily state the reasons on which my reaction is based.*

Finally, we postulate that the equity crowdfunding investor is driven by a triptych of rationality: instrumental, axiological and affective. Our representation of the investor's rationality (presented in Figure 1.1) is as follows: an individual placed in a given situation will behave according to a three-dimensional rationality whose center of gravity is within a triangle defined by the following three vertices: instrumental rationality, axiological rationality and affective rationality.

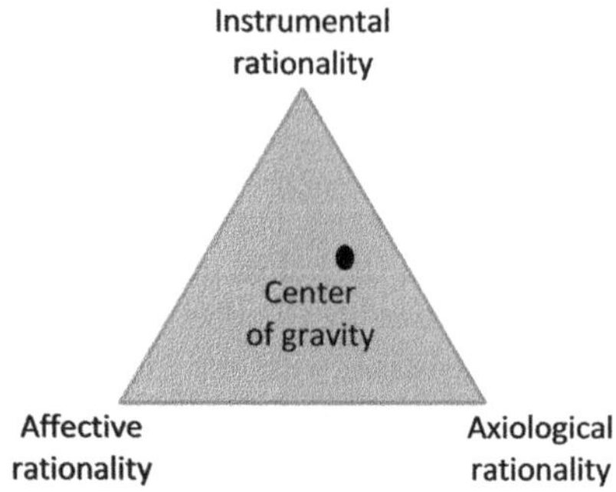

Figure 1.1. *Contextual rationality of the investor*

We made the assumptions of our modeling with regard to the nature of uncertainty, the nature of consequences and the rationality of investors. We are therefore in a framework where the consequences determining the choice of investment are multifold, financial and non-financial, and are associated with the specific objectives of the investor. These consequences have no associated objective probabilities; we are in uncertainty.

Furthermore, we believe that the choice of investment is only partially based on its consequences, because the investment can, in itself, have a decisive value for the investor. Finally, the considered triptych of rationality requires the enrichment of the framework with another determinant of decision: anticipatory emotions (the affective reactions felt at the time of the choice).

Obviously, the complexity of this framework, like the explanatory objective of this research, is not compatible with the normative models derived from the expected utility. Let us recall that if these models operate in uncertainty, the rationality of the economic agent is exclusively consequentialist, including when they integrate anticipated emotions as components of the consequences.

Our approach is empirical and aims to identify the psychological mechanisms underlying the choices of investors in the singular context of investment in equity crowdfunding, which justifies the development of an *ad hoc* and original explanatory model, which is the subject of section 1.2.

1.2. Explanatory model

This section is devoted to developing an explanatory model for the choice of investment of individual equity crowdfunding investors.

We start by identifying the variables and constructs of the model (section 1.2.1). Analyzing the qualitative material then allows us to confirm these variables and constructs as well as to explore the dimensions of the constructs (section 1.2.2). In the third step, we operationalize the constructs (section 1.2.3) before linking them causally by hypotheses (section 1.2.4). Finally, we propose several reading grids of the explanatory model obtained through several theories of our conceptual framework (section 1.2.5).

1.2.1. *Choice of model variables by the combined hypothetico-deductive and inductive/abductive approach*

As we specified when presenting the methodology adopted for this work, the variables of the explanatory model (here, variables must be taken in the broad sense, meaning indifferently observable or constructed variables) result from an approach combining abductive, inductive and deductive reasoning due to two concomitant processes: the first phase of literature review and the analysis of a body of qualitative data.

In section 1.2.1.1, we first specify the case of two variables first identified by induction (pure or associated with *a priori* abduction) by reading and then analyzing the data corpus before providing a theoretical justification for all the variables in the model, irrespective of the reasoning method that led to their identification (section 1.2.1.2).

1.2.1.1. *Variables from inductive/abductive inference by skimming associated with manual content analysis*

Before presenting the two variables identified by inductive and/or abductive inference, let us recall that the qualitative corpus is made up of 3,020 verbatim of investors justifying *ex post* their choice of investment in equity crowdfunding. These public testimonies were collected manually (by copy-pasting) on the website Wiseed.com in two stages prior to July 31, 2017.

Concerning the study of this corpus, we successively proceeded to skimming, and then to a manual thematic analysis (by resorting to an Excel spreadsheet for counting occurrences).

Our content analysis approach was essentially exploratory and aimed to bring out themes (the determining variables of investors' choices) that would not have emerged from the first literature review on crowdfunding. A preanalysis by skimming allowed for the identification of a recurring theme: the "interest" for the project (more specifically for its field of activity or its concept). A second theme centered on "values" had emerged from discussions prior to the analysis of the data, and so we sought empirical confirmation of its importance. The analysis of a sample of verbatim on these two themes resulted in the emergence of coding that were not based on *a priori* theories, according to the approach of the theory anchored in the data or "grounded theory" (Glaser and Strauss 1967). It should also be noted that while we did not compare these coding with those of a second researcher (with a view to guaranteeing the quality and validity of the analysis carried out), we have triangulated the theme obtained by a complementary literature review offering theoretical support to the two variables concerned.

1.2.1.1.1. Two variables identified by induction and/or abduction: congruence to values and interest

For these two variables, we successively present a series of verbatim illustrating their relevance and then give a measure of their intensity in the text (by a measure analogous to lexical intensity), calculated manually by thematic analysis in Excel.

Let us note that lexical intensity is a measure of the weight of a theme in a text; it is calculated as the percentage of occurrences of words in the text associated with the theme. Lexical intensity is a lexicometric tool that can be defined as an approach to statistical analysis of the lexicon of a text and falls within the currents of discourse analysis. It is therefore a quantitative approach to the text based on a postulate of the relevance of recurrent phenomena. Thus, the tools of lexicometry are based on counting and calculating the frequency of words, most often lemmatized, with lemmatization consisting of grouping the variations of a word in the same "form", for example, by associating the different occurrences of the same conjugated verb to their infinitive using a dictionary (Lejeune 2010).

In our case, the measurement of the intensity of the two variables is the result of the ratio between the number of occurrences of the forms associated with the variables (or themes) on the number of verbatim of the corpus and not on the total number of words of the text. This measure of intensity and the traditional lexical intensity are proportional, the passage from one to the other being made by the product of the average number of words per verbatim (or its inverse). This measure seems to be more significant to us in the particular case of our corpus, as it aggregates a large number (3,020) of short testimonials (19 words per testimonial, on average). Thus, an intensity of 10% means that the variable (more precisely, the associated words) appears in 10% of the testimonials, that is to say, at the most, 10% of the investors (because some investors were able to successively invest several times during the same exercise; however, this phenomenon is not frequent).

A first variable linked to the congruence to the talues of investors

The theme of values does not arise directly from the state of the art on crowdfunding but comes from an abductive inference from my thesis director about the work of sociologist Raymond Boudon. Almost at the same time, a first content analysis of the qualitative corpus confirmed the importance of values for the choice of investors on the wiseed.com platform. Also in the case of this variable, lexical analysis aimed to confirm the relative importance of the theme of values in the corpus.

Skimming and verbatim on the congruence to values

In Box 1.2, we present a selection of representative testimonials (translated from French) from investors, highlighting the adequacy of the values of the financed project with their own values as the determining reason for their choice of investment.

"I invested in Glowee because it is a project I believe in, *corresponding to the values I stand for*. I believe in the growth of its business".

"I invested in Poietis because *this company seems, to me, to be aligned with my values* and I think that the bioprinting sector is very promising. Poietis has adequate potential to establish its credibility in this market and take the market share necessary for its success".

"I invested in Stayhome because *the presented project seemed, to me, to be in line with my values* of solidarity, support for initiative and great creativity".

"I invested in Altern Mobil because I am an employee of this company and I believe that it is sustainable. It bears the *values to which I adhere*".

"I invested in Forestera because the project seems sound and *in line with my values*".

"I invested in Mamie & Compagnie because *I adhere to the values of this company* (local production and respectful of the environment)".

"I invested in Pumpart System because the seriousness of the project, the outcome of the product, and *the ecological values correspond to my criteria*".

"I have invested in Gifts For Change/Treez because it is a promising company that *bears values important for our society*".

Box 1.2. *The concept of value in investor testimonials*

Manual thematic analysis on congruence to values

For this thematic analysis, we have identified a list of words that emerged in the preanalysis stage through skimming the testimonies mentioning values and, more precisely, a congruence between the values of the investor and those put forward implicitly or explicitly by the project or its management team. The words associated with the values are as follows:

> {Valeur, sens, durable, responsable, humain, proximité, social, progrès, respec-tueux, écologique, honnête, éthique}
>
> (Value, meaning, sustainable, responsible, humane, proximity, social, progress, respectful, ecological, honest, ethical)

The calculated lexical intensity is 18%.

It is certain that this figure is crude in the sense that "value" can be used contextually in different ways (for example, added value). However, a check by a concordancer[3] reveals that a majority of the occurrences of the word value are used with the expected meaning.

A second variable linked to investor interest

Like the congruence of values theme, that of Interest does not come from the state of the art on crowdfunding but results from an inductive inference through skimming, which is then confirmed by data analysis.

Skimming and verbatim on interest

In Box 1.3 we present a selection of representative testimonies from investors highlighting their interest in one of the dimensions of the funded project, essentially the field or concept, as the determining reason of their choice of investment.

"I invested in Pearl because *the field of ecology interests me* greatly".

"I invested in Poietis because *the field of activity interests me*. The presentation of the project is very clear and fascinating".

"I invested in Advansolar *out of personal interest in cleantech startups* and in connection with my professional activities in the world of energy".

"I invested in Fib & Co because *I am interested in green finance*".

"I invested in Leko because *home automation and ecology interest me*".

"I invested in Save Innovations because this French technology relates to *a sector of the future that interests me a lot (renewable energies)* and seems to have good growth".

---

3 "Concordancers are expression-searching tools whose results are presented in a unique way: all the text segments are displayed one below the other, vertically centered on the word or expression sought" (Lejeune 2010).

"I invested in Oncomedics because *this topic of medical research interests me*".

"I invested in Naïo Technologies, I decided to invest in Naïo Technologies because *I am interested, among other things, in any innovation reducing the arduousness of tasks*, in particular in the agricultural field and that of building and public works".

"I invested in France Barter because *the concept interests me greatly*".

Box 1.3. *The concept of interest in investor testimonials*

Manual thematic analysis on interest

Regarding this thematic analysis, we proceeded in the same way as for the variable of Congruence to values. The words associated with the values are as follows:

{Intéressant, intérêt, passion, adore, plaît, curiosité}

(Interesting, interest, passion, adore, please, curiosity)

The calculated lexical intensity is 16%.

Again, the remark on the contextual meaning of the word interest is valid (for example, economic interest). However, a concordance analysis shows that the word interest is mostly used with the desired meaning.

1.2.1.2. *Theoretical support for variables and constructs, and first modeling hypotheses (hypotheses H1–H5)*

This section proceeds with a hypothetico-deductive approach to give a theoretical justification to the variables of the proposed explanatory model, with the principle being that a variable (or construct) is selected if it can explain the choice of investment, that is to say, the explained variable of the model.

In other words, we give a theoretical basis for the direct effect of the concerned variable on the Intensity variable of the investment choice, and in doing so, we make our first modeling hypotheses.

1.2.1.2.1. Intensity variable of investment choice

The Intensity variable of investment choice is the explained variable of the model. It measures the intensity of investment behavior in a given asset A and is calculated as the ratio[4] of the amount invested in asset A to the total amount to be invested in equity crowdfunding.

We have chosen to measure an investment intensity rather than a choice or rejection of investment because the information provided is finer and provides more information for analysis. Naturally, we do not associate a hypothesis with this variable since it is the explained variable.

1.2.1.2.2. Perceived signal quality variable

In the sphere of private equity, the investor tries to overcome the asymmetry of information by reducing agency risks through the collection of indicators (Manigart *et al.* 1997). In particular, business angels are more concerned with agency risks than venture capital, with the latter being more in touch with market risk (Mason and Stark 2004).

Like business angels, equity crowdfunding investors are faced with agency risk but with greater intensity, in particular because they rely largely on investigations and due diligences carried out on their behalf by the intermediation platform.

Nevertheless, the book by Ahlers *et al.* (2015) on equity crowdfunding reveals that certain signals communicated by entrepreneurs (composition of the board of directors, level of education of managers, quality of the network, intention to exit by initial public offering or buyout, etc.) have a positive impact in terms of attracting investors as well as their number and the amount raised. This result supports the idea of individual investors seeking to assess the unobservable characteristics of startups by interpreting signals communicated by entrepreneurs (Connelly *et al.* 2011).

Beyond this study, we refer the reader to section 1.2.2.1 of the first chapter of Volume 1 on the treatment of the choice of investors in equity crowdfunding by the literature and in which we show that the bibliographical references on this subject essentially adopt the theoretical prism of information asymmetry. Articles fall into two groups; the first brings together studies aimed at identifying the signals on which investors base their decision-making and the second brings together research on the success factors of fundraising campaigns, the results of which may also reveal important signals for investors.

While the perceived quality of the signal has an effect on the choice of investment, we have chosen to model it as an indirect effect, which is why we do not make any assumptions about this variable at this stage.

---

4 In the context of the experiment described in Chapter 2, the possible values for this variable are 0%, 25%, 50%, 75% and 100%.

1.2.1.2.3. Trust variable

For personality theorists, trust is a belief or expectation rooted in the personality, with its roots in the psychological development of the subject, while, for social psychologists, trust is based on the hope and consent of a third party engaging in a risky transaction to which the individual is vulnerable (Simon 2007). Joel Brockner and Phyllis Siegel (cited by Bonnet 2005) described trust as the presumption of a party (A) vis-à-vis the future behavior of a party (B), the level of trust of (A) towards (B) being proportional to (A)'s belief in (B)'s ability and determination to keep its commitments to it.

Books on private equity underline the importance and the need to establish a relationship of trust between investors and entrepreneurs, the latter needing to be trustworthy by revealing accurate and sincere information on the prospects of future activity. According to Bonnet (2005), "A private equity operation does not take place if a certain level of mutual trust has not been reached beforehand, during the studies and negotiation period that precedes the investment".

The challenge for managers is to reduce information asymmetry to gain the trust of investors, a *sine qua non* of funding (Scarbrough *et al.* 2013; Bammens and Collewaert 2014; Ola 2016).

Thus, trust naturally takes place in the context of agency relationships. According to Simon (2007), "When we talk about trust between two partners, there is an agency relationship in which the principal, called a trustor, trusts an agent or trustee. In principle, the trustor places their trust in the trustee so that the latter carries out the mandate while respecting the expectations of the former". Trust therefore acts as a natural governance mechanism associated with transactions and cooperation by accompanying and complementing the traditional economic mechanisms of the market and hierarchy (Charreaux 1998).

Then, according to Taffler (2014), emotional finance, the branch of behavioral finance focused on the role of conscious, but above all unconscious[5], emotions in the behavior of financial actors, sees trust as playing a key role enabling individuals to alleviate the anxiety resulting from investments whose future is unknowable. According to this author: "To trust is to invest!".

In the e-commerce sector, Gefen (2000) showed that trust and familiarity, which he modeled as its direct antecedent (while, in our specification, it is an indirect

5 According to Taffler, the theoretical framework of emotional finance is backed by psychoanalytic theory, which explains why our book fits into the field of behavioral finance but not that of emotional finance.

causal factor), have a strong effect on purchase intention, in accordance with Luhmann's theory (see, for example, Luhmann 2001).

Trust is therefore a determining ingredient for the good functioning of the economy. Arrow (1974) highlighted its importance and described it as an "invisible institution", while for Dasgupta (2000), trust is central in any transaction. According to Le Heron (2012), it is possible to go back to Keynes's seminal book to find traces of this concept. Keynes (1936) incorporated into his general theory the concept of a state of trust, which represents the solution on which individuals faced with decisions in radical uncertainty rely in order to cope. Thus, this concept, developed since his first thesis work on probabilities, tells us that individuals mainly rely on the trust they have in their own forecasts to make decisions; Keynes placed this concept at the heart of capitalism.

Naturally, trust appears in the literature on crowdfunding. Agrawal *et al.* (2014) confirmed that, in terms of equity crowdfunding, the managers of companies seeking funding disclose as much information as possible in order to establish a "have trust" ethos. They also believe that the development of mechanisms to guarantee the reputation of companies seeking funding is inevitable in order to ensure the trust of investors. These mechanisms will be substitutes for those (due diligences and interpersonal interactions) that prevail in traditional business financing markets at the seed stage. In their exploratory qualitative study on crowdfunding, Gerber and Hui (2013) identified trust in entrepreneurs as a motivation for investment. Ryu and Kim (2014) made trust in the creator the vital criterion necessary for the funder to develop a favorable attitude to the project; the associated hypothesis is nevertheless not significant in their study. Finally, the empirical study by Cholakova and Clarysse (2015) confirms the causal relationship between trust and the decision to subscribe in equity crowdfunding. According to these authors: "Trust is the only nonfinancial motivation that plays a role in the decision to pledge".

HYPOTHESIS 1 (H1).– *Trust in the project has a positive influence on the Intensity of the Investment Choice.*

1.2.1.2.4. Congruence to base values variable

As we indicated in Chapter 2 of Volume 1 (section 2.2.7.4.1), value theorists describe this concept as a motivational force that guides behavior (Rokeach 1973; Feather 1995; Schwartz 2006; Mucchielli 2011). Thus, actions are subjectively attractive when they allow for the expression of values that are important for the individual and can be assimilated to goals (Schwartz 1994). Like interest, values are classified as secondary motivations (Fenouillet 2016).

However, let us recall two characteristics of values according to Schwartz (2006)[6], which illustrate the motivational dimension of values and their role in questions of choice:

> Characteristic 2: "Values relate to desirable goals that motivate action".
>
> Characteristic 4: "Values serve as a benchmark or criteria. Values guide the selection or evaluation of actions".

Moreover, according to Schwartz (2006), all empirical studies confirm a, sometimes substantial, correlation link, between declared values and behavior, while Feather (1995) highlighted a causal relation between Schwartz values and decision by an experimental study. In this study, the actual choice of subjects was influenced by their personal values and by the values assigned to each alternative of the choice.

Literature on equity crowdfunding implicitly states the role of certain values as a motivational determinant, in particular, the values of stimulation, power, benevolence and universalism of the typology of Schwartz (1992) values. It is implicitly mentioned because, while the authors refer to motivations and not values, these motivations express the desire to achieve goals identifiable with listed values.

For example, Gerber and Hui (2013) and Bretschneider *et al.* (2014) identified the altruistic motivation of investors driven by the desire to help entrepreneurs with whom they share the project objective: "crowdfunding supporters are motivated to support causes analogous with their personal beliefs" (Gerber and Hui 2013). Similarly, Ryu and Kim (2014) discuss philanthropy and the desire to assist creators. These motivations can be associated with the benevolence value. Symmetrically[7], the article of Cholakova and Clarysse (2015) highlighted a primarily utilitarian and financial motivation of investors; however, this corresponds to a value: that of power through the control of financial resources. Moreover, the "fun to make investments" motivation of Bretschneider *et al.* (2014) can be associated with the stimulation value, while the "support a cause" motivation of Gerber's and Hui's (2013) can be associated with the universalism value.

Schwartz (2007) showed in his book that values are considered moral or amoral by respondents. They are viewed as moral (especially the values of benevolence and universalism) when they promote positive and protective relationships with others

6 Schwartz's theory of basic values is the one that we will take as a reference for the operationalization of this concept; we come back to this point later.

7 The values of benevolence and power are almost symmetrical in the circumplex of Schwartz values.

and are viewed as amoral (especially the values of stimulation and power) when they lack consideration for others. Also, in this theory, an individual valuing power through the accumulation of wealth is moved by a value, even if this can be considered as amoral. This theory, therefore, makes it possible to capture both intrinsic motivations (I invest in this project because its vision and its objectives are in line with my own vision of the world) as well as extrinsic motivations (I invest not for the project itself, but for the returns that I hope to obtain), which go beyond the choice of order 1, which consists of choosing to invest in equity crowdfunding rather than in any other financial product.

Finally, let us specify that axiological rationality is the form of rationality that corresponds to behaviors induced by personal values or strong reasons or perceived as such by individuals (Boudon 2011).

HYPOTHESIS 2 (H2).– *Congruence to base values has a positive influence on the intensity of the choice of investment.*

1.2.1.2.5. Affective reaction variable

Affective reactions naturally find their place in our model because (1) they are intimately linked to motivations and (2) they participate in the decisions of individuals and, therefore, in their choices.

1) They are closely linked to motivations; this assertion is confirmed by many researchers (Darwin 1872; Plutchik 1970; Izard 1977; Frijda 1988; Lang 1994; Davidson 1998; Fredrickson 2001; Frijda 2006; Sander and Scherer 2014; Fenouillet 2016), for whom the role of emotions is to motivate behaviors to achieve goals and meet the needs of individuals. Thus, Dantzer (2010) stated that

> Emotions also play an important organizing role in evaluating the world around us. Among the categorizations we form on the outside world, it is difficult to find one more fundamental than the pleasant-unpleasant or the beneficial-harmful dichotomy. This categorization motivates and directs action.

According to Fenouillet (2016), many motivational theories integrate a certain vision of emotions, which results from bringing together the fields of emotional psychology and motivational psychology. In particular, the theory of realization of interests of Frijda (1988, 2006) presented above identified emotion and action tendency. Loewenstein *et al.* (2001), agreeing with Frijda, explained the motivational role of emotion as follows: "Emotions serve to situate us vis-à-vis our environment, attracting us to certain people, certain objects, actions and ideas, keeping us away from others".

2) Affective reactions participate in the decisions of individuals; we previously presented (section 2.2.3 of Volume 1) several theories and decision-making models integrating affects and which justify this statement. We especially select the affect heuristic hypothesis (section 2.2.3.3.7 of Volume 1) adapted to a risk/benefit decision-making context such as a financial investment situation and which is closely linked to the hypothesis of somatic markers (section 2.2.3.3.8 of Volume 1). Let us recall that this last hypothesis links the capacity of individuals to make favorable choices to an emotional mechanism whose role is to send immediate signals on the anticipated consequences of actions to assist in the selection of advantageous options.

Then, as we indicated in section 1.2.2.3 of Volume 1, the context of persuasive advertising (a concept studied in marketing and presented in section 2.2.5.1 of Volume 1) that prevails in equity crowdfunding investment is conducive to the generation of affective reactions. Storytelling techniques, used by rich media, and, in particular, the decisive role of the entrepreneur's pitch video, provoke an emotional state, capable of modifying the favorable or unfavorable orientation of the investor toward the evaluated project.

Finally, we have also already mentioned an emerging stream of literature on crowdfunding that introduces affective reactions as one of the determinants of the choice of the investor (Bretschneider *et al.* 2014; Bessière and Stéphany 2015; Milovac *et al.* 2015; Wuillaume *et al.* 2016; Davis *et al.* 2017).

HYPOTHESIS 3 (H3).– *Affective reaction has a positive influence on the intensity of the choice of investment.*

1.2.1.2.6. Familiarity variable

In our review of literature, we presented Zajonc's (1968) effect of mere-exposure. Let us recall that the mere-exposure of an object is capable of creating a positive attitude and a preference for the object. Typical studies on the mere-exposure effect involve presenting sentences, faces and pictures to subjects, with varying frequencies, and then asking participants to judge their preferences for these stimuli. The higher the frequency of exposure, the stronger the preference. The mere-exposure effect also demonstrates the link between familiarity and a positive affective attitude, the latter predisposing to approach behavior.

Familiarity is also linked to an eponymous cognitive bias: the familiarity bias. This occurs when an individual prefers one option over another simply because it is more familiar to them. Heath and Tversky (1991) showed that between two bets of the same probability, individuals prefer the one they know the most, with this preference being able to persist even for a familiar bet having a lower probability of success. This bias is confirmed in financial markets, for example, Frieder and Subrahmanyam (2005) showed that individual investors increasingly choose companies whose brand is better known, i.e. more familiar. Grullon *et al.* (2004) showed that the number of individual investors in a company increases with the amount of advertising spending, whereas Huberman (2001) showed the existence of a geographic familiarity bias pushing investors to invest in companies established in their region.

Crowdfunding literature makes familiarity a determinant of the success of fundraising campaigns, but, generally, without explicitly naming it. Gerber and Hui (2013) noted that crowdfunders expressed a strong desire to help projects with which they have a direct or indirect personal link. Agrawal *et al.* (2011) showed that friends and family play a key role in initiating fundraising in reward-based projects. Mollick (2013) and Wechsler (2013) showed the importance of the size of the entrepreneur's social network for the success of campaigns. Bessière and Stéphany (2014) believed that familiarity plays an important role in equity crowdfunding, and Bretschneider *et al.* (2014) made a direct identification hypothesis with managers who are part of the investor's friends and family.

Beyond direct or indirect familiarity with entrepreneurs, geographic familiarity could play a role in crowdfunding, although this point remains controversial. On the other hand, geographic bias is documented in market finance, with investors inclined to hold portfolios of domestic, national and even local equities (Mangot 2008). It is also important in private equity, where the investment decision is based on personal interactions and the face-to-face due diligence necessary to reduce information asymmetry in high-risk situations (Agrawal *et al.* 2014). However, in the context of crowdfunding, Mollick (2013) noted a decrease in the importance of geographic constraints on the choice of funding. Moreover, Agrawal *et al.* (2011) showed that geographic distance has little effect on investment if we control social relationships. For the authors, geographic familiarity results from the geographic location of friends and family. In contrast, Bretschneider *et al.* (2014) hypothesized regional identification by supposing that investors establish links with regional startups based on the study by Lin and Viswanathan (2015); their study shows that geographic familiarity bias is a robust phenomenon, including in crowdfunding.

HYPOTHESIS 4 (H4).– *Familiarity has a positive influence on the intensity of the choice of investment.*

1.2.1.2.7. Interest variable

As we mentioned previously, this variable was initially the result of skimming the qualitative corpus, highlighting the testimonies of investors justifying their choice by the interest they have in the project, its concept, or the field of activity associated with it. However, the field of cognitive psychology attests to the motivational dimension of interest. Interest is classified among the secondary motivations, that is to say, those which do not give an absolute psychological origin (like instinct or needs), but rather a contextual origin to the motivation (Fenouillet 2016). Interest results from an interaction between a particular content and an individual; it engages or predisposes a person toward different objects, ideas or events.

Literature on equity crowdfunding highlights interest as a motivational determinant of investment. Schwienbacher and Larralde (2010) believed that in this area, not only are investors guided by profitability, but they also need to be interested in the project; innovation is then a catalyst for interest. In developing their empirical model, Ryu and Kim (2014) chose interest as a motivational variable explaining the choice of investment. For the authors, interest sparks attention to projects that match investor preferences. Like Schwienbacher and Larralde, Ryu and Kim made innovation the antecedent of interest and curiosity. Bretschneider *et al.* (2014) chose the self-determination theory of Deci and Ryan (1985) as the theoretical framework of their explanatory model and, according to this theory, identified in particular interest and curiosity as determinants of the intrinsic motivation of investors. As we have indicated, curiosity and interest are two interrelated concepts, since it is possible to, and we will, conceptualize curiosity as a dimension of situational interest. However, the capacity of curiosity to engage consumers in the development of new products, in which investors in equity crowdfunding participate, is demonstrated by the work of Füller (2006). Finally, Ordanini *et al.* (2011) considered that the interest in the functioning of crowdfunding constitutes a reason for the participation of investors.

HYPOTHESIS 5 (H5).– *Interest has a positive influence on the intensity of the choice of investment.*

1.2.2. *Confirmatory study of the variables of the model on qualitative material*

At this point, we have identified the variables of the explanatory model by both abduction/induction and hypothetico-deductive reasoning. We now return to the data with the objective of confirming the relevance of the chosen variables by comparing the contributions of two free softwares, TXM (version 0.7.7) and IRaMuTeQ (version 0.7 alpha 2).

Let us recall that the depth of our qualitative corpus of 3,020 testimonies lends itself to speech analysis by the use of textual analysis tools.

First (section 1.2.2.1), we calculate the lexical intensities (according to the method explained above) of the variables using the TXM software. Therefore, the approach is of the *a priori* kind, since we start from a list of variables known and supported by the theory. The objective is to check that the lexical intensities of the variables are not marginal, that is to say, that the codes associated with them appear in the speech of a reasonable number of investors.

Second, we use the IRaMuTeQ software to provide a hierarchical analysis, followed by a factorial correspondence analysis (FCA) (section 1.2.2.2). This typology is a structure underlying the data normally used in the context of an exploration; it does not proceed *a priori*, but according to a logic that we will recall briefly. But it is precisely for this reason that, from a viewpoint of triangulation for internal validity purposes (Gavard-Perret *et al.* 2013), it seems relevant to us to compare the information contained in this classification with the list of variables that we previously obtained. The question is, does this data structure that emerges spontaneously with hierarchical classification corroborate our variables?

1.2.2.1. *Confirmation of variables and thematic content analysis by* a priori *coding*

This time, we are abandoning the Excel spreadsheet for counting occurrences, which we will do with the TXM tool, through queries in Corpus Query Language (CQL), the language associated with this tool. It is a "formal language, with a lexicon and a syntax of operators, which form a metalanguage making it possible for elements to be combined for the search of structured patterns"[8].

Our method is as follows. For each variable, we coded by defining a list of simple or compound, and sometimes generic, forms, and occasionally excluded certain words. The list of forms chosen results from our knowledge of the corpus, the definition of the variable and its synonyms or even the theory. The reason behind excluded forms is that they have a different meaning from that which interests us.

We present below the CQL of the corpus, a results table displaying the count of the occurrences of each form, the total occurrences of the variable and indicate the lexical intensity calculated as the ratio between the total (figure) and the number of verbatim (3,020).

The analysis indicates that the Interest variable stands out clearly by the significance of its score, which is two to three times higher than the score of the other variables. No variable obtains a marginal score insofar as we consider that, compared to the size of our corpus, a hundred investors mentioning the same theme is significant.

8 See the TXM manual available at: http://textometrie.ens-lyon.fr/files/documentation/Manuel%20de%20TXM%200.7%20FR.pdf.

1.2.2.1.1. Interest variable

We searched for all words prefixed with "*intér*" (inter) using the generic form intér.* and excluded the word "*intérieur*" (interior). This family of words alone is sufficient to group a significant percentage of testimonials.

CQL request:

[frlemma="**intér**.*" & frlemma!="intérieur"]

intéressant	126
intéressante	39
Intérêt	35
Intéressé	29
Intéresse	27
intéressants	8
intéressantes	7
Intéresser	5
intéressent	4
intéressée	2
Intérêts	2
intéressais	1
intéressant	1
intéressante	1
Intéressé	1
intéressés	1
intéressons	1
Total	**290**

Table 1.1. *Lexical intensity of words with the prefix "intér-"*

The lexical intensity of the Interest variable is 10%; in other words, 10% of the investors in the corpus mention interest as the reason for their choice.

1.2.2.1.2. Familiarity variable

This time, we relied on our knowledge of the corpus and on theory. Because the investors do not explicitly declare themselves "familiar" with the project, we looked for indicators of familiarity. The chosen forms touch on the fact of being familiar with one of the attributes of the project because one "knows" (*connaît*) (a founder, the product, the company, etc.), because one "works" (*travaille*) (in the company's field of activity), because one "lives" (*habite*) in the company's "city" (*ville*) or "region" (*région*) or because one has "already invested" (*déjà investi*) in the project.

CQL request:

[word="connais"]|[word="travail.*"]|[word="habite"]|[word="ville"]|
[word= "région"]|[word="déjà"][word="investi"]

connais	57
Région	25
Travail	19
travaille	14
déjà investi	12
travailler	8
travaillé	7
Ville	7
Habite	4
travaillant	2
travaillons	1
Total	**156**

Table 1.2. *Lexical intensity of words representative of the Familiarity variable*

The lexical intensity of the Familiarity variable is 5%; in other words, 5% of the investors in the corpus mention familiarity as the reason for their choice.

1.2.2.1.3. Trust variable

For the Trust variable, we looked, knowing that the theory specifies that trust is attached to leaders, both for the forms resulting from the generic form confian.* and the forms qualifying the leaders likely to instill trust. An investor can trust the leaders of a startup because they are "credible" (*crédibles*), seem "sincere" (*sincères*) or even "honest" (*honnêtes*).

CQL request:

[confian.*|crédib.*|sincèr.*|honnêt.*]

confiance	75
crédible	14
crédibilité	3
crédibles	3
sincère	3
sincèrement	3
confiant	1
crédibiliser	1
honnêtes	1
sincères	1
Total	**105**

Table 1.3. *Lexical intensity of words representative of the Trust variable*

The lexical intensity of the Trust variable is 3.5%; in other words, 3.5% of the investors in the corpus cite trust as the reason for their choice.

1.2.2.1.4. Congruence to base values variable

We have searched for all compound forms where the first word is "value", excluding the compound form "added value" (*valeur ajoutée*).

CQL request:

[frlemma="valeur"][word!="ajouté.*"]

The lexical intensity of the Congruence to Base Values variable is 3%; in other words, 3% of the investors in the corpus mention values as the reason for their choice.

This percentage is relatively modest, because it only relates to the explicit expression of the word "value". In the manual thematic analysis presented in section 1.2.1.1.1, we used a list of indicators mentioning the basic values of universalism and benevolence, which are particularly present in the community of investors of the Wiseed platform with the following list of forms: {Valeur, sens, durable, responsable, humain, proximité, social, progrès, respectueux, écologique, honnête, éthique} (Value, meaning, sustainable, responsible, humane, proximity, social, progress, respectful, ecological, honest, ethical), which gave a significant score of 18%.

valeurs de	12	valeur partagée	**1**
valeurs et	7	valeur pour	1
valeurs.	5	valeur qui	1
valeurs écologiques	4	valeurs ;	1
valeur.	3	valeurs !	1
valeur de	3	valeurs (	1
valeurs auxquelles	3	valeurs agriculture	1
valeurs environnementales	3	valeurs au	1
valeur d'	2	valeurs bénéfiques	1
valeur et	2	valeurs défendues	1
valeurs,	2	valeurs économiques	1
valeurs défendues	2	valeurs éthiques	1
valeurs éthiques	2	valeurs humaines	1
valeurs importantes	2	valeurs incarnées	1
valeurs je	2	valeurs ont	1
valeurs que	2	valeurs portées	1
valeur ;	1	valeurs qui	1
valeur à	1	valeurs sur	1
valeur basée	1	valeurs universelles	1
valeur en	1	valeur sûre	1
valeur énergétique	1	valeurs véhiculées	1
valeur la	1	valeur testée	1
valeur m'	1	valeur un	1
Total		**86**	

Table 1.4. *Lexical intensity of expressions containing the form "value" (valeur)*

1.2.2.1.5. Perceived Signal Quality variable

Concerning the Perceived Signal Quality variable, knowing that the theory specifies that it is the result of the assessment of the manager's profile and the quality of the business plan, we looked for both the composite form “business plan” as well as the words deriving from the generic form dirigeant.* (manager) and fondateur.* (founder).

CQL request:

[word=“business”] [word=“plan”] | [word=“dirigeant.*”] | [word=“fondateur.*”]

Dirigeants	34
Dirigeante	28
Fondateurs	20
business plan	18
Dirigeant	11
Fondateur	9
Dirigeantes	1
Total	**121**

Table 1.5. *Lexical intensity of the Perceived Signal Quality variable*

The lexical intensity of the Perceived Signal Quality variable is 4%; in other words, 4% of the investors in the corpus mention one of the dimensions of the Perceived Signal Quality variable as the reason for their choice. Note that this score is overvalued, as the words deriving from the forms “dirigeant.*” and “fondateur.*” can also relate to trust.

1.2.2.1.6. Affective Reaction variable

Identifying forms serving as an indicator of affective reactions results from our knowledge of the corpus; the following CQL request aggregates a list of forms that clearly express the role of the affective in the testimony of the investor.

CQL request:

[word=“séduit.*”|word=“sensib.*” |word=“appréci.*” | word=“passion.*” | word=“ador.*”| word=“plaît”| word=“séduisant.*” | word=“touch.*”| word=“ cœur”| word=“sentiment.*”]

Séduit	28	séduisante	2
Sensible	26	sentiment	2
apprécie	24	touché	2
Plaît	15	toucher	2
Adore	13	touchés	2
séduisant	12	appréciés	1
Touche	9	passion	1
apprécié	6	passion'	1
cœur	6	passionné	1
passionnant	5	passionnée	1
passionné	4	passionnent	1
Séduite	4	sensibilisant	1
sensibilisé	4	sensibilisation	1
sensibilité	3	touchent	1
apprécier	2	touches	1
passionnés	2		
Total		**183**	

Table 1.6. *Lexical intensity of the Affective Reaction variable*

The lexical intensity of the Affective Reaction variable is 6%; in other words, 6% of the investors in the corpus use a vocabulary that evokes the role of affect as the reason for their choice.

1.2.2.2. *Confirmation of variables and typology of investors*

In this section, we proceed to a descending hierarchical classification according to the method of Reinert (1983). This classification makes it possible for forms to be grouped into classes according to their independence, measured by a chi-square test.

The principle is as follows: the algorithm operates on an initial lexical (or contingency) table whose lines are the forms of the corpus (the words) and the columns are the text segments, that is to say, sentence extracts of a fixed length. A cell (i,j) of this table, located at the intersection of the *i*th row and the *j*th column indicates the presence (by number 1) or the absence (by number 0) of the form *i* in the segment *j*. The segments presenting the same profile, that is to say, a similar series of 0 and 1, are grouped together in the same class. At the end of the cycle of iterations, the classification algorithm produces a dendrogram, that is to say, a tree of classes.

In our case, using the default setting, the number of classified text segments (3,191) is close to the number of investor testimonials (3,020). Moreover, the division into four classes obtained makes it possible to classify 87.90% of the segments.

```
+-+-+-+-+-+-+-+-+
|i|R|a|M|u|T|e|Q| – Mon Sep 11 18:27:40 2017
+-+-+-+-+-+-+-+-+

Number of texts: 3020
Number of text segments: 3191
Number of forms: 5458
Number of occurrences: 60634
Number of lemmas: 3816
Number of active forms: 3521
Number of complementary forms: 294
Number of active forms with a frequency >= 3: 1415
Average forms per segment: 19.001567
Number of classes: 4
2805 segments classified out of 3191 (87.90%)

###########################
time : 0h 0m 17s
###########################
```

Figure 1.2. *Dendrogram statistics*

Figure 1.3 shows the dendrogram obtained; the percentages represent the amount of information summarized for each class. Class 1 includes 27.7% of the data (without considering the classes not selected). The sum of these percentages is naturally equal to 100%.

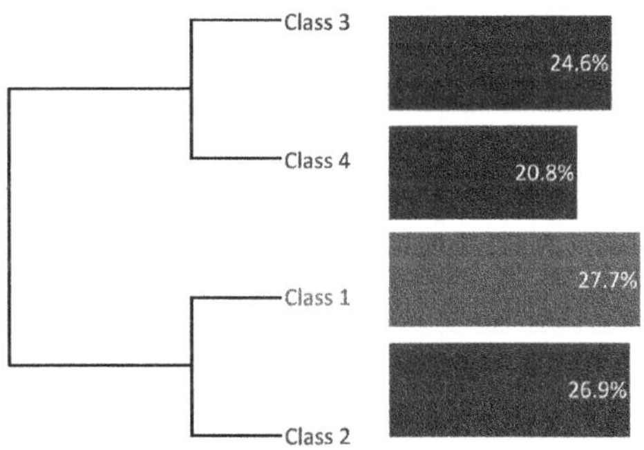

Figure 1.3. *Dendrogram of the qualitative corpus by Reinert classification. For a color version of this figure, see www.iste.co.uk/goglin/investment2.zip*

We note that classes 1 and 2 and 3 and 4, respectively, are associated and form two distinct sets. In order to give an interpretation of these classes, we need to know the forms that they are composed of. Table 1.7 lists the first 20 forms associated with the four classes in decreasing order of the strength of their association. The p-value is a probability; it is the risk that the chi-square test of independence could be false. The lower the p, the lower the risk of error of the test of independence.

	Class 1			Class 2			Class 3			Class 4		
	Chi-square	Form	*p*-value	Chi-square	Form	*p*-value	Chi-square	Form	*p*-value	Chi-square	Form	*p*-value
1	347.91	Projet	1.209521e-77	231.83	équipe	2.383778e-52	150.93	environnement	1.083871e-34	540.18	énergie	1.723815e-119
2	163.68	Trouver	1.781098e-37	142.73	dirigeant	6.724077e-33	101.07	agriculture	8.862846e-24	163.52	avenir	1.930367e-37
3	128.82	Intéressant	7.420532e-30	106.92	confiance	4.645626e-25	90.18	économie	2.179245e-21	127.90	énergétique	1.182090e-29
4	109.82	Concept	1.072170e-25	83.51	entreprise	6.349684e-20	73.15	respectueux	1.199670e-17	112.70	renouvelables	2.507979e-26
5	97.33	Innovant	5.861760e-23	72.41	aventure	1.747954e-17	71.30	local	3.062859e-17	85.19	électricité	2.710884e-20
6	71.00	novateur	3.567219e-17	69.65	wiseed	7.077201e-17	67.00	circuit	2.710562e-16	80.42	renouvelable	3.026586e-19
7	45.71	piscine	1.373977e-11	66.25	marché	3.962785e-16	62.44	soutenir	2.749972e-15	78.94	solaire	6.410804e-19
8	39.37	écologique	3.512150e-10	63.55	potentiel	1.566189e-15	61.86	équitable	3.681202e-15	78.94	source	6.410804e-19
9	30.88	idée	2.742667e-08	59.89	stratégie	1.001100e-14	59.29	produit	1.360472e-14	73.06	alternative	1.257591e-17
10	29.77	dimension	4.865276e-08	58.00	business	2.623223e-14	50.73	durable	1.061511e-12	68.07	utilisation	1.580756e-16
11	29.32	plait	6.148797e-08	52.90	long	3.508549e-13	50.60	sain	1.130282e-12	65.74	ressource	5.138006e-16
12	28.11	utile	1.144440e-07	49.51	porteur	1.977391e-12	49.42	chocolat	2.066519e-12	59.57	géothermie	1.181061e-14
13	26.77	social	2.288058e-07	43.35	solide	4.572226e-11	47.86	planète	4.570721e-12	57.38	propre	3.584533e-14
14	26.13	design	3.192570e-07	42.58	compétent	6.775459e-11	44.74	emploi	2.248105e-11	57.35	électrique	3.642198e-14
15	23.18	séduire	1.472211e-06	40.87	plan	1.630882e-10	44.65	court	2.350143e-11	50.33	transition	1.298329e-12
16	21.16	apprécier	4.232763e-06	39.34	risque	3.560547e-10	43.21	population	4.913565e-11	47.26	eau	6.232624e-12
17	21.08	propriétaire	4.401724e-06	38.13	capacité	6.612398e-10	42.70	filière	6.383439e-11	46.63	fossile	8.576826e-12
18	18.28	intéressant	1.903571e-05	38.11	diversifier	6.702685e-10	41.81	bois	1.008394e-10	41.64	nombreux	1.099869e-10
19	17.95	utilisateur	2.265729e-05	37.39	technologie	9.654613e-10	41.66	maison	1.084173e-10	35.14	utiliser	3.070409e-09
20	16.12	écolo	5.960225e-05	36.61	expérimenté	1.443610e-09	39.99	contribuer	2.555084e-10	32.94	production	9.495898e-09

Table 1.7. *List of forms associated with each class in order of the strength of the association*

1.2.2.2.1. Interpretation of classes

Class 1 groups together the forms qualifying the project, concept or idea. The main adjectives are as follows: *intéressant* (interesting), *innovant* (innovative), *novateur* (novel), *utile* (useful) and *social* (social). Several verbs (*plaire*, *séduire*, *apprécier*) describe the investor's feeling toward the financed project.

This class shows the Interest and the Affective Reaction variables insofar as the verbs *plaire* (to please), *séduire* (to attract) and *apprécier* (appreciate) are judgments of positive valence with an affective connotation.

Class 2 includes the forms qualifying the management team and the business plan. The forms *confiance* (trust), *compétence* (competence), *capacité* (ability) and *expérimenté* (experienced) can be attached to the management team. The forms *marché* (market), *potentiel* (potential), *stratégie* (strategy), *business* (business), *porteur* (promising), *solide* (sound), *plan* (plan), *risque* (risk) and *technologie* (technology) can be linked to the business plan. This second class implicitly shows the Perceived Signal Quality and Trust variables.

Class 3 brings together a lexical universe linked to ecology: *environnement* (environment), *agriculture* (agriculture), *respectueux* (respectful), *local* (local), *équitable* (fair), *durable* (sustainable), *sain* (healthy), etc.

Class 4 includes a lexical universe related to energies: energy, renewable, electricity, solar, source, alternative, geothermal, etc.

Classes 3 and 4 refer to the line of business of startups. These two classes mark the attachment to the subject of sustainable development, which is important for investors, and which echoes the value of altruism and the Congruence to Base Values variable.

In order to ensure the correct interpretation of the classes, we now return to the initial text and identify for each class a selection of testimonies associated with several companies, which are themselves associated with the class concerned. To do this, we run an FCA on the variables defined in the imported text file. Note that in the latter, we have defined three variables (the name of the company, its line of business and its geographical location) for each testimonial.

The FCA synthesizes information and facilitates its interpretation; it is performed according to a Reinert classification. The FCA under IRaMuTeQ generates a graph with the two dimensions that summarize the most data. The shapes are colored according to the classes resulting from the Reinert classification.

In our case, as shown in Table 1.8, the first two factors summarize 70.77% of the information, which is satisfactory (with 39.26% for factor 1 and 31.40% for factor 2).

	Eigenvalues	Percentages	Cumulative percentage
Factor 1	0.301502698011881	39.3651630786116	39.3651630786116
Factor 2	0.240556802276859	31.4078706881911	70.7730337668027

Table 1.8. *Eigenvalues, percentage of inertia extracted and cumulative percentage of factors*

Figure 1.4 shows the graphical result of the FCA. Our objective here is not to interpret the axes, but simply to randomly collect several project names associated with each class in order to validate our interpretation by returning to the text, that is to say the verbatim relating to the projects of classes 1 and 2 and complementarily by checking the line of business of projects associated with classes 3 and 4.

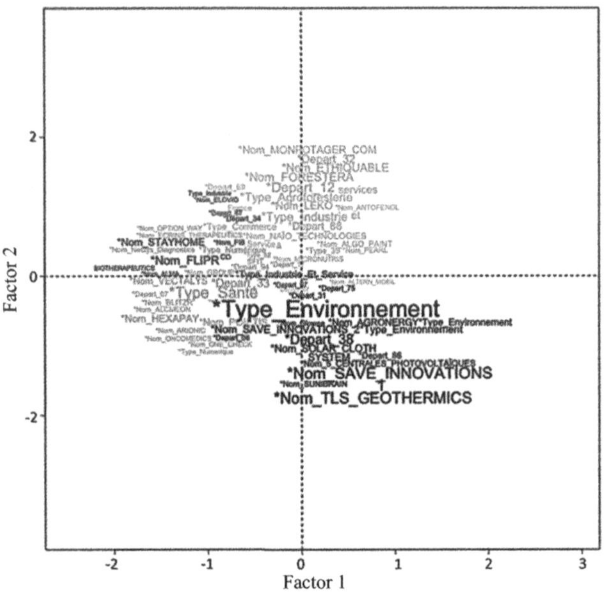

Figure 1.4. *FCA graph based on the variables. For a color version of this figure, see www.iste.co.uk/goglin/investment2.zip*

Class 1

The verbatim (here translated) from projects randomly chosen in class 1 (red) confirm our interpretation and highlight the project, idea or concept.

Project Stay Home

> "I invested in Stay Home because the project is innovative and I think it will be a great success".
>
> "I invested in Stay Home because the project seems very attractive and novel".

Project Flipr

> "I invested in Flipr because it is innovative and meets a growing need…" .
>
> "I invested in Flipr because it is a project I believe in because of its usefulness and its efficiency in terms of pool maintenance".
>
> "I invested in Flipr because I was won over by the design of the product and its ease of use".

Class 2

Some verbatim from projects randomly chosen in class 2 (green) confirm our interpretation by highlighting the management team and the business plan.

Project Hexapay

> "I invested in Hexapay because an experienced and visionary team working for an original offer […]".
>
> "I invested in Hexapay because […] the high availability of the teams to answer Wiseeders' questions ended up convincing me to invest!"
>
> "I invested in Hexapay because the field is promising. Serious and credible business plan".

Project Vectalys

> "I invested in Vectalys because I think the team is very competent and that the validation of their process is well advanced".
>
> "I invested in Vectalys because here are the reasons that led me to invest in Vectalys: 1. There is a background already and capacity to generate turnover already. 2. Well positioned in a rapidly growing sector".

> "I invested in Vectalys because it is a promising biotech and (a rarity!) has already found its market (substantial turnover). The management seems top-notch".

> "I invested in Vectalys because the market is promising and Vectalys seems well positioned to handle it".

Class 3

Concerning class 3 (blue), several startups chosen randomly correspond to a lexical universe linked to ecology.

Project Forestera

> "A lumber company for developing an agroforestry project based on cocoa farming in Peru".

Project Ethiquable

> "Fair trade demanding and supporting peasant farming with 49 cooperatives of small partner producers".

Project Leko

> "When home automation, ecology and design become one".

Class 4

Likewise, several startups randomly chosen from class 4 (purple) are doing well in the energy sector.

Project Save Innovations

> "Pico turbine for revolutionary production of electricity from water or low speed air currents not yet used".

Project Solar Cloth System

> "Thin and rollable photovoltaic textiles allowing for energy autonomy in nomadic situations or outside the grid".

Project TLS Geothermics

> "Developer of deep geothermal power plants. Geothermal energy is clean, local, and an available renewable energy".

study of the market and competition, financial prospects, etc.) and the "management team", with these two dimensions being supported by our data as evidenced by the selection of (translated) verbatim in Box 1.4.

Business plan dimension

"For *the relevance of their project* and *their business plan*".

"*The business plan seems feasible* once the resources can be gathered to achieve these objectives".

"Furthermore, *the project's business plan is convincing*".

"*The business plan seems coherent to me*".

"*The business plan is very well drawn up*: there is a real need and they have developed a 'breakthrough' technology for this application that will address two needs in one".

"[...] a good dose of marketing and *well-structured business plan*, guaranteed success".

"I find this new adventure refreshing. *The business plan is realistic* and it is a great regulatory challenge".

"In addition, the team seems to have good technical and commercial expertise, as can be seen from *the well-crafted business plan*".

"*The detailed business plan* and the presentation convinced me of the motivation of the managers".

"*I believe in their business plan*".

Management team dimension

"*I believe in the management team*, to support entrepreneurs in a country of civil servants!"

"For having had the chance to meet *the management team who made an excellent impression on me*".

"Because of the experience of the management team and for the ethical aspect – responsible".

"[...] *I know members of the management team* and trust them to succeed in this great adventure".

"*I believe in his/her management team* and his/her project".

"*I trust the management team*, and believe in the Option Way solution".

"It is also supported by *an excellent management team* that should absolutely be supported".

"I was won over by the uniqueness of its technology and *the proven skills of its management team*".

"*The management team seems very competent* and it shows in the business plan".

"*I trust the management team*, because of past results and the partnerships".

Box 1.4. *Selection of verbatim illustrating the business plan and management team dimensions*

Regarding the business plan dimension, we agree with Bessière and Stéphany (2014) that in the equity crowdfunding sector, the product/market approach dominates the financial approach. Thus, returning to our qualitative corpus tells us that investors only marginally justify their investment by the exit prospects: the IPO is only mentioned twice and the acquisition five times, while the amount of securities offered is not mentioned. In contrast, the occurrences of testimonies evoking the innovation of the product or the service, the market dynamics, the competition and the financial prospects are abundant. The words "*solution*" (solution, 175 occurrences), "*prometteur*" (encouraging, 69 occurrences), "*novateur*" (novel, 54 occurrences), "*marché*" (market, 203 occurrences), "*porteur*" (promising, 86 occurrences), "*croissance*" (growth, 41 occurrences) and "*perspectives*" (prospects, 46 occurrences) are overrepresented in the corpus. This is why we associate the following four items with the business plan dimension: product/service innovation, market growth, intensity of competition, and financial prospects.

Concerning the management team dimension, we summarize the aforementioned research using four items relating to the number of managers, their complementarity, their experience and the adequacy of their level of qualification. While the number of managers does not appear explicitly in our evidence, we believe that evoking the complementarity of managers presupposes that there is a sufficient amount in order to cover the spectrum of skills required for developing the business. Likewise, we form the hypothesis that investors consider the level of education satisfactory when they consider the management team to be competent.

Finally, given the little research on the criteria for selecting investors in equity crowdfunding, we choose to define an *ad hoc* construct, based on traditional criteria for private equity and the study by Ahlers *et al.* (2015), but keeping only the items supported by our qualitative corpus.

Also, we define the latent Perceived Signal Quality variable as a formative construct (see Figure 1.5) or index based on the subjective evaluation of the perceived quality of the business plan (index made up of four items) and the subjective evaluation of the perceived quality of the management team (index made up of four items). Table 1.9 explains the eight items of this construct. The construct is formative and non-reflective; as these eight items literally form the construct, they are not interchangeable, do not necessarily covariate, do not share a common subject and are antecedents of the quality perceived by the investor (Jarvis *et al.* 2003). Finally, it should be noted that this is not a "signal" within the meaning of signal theory (Spence 1973), as each investor carries out a subjective evaluation that leads to a personal assessment.

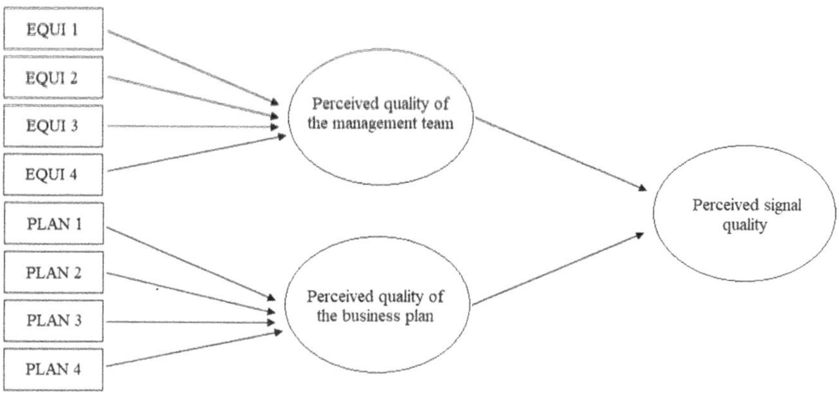

Figure 1.5. *Perceived Signal Quality formative construct*

EQUI1	The size of the management team is appropriate for this project
EQUI2	Managers have complementary profiles
EQUI3	Managers' degrees are appropriate for this project
EQUI4	Managers' experience is appropriate for this project
PLAN1	I find this product/service innovative
PLAN2	I think this market is growing
PLAN3	I think competition does not prevent a newcomer from entering the market
PLAN4	Financial prospects look good

Table 1.9. *Indicators of the Perceived Signal Quality formative construct*

The data for the Perceived Signal Quality variable are collected using eight items measured on a 5-point Likert scale ranging from "strongly disagree" to "strongly agree".

In order to further anchor this construct in the data, we combine a selection of five illustrative verbatim for each of these items[9] in Box 1.5.

Items EQUI1 and EQUI2 (the size of the management team is appropriate for this project/managers have complementary profiles)

"The management team seems very *complementary* to me".

"I am confident in the creativity, the *complementarity*, the work of the management team".

"Because the team seems *complementary* and the target market is growing".

"Because I believe in the innovative project of building high-tech smart wooden houses, in the *complementarity* and commitment of a team of passionate professionals".

"Because its technology seems to be one step ahead of the competition, the partners are *complementary*, and the partnership with Airbus is proof that things are taking off".

Items EQUI3 (managers' degrees are appropriate for this project)

"*The management team is competent* and the market very promising".

"*The management team is completely credible and competent* for transforming this project into a success".

"Because not only does the project seem exciting to me, but above all the team has *well-balanced competencies*: Finance, Technical and Marketing, which gives us every opportunity for the proper execution of the project".

"I believe in *the competence of the team* to carry out the project and I want to encourage them".

"Because I believe in these technologies for our near future and *in the competencies of this entire team*".

Items EQUI4 (managers' experience is appropriate for this project)

"Because I believe in the mobile digital transformation, and in *the team's experience* in the hotel industry (*network*)".

9 With the exception of the items EQUI1 and EQUI2, voluntarily categorized together due to the justification provided above.

"Because I think the project is driven by *the managers' extensive experience in the hotel industry*".

"Because the company presents an innovative solution in the spirit of the current societal change – local food systems, the fight against global warming and support for agriculture by recovering waste. In addition, the staff's experience demonstrates the company's ability to succeed".

"Furthermore, *the entrepreneur already has some experience* in business creation and this green sector, which will therefore limit the risks and make it easier for them to find clients quickly".

"Because of *the experience of the management team* and for the ethical aspect – responsible".

Items PLAN1 (I find this product/service innovative)

"Because it is a *simple and innovative technological solution* for the hotel industry – an important market in France".

"Because *the concept is innovative* and it is a solution of the future, the applications affect the public but also the private sector".

"Because this company offers *an innovative technical solution* that respects the environment".

"Because the company presents *an innovative solution* in the spirit of the current societal change – local food systems, the fight against global warming and support for agriculture by recovering waste. In addition, the staff's experience demonstrates the company's ability to succeed".

"Because the company offers *an innovative solution* for reducing greenhouse gases".

"Because *the technical solution is truly innovative* and virtuous by allowing for the recovery of previously unused waste".

Items PLAN2 (I think this market is growing)

"Because *online commerce is constantly growing* and I think the sector is promising".

"Because the project is positioned *in a very promising sector* which can generate good margins".

"Because I believe in *the expansion of the insect-based food market* in Europe".

"Because the project and the concept are very interesting *in a growing market*".

"Because this project is exciting! Artificial intelligence and social networks: two *themes driven by a growing market*, at the heart of the concerns of young people, and therefore a project resolutely oriented towards the future".

Items PLAN3 (I think competition does not prevent a newcomer from entering the market)

"Because the solution developed by Pumpart System has many advantages and must quickly gain momentum through crowdfunding or other kind of funding, *which will enable it to stay one step ahead of the competition* who will not fail to copy this exciting concept".

"Because this project is innovative and is placed in a market with *certain demand and little competition*, all while respecting a certain ethics".

"Because its technology seems *to be one step ahead of the competition*, the partners are complementary, and the partnership with Airbus is proof that things are taking off".

"The project is innovative, part of the 'cleantech' movement, *with zero competition* at the moment".

"The detailed business plan and the presentation convinced me of the motivation of the managers. The market positioning of the wooden house/smart house is also interesting. A well-positioned service price *compared to the competition*".

Items PLAN4 (Financial prospects looks good)

"For me, it is a financial investment with *good prospects* and a showstopper".

"Because in addition to helping the development of personalized cancer care, *the project seems very interesting from a financial point of view!*"

"Because *the prospects seem financially attractive*".

"I found the project interesting and *the financial data valid*".

"Because *their financial and investment record seems sound*".

Box 1.5. *Verbatim of investors and items of the Perceived Signal Quality construct*

1.2.3.2. *Trust variable*

As we have already mentioned, Brockner and Siegel, quoted by Bonnet (2005), considered that trust referred to the presumption of a party (A) vis-à-vis the future behavior of a party (B), the level of trust of (A) in (B) being proportional to the belief of (A) in the capacity and the determination of (B) to keep their commitments toward them.

Trust is therefore a belief, not necessarily based on knowledge, which represents the intermediate degrees between absolute certainty and ignorance (Neveu 2004).

Trust is also future oriented; it can also be conceptualized as a behavioral intention or a will (Moorman *et al.* 1992). In addition, this concept is cognitive and affective in nature; cognitive because trust is based on the processing of available experience and affective information as the trustful individual tries to overcome future uncertainty about interactions with the partner, to whom the former attributes motivations (Mcallister 1995).

Through his study that aimed to take stock of the concept and definitions of trust in the field of management, Neveu (2004) identified several recurring characteristics in the definitions of trust:

– trust is "an optimistic expectation on the part of an individual as to the outcome of an event or the behavior of another individual";

– trust "usually occurs under conditions of vulnerability and dependence on the behavior of the other party";

– "the loss in case of breach of trust will be more intense than the gain in case of respect for trust";

– "the belief that the likelihood of a breach of trust is both unknown and beyond the control of the person who trusts is also integral to trust";

– "trust is generally accompanied by the assumption of an obligation accepted or recognized by the other party to protect the rights and interests of all. These voluntarily accepted obligations go beyond the promise to neither harm nor impede the interests of the other".

These characteristics outline a multidimensional construct; the first point refers to the notion of credibility (optimistic expectation of another individual's behavior), while the last point refers to benevolence (going beyond the promise to not harm). Specifically, the literature on organizational research and that on marketing (Morgan and Hunt 1994; Cummings and Bromiley 1996; Ganesan and Hess 1997) define the facets of trust and show that this concept is based on three distinct types of presumptions regarding the behavior of the individual who is trusted:

– benevolence: the other party is supposed to act in a benevolent way, not harm, in the adhering to its commitments;

– coherence: trust is built on the predictability of the behavior of the other party;

– competence: trust is based on the assumption that the other party is able to meet its commitments by virtue of its competence.

Bonnet (2005) developed an explanatory model of the influence of the level of interpersonal trust between capital-investors and managers on the interaction processes, the roles of capital-investors in the post-investment phase and on the financial performance of investments. It operationalizes a trust construct with eight items based on the dimensions of benevolence, coherence and competence.

Sapienza and Korsgaard (1996) presented a second study measuring the trust between capital-investors and managers, which focuses on another dimension: integrity. The authors use a four-item measure of trust, in which capital-investors indicate how much they believe in honest, sincere and trustworthy leaders.

A third study focuses on trust in the sphere of venture capital; Zidi (2009) examined the influence of the relationship of trust between the venture capitalist and the entrepreneur on the creation of added value for the company and its stakeholders. In his work, the author adapted a scale borrowed from the field of marketing (Gurviez and Korchia 2002). This scale is articulated in three dimensions: credibility, integrity and benevolence.

Table 1.10 lists the measurement items for this scale; the first three items (FIKRSECU, CONFEGKR and GARANTKR) measure credibility, the next three items (SINCERKR, HONETKR and INTEREKR) measure integrity, and the last two items (AFIKRDEV and AMREPOKR) measure the benevolence of the venture capitalist.

The trust scale developed by Gurviez and Korchia (2002) is a measure of the relationship of trust between the consumer and the brand, the conceptualization of which is based on work in social psychology and marketing. Let us add that in addition to being used within the framework of research on investment capital, this scale has the advantage of presenting satisfactory psychometric qualities. Table 1.11 presents the trust construct, its dimensions and the associated items.

We choose to use this scale by adapting it to the specific context of equity crowdfunding investment. To do this, we first return to the data.

Item	Description
FIKRSECU	The strong involvement of the venture capitalist (KR) provides the entrepreneur (E) security
CONFEGKR	The E trusts the commitment of the KR in their business
GARANTKR	Cooperation with the KR is a guarantee
SINCERKR	The KR is sincere
HONETKR	The KR is honest
INTEREKR	The KR shows interest in the entrepreneur
AFIKRDEV	Financial support provided by the KR helps develop our structure
AMREPOKR	The KR continuously seeks, during their presence, to improve their responses to the needs of the company

Table 1.10. *Trust measurement scale in Zidi's study (2009)*

Credibility	This brand's products bring me security (CREDI1)
	I trust the quality of the products of this brand (CREDI3)
	Buying products from this brand is a guarantee (CREDI4)
Integrity	This brand is sincere towards consumers (INTE2)
	This brand is honest with its customers (INTE4)
	This brand shows interest in its customers (INTE5)
Benevolence	I think this brand is renewing its products to take into account the advancement of research (BIENV1)
	I believe this brand is continually looking to improve its responses to consumer requirements (BIENV2)

Table 1.11. *Trust measurement scale of Gurviez and Korchia (2002)*

A first textual analysis of our corpus initially confirms that the concept of trust is well directed toward the management team, as shown in the screenshot (Figure 1.6). This is the result of a CQL search query for co-occurring forms classified according to a specificity index[10] (indicator of probability for the co-occurrence) and located in a 20-word segment[11] centered on the generic form "confian.*".

10 "The exact calculation of the specificity index used in TXM is that of calculating the probability that the event occurs as many times as it is actually observed in the segment or even more frequently up to the size of the segment" in http://textometrie.ens-lyon.fr/files/documentation/Manuel%20de%20TXM%200.7%20FR.pdf.

11 Let us remember that the average length of testimonials is 19 words.

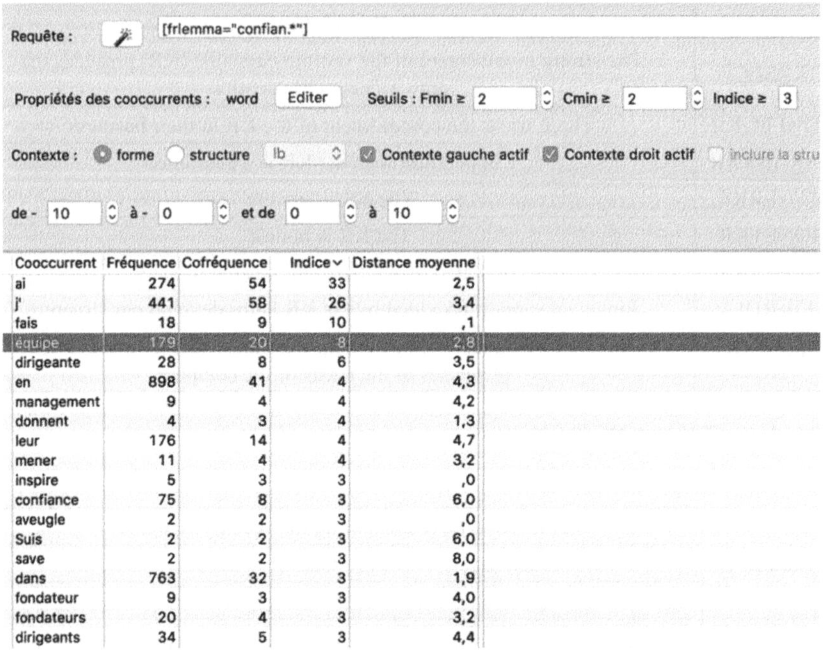

Cooccurrent	Fréquence	Cofréquence	Indice	Distance moyenne
ai	274	54	33	2,5
j'	441	58	26	3,4
fais	18	9	10	,1
équipe	179	20	8	2,8
dirigeante	28	8	6	3,5
en	898	41	4	4,3
management	9	4	4	4,2
donnent	4	3	4	1,3
leur	176	14	4	4,7
mener	11	4	4	3,2
inspire	5	3	3	,0
confiance	75	8	3	6,0
aveugle	2	2	3	,0
Suis	2	2	3	6,0
save	2	2	3	8,0
dans	763	32	3	1,9
fondateur	9	3	3	4,0
fondateurs	20	4	3	3,2
dirigeants	34	5	3	4,4

Figure 1.6. *Co-occurrences of the "confian.*" forms*

Next, Box 1.6 confirms that the three dimensions of the Trust construct, proposed by Gurviez and Korchia (2002), can be identified in the testimonies of the investors in our corpus; all items are also represented. The box associates a selection of five illustrative verbatim to each dimension.

Credibility dimension

"For the obvious interest in the development of clean energies + *the obvious involvement* of the project team".

"The team is *competent and inspires trust*".

"[…] *I trust the ability of the management team* to realize this potential".

"I believe in the innovative project of building smart high-tech wooden houses, in the complementarity and *commitment of a team of passionate professionals*".

"I have already invested the first time and *I trust the management, which has kept* its roadmap and *its commitments*. [...]"

Integrity dimension

"This project is sincere in its approach, created by *people who are confident and honest*, and must not fall into the hands of people who are only greedy".

"The values held by the company are similar to the DNA of the company that I lead and we have already worked with Treez, so I know their professionalism *and their sincere commitment*".

"*For the quick, clear, in-depth and compelling answers* given by leaders on the forum".

"*I got all the answers to the questions put to Mr. Popov*".

"[...] and *I was reassured by the serious answers of the leaders to the questions* raised by investors".

Benevolence dimension

"[...] In addition, the Fibandco *executives*, whom I met during the presentations organized by Wiseed at the BPI, *are always available to give the Wiseeders all the details on their development strategy*".

"I renewed my investment because i received an explanatory letter that I valued with an invitation to visit the laboratory. Even if I can't come to it, *I find the process transparent*".

"The project seems viable to me. *The leaders are responsive and quite precise*; this is clear in the discussions".

"The business plan is robust, it is the technology of the future, and *the leaders have a realistic vision of their strengths, weaknesses, and their short and long term potential*".

"[...] *I have complete trust in the team* to carry out this project".

Box 1.6. *Verbatim of investors and items of the Trust construct*

Below, we give our definition of trust, which results from a direct transposition of that of Gurviez and Korchia (2002) to our research context.

DEFINITION 1.1.– Trust in the management team of an entrepreneurial project raising funds by equity crowdfunding, from the investor's point of view, is a psychological variable that reflects a set of accumulated presumptions about the credibility, the integrity and the benevolence that the investor attributes to the founders:

– *the credibility* attributed to the management team is the assessment of its ability to meet the terms of trade in terms of expected performance, that is to say to meet the financial expectations of the investor. It is based on the investor assigning the management team a degree of competence in terms of financial expectations and the level of risk borne;

– *integrity* is the attribution of fair motivations to the management team in following up on its promises regarding the terms of trade, in other words the honesty of its "discourse" taken in the broadest sense;

– *benevolence* is the attribution of a sustainable investor orientation to the management team in terms of considering the investor's interests, including before their own interests in the short term. The presumption that the management team has a benevolent orientation toward him/her allows the investor to imagine a less uncertain future with respect to a future exit.

Finally, our adaptation of the Gurviez and Korchia (2002) measurement scale is minimal; we retain the three dimensions and all its items but, drawing on the adaptation of Zidi (2009) and drawing on our knowledge of the data corpus, we specify the items in a way that is specific to our research context. We therefore define trust as a three-dimensional reflective construct, represented by Figure 1.7, supplemented by Table 1.12, which gives the definition chosen for each item.

Finally, we would like to specify that the Trust variable, collected from the eight items above, is measured on a 5-point Likert scale ranging from "strongly disagree" to "strongly agree".

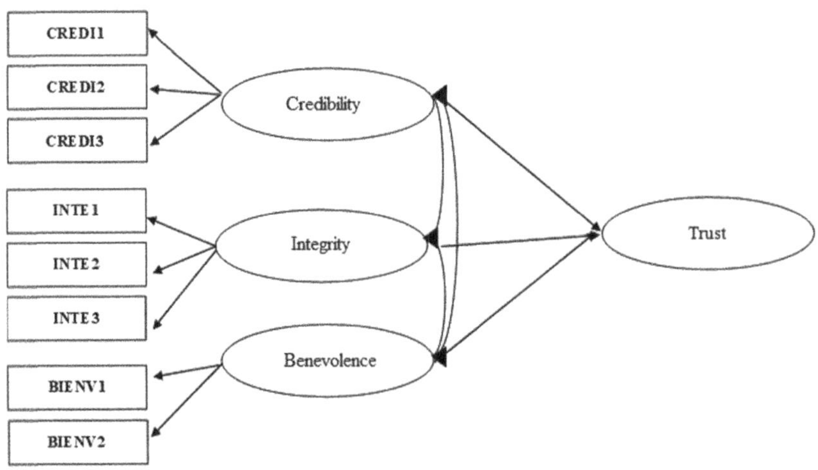

Figure 1.7. *The reflective Trust construct*

CREDI1	The management team's involvement makes me feel safe
CREDI2	I trust the commitment of the leaders
CREDI3	Partnering with this management team is a guarantee
INTE1	The management team is sincere toward investors
INTE2	The management team is honest with investors
INTE3	The management team shows interest in investors
BIENV1	I think this management team is committed to continuous improvement to develop its business
BIENV2	I think this management team continuously seeks to improve the information given to its investors

Table 1.12. *Indicators of the reflective Trust construct*

1.2.3.3. *Congruence to base values variable*

We have justified the motivational role of values above, in general as well as in the particular case of equity crowdfunding; this role justifies the presence of a variable relating to the investor's values in our explanatory model. We then decided to define a variable representing the strength of the congruence (or axiological distance) between the investor's values and the main value promoted (or implicitly associated) to the entrepreneurial project for two reasons – a theoretical reason and an empirical reason.

The theoretical reason is that for them to have an effect on behavior, the literature tells us that values must be activated (Verplanken and Holland 2002). For example, in the context of consumption, when stimulus is an object, it becomes desirable when its characteristics are linked, adjusted or when they are in congruence with the buyer's values: these are then activated. This relationship between characteristics and values is described by cognitive chains, a previously discussed theory (Valette-Florence 1994). Moreover, the processing can be conscious or unconscious, during the activation of a value, resulting from the encounter between the individual and a situational stimulus. Also, the more accessible the value concerned – i.e. if it easily comes to mind – the greater the probability that it will be activated (Schwartz 2006). Accessibility is therefore a function of the hierarchy of values, i.e. the subjective importance that the individual gives them. The determination of situational behaviors depends on this hierarchy of values. These rules correspond precisely to two characteristics of the values stated by Schwartz (2006):

> Characteristic 5: "Values are ranked in the order of importance to each other. A person's values can be classified according to the order of priority, and this hierarchy is a characteristic of that person".

> Characteristic 6: "The relative importance of multiple values guides action. […] Values contribute to action insofar as they are relevant in the context (and therefore likely to be activated) and important for the one who acts".

It is therefore the strength of the congruence between the values of the individual and the characteristics of the object encountered that activates the value with more or less intensity and ultimately guides the action.

Chataigné (2014) summarized this idea when she declared that for several value theorists, it was the need for consistency between values and actions that explained the choices and attitudes of individuals. Thus, the link between value and behavior is explained by a need for consistency that we operationalize using a congruence by making the values of the individual and the characteristics of the object of attention coincide.

The second reason is empirical because of the TXM software; we examined our qualitative corpus in order to better identify the words "*proches géographiquement*" (geographically close) from the form "*valeur*" (value) in the testimonies. The lexicographic tool adapted to this objective is the search for co-occurrences, that is to say the "particular attractions between pairs of forms within a given context unit" (Lebart and Salem 1994). The screenshot in Figure 1.8 is the result of a CQL query to find co-occurring forms classified according to a specificity index and located in a 20-word long segment centered on the form "*valeur*" (value).

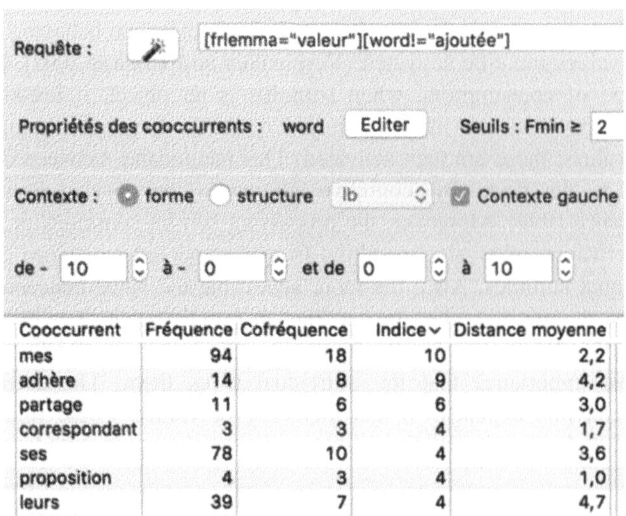

Figure 1.8. *Co-occurrences of the form* "valeur" *(value)*

The co-occurring verbs "*adhérer*" (to adhere), "*partager*" (to share) and "*correspondre*" (to correspond) seem to indicate that the investors connect their values to those of the project, because they fit and coincide, in other words they are in congruence. Returning to the text by concordance confirms this impression, as evidenced by the following verbatim (Box 1.7).

"The project is *coherent* with my values and has a very good chance of being profitable".

"Their innovation *corresponds* with my values!"

"I know this company and *I adhere* to its values, I know the products that I prefer when shopping and I must say that the quality is really impeccable".

"Fair trade *corresponds* well to my values. Their efforts deserve to be encouraged".

"Their organic and fair trade approach *meet* my values and my vision of tomorrow's world trade".

"I want to save intelligently, in *correlation* with my ecological values and values of solidarity, in the real economy".

"This company seems to be *aligned* with my values and I believe that the bioprinting sector is very promising".

"The presented project seemed to me to *conform* to my values of solidarity, support for initiative and great creativity".

"It *conforms* with my values of sustainable agriculture".

"This is exactly the type of project that *corresponds* to my economic and ethical values".

"It's a project *in line* with my values (social, ecological)".

"This project has an environmental, social and humane impact. It is interesting to follow a complex project from the inside *corresponding* to our values. This project *corresponds* to my environmental, economic and social values".

"This project *corresponds* to my environmental, economic and social values".

"The project seems relevant to me and *conforms* with my values".

"The project seems solid to me and *in line* with my values".

"*It represents my values* and its development potential lies in returning to better living, product outcome and the ecological values correspond to my criteria".

"In my opinion, the future is no longer nuclear and this is a transition *corresponding* to my values".

"I fully *adhere* to their values, regularly consume their products and wish to contribute to their development".

"In addition, I fully *adhere* to their values, and I am happy to be able to do my bit".

"I know this company and *I adhere* to its values, I know the products that I prefer when shopping and they are brilliant people who have values to which I adhere".

"It has values to which I *adhere*".

"*I adhere* to the values of this company (local production, and environment-friendly)".

"I *share* the same values and want to encourage people who are really involved".

"I *share* the same values and want to encourage people who really involved and go out of their way to create new things that better fit the world we live in".

"In addition, I *share* the values of Ethiquable, which represents a good way to diversify my investments".

"Project with a new vision and which *shares* the same values as me".

"It's a project that carries values of *sharing*".

"I believe in the team's ability to quickly develop sales and I *share* the brand values adopted by David Couthon".

"I *share* the values and the concept of the company. A complete enthusiast of products for almost 3 years".

Box 1.7. *Verbatim of investors and congruence of values*

For this reason, we have chosen not to develop an *ad hoc* measuring instrument, reflective or formative construct for this concept, but preferred to propose an original variable calculated as a "distance" (more precisely a measure of similarity) between the hierarchy of values of the individual and the value associated with the project. Box 3.1 of Chapter 3 of this volume describes the calculation of the Congruence to Base Values variable (the code for which is CONGR AXIO) for the data of an axiological preference structure (i.e. a hierarchy of values) and of the value associated with a project being funded.

From a theoretical point of view, we have opted for the typology of 10 values of Schwartz (1992) that the author called basic values by virtue of a postulate that is the basis of his theory; the author considered that human values are endowed with content and a universal structure that correspond to three requirements: "Biological needs, coordination of social interactions and survival or continuity in a society".

In order to determine the axiological preference structure, we chose the Short Schwartz's Value Survey (SVSS) questionnaire for measuring values for its simplicity as well as for its psychometric qualities. In fact, the Schwartz Value Survey (SVS) questionnaire by Schwartz (1992) presents 57 items, which, inserted in our questionnaire, would have increased the data collection time too much and induced cognitive fatigue in the subjects. Its short version proposed by Lindeman and Verkasalo (2005) only has 10 items, one per value. The study by the two authors shows that the simplified SVSS scale has satisfactory reliability and validity while offering an appreciable gain in terms of time.

The items of our questionnaire are freely translated according to the original scale in English. The wording of the question relating to this variable in the questionnaire is as follows.

"Please rate the importance of the following VALUES by putting them in the order of their importance to you, placing the most important to you on top and the least important to you at the bottom:

– power (social power, authority, wealth);

– achievement (success, skills, ambition, influence on people and events);

– hedonism (satisfaction of desires, enjoyment in life, indulgence for oneself);

– stimulation (daring, variety and stimulating life, exciting life);

– autonomy (creativity, freedom, curiosity, independence, choosing your own goals);

– universalism (open-mindedness, beauty of nature and the arts, social justice, a world of peace, equality, wisdom, unity with nature, protection of the environment);

– benevolence (help, honesty, forgiveness, loyalty, responsibility);

– tradition (respect for tradition, humility, accepting one's place in life, dedication, modesty);

– conformity (obedience, honoring parents and elders, self-discipline, politeness);

– security (national security, family security, social order, cleanliness, reciprocity of services rendered)".

This questionnaire results in an axiological preference structure, that is, the ordered list of base values V1<V2<…<V10.

1.2.3.4. *Affective reaction variable*

We have previously presented (see Table 2.1 of Volume 1) the components of Scherer's emotional construct, adapted from Sander and Scherer (2014). This model distinguishes cognitive, peripheral, efferent, motivational, and expressive motor components, as well as a subjective feeling.

Concerning the measurement of affective reactions, the recommendations of theorists suggest the use of multimethod approaches. This involves combining physiological measures with the observation of motor behavior (facial expression) as well as with subjective verbal and self-reported measures (Derbaix and Pham 1989; Derbaix and Poncin 2005). However, due to the time constraints associated with our data collection experiment, we opted to administer a questionnaire, even though this choice limits the measurement of affective reactions to a subjective self-reported approach. More precisely, we used the PAD scale developed by Mehrabian and Russel (1974), which finds its origins in the work of Osgood *et al.* (1957). While we are aware that measuring affective reactions from a single technique has its limits, some authors, like Ericsson and Simon (1980), believed that this may have nevertheless been sufficient to produce reliable data, provided that the time between the emotional feeling and the administration is reasonably short. We applied this advice rigorously by immediately following the induction sequences of affective reactions by administering questions pertaining to their measurement.

The PAD scale is based on a continuous approach based on a hypothesis of representation of affective reactions in a multidimensional space in which a given affective reaction is then identified at a point in space. According to Mehrabian and Russel, any affective response can be understood through three bipolar dimensions: pleasure, arousal and dominance. The valence distinguishes pleasant/positive emotions (like joy) from unpleasant/negative emotions (like sadness). Arousal represents the level of bodily arousal. Finally, dominance corresponds to the individual's ability to control the situation.

Two of these three dimensions are commonly used: valence (positive/negative) and arousal (calm/excited). This is why, in accordance with many authors (Russell 1980; Russell and Pratt 1980; Lemoine and Plichon 2000), we have excluded the dimension of dominance that finds little theoretical support in the field of emotions (Derbaix and Filser 2011) and whose explanatory power on the variance is limited. The chosen dimensions are therefore valence and arousal. Valence, in particular, is a cardinal dimension in the cognitive assessment of a stimulus, because the concordant results of work in behavioral psychology and neurophysiology show that it naturally induces approach-avoidance attitudes and determines preferences (Kahneman 2003). Zeelenberg *et al.* (2008) recalled that this term, borrowed from physics and chemistry, answers the question of knowing to what extent the results of an experiment are positive or negative, good or bad, pleasant or unpleasant.

As part of our experimental protocol, we measured "integral" affective reactions, i.e. reactions generated by exposure to stimuli: project pitch videos.

The measurement of the Affective Reaction variable is based on a 5-point scale (differential semantics), adapted[12] from Mehrabian and Russel (1974). The indications provided in the questionnaire are as follows:

"Among the eight following statements, concerning the video previously watched, please tick the box that best corresponds to your feelings:

1) unhappy/happy;

2) upset/happy;

3) unsatisfied/satisfied;

4) sad/cheerful;

5) hopeless/optimistic;

6) without energy/full of energy;

7) asleep/awake;

8) unstimulated/stimulated".

Figure 1.9 presents a graphic representation of the construct and specifies the codes associated with its indicators.

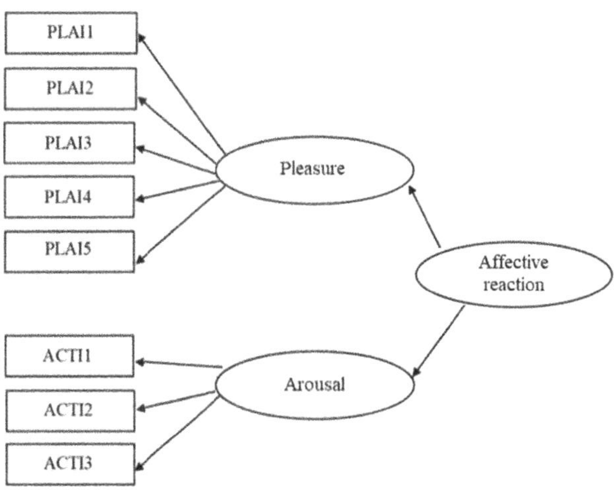

Figure 1.9. *Reflective construct of the Affective Reaction variable, dimensions and indicators*

---

12 The original semantic scale has six points; the constraints of the LimeSurvey tool led us to define a semantic scale with five points, which however has the advantage of consistency with the number of levels (also five) of the questions, measured using a Likert scale.

1.2.3.5. *Familiarity variable*

To our knowledge, work in the field of finance on the familiarity that investors maintain with assets is rare and does not conceptualize familiarity as a latent multidimensional construct. Thus, the research by Ganzach (2000) on the effects of the familiarity of financial analysts with assets and on their perception of profitability–risk relationship is based on a series of experiments in which subjects must make a judgment on lists of securities considered *a priori* as familiar and then unfamiliar.

In order to operationalize the concept of familiarity more precisely, it seemed necessary to borrow from work on consumer theory in the field of marketing. In this field of research, familiarity is part of the more general concept of "brand awareness". According to Korchia (2004), this concept is used in many explanatory models of consumer behavior and can be defined as follows: "Knowledge of a brand represents information relating to this brand stored in the consumer's long-term memory".

According to Alba and Hutchinson (1987), this concept can be subdivided into two major components: familiarity and expertise. Korchia (2004) clarified the relative relationship of these concepts by considering that familiarity is an antecedent of knowledge, since the stored information follows the experiences of the consumer, while expertise is a consequence of the stored knowledge that allows, or prevents, the consumer to perform tasks.

According to Alba and Hutchinson (1987): "Familiarity can be defined as the 'number of experiences accumulated by the consumer in relation to the product'". And Korchia (2004) specified: "That is to say exposures to advertising, the quest for information such as discussing with sellers or friends as well as frequenting points of sale or even possessing a product…" .

This definition echoes that of the *Centre national de ressources textuelles et lexicales* (the French National Center for Textual and Lexical Resources) of the CNRS, indicated below, in the sense that "the accumulation of experiences" of the first complements well the "repeated practice" of the second: "The habit we have of something, resulting from a deep knowledge that we have acquired through learning or repeated practice".

Like Korchia, Lebrun (2002) listed the multiple sources of familiarity with the brand: exposure to advertising, seeking information at the point of sale, interactions with those around us or with sales staff, or even direct familiarity with the product or service.

We take these defining elements and adapt them to the specific context of equity crowdfunding investment on the basis of our knowledge of the qualitative corpus and propose the following definition:

> Familiarity can be defined as "the number of experiences linked to the company in investment research or to its context and accumulated by the investor", that is to say the exposure to the company, its founders, its products or services, its field of activity, its geographical area, or even the problem solved by what it offers.

With a view to operationalizing familiarity with the brand, Korchia (2004) summarized the measures proposed in the literature, starting with the first definition of familiarity by Baker *et al.* (1986). This is one-dimensional; familiarity is "[...] linked to the amount of time spent processing information about the brand, regardless of the nature or content of that processing". This definition is rudimentary in view of subsequent studies that pointed out the difference in the effects induced on the consumer by the direct (use of the product) or indirect (exposure to advertising material) nature of the information. Also, Korchia considered that familiarity with the brand is a three-dimensional construct whose facets are: direct experience (purchase and use), exposure to communication, and interpersonal familiarity. Moreover, since the relationships linking these three dimensions to familiarity are causal, the construct is formative. Table 1.13 describes his proposal for this latent variable.

Dimensions	Possible components (or measurements)
Purchase and use (or direct experiences, or even familiarity with products)	Number of products purchased and/or owned, frequency of use, exposure to products at the point of sale, etc.
Communication exposure (or familiarity with communication)	Exposure to traditional media advertisements, non-media stocks, or to information not issued by the company (press).
Interpersonal familiarity	The individual has relationships and discussions about it (word-of-mouth) with other people around them, or with sellers.

Table 1.13. *The three dimensions of familiarity and their components according to Korchia (2004)*

Although there are similarities, the context of equity crowdfunding investment is significantly different from that of consumption, familiarity through purchase and use, associated with consumption, is relatively similar to that attributable to an investment previously carried out in a startup as well as the use of its products. Familiarity due to exposure and communication does not seem relevant to us in the context of investing, as funded startups are in the seed stage and, therefore, are generally unknown to investors. They also do not have the financial capacity to afford media advertising campaigns. Finally, the personal familiarity of the consumption context can be linked to the concept of friends and family that is well known in the investment sphere. This is why, based on the work of Korchia (2004) and relying on the analysis of the qualitative corpus, we propose an *ad hoc* Familiarity construct to the context of equity crowdfunding investment, the dimensions and indicators of which are shown in Table 1.14 and are represented in Figure 1.10, supplemented by Box 1.8.

We classify interpersonal familiarity (with managers) under the "Familiarity with the company" dimension because, at the beginning of the entrepreneurial adventure, the startup and its management team are inseparable; the startup only exists through its founders, while the attributes of the company (geographical location, product and field of activity) may change from the start-up phase onwards, for example in the event of a startup pivot (i.e. in the event of radical change of business model and/or the products or services offered).

Although familiarity through work in the field of activity of the funded startup appears clearly in the data, we did not retain the associated item because the data collection experiment (described in Chapter 2) mobilizes the exclusive participation of students. However, most of them have not yet entered the labor market.

Dimensions	Indicators
Familiarity with the company	*Direct familiarity* – Has already invested in the company – Already uses the products or services *Interpersonal familiarity* – Personally knows one or more managers
Familiarity with the company's attributes	*Familiarity with the field of activity* – Their job is related to the field of activity of the company – Their hobbies or passions are related to the field of activity of the company *Geographical familiarity* – Lives in the same city or region of the company being funded *Familiarity with the problem* – Is or has already been confronted with the problem solved by the company's offer

Table 1.14. *Dimensions, components and indicators of the Familiarity construct in the context of equity crowdfunding investment*

We should also remember that familiarity attributable to the geographical location of the company (Item ATTR2) finds theoretical legitimacy in the work of

Mollick (2013), while interpersonal familiarity (Item ENTR3) is supported by Agrawal *et al.* (2011), Mollick (2013) and Wechsler (2013).

Finally, in order to anchor this construct in data, we associate, in Box 1.8, a selection of five illustrative verbatim for each of its items.

Item ATTR1 (my hobbies or passions are related to the field of activity of the company)

"I am *passionate about their field of activity* and their skills".

"I am *passionate about renewable energies.* I support this innovation because I wanted this type of turbine to exist and I discovered through Wiseed that Save Innovation does it [...]".

"As an engineer, I love the concept. *I am also a big fan of sailing*".

"Startups that improve *disease treatment processes fascinate me*".

"I have always been *passionate about 3D printing/*3D factory and I have also registered dozens of .fr and .com domain names, in French and in English, skin printing is even more revolutionary and exciting… To be continued!"

Item ATTR2 (I live in the same city or region of the company being funded)

"*I even live in the same department* and for many other reasons".

"A great adventure that I can't wait to see *land in my city*!"

"This is an important step forward in the fight against cancer, and I'm quite proud that this *project comes from my city*".

"The company is also *located in the region where I currently live.* It's a startup from my region with great potential".

"In addition, Ethiquable is located in the Gers, and being from the South-West, it is an investment to *support the activity of my region*".

Item ATTR3 (I have already confronted the problem solved by the company's offer)

"*I own a swimming pool myself* and I understand the interest of Flipr for users. Regulating the water in a swimming pool is complicated and expensive. Flipr will be successful because it is a great product that is paid for directly with the savings".

"I find the product great. *Being a user of cosmetic tubes*, which I already find more hygienic than jars, I am sure that this airless tube corresponds to a real need!"

"*I myself am an internet consumer* via *my smartphone* and want a simple, secure and fast interface to place orders".

"I appreciate the social project and the concept, *I myself am a locavore* and from my point of view the business model seems coherent to me".

"*I myself am affected by cancer*, and think that solutions like the ones you are considering will effectively contribute to more precise targeting to better identify it and therefore better eradicate it".

Item ENTR1 (I have already invested in the company)

"*I have already invested* in the first fundraiser".

"*I have already invested* the first time and I trust the management, which has kept its roadmap and its commitments. From a personal point of view, I want to make my small contribution in the fight against cancer".

"*I was already an investor* when I first raised funds. I still believe in the potential of this company and its medicine".

"*I have already invested in three projects of the company* Forest Finance in 2014 and 2015 and I think that it is a strong and serious company that offers excellent projects with a realistic remuneration objective as well as a consideration of environment and good agricultural practices".

"*I had already invested* via Wiseed"

Item ENTR2 (I know the products or services of this company)

"*I am a customer myself* and love the concept".

"*I am already a consumer of the brand's products.* I appreciate them and I support the united approach of this cooperative".

"*I am already a consumer of several of their products*, so it's a complementary way to support their interesting initiative!"

"*I have used this paint before in our house* and I am very satisfied with it".

"I have *already had the opportunity to eat in their restaurants on several occasions.* Because I deeply believe in the values defended by the company, and its business model. And because I think this company is responding to consumer demand".

Item ENTR3 (I directly or indirectly know one or more founders of this company)

"*I know the founder* and find the project useful".

"*I know the founder*, and I trust them".

"*I know the founder personally* and his innovative concept fits in with the times".

"*I have known the founder, Fabien, for 7 years* and I was able to follow his trajectory from the laboratory to the startup".

"*I know the founder very well* and I fully believe in the success of his project".

Box 1.8. *Investor verbatim and familiarity construct items*

The Familiarity construct is presented in Figure 1.10, and supplemented by Table 1.15 which lists the associated items. This construct is formative and non-reflective, since its items are not interchangeable and do not necessarily covariate; they do not share a common theme and are antecedents of Familiarity (Jarvis *et al.* 2003). For example, investors may be familiar with the project because they have already invested during prior fundraising by equity crowdfunding, without having any personal link to the leaders, the geographical location, the field of activity of the company, etc. Conversely, living in the city or region of the company, or being passionate about robotics when the company is positioned in this field of activity, arouses a feeling of familiarity; the causality is therefore from items toward the construct and not the reverse.

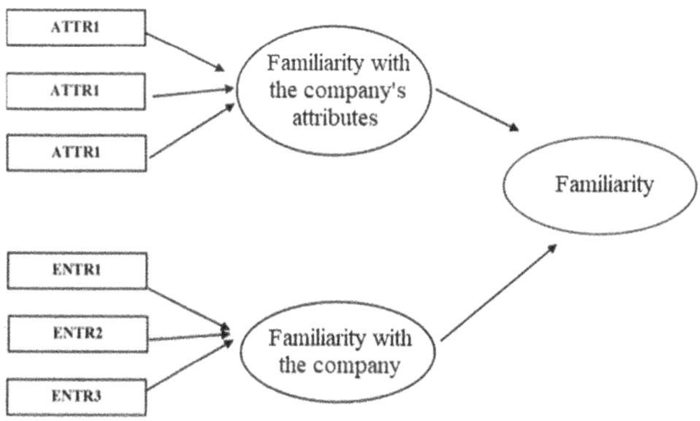

Figure 1.10. *Formative familiarity construct*

ATTR1	My hobbies or passions are related to the field of activity of the company
ATTR2	I live in the city or region of this company
ATTR3	I have already faced the problem solved by what this company offers
ENTR1	I have already invested in the company
ENTR2	I know the products or services of this company
ENTR3	I directly or indirectly know one or more founders of this company

Table 1.15. *Indicators of the formative familiarity construct*

The data for the Familiarity variable are collected using six items measured on a 5-point Likert scale, ranging from "strongly disagree" to "strongly agree".

1.2.3.6. *Interest variable*

Since the early 1990s, research in educational science has revealed the importance of the concept of interest as a motivational factor. For some theorists, interest is an emotion (Izard 1977; Frijda 1986; Silvia 2006). Silvia showed, for example, that the emotion of pleasure is different from interest; while the function of pleasure is to strengthen the attachment to an object or achievement of a goal, interest promotes exploration of new domains or objects (Schiefele 2009). According to Nico Frijda, interest is also an emotion that differs from pleasure, which results from preferences and whose function is to induce increased attention toward a specific object.

In a second line of research, other theorists have mainly carried out empirical studies to understand the link between interest and professional activities, for the purpose of career guidance (Fenouillet 2016).

A third stream is based on the work of Deci and Ryan on intrinsic motivation (for example, Deci and Ryan (1985)) in which interest is the fact of practicing an activity for oneself. In this line of research, the work initiated by Hidi and Baird (1988) made it possible to distinguish two distinct conceptual forms of interest, understood as a two-dimensional construct: individual and situational. Individual interest is understood as an enduring individual preference for certain subjects or activities, while situational interest is an emotional state triggered by a situational stimulus (Yennek 2014).

More precisely, in Schiefele's conception of individual interest (1991), interest is a latent characteristic that represents the long-term orientation that an individual maintains with an object, a domain of knowledge or an activity. This dimension of interest has three facets: the first relating to positive feeling, particularly joy, and the second relating to value, that is to say the importance given to the object of interest per se.

In Schiefele's approach, interest is a content-specific concept that directs behavior and involves attaching significant value to a subject or activity for itself, also individual interest therefore presents an intrinsic motivational character in the sense of Deci and Ryan (1985), which constitutes the third facet of the concept.

Situational interest is associated with immediate reactions of varying duration, triggered by an environmental stimulus that attracts the attention of the individual and arouses his/her curiosity; it is therefore a psychological state (Hidi and Baird 1986; Hidi and Renninger 2006). We go back to the data in our corpus to determine whether they reveal the two dimensions of interest. First, we run a co-occurrence query to identify forms close to the word interest.

The result of this query indicates that the forms which are significantly co-occurring (that is to say with a specificity index ≤ 3) in relation to the two dimensions of interest are the "*projet*" (project), the "*concept*" (concept), the "*idée*" (idea) and the "*domaine*" (domain), the latter referring to the "*domaine d'activité*" (domain of activity) of the startup. From our knowledge of the corpus, we can specify that, among these four forms, the first three can be associated with the dimension "*intérêt situationnel*" (situational interest), while the domain (of activity) can be associated with the dimension "*intérêt individuel*" (individual interest)[13]. This statement can be understood by reading the verbatim text. When we come back to the text using the TXM concordance tool, the distinction is obvious. Box 1.9 brings together a random selection of testimonials from investors mentioning these four forms (project, concept, idea and domain, the latter form does not necessarily appear explicitly, with the domain itself being mentioned more frequently). The testimonies relating to the field of activity mention "*intérêt constant*" (a constant interest), "*intérêt personnel*" (a personal interest), or a field of activity related to the passion or the profession of the investor. This suggests a stable interest, linked to non-circumstantial preferences, as seems to be the case for the testimonies associated with the situational interest dimension mentioning the project, idea or concept.

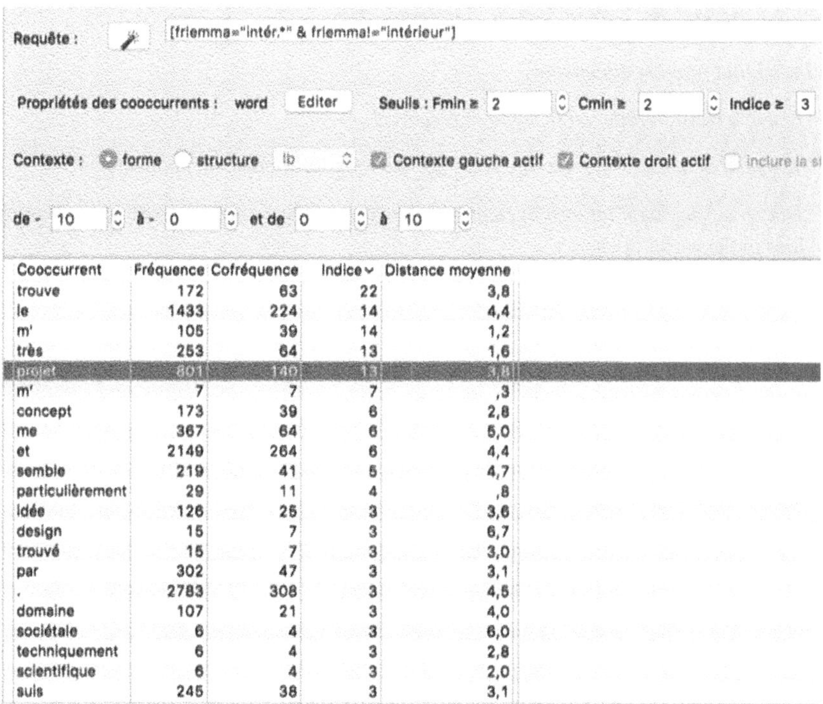

Cooccurrent	Fréquence	Cofréquence	Indice	Distance moyenne
trouve	172	63	22	3,8
le	1433	224	14	4,4
m'	105	39	14	1,2
très	253	64	13	1,6
projet	801	140	13	3,8
m'	7	7	7	,3
concept	173	39	6	2,8
me	367	64	6	5,0
et	2149	264	6	4,4
semble	219	41	5	4,7
particulièrement	29	11	4	,8
idée	126	25	3	3,6
design	15	7	3	6,7
trouvé	15	7	3	3,0
par	302	47	3	3,1
.	2783	308	3	4,5
domaine	107	21	3	4,0
sociétale	6	4	3	6,0
techniquement	6	4	3	2,8
scientifique	6	4	3	2,0
suis	245	38	3	3,1

Figure 1.11. *Co-occurrences of interest ("inter.*" form)*

13 This second dimension is less present (with a frequency of 107 against a frequency of 1,100 = 801 + 173 + 126 for the "situational interest" dimension) and also less strongly linked to the form "*intérêt*" (interest) (with the weakest specificity index of the four forms). It should be noted from the outset that we will find this predominance of situational interest over individual interest in our empirical results.

Situational interest dimension

"*I found the project interesting* and the financial data valid".

"*The concept seems interesting* and promising to me".

"*The project seems interesting to me* combining the use of non-recovered waste with the production of energy".

"*The concept of the product is interesting* and local".

"Because *the project is interesting* and offers medium-term potential".

"*I find the idea interesting* as it combines design and environmental protection. Good luck to the founders".

"*I like the idea and I am interested in the project*".

Individual interest dimension

"*I have a constant interest in medical research*".

"*The field of activity interests me* and I see the interest of practical applications".

"*Due to my personal interest in cleantech startups* and in connection with my professional activities in the world of energy".

"*I have a special interest in biodiversity* and societal projects".

"I have *a great interest in robots*".

"*I am a health manager (medical-technical) and therefore very aware and interested in medical progress*. I think this must be a big step forward for oncology".

"It's an innovative project *in the field of technical textiles and energy, which are subjects that particularly interest me*".

Box 1.9. *Verbatim of interested investors broken down according to the situational interest and individual interest dimensions*

The two dimensions of interest appear in our data; we therefore decided to operationalize them.

However, according to Schiefele (2009), states of interest, whether individual or situational, are very similar, which may justify the use of a single construct of interest. Supporting this proposition, Linnenbrink-Garcia *et al.* (2010) also hypothesized that these two forms of interest, although distinct, are structurally similar, since the model of

Hidi and Renninger (2006) showed the potential evolution of situational interest toward individual interest. We have chosen to re-categorize the two dimensions of interest under an "umbrella construct" of interest. Then, the author added that, with regard to situational interest, the measurement scales usually question respondents about their level of interest (implicitly considered as situational) with regard to the object concerned. Further, Schiefele advocated the development of a measuring instrument based on existing theories of situational interest. According to the definitions of situational interest given by Silvia (2006) and Hidi (2000), Schiefele believed that an instrument for measuring situational interest should include an assessment of attention, curiosity and affective implication toward the object of interest.

In her doctoral work, focusing on situational interest in the context of continuing education for adults, Yennek (2014) developed a scale for measuring situational interest (see Table 1.16), which is conceptually based on two dimensions: attention and emotional involvement. Only the items in italics are retained after an exploratory factor analysis. We were inspired by the formulations of these items, by transposing them to our context ("*projet*" (project) therefore replaces "*intervenant*" (speaker)), to define the items of the affective involvement and attention subdimensions of the situational interest dimension of our construct of interest. We added a specific item for the curiosity subdimension (item CURI1) in accordance with the recommendation of Schiefele (2009).

TRIG1	*The speakers were fascinating.*
TRIG2	The speakers were able to capture my attention during this training.
TRIG3	This training was so stimulating that it was easy to pay close attention to it.
TRIG4	*The speakers were able to capture my attention during this training.*
TRIG5	This training attracted my full attention.
TRIG6	*The speakers were really interesting.*
TRIG7	*I really appreciated the speakers.*

Table 1.16. *Items of the activated situational interest (Yennek 2014)*

Concerning the measurement of individual interest, we transposed the Study Interest Questionnaire (SIQ) from Schiefele *et al.* (1993). The extensive version of the SIQ has 18 items referring to the intrinsic motivation linked to a specific domain, as well as to the different valences of intrinsic feelings and the different valences of value associated with it. Box 1.10 presents a version of the SIQ scale[14], translated from German; the nine questions highlighted in italics (questions 3, 5, 6, 8, 11, 12, 13, 16, 18) can, according to the authors, reflect a short version of the questionnaire.

14 Available at: https://www.researchgate.net/publication/281228309_New_version_of_Study_interest_questionnaire.

Valences related to feelings

1) Working with the topic and issues in my field is not really one my favorite activities.*

2) I don't really like to talk about subjects related to my studies.*

3) *After a long weekend or vacation, I can't wait to go back to school.*

4) Involving myself with my field of activity puts me in a good mood.

5) *I prefer to talk about my hobbies rather than my activity.**

6) *When I'm in a library or bookstore, I like to browse magazines or books on topics related to my field of activity.*

7) Many subdomains within my field of activity mean nothing to me.*

Valences linked to value

8) *It was very important for me to be able to study this particular subject.*

9) To be completely honest, I am sometimes quite indifferent about my field of activity.*

10) The subject of my field of activity actually has very little to do with my personal achievement.*

11) *Compared to other things that are of great importance to me (for example, hobbies, social life), my studies are significantly less important to me.**

12) *Working with a particular subject is more important to me than hobbies and entertainment.*

13) *Even before I started my studies, my current field of activity was important to me.*

14) I am sure that studying my field of activity has a positive influence on my personality.

Intrinsic orientation

15) If I had enough time, I would work more intensively on certain aspects of my studies, even if they had nothing to do with the requirements of the course.

16) *I am convinced that I have chosen the field of activity which corresponds to my personal preferences.*

17) Even before coming to college, I spent time on purpose thinking about my field of work (for example, reading books, going to conferences, having conversations with other people).

18) *I chose my specialization mainly because of its interesting subject.*

**Reversed coding.*

Box 1.10. *SIQ scale for measuring individual interest*

We have chosen to operationalize the individual interest dimension by transposing, to the specific context of our research, the questions forming the short version of the SIQ questionnaire by Schiefele *et al.* (1993). Finally, we conceptualize interest as a reflective construct, grouping together 14 items spread over two dimensions. Figure 1.12 represents our construct; Table 1.17 specifies its items.

Although we have relied on theory by adapting existing scales, the field of application of this construct, the sciences of education and more especially the reading make conceptual borrowing difficult. That is why we will pay particular attention to this construct in the data analysis within Chapter 3 to ensure that the two dimensions of interest – although combined under the same umbrella construct – separately meet the psychometric quality criteria of reliability and validity. We will also ensure that items on the situational interest scale form a single key component, distinct from those formed by indicators associated with individual interest.

Finally, the data from the Interest variable, collected from the 14 items below, are measured on a 5-point Likert scale, ranging from "strongly disagree" to "strongly agree".

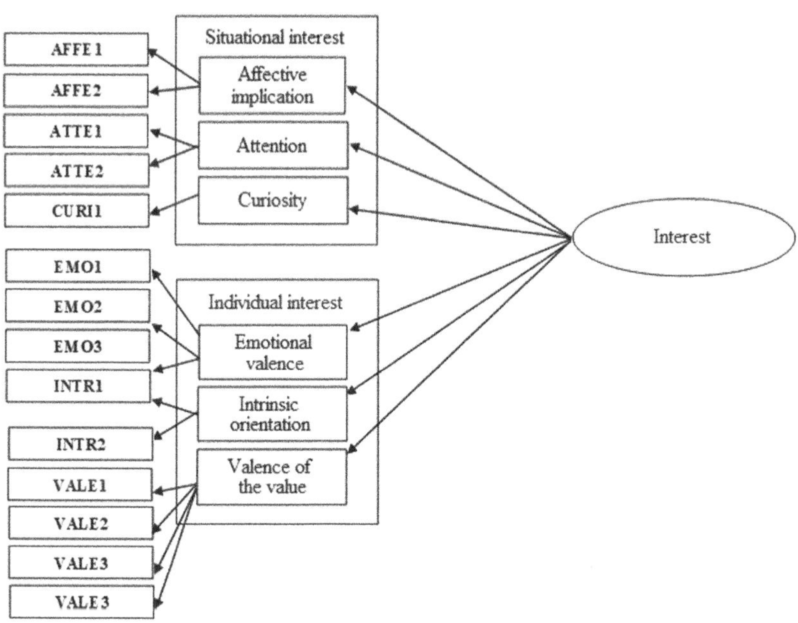

Figure 1.12. *Reflective interest construct*

Interest	**Situational interest**	Affective implication	AFFE1	I really appreciate this project
			AFFE2	I found this project to be stimulating
		Attention	ATTE1	This project caught my attention
			ATTE2	This project captivated me
		Curiosity	CURI1	This project aroused my curiosity
	Individual interest	Emotional valence	EMO1	After a long period without contact with this domain, I look forward to having information related to it again
			EMO2	I prefer talking about my hobbies rather than this domain
			EMO3	When I'm in a bookstore, I like to browse magazines related to this domain
		Intrinsic orientation	INTR1	With (COMPANY NAME), I am convinced that I have chosen an investment that corresponds to my personal preferences
			INTR2	I chose this investment first because of this interesting domain
		Valence of the value	VALE1	This domain has real personal value for me
			VALE2	Compared to the other subjects that matter to me (in connection with my hobbies), this domain is much less important to me
			VALE3	Acquiring new knowledge in this area is more important than acquiring new knowledge about my hobbies
			VALE4	Before I decided to invest, this domain was important to me

Table 1.17. *Indicators of the reflective interest construct*

1.2.3.7. *Moderating variables*

1.2.3.7.1. Personality type variable

The Myers-Briggs Type Indicator (MBTI)[15] is based on the theoretical work of Carl Jung, who observed that psychological preferences play a role in judgment and the relationship between individuals and the world (Filbeck *et al.*, 2005). In addition, the MBTI describes a person's preferred ways of making decisions based on psychological types identified by Jung (1923). Based on self-assessment, the MBTI questionnaire measures the strength of individuals' preferences over four dimensions, indicating: (1) the direction in which individuals prefer to focus their attention (extraversion or introversion); (2) how they acquire information about their environment (by sense or intuition); (3) how they make decisions (by thought or feeling); and (4) how they relate to the environment (by judgment or perception) (Filbeck *et al.* 2005).

Table 1.18 presents the two dimensions that we use as moderating variables: information acquisition preferences and decision-making preferences.

The Personality Intuition variable corresponding to the Preferences for Information Acquisition dimension is collected by a single item, measured by a binary nominal scale recognizing the "S" and "N" modalities; the associated code is MBTI1.

The question asked is: "In the below table[16], choose the statement that best suits you for each line. There is no right or wrong answer. Summarize the sentences that correspond to you for the two columns of each table to establish your S-N score and thus determine whether you are more S or more N".

Please select one of the following:

– you are more like S;

– you are more like N.

The Feeling Personality variable corresponding to the Decision-Making Preferences dimension is collected by a single item measured by a binary nominal scale recognizing the "T" and "F" modalities; the associated code is MBTI2.

---

15 See, for example, Quenk (2009).

16 There are four forms of the American MBTI, which differ in the number of questions asked (from 93 to 222). Given the length of our questionnaire, we opted for a simplified version, freely translated from Tieger *et al.* (2014).

Information acquisition preferences	Decision-making preferences
Sensing (S) Individuals focus on the concrete aspects of a situation. They value what can be seen, touched, felt, smelled or heard. They tend to be practical minded and grounded in the present. Their concern for details and facts tends to make them more accepting of the world as it is.	Thinking (T) Individuals focus on objective decision-making based on a desire for fairness and detachment. They seek logic in their analyses of situations and any consequences that result. They desire objectivity and prefer to work to discover what may be wrong in situations that arise.
Intuition (N) Individuals focus on the abstract, even using a "sixth sense" or "gut feeling" to acquire information. They value relationships which are not immediately recognizable to the senses. Rather, they strive to understand the "big picture", are change-oriented and interested in future possibilities.	Feeling (F) Individuals focus on subjective decision-making, based on a desire for harmony. They seek to consider the impact on people in their analysis of a situation. They value interpersonal relations, preferring to affirm what is right with situations and offering appreciation and sympathy as needed.

Table 1.18. *MBTI information acquisition preferences and decision-making preferences (Filbeck and Smith 1997)*

"S" (Sensing) in general	"N" (Intuition) in general
Focus on facts and specific details	Interested in ideas and general summaries
Appreciate practical solutions	Notice everything that is new and different
Note the details and remember facts	Think about the future implications
Live in the present moment	Follow their instincts
Trust the experience	Seek to understand
Prefer to rely on recognized competence	Like to learn new skills
Prefer step-by-step instructions	Are imaginative: see what could be done
Work at a steady pace	Overflowing with energy
Are realistic	Are attracted by original ideas

Table 1.19. *MBTI short questionnaire, Intuition variable*

Please select one of the following:

– you are more like T;

– you are more like F.

It should be added that, according to a meta-analysis by Capraro and Capraro (2002), MBTI's measurements are generally reliable.

"T" (Thinking) in general	**"F" (Feeling) in general**
Strive to be objective in their decisions	Base their decisions on their values and feelings
Appear calm and reserved	Are warm and friendly
Appreciate loyalty and justice	Appreciate harmony and compassion
Get involved in few things	Take things to heart
Quickly notice flaws and defects	Are quick to compliment
Love arguing for fun	Avoid discussion and conflict
Are motivated by the fruition of what they undertake	Are motivated by praise
Are sensitive to logic	Trust their insights
Are honest and direct	Are diplomatic and tactful

Table 1.20. *MBTI short questionnaire, Feeling variable*

1.2.3.7.2. Investor Sophistication variable

Sophistication corresponds to the level of knowledge on financial markets and expertise on financial products (Magron 2014). In terms of equity crowdfunding investment, the sophistication of investors corresponds to their ability to understand and analyze the business plan.

As part of the data collection experiment, we have chosen to consider management science students as sophisticated (apart from those enrolled in the first year of an undergraduate degree).

The Investor Sophistication variable is collected by a single item, measured by a nominal binary scale recognizing the modalities "Yes" and "No"; the question asked, along with its code, is as follows: "Are you studying at IAE (IAEs are Graduate Schools of Management within the French Public Research Universities) in the second year of the undergraduate degree or beyond?" (IAE1).

1.2.3.7.3. Risk Aversion variable

Risk aversion can be defined as "an economic behavior. Investors and bettors usually have a certain aversion to risk. They prefer a relatively safe gain to a much larger but uncertain gain"[17]. In economics, the risk aversion is traditionally measured

17 Available at: https://fr.wikipedia.org/wiki/Risque#Aversion_au_risque.

by means of successive choices between two or more possibilities, at least one of which includes a hazard, formalized by a probability. However, we opted for a workaround, given the length of our questionnaire and the cognitive fatigue induced, as well as to avoid inserting complex explanations within the experiment, which are nevertheless necessary for understanding the choices between lotteries. Nivoix (2008) specifically proposed a simple and quick alternative solution consisting of collecting, in a declarative manner, the expression of the subject's attitude toward risk in two questions.

Thus, the Risk Aversion variable is collected using two items measured on a 5-point Likert scale, ranging from "strongly disagree" to "strongly agree". The questions asked, along with their code, are as follows: "I would rather be sure of winning a little than unsure of winning a lot" (AVER1); "I prefer to be sure of losing a little, than uncertain of losing a lot" (AVER2).

1.2.3.7.4. Gender variable

The Gender variable is collected by a single item, measured using a nominal binary scale recognizing the "Male" and "Female" modalities; the question asked, along with its code, is as follows: "What is your gender?" (GENR1).

1.2.3.7.5. Activated values variable: power through resources or personal safety

This variable is not formalized in the questionnaire but is calculated according to the hierarchy of values entered by the subject. This variable is binary and takes the value 1 if the subject has declared the power value as being most important to him/her and the value 0 otherwise.

1.2.3.7.6. Relative amount of the investment

This variable is not formalized in the questionnaire; it is possible to take into account the potentially moderating effect of the relative amount of the investment insofar as, in the questionnaire, the subjects make two successive asset allocations. The first time, the allocation is €200; the second time, the allocation represents virtually all of the subject's assets. Thus, it is possible to compare the proportion of allocation for a given asset in the two cases. For example, a subject may have invested 100% of the €200 in the Ethiquable company but only 25% of his/her assets.

1.2.3.8. *Control variables*

Finally, we specified two control variables that we felt should be taken into account.

1.2.3.8.1. Age variable

Behaviors and decisions in the face of risk are not constant over the course of an individual's life. Studies in epidemiology, psychology and on brain development converge to describe individuals more and more averse to risk as they move away from adolescence (Cauffman *et al.* 2010). These behavioral variations could be explained by the modifications of a system, regulated by dopamine, and involved in the functioning of the brain and the nervous system. This system is involved in the reward system; it ensures affective and motivational regulation and promotes the survival of the organism. Furthermore, it is not unthinkable that young investors take more risks than their elders by making less thoughtful and more affective choices.

The Age variable is collected by a single item measured using a proportion scale. The question asked, along with its code, is: "How old are you?" (AGE1).

1.2.3.8.2. Have Already Invested in Equity Crowdfunding variable

Startups can sometimes do several financing rounds by soliciting the same crowdfunding platform, which gives investors the opportunity to invest several times in the same company. However, a study carried out by Lemoine and Onnée (2003) showed that French listed companies are implementing a relational strategy of building loyalty and increasing the share of capital held by individual investors, because the latter tends to recommit to a company in which they already hold shares. Also, it seems reasonable to think that an investor who has already supported a company has a tropism that encourages him/her to reinvest again.

The Have Already Invested in Equity Crowdfunding variable is collected by a single item measured using a nominal binary scale, recognizing the "Yes" and "No" modalities. The question asked, along with its code, is: "Have you ever invested in equity crowdfunding?" (INVE1).

Figure 1.13 provides a synthetic schematic presentation of the main variables and constructs of the explanatory model (excluding mediating and control variables), classified into three groups: formative constructs, reflective constructs and calculated variables. The original measurement scales that served as the basis for adaptation are also specified.

1.2.4. *Other hypotheses of the model*

In this section, we specify the remaining hypotheses of the explanatory model, distributed between "indirect" effects (section 1.2.4.1) and moderation effects (section 1.2.4.2). We can recall that the hypotheses H1 to H5, relating to the direct effects of the variables of the model, have been discussed above (see section 1.2.1.2). Figure 1.14 gives a schematic representation of the explanatory model.

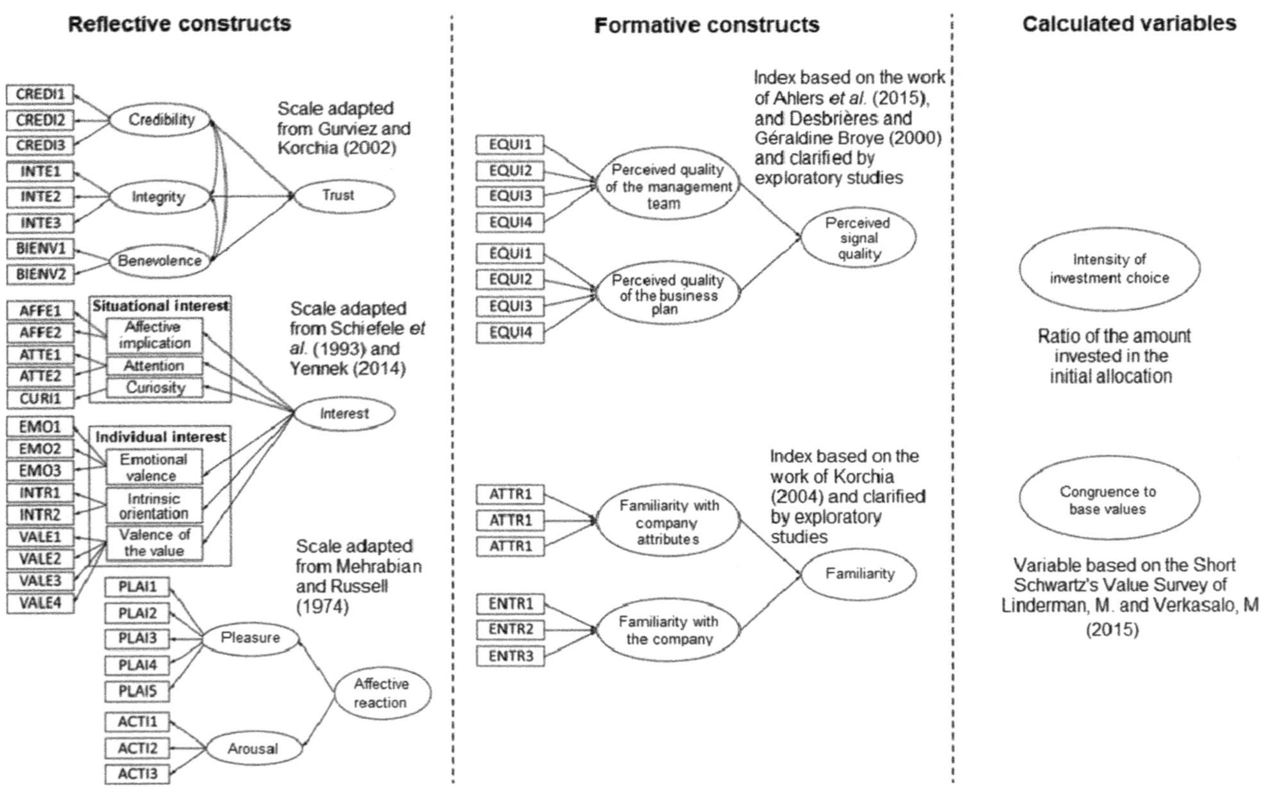

Figure 1.13. *Summarized representation of the main variables and constructs of the explanatory model*

In this diagram, in addition to the variables, constructs and the dependency relationship that links them, we have represented the information relating to the evaluated project. According to Loewenstein *et al.* (2001), the information is divided into "cold information" (the business plan in our case) and "hot information" (entrepreneurs' pitch video in our case). Hot information generates affect-driven decisions while in the case of cold information, decisions are cognition driven. We have also included a "preference structure" associated with the Congruence to Base Values, Familiarity and Interest variables in the form of a database, since preferences are a memory characteristic of the individual, stored in one's long-term memory. These preferences implicitly determine the score of these three constructs; we will discuss them in more detail in the next section.

We will also note the position of the affect (Affective Reaction variable), located at the heart of the model, while the importance of the axiological variable (Congruence to Base Values) is appreciable by its role as the antecedent of all the variables of the model, except for the Perceived Signal Quality variable. Finally, the solid arrows represent direct effects (hypotheses H1 to H5), linking the construct to the explained variable, while the dotted arrows represent indirect effects (hypotheses H6 to H11), that is to say, linking the construct to the variable explained by means of at least one mediating variable.

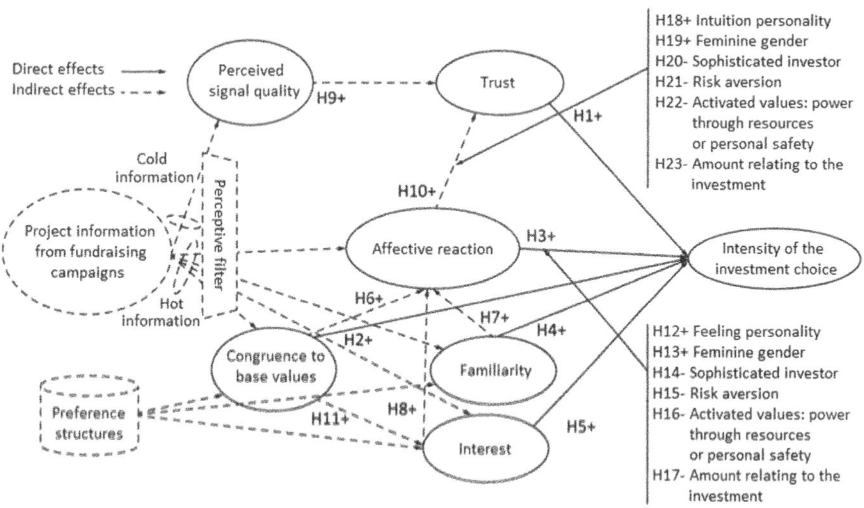

Figure 1.14. *Explanatory model of investment choices in equity crowdfunding*

1.2.4.1. *Hypotheses of the explanatory model (hypotheses H6 to H11)*

This section provides an argument for the six hypotheses relating to the indirect effects linking the explanatory variables to the explained variable.

According to Rimé (2009), emotions result from an encounter between an object (a situation, an event, etc.) and the representations of the individual (needs, desires, aspiration), the strength of the emotion depending on the gap, that is to say the distance that separates them or, in other words, the quality of the congruence that links them.

This proposition is shared by Schwartz (2006) for whom the activation of values by an event (encounter with an individual, an object, etc.) automatically generates an affective response, accompanied by movement toward the objective that relates to the value at stake and its expression. This emotion is all the stronger as the value is subjectively important. This mechanism is based on the inseparable relationship between values and affects. In their experimental studies, Maio and Olson (1998) showed that values and affects are intimately linked to the extent that values are truisms that are first based on an emotional substrate and to a lesser extent on behavioral information, which is defined as the sum of the memories of behavior that confirms the value.

Cognitive evaluation theory offers an explanation for the association between activation of values and aroused emotion. This means that values must be considered as desirable goals, which corresponds precisely to the definition by Schwartz (1996). However, in cognitive evaluation models, the individual's goals are the main evaluation variable (Lazarus 2001). Thus, in the Stimulus Evaluation Checks model of Scherer (see Sander and Scherer 2014) or in the OCC model of Ortony *et al.* (1988), the relevance of an event vis-à-vis the goals of the individual, conditions the triggering of the emotion.

Let us add that work in marketing and consumer theory also identifies values as the main psychographic characteristic capable of influencing the emotional states of the subject (Lemoine and Plichon 2000), following the example of Holbrook and O'Shaughnessy (1984) for whom personal values can have an effect on the emotions induced by advertising screens. Holbrook (1986) added that values induced a preference that determined the valence of emotions in the consumption experience. These arguments lead us to hypothesis 6.

HYPOTHESIS 6 (H6).– *Congruence to Base Values has a positive influence on Affective Reaction.*

In his first studies using subliminal exposures of objects to subjects, Zajonc (1968) demonstrated a correlation between affect and frequency of exposure.

This effect, called the mere-exposure effect, induces a positive attitude or preference for what is familiar, even in the absence of any recognition. The more frequent the exposure prior to a stimulus, the more the preference is reinforced. However, preferences are classified among affective reactions by Derbaix and Pham (1989); familiarity therefore induces a preference, that is to say an affective reaction. A meta-analysis by Bornstein (1989) of more than 200 studies, published between 1968 and 1987 on the exposure–affect relationship, supports this hypothesis: exposures have been shown to reliably improve affects toward visual, auditory, taste, abstract and social stimuli.

Also, investors who have developed – using mere-exposure – a preference for the sector of activity in which they work, and who find they have a choice of projects on an equity crowdfunding platform, will feel an emotional reaction of positive valence at the time of exposure to an entrepreneur's pitch video relating to their professional sector of activity (the familiar stimulus), because of their sectoral preference.

Let us recall that preferences generate positive feelings relative to an attractive stimulus (Scherer 2005), hence we propose hypothesis 7.

HYPOTHESIS 7 (H7).– *Familiarity has a positive influence on Affective Reaction.*

Some researchers conceptualize the interest as an emotion (Izard 1977; Frijda 1986; Silvia 2006). We preferred to conceptualize this construct with two dimensions: situational interest and individual interest, in line with the seminal work of Hidi and Baird (1988).

In this conception, interest is both a cognitive and an affective construct. According to Schiefele (1991), there is a causal relationship between individual interest and a set of positive emotions like the joy felt when in contact with the object of interest. This can be explained by the very nature of individual interest which, for the author, can be understood as a stable preference for a domain, a subject or an activity, with the encounter between the object of interest and the individual eliciting a positive emotional reaction.

Hidi (2000) also argued that while immediate attention is one aspect of interest that contributes to the facilitating effect that interest has on cognitive function, a second aspect considered by many researchers is the association of affective reactions to the experience of interest, mainly positive like joy, hence we propose hypothesis 8.

HYPOTHESIS 8 (H8).– *Interest has a positive influence on Affective Reaction.*

According to Simon (2007), trust fits naturally into the context of agency relationships between principal or trustor and agent or trustee. In this context, the potential investor tries to collect as many quality indicators or signals as possible from entrepreneurs in order to overcome the information asymmetry that he/she encounters (Manigart *et al.* 1997). Harrison *et al.* (1997) researched, by means of questionnaires, the determinants of the trust of business angels. During the initial selection phase, they identify inferences based on the business plan. Huang and Pearce (2015) also based the trust of business angels on the formal analysis of the business plan, as well as on the intuition on the competence of the team.

Symmetrically, many authors (Scarbrough *et al.* 2013; Bammens and Collewaert 2014; Ola 2016) believe that in the sphere of venture capital, managers try to reduce the information asymmetry borne by the potential investor by providing reliable information on the activity, which are good quality signals that allow for gaining the investor's trust. This need is even stronger in the case of small investors because they do not have the capacity to carry out an in-depth assessment, which is why startups have an interest in sending them clear signals about the value of their business (Ahlers *et al.* 2015). This argument is shared by Agrawal *et al.* (2014) for whom equity crowdfunding platforms must establish trust mechanisms for investors, in particular through signals on the quality of the projects presented, which leads us to hypothesis 9.

HYPOTHESIS 9 (H9).– *The Perceived Signal Quality has a positive influence on Trust.*

Like Bessière and Stéphany (2014), we believe that the holistic and immediate nature of the affective reaction alters the perceptions that shape the investor's judgments. Trust is a construct made up of beliefs (divided into three dimensions: credibility, integrity and benevolence) toward the leaders of the startup being evaluated. These beliefs are shaped by judging perceptions pertaining to the project team. However, two effects induced by the affect, which can be used jointly, explain why a positive affective impression modifies perceptions: the affective halo effect (see section 2.2.5.2 of Volume 1) and the affect heuristic (see sections 2.2.3.3.7 and 2.2.4.2.2 of Volume 1).

Let us recall that the Halo effect of Thorndike (1920) describes the influence of the judgment of a single characteristic on the judgments concerning all the characteristics of a person. The affective halo effect is a variant of the halo effect, describing the influence of the affect on consumer perceptions (Wilkie 1990). Derbaix and Pham (1989) illustrated the case of a consumer captivated by a first impression favorable to the sight of a car; the affective halo effect then influences the evaluation of the consumer in all its dimensions. Thus, in our case, the positive emotional reaction (the pleasure felt) in discovering that a member of the management team of the evaluated startup is a friend (trustworthy) will lead, by the halo effect, to a positive overall perception with regard to the management team as a whole, which will *ipso facto* benefit from a favorable presumption and the investor's trust.

The second effect attributable to the affect is the affective heuristic. Let us recall that according to this heuristic, individuals use their emotional feelings to judge the benefits and risks associated with an object, without relying on cognitive reasoning (Slovic *et al.* 2002). However, as Simon (2007) indicated, risk and interdependence are two necessary conditions for the development of trust. It is therefore relevant to use the affectivity heuristic in our context. Also, several studies in finance show that an affective reaction of positive valence (induced by knowledge, familiarity or emotional attachment) linked to a financial product reduces the associated objective measure of risk, and the investor is showing an optimistic bias in the evaluation of information (Ganzach 2000; Nofsinger 2001; Wang *et al.* 2011). Again, perceptions are distorted, and the financial product is viewed more favorably, which, together with the halo effect, builds trust in the leadership team; hence, our 10th hypothesis.

HYPOTHESIS 10 (H10).– *Affective Reaction has a positive influence on Trust.*

According to Schiefele (1991), from whom we borrow the construct operationalizing the individual interest dimension of interest, personal values orient individuals toward objects of interest, because of their importance for personal development or for the understanding of important problems. One of the two subdimensions of individual interest refers to the value of the object of interest, i.e. the subjective and intrinsic importance of the object of interest for the individual, with the value connected to his/her personal values, that is to say to his/her main basic values. Further, the activation of an individual value by encountering an object can be a reason for the interest that the individual has in it. Based on the work of Schiefele (1991) and Fenouillet (2016) made values the antecedent of interest. Moreover, Krapp (2005) conceptualized interest as an aspect of the person–object relationship; he also made values an antecedent of interest. In his approach, interest is the result of a cognitive–affective system of regulation; the cognitive system, of a rational analytical type, forms the intentions, which explains why certain activities deemed unpleasant will nevertheless interest the individual, and this is because of their importance in relation to his/her personal values. Hence, we propose hypothesis 11.

HYPOTHESIS 11 (H11).– *Congruence to Base Values has a positive influence on Interest.*

1.2.4.2. *Moderation hypotheses of the explanatory model (H12 to H23)*

This section provides an argument for the 12 moderation hypotheses of the explanatory model, all of which relate to the effects of the Affective Reaction variable on the Intensity of the Investment Choice variable (H3) and Trust variable (H10). In addition, with the exception of the two moderation hypotheses linked to the investor's personality traits (H12 and H18), the 10 remaining hypotheses are grouped together using the concerned moderating variable and form pairs of hypotheses. For example, hypotheses H13 and H19, associated with the "gender" moderating variable, are grouped together because the argumentation used shows that women are overall more sensitive to emotions than men, which implies that the causal link connecting the Affective Reaction variable to any variable is affected by this moderation. Also, with some exceptions, we will logically test these hypotheses using a multigroup analysis (see Chapter 3).

According to Filbeck *et al.* (2005), in the MBTI approach, the Thinking/Feeling axis described behaviors relating to the assessment and decision-making of individuals. This personality axis makes it possible to distinguish between individuals who base their decisions and evaluations on a logical analytical judgment (the individual has a Thinking preference) or, on the contrary, will subjectively rely on their emotions, feelings and values (the individual has a Feeling preference). Henderson and Nutt (1980) stated:

> The second dimension focuses on the approach used for evaluation. At one extreme is the "sentimental" individual who takes into account individual feelings and emotions as well as values as an important criterion in decision-making. In contrast, the "thinking" individual tends to be very impersonal in the assessment, relying on logical and pragmatic analysis to guide him in his decision-making.

We propose our first moderation hypothesis (H12).

HYPOTHESIS 12 (H12).– *MODERATION OF H3. The more the investor has a Feeling-oriented personality type (Thinking/Feeling axis) in the MBTI model, the more the positive relationship between the Affective Reaction and the Intensity of the Investment Choice will be reinforced.*

According to Brody and Hall (2008), many studies show significant differences between men and women when they face emotional situations. More specifically, the theories of emotional intelligence define several skills related to emotions recognized as important for adaptive functioning, such as the precise perception of emotions, their use for thinking and understanding or for managing emotions. However, studies on emotional intelligence tests show that women score higher on all of these components (Mayer *et al.* 1999; Day and Carroll 2004). These results are consistent with research in psychopathology: Boyle (1989) showed that women are more concerned by affective illnesses than men; they obtain higher scores in terms of depression and fatigue. This difference in sensitivity to emotions is naturally found in the work on consumer theory in the field of marketing. In an empirical study on the affective reactions of consumers placed in different contexts of consumption, Derbaix and Pham (1991) highlighted the greater emotional sensitivity of women: "The average range of affective reactions reported by females were larger than the ones reported by males. Women seem to have more important and maybe more differentiated emotional experiences". Also, in a study comparing the differences in cognitive-affective processes between the genders with regard to impulse purchases, Coley and Burgess (2003) showed significant differences in the emotions felt during the purchase, with women appearing to be more guided by their emotions and their image than men. This is why we propose the moderation hypotheses H13 and H19.

HYPOTHESIS 13 (H13).– *MODERATION OF H3. If the investor is female, the positive relationship between Affective Response and Intensity of Investment Choice is strengthened.*

HYPOTHESIS 19 (H19).– *MODERATION OF H10. If the investor is female, the positive relationship between Affective Response and Trust is strengthened.*

In market finance, Magron (2014) reiterated that sophistication corresponds to the investor's level of knowledge of financial markets and expertise in financial products. However, many studies show that sophisticated investors are less prone to psychological biases than unsophisticated investors (Dhar and Zhu 2006; Calvet *et al.* 2009; Grinblatt *et al.* 2011). These results can be explained by increased exposure of sophisticated investors to statistics and logical thinking, as this type of exposure is correlated with more rational decisions, based on system 2 rather than system 1 (Kahneman 2003).

Furthermore, work in the field of marketing shows that the consumer who lacks expertise relies more on the affect (Cohen *et al.* 2008). For these reasons, we believe that sophisticated investors further rationalize their judgments and choices and rely less on their emotional feelings; hence, we propose here moderation hypotheses H14 and H20.

HYPOTHESIS 14 (H14).– *MODERATION OF H3. If the investor is sophisticated, the positive relationship between the Affective Reaction and the Intensity of Investment Choice is mitigated.*

HYPOTHESIS 20 (H20).– *MODERATION OF H10. If the investor is sophisticated, the positive relationship between the Affective Reaction and Trust is mitigated.*

The risk-averse investor favors safe options – those that reduce uncertainty. Caution is a character trait defined as "the attitude of someone who is attentive to anything that may cause harm, who reflects on the consequences of his/her actions and who acts in a way that avoids error"[18]. Therefore, the investors who are averse to risk, and thus prudent, are wise. They process information and depend more on analytical and logical reasoning. This deduction is consistent with the summary of Cohen *et al.* (2008) who stated that when the motivation to process information is low, consumers rely more on the affect, which is equivalent to saying that when the motivation to process information is strong, consumers rely less on the affect. Hence, we proposed hypotheses H15 and H21.

HYPOTHESIS 15 (H15).– *MODERATION OF H3. The more risk-averse the investor, the more the positive relationship between the Affective Reaction and the Intensity of Investment Choice is mitigated.*

HYPOTHESIS 21 (H21).– *MODERATION OF H10. The more risk-averse the investor, the more the positive relationship between the Affective Reaction and Trust is mitigated.*

We believe that the investor who is driven by an expectation of high gains should be motivated to process the business plan to identify quality signals. Again, the article of Cohen *et al.* (2008) serves as an argument for us: when the motivation to process information is high, consumers rely less on the affect, which brings us to the two moderation hypotheses H16 and H22.

HYPOTHESIS 16 (H16).– *MODERATION OF H3. If the Power Through Resources or Personal Security values are ranked higher in the investor's hierarchy of values, then the positive relationship between the Affective Reaction and the Intensity of Investment Choice is mitigated.*

HYPOTHESIS 22 (H22).– *MODERATION OF H10. If the Power Through Resources or Personal Security values are ranked higher in the investor's hierarchy of values, then the positive relationship between the Affective Reaction and Trust are mitigated.*

In Kahneman's Prospect Theory (2003), choices depend on gains or losses relative to a benchmark, i.e. relative gains or losses.

We also believe that a study of the psychological impact of the amount involved in an investment on behavior should consider the amount at stake in relation to the individual's wealth. Clearly, investing €1,000 is not the same as investing the entirety of your wealth or when it represents only a tiny proportion.

In venture capital, Ahlers *et al.* (2015) pointed out that screening (the selection procedure) is expensive, so it must be consistent with the stakes, the latter being

18 Definition from the Larousse dictionary.

proportional to the amount invested. For these authors, the small amounts invested by individual investors do not justify disproportionate analysis times.

Conversely, an individual investor investing a substantial amount of wealth should have a strong incentive to process information and depend less on the affect (Cohen *et al.* 2008); hence, the two hypotheses H17 and H23 are proposed.

HYPOTHESIS 17 (H17).– *MODERATION OF H3. The larger the amount invested with respect to the investor's wealth, the more the positive relationship between the Affective Reaction and the Intensity of Investment Choice is mitigated.*

HYPOTHESIS 23 (H23).– *MODERATION OF H10. The larger the amount invested with respect to the investor's wealth, the more the positive relationship between the Affective Reaction and Trust is mitigated.*

Henderson and Nutt (1980) explained that the sensing/intuition axis of the MBTI personality test describes how individuals acquire and process data. While people with a sensing preference prefer structured and detailed problems, those whose preference is intuition have a global, non-analytical perception; they do not like precise work and rely more on their intuition: "The sensing person prefers detailed structural problems, and has the patience for routine, precise work. In contrast, intuitive individuals perceive problems as a whole, rarely focusing on individual elements in isolation. They dislike routine and precise work, tend to rely on hunches and prefer new unstructured problems". This is why a person who prefers intuition should logically be more prone to the affective halo effect and trust in the management team intuitively. This brings us to our last moderation hypothesis.

HYPOTHESIS 18 (H18).– *MODERATION OF H10. The more the investor has an intuition-oriented personality type (Sensing/Intuition axis) in the MBTI model, the more the positive relationship between the Affective Reaction and Trust is amplified.*

1.2.5. *Reading grids for the explanatory model*

In this section, we propose several complementary reading grids for the explanatory model. The first step is to consider certain components of the theoretical framework to understand, by juxtaposition, how they can be understood as metamodels. Other theoretical components are then articulated with the explanatory model; a dynamic perspective is put forth and then we propose to attempt to put into perspective the triptych of rationality of the equity crowdfunding investor (as defined in the previous assumptions) with the explanatory model. These different reading prisms are presented with the help of a figure accompanied by a short explanation.

The perspective of the dual system 1 and system 2 of Stanovich and West (2000) is analyzed fairly directly on the graph of the model (Figure 1.15). System 1, backed by experience and the affect, combines the cognitive evaluation variables (Congruence to Base Values, Interest and Familiarity) as well as the variable outcome of the assessment: the Affective Reaction. The three evaluation variables are related to the memory and preferences of the individual, and they correspond to the experiential dimension of system 1; the Affective Reaction naturally correlates with the emotional dimension of this system. System 2 – analytic, logical, explicit, rational – corresponds to the cognitive variable of the explanatory model: the Perceived Signal Quality.

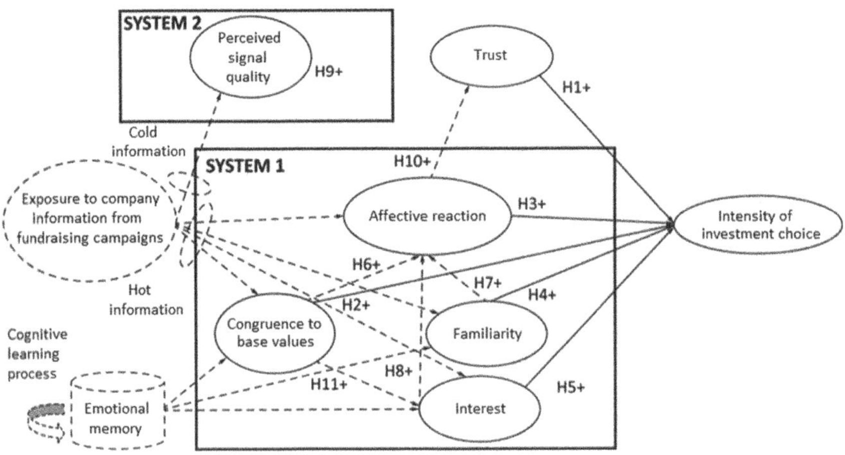

Figure 1.15. *Psychological perspective: system 1/system 2*

This dual perspective may be related to the secondary issue of the problem that questions the relative importance of affect and cognition in the decision-making of equity crowdfunding investors in an artificial context, deprived of social interactions. In addition, this reading grid highlights the originality of this decision model, which places a central emphasis on the affective reactions felt at the time of choice rather than those associated with the consequences of choice. According to Bechara and Damasio (2005):

> There are […] few theories that deal with emotion as a decision-making factor […]. Moreover, these rare theories deal only with emotions that are the result of a decision (for example, disappointment or regret after a risky and wrong decision), rather than affective reactions arising directly from the decision itself at the time of

deliberation. The somatic marker hypothesis provides neurobiological evidence that supports the idea that people often make judgments based on "intuitions", "gut-level feelings" and a subjective assessment of the consequences.

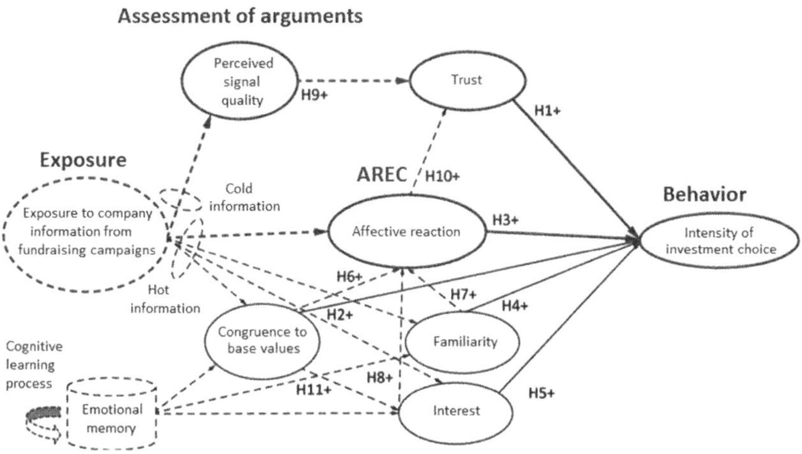

Figure 1.16. *Marketing perspective: persuasive advertising. For a color version of this figure, see www.iste.co.uk/goglin/investment2.zip*

The version of the basic persuasive advertising model (see Derbaix and Filser 2011), borrowed from marketing and consumer theory and adapted by us to the context of our research (see Figure 2.6 of Volume 1) is naturally juxtaposed with the explanatory model (Figure 1.16). The two causal paths – the first is the cognitive assessment of arguments, and the second is related to AREC (affective reaction elicited by commercials) – appear distinctly. The assessment of the arguments in the pitch video of entrepreneurs corresponds to the Perceived Signal Quality construct when the AREC corresponds to the Affective Reaction. The main difference lies in the substitution of a variable representing a behavior (the Intensity of Investment Choice is a choice) to the two attitudinal constructs (Attitude toward the video pitch and attitude toward the project). This perspective echoes the argument that we put forward when justifying the problem, which said that investment in equity crowdfunding has this particularity – within wihin the world of investment products – that it is done in a context of persuasive advertising; this induces an affective dimension in decision-making, the latter being insufficiently taken into account by the literature of the field of finance.

This third perspective (Figure 1.17) proposes to link several concepts of the theoretical framework to the upstream and downstream of the affective reaction.

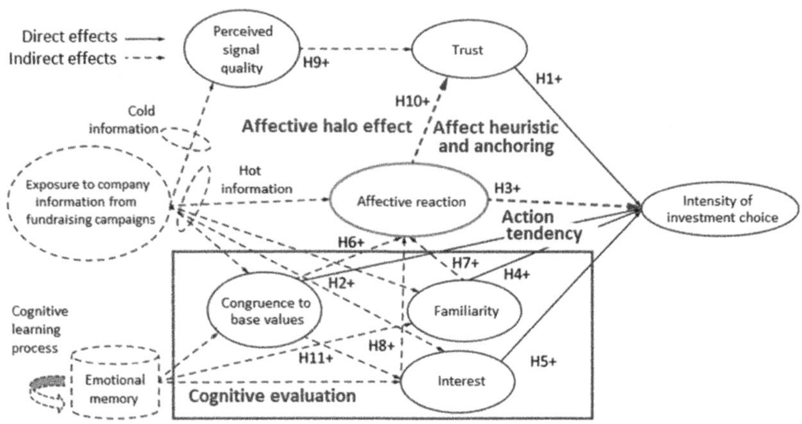

Figure 1.17. *AR-focused perspective: upstream and downstream effects of AR. For a color version of this figure, see www.iste.co.uk/goglin/investment2.zip*

Upstream, if we look at the cognitive evaluation theory (see Sander and Scherer 2014), then the antecedent variables of the affective reaction are the evaluation variables that determine the consequent emotion.

Downstream of the affective reaction, several quasi-immediate phenomena operate toward the investment and trust behavior of the investor: the action tendency of Frijda (1986) links the affective reaction and investment behavior; emotion is an action tendency, an affective reaction of positive valence such that pleasure creates *ipso facto* an approach movement that can be translated, in our context, as a motivation to invest.

Furthermore, three concurrent and intriguing phenomena affect investor trust:

– immediate anchoring of Trust at a higher or lower level depending on the valence and intensity of the Affective Reaction;

– the sense of trust is all the stronger because the Affective Reaction is of positive valence and high intensity under the affect heuristic hypothesis;

– the characteristics of the three facets of trust (credibility, integrity and benevolence) are assessed in a homogeneous way as long as the intensity of the Affective Reaction is sufficient from the affective halo effect.

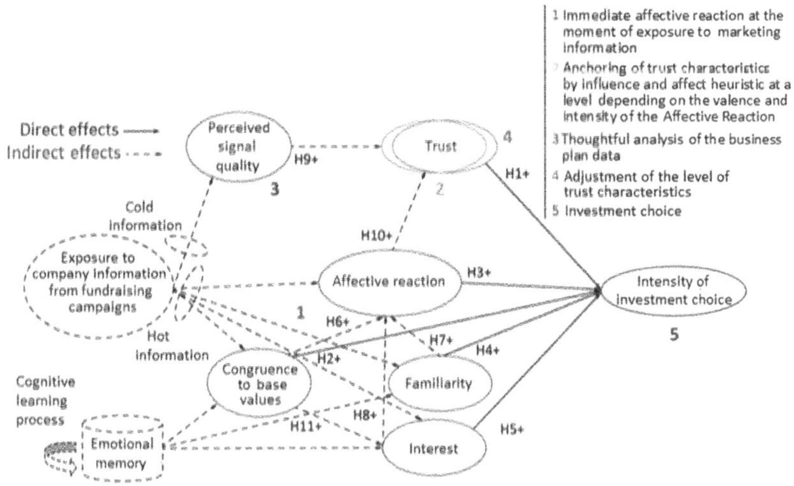

Figure 1.18. *Dynamic perspective: the dynamics of investment choice. For a color version of this figure, see www.iste.co.uk/goglin/investment2.zip*

Based on the articulation procedure of the two Kahneman (2003) dual decision-making models below, we offer a dynamic reading of the five-step explanatory model (see Figure 1.18):

1) An intuitive judgment or intent is initiated, and:

a) approved by system 2;

b) adjusted (insufficiently) with other characteristics, recognized as relevant;

c) corrected (sometimes overcorrected) for an explicitly recognized bias or;

d) identified as violating a subjectively valid rule before being blocked.

2) No intuitive answer comes to mind and judgment is calculated by system 2.

In the same article, Kahneman also linked affect heuristics, anchoring and subsequent analytical adjustment:

> [...] the affect heuristic fits the present model of attribute substitution. [...] Because it is based on salient information and because it comes first, the intuitive impression is likely to serve as an anchor for subsequent adjustments, and the corrective adjustments are therefore likely to be small. Variations on this theme of anchoring on intuition are common in the literature.

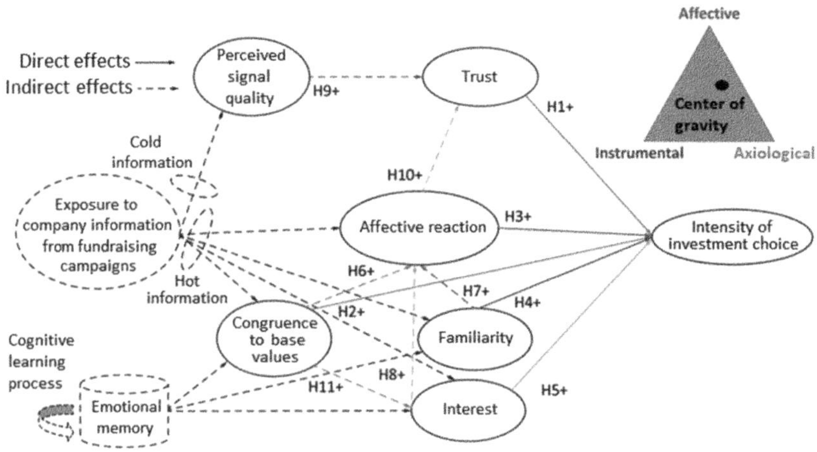

Figure 1.19. *Explanatory model: investor rationality. For a color version of this figure, see www.iste.co.uk/goglin/investment2.zip*

Figure 1.19 attempts to link the effects of the explanatory model and the triptych of rationality. Three primary colors (blue, red and green) are associated, respectively, with the three forms of investor rationality: instrumental, affective and axiological.

The figure represents the associations between causal links and colors; the colors of some links are one of the primary colors. For example, the links taking Congruence to the Base Values as a starting point (source) are green, which is the color of axiological rationality. Some links have mixed colors. Like the green (resulting from the mixture of yellow and blue) of the segment linking Trust and Intensity of Investment Choice; or the yellow (resulting from the mixture of green and red) of the segment connecting Affective Reaction and Trust.

Finally, no causal route is purely cognitive because the causal route from the Perceived Signal Quality to the explained variable is blue in its first segment (the individual coldly analyzes the signals of the project from a maximization perspective, then chooses the project that minimizes agency risk), then green (resulting from the mixture of yellow and blue but a green distinct from that attributed to axiological rationality) in the segment connecting Trust and the Intensity of Investment Choice.

Similarly, no causal path is purely affective, since the affective rationality, as we perceive it, can be understood as a form of instrumental rationality (see the brief comment on the third point of the pre-postulates of this chapter).

1.2.6. *Conclusion*

This section opened with a comment, prior to the modeling itself, which articulates three key concepts that are intimately linked: the nature of uncertainty, the concept of consequentialism and the rationality of the equity crowdfunding investor. As indicated, we chose to situate ourselves in an uncertain universe whose consequences are non-probabilizable, if not by subjective probabilities. The consequences "that matter" were defined; they are of great variety and complexity in view of the idiosyncratic motivations of the investor. The latter does not necessarily act in a consequentialist way, for example, when he/she makes a choice on a purely axiological basis. As for the rationality of the investor, we defined it as being at the crossroads of the peaks of a triptych, composed of instrumental, axiological and affective rationalities. We specified how the theories of cognitive evaluation and actions tendency of our conceptual framework encourage us to talk about affective rationality, while this rapprochement seems to stem *a priori* from an oxymoron.

Next, we explained the approach taken to identify the variables of the explanatory model, based in particular on the analysis of the collected corpus. The latter allowed us to go back and forth between theory and data.

Thus, the Interest variable, the importance of which is revealed in the continuation of this research, appeared to us in the data, even though it had eluded us during our literature review. The variable relating to investor values, the Congruence to Base Values, originally derived from an abductive inference, is clearly in the data; it is also reinforced by the theory of values borrowed from the field of social psychology. Lexicographic textual analyses of the qualitative data corpus were used to confirm the choice of variables and, in an exploratory approach, to identify the dimensions of some constructs in the operationalization phase. We have also systematically backed the variables of the model with theory. To the extent that the condition for retaining a variable was based on the potential to explain the investment choice, the argument employed was used as justification for the first hypotheses of the model, directly linking explanatory and explained variables.

Then, in the development phase of the measurement model, we specified the source of the constructs and the adaptations applied to the original scales.

Two constructs are rooted in marketing (the Trust and Familiarity constructs); the Interest construct is adapted from educational science. The Congruence to Base Values variable finds its source in social psychology. The measurement of the Affective Reaction comes from works in environmental psychology, and that of the Perceived Signal Quality from work on equity crowdfunding, as well as older works on venture capital. Two constructs are formative (Familiarity and Perceived

Signal Quality) to reflect the specific context of this research. The mixed nature of the model constructs, as well as the lack of stability of some of them (particularly formative constructs) given the exploratory nature of this research, will be two strong arguments for using the Partial Least Squares approach for modeling the explanatory model. The operationalization of the Congruence to Base Values variable is original; it was calculated and we theoretically and empirically justified this choice of modeling. The remaining hypotheses were then made explicit and justified.

Finally, the explanatory model was presented, with several complementary reading grids that again link with certain components of the theoretical framework.

1.3. Individual predictive model

In this section, we present a second model, individual this time, as it is set by the characteristics of an individual, which derives directly from the explanatory model developed in the first section.

We begin by presenting this second model (section 1.3.1), underpin it with theory (sections 1.3.2 and 1.3.3) and then define several concepts as well as a mathematical function that puts it to use and makes it operational (section 1.3.4).

1.3.1. *Presentation*

This perspective outlines the origin and purpose of the model (section 1.3.1.1), links it to the model of the first section (section 1.3.1.2) and then presents this individual model as a new theoretical perspective, complementary to the explanatory model (section 1.3.1.3).

1.3.1.1. *Origin and objectives of the model*

1.3.1.1.1. Model origin

At the beginning of this thesis, the first thought experiments carried out lead to two intuitions, even before the literature review, and thus without theoretical preconceptions. These two interconnected intuitions structured the development of this book[19]. The first intuition, which became conjecture, was that, *a priori*, the choices of equity crowdfunding investors were necessarily strongly imbued with an affective dimension; the second was that these same investors chose the projects that

19 It should also be noted that the avenues of reflection of my thesis director contributed to the emergence of the axiological variable of the explanatory model, as well as to the concept of affective rationality.

suited them the most. To put it another way, they chose the projects that matched them the best. These proposals, inferred by mere naïve psychology, later found theoretical support in the literature, starting with that on equity crowdfunding. While Bessière and Stéphany (2015) pointed out the affective dimension of the choice: "Given the information used, the evaluation of the project carried out by the crowd is rather intuitive, even affective, in nature, possibly reinforced by certain knowledge or beliefs about the sector of activity", Schwienbacher (2015) explicitly mentioned the matching (project/investor) organized by the platforms: "The main role of the platform is to offer a 'matching' service between the issuing company and the crowd".

1.3.1.1.2. Objectives of the model

The first objective of this model is intrinsic; it concerns predicting (as well as explaining, one does not go without the other in a stable if not stationary context) the choices of investors *a priori*, given the knowledge of certain characteristics of the individual. "*A priori*" here means before the investor has become aware of the projects competing on a platform. To be more specific, the individual predictive model allows a given investor to define *a priori* an ordinal relationship between several financing projects based on his/her preference structure, the latter being provided by declarative means. We further clarify the scope and content of this structure of individual preferences.

A second objective is extrinsic and utilitarian in nature; the results of this individual predictive model allow us to add additional evidence to the thesis defended in this work and so the approach is confirmatory.

1.3.1.2. *Individual predictive model as an extension of the explanatory model*

The formalization of this second model derives directly from the explanatory model taken as a starting point, the latter being assumed to be previously estimated on a sample. The explanatory model is transformed, essentially by truncation of the Perceived Signal Quality cognitive variable which, by virtue of the thesis we defend, is not determinative in the choice of investors in equity crowdfunding, in a private context of social interactions, the choice being essentially determined by the affect and the values of the investor. In other words, this second model assumes that our thesis is true, which is consistent with the fact that it implements the theory of affective matching that makes this hypothesis a postulate (see below).

Thus, the additional evidence of our thesis by this second model, referred to as an extrinsic objective of the individual predictive model above, is based on the following reasoning: if the thesis is true, then a model based on this hypothesis should give quality predictions; *a contrario*, if the thesis is false, then a model based on this hypothesis should not produce good quality predictions.

Given the nature of the thesis defended, it seems to us that it cannot be argued that it may be unrelated to the quality of the prediction of the investor's choice, which would invalidate the previous reasoning since, by nature, the defended thesis (the choice is affective, the quality of the signal is not an obvious antecedent in a private context of social interactions) is an explanation of the choice.

1.3.1.3. *A new reading prism*

The individual predictive model places emotion at the heart of the choice – a project that is "emotionally close" to us and attracts us. Let us note that the individual predictive model is based on emotions, but in an implicit manner because the Affective Reaction variable is absent (if not in the expression of its exogenous variables which are precisely the "cognitive evaluation variables"). Only the cognitive evaluation variables, which we also call "affective variables" by malapropism, that is, the variables that generate the affective reaction by appraisal, constitute the model.

Nevertheless, as Affective Reaction is the result of a monotonically increasing linear function of the cognitive evaluation variables that are its antecedents, a model based on the maximization of the values of these variables also maximizes the relevant Affective Reaction.

This model is based on a matching calculation that matches the investor with a given project. More specifically, the match relates to the individual's preference structure and the project data relevant to this data structure. We note that Ryu and Kim (2014) had already developed a model (the Crowdfunding Participation Model) matching the characteristics of the project with those (the motivations) of the investor, the objective however being different: to relate the characteristics of the founder to the motivations of the investor via the characteristics of the project, which is reminiscent of the cognitive chains in consumer marketing theory.

This second model offers a new prism for reading investor behavior, the reading of which is as follows: the *choice results from the strength of the match linking the projects to the investor*.

Figure 1.20 shows matching, i.e. the mapping of project information with the individual's preference structure, the first result of which is a data structure, the *a priori* congruence structure, or the three "affective variables" or cognitive assessment, then the Intensity of the Investment Choice predicted or attraction in a second step. *In this perspective, the choice depends only on the values of the 3 "affective variables" resulting from the matching without the Perceived Signal Quality being taken into account.* It should also be noted that the Trust and Affective Reaction variables are integrated into the model in their expanded form, that is to say as a linear function of the "affective variables".

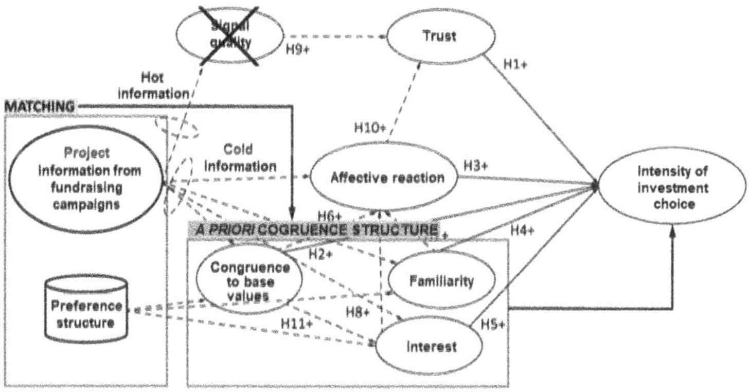

Figure 1.20. *Reading prism of affective matching*

1.3.2. *Affective matching theory*

As mentioned, our first hunch, that of a choice based on a match between investor and project, resonates with the financial literature; we have cited Schwienbacher (2015) explicitly referring to the term matching. While remaining in the sphere of equity crowdfunding, we also referred to the work of Ryu and Kim (2014), matching the motivations of investors with the characteristics of the project. In venture capital, we can add Mason and Stark (2004), for whom business angels rely on a subjective feeling of affinity: "In particular, because BAs are looking to take a more hands-on role in their investee businesses than are VCFMs, they place greater importance on the 'chemistry' between themselves and the entrepreneur". In the field of market finance, the work of Aspara and Tikkanen (2011) empirically shows that most investors have an additional motivation, based on affect, to invest in equities, beyond expected returns. The two authors rely on the Affective Self-affinities (ASA) theory of Aspara *et al.* (2008), an integrative theory (in particular of the theories of attachment and social identity) that we could have chosen, alternatively to those chosen, as the basis for the theory of affective matching given their theoretical proximity:

> The affective Self-affinity (ASA) of an individual for a given thing is defined as the measure that an individual has of perceiving a positive affective congruence between the thing considered and his/her identity. […] A person having an emotional affinity relationship with a company will tend to give it preferential treatment and support it by being ready to devote more of his/her scarce resources to it.

After having mentioned several references in the financial literature, highlighting the role of an "investor–financial asset" match, we set out in Box 1.11 the theory of affective matching.

> *The theory of affective matching postulates that under certain conditions, investors choose the financial asset that suits them the most, independently of any analytic procedure.*
>
> The correspondence or matching relates, on the one hand, to the preferences of the investor and, on the other hand, to the characteristics of the financial asset.
>
> Preferences constitute a structure called "preference structure" that covers axiological preferences, preferences on interest in the field of activity underlying the financial asset as well as preferences associated with other "affective variables", depending on the nature of the financial asset.
>
> The variables on which preferences are defined are called "affective variables", as they are necessarily input evaluation variables of the appraisal process; they are antecedents of the affective reaction.
>
> The intensity of the affective reaction associated with the exposure of a financial asset is proportional to its attraction.
>
> The attraction or Intensity of the Investment Choice predicted by a financial asset for an investor is the result of matching.
>
> Affective distance is defined as the inverse of the attraction or the predicted Intensity of Investment Choice (ICIp).
>
> *The theory of affective matching can be reformulated: under certain conditions, the investor chooses the most attractive financial asset – the one which minimizes the affective distance or in an equivalent manner, maximizes the ICIp – and, as a result, maximizes the affective reaction.*

Box 1.11. *Theory of affective matching*

These elements call for several remarks:

– we open the field of application of this theory to unrestricted finance because we believe that the concept is extendable beyond investment in equity crowdfunding (see sections C.3.1 and C.3.2);

– the choice of the term matching, rather than fit, is explained first by the financial connotation of matching – a procedure for executing stock market orders for updating order books – and second, by the purpose of the theory of affective

underlying the financial asset for the case of equity crowdfunding. However, this difference is noticeable, as shown by the analysis of the results of the explanatory model (see Chapter 3). These show that, in the context of our research, the P-O fit alone would not be enough to explain the choices of investors. This justifies the need for an *ad hoc* theory, specific to the field of finance. Nevertheless, the relationship of these two theories is strong, as evidenced by their respective mode of implementation, a point that we will discuss in the following.

1.3.4. *Definitions and operationalization*

1.3.4.1. *Preference structure*

DEFINITION 1.2.– The *preference structure* of the investor is a data structure made up of three ordered sets (or hierarchical rankings), an ordered set of values, an ordered set of familiarity data and an ordered set of data of interest.

As part of our research, we have chosen to associate interest and familiarity with the field of activity of the projects for the sake of simplicity, as well as because the field of activity is a relevant characteristic revealed by the analysis of our corpus and shared by these two variables: indicator ATTR1 for the Familiarity construct and all the indicators of the individual interest dimension for the Interest construct. The collection of the investor preference structure is carried out by the contingent valuation method, which consists of collecting preferences using a questionnaire. According to Ruffieux *et al.* (2008):

> For an economist, the preferences of individuals are expressed through purchasing behavior in the markets. [...] When it is not possible to deduce WTP[20] from direct observation of purchasing behavior in the markets, it is often possible to use other methods. One of them, widely used, is *the contingent valuation method. It makes it possible to reveal the preferences directly expressed by individuals. It is based on the statement of intentions declared by individuals and not on actual behavior.*

Example of preference structure

Preferences for base values are as follows:

> Autonomy > Stimulation > Universalism > Safety > Benevolence > Achievement > Power > Tradition > Hedonism > Conformity

20 WTP is an acronym for willingness to pay; it is the maximum price that the economic agent is willing to pay, under normal market conditions, to acquire a good or a service.

Preferences for interest relating to the field of activity are as follows:

Fair trade > Medical field > Traditional remedies or recipes > New technological uses

Preferences for familiarity relating to the field of activity are as follows:

Medical field > Fair trade > Traditional remedies and recipes > New technological uses

1.3.4.2. A priori *congruence structure*

DEFINITION 1.3.– The *a priori congruence structure* is defined by the numerical values taken by the variables *CVB*, *Fam* and *Int* (included in the interval [0-1]) relating to the Congruence to Base Values, Familiarity and Interest constructs for an investor and a project. These three numerical values are the result of the matching procedure (presented below) between, on the one hand, the data associated with a project (promoted value and field of activity) and, on the other hand, the preference structure of the investor. These three numerical variables measure the quality of the congruence or correspondence between an individual and a project: the closer their value is to 1, the better the congruence.

1.3.4.3. *Matching procedure, IClp or attraction and the affective distance*

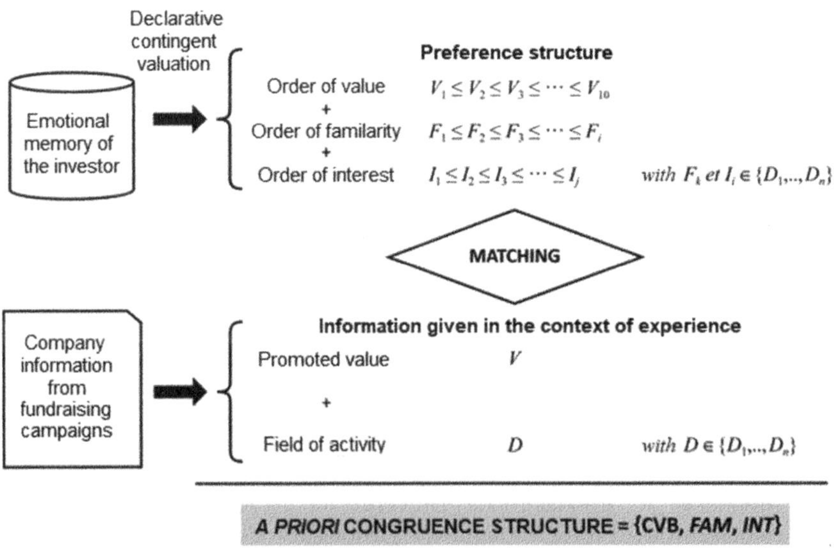

Figure 1.21. *First step in matching*

DEFINITION 1.4.– The *matching procedure or "matching"* results in the attraction or the ICIp. This procedure is divided into two stages, the first of which establishes a match between the individual and the project, depending on which has as operands the project information and the preference structure of the investor, and results in the congruence structure of the individual (in $[0,1]^3$):

matching (individual, project) =

matching (project information, preference structure) = {*CVB, Fam, Int*}

This function is based on a similarity measure presented below. Figure 1.21 illustrates the first step of the matching procedure.

Attraction or predicted intensity of choice

Variables

ICI	:	Intensity of investment choice
Conf	:	Trust
RA	:	Affective reaction
Fam	:	Familiarity
Int	:	Interest
QS	:	Signal quality
CVB	:	Congruence to base values

Equations

$$\left.\begin{aligned} ICI &= \alpha_1 Conf + \alpha_2 RA + \alpha_3 Fam + \alpha_4 Int + \alpha_5 CVB + \varepsilon_1 \\ Conf &= \beta_1 QS + \beta_2 RA + \varepsilon_2 \\ RA &= \gamma_1 CVB + \gamma_2 Fam + \gamma_3 Int + \varepsilon_3 \\ Int &= \delta_1 CVB + \varepsilon_4 \end{aligned}\right\} \Rightarrow$$

$$ICI = \alpha_1\left(\beta_1 QS + \beta_2(\gamma_1 CVB + \gamma_2 Fam + \gamma_3(\delta_1 CVB))\right) + \alpha_2(\gamma_1 CVB + \gamma_2 Fam + \gamma_3(\delta_1 CVB)) + \alpha_3 Fam + \alpha_4(\delta_1 CVB) + \alpha_5 CVB + \varepsilon_5 \quad [1.1]$$

$$\Leftrightarrow$$

$$ICI = (\alpha_1\beta_1)QS + (\alpha_1\beta_2\gamma_1 + \alpha_1\beta_2\gamma_3\delta_1 + \alpha_2\gamma_1 + \alpha_2\gamma_3\delta_1 + \alpha_4\gamma_1 + \alpha_5)CVB + (\alpha_1\beta_2\gamma_2 + \alpha_2\gamma_2 + \alpha_3)Fam + \varepsilon_5 \quad [1.2]$$

$$\Leftrightarrow$$

$$\boldsymbol{ICI = A.QS + B.CVB + \Gamma.Fam + \varepsilon_5} \quad [1.3]$$

$$[1.1] \Leftrightarrow$$

$$ICI = \alpha_1\left(\beta_1 QS + \beta_2(\gamma_1 CVB + \gamma_2 Fam + \gamma_3(\delta_1 CVB))\right) + \alpha_2(\gamma_1 CVB + \gamma_2 Fam + \gamma_3(\delta_1 CVB)) + \alpha_3 Fam + \alpha_4 Int + \alpha_5 CVB + \varepsilon_5 \quad [1.4]$$

$$\Leftrightarrow$$

$$ICI = (\alpha_1\beta_1)QS + (\alpha_1\beta_2\gamma_1 + \alpha_1\beta_2\gamma_3\delta_1 + \alpha_2\gamma_1 + \alpha_2\gamma_3\delta_1 + \alpha_5)CVB + (\alpha_1\beta_2\gamma_2 + \alpha_2\gamma_2 + \alpha_3)Fam + \alpha_4 Int + \varepsilon_5 \quad [1.5]$$

$$\Leftrightarrow$$

$$\boldsymbol{ICI = A.QS + B'.CVB + \Gamma.Fam + \Delta.Int + \varepsilon_5} \quad [1.6]$$

Figure 1.22. *Intensity of Investment Choice and structural equations of the explanatory model*

Let us recall that the Intensity of Investment Choice is the explained variable of the explanatory model in section 1.2.

Figure 1.22 proceeds by factorizations on the model of structural equations in section 1.2 to highlight the relationship between the explained variable and the exogenous variables (equation [1.3]), but above all to reveal the relationship between the Intensity of Investment Choice in the cognitive variable (*QS*) as well as in the three variables of affective evaluation of the *a priori* congruence structure: *CVB*, *Fam* and *Int* (equation [1.6]).

DEFINITION 1.5.– The *IClp or attraction is the final result of the matching*. The IClp is a proxy of the Intensity of the Investment Choice, calculated exclusively from the *a priori* congruence structure; it is the second step of the matching procedure.

For an individual I and a project P, it is:

$$Attraction\,(I,P) = IClp(I,P) = \alpha.CVB + \beta\,.Fam + \gamma.Int \qquad [1.7]$$

with $\alpha, \beta, \gamma \in \mathcal{R}$ the coefficients of the linear equation obtained by estimation (via the SmartPLS approach presented in Chapter 3), and *CVB*, Fam and *Int* $\in [0,1]$ being the *a priori* congruence variables for the values, familiarity and interest.

Equation [1.7] is derived directly from the explanatory model and from the investor's individual preference structure (necessary for the calculation of the *a priori* congruence structure). The transition from [1.6] to equation [1.7] is not mathematically formal; the approximation essentially results from the elimination of the Perceived Signal Quality variable by virtue of the thesis that we defend.

Finally, the affective matching theory asserts that, under certain conditions, investor I should choose the project that best suits them on the investment platform, *Plateforme* i.e. the most attractive project P_α, a local optimization solution (i.e. optimization limited to *Plateforme* projects):

$$arg \max_{P_\alpha} Attraction(I,P) = \{P_\alpha | \forall\, P \in Plateforme : \\ Attraction(I,P_\alpha) \geq Attraction(I,P)\}$$

We also define the affective distance, which will be useful for interpreting the results (see section 3.5 of Chapter 3).

DEFINITION 1.6.– *Affective distance* is the inverse of the IClp:

$$DA(I,X) := \frac{1}{IClp(I,X)}$$

1.3.4.4. A priori *choice vector*

DEFINITION 1.7.– The *a priori choice vector* is a vector of projects, ranked by an ICIp that increases with the index of the vector component.

Calculating the ICIp or, in an equivalent manner, the Affective Distance therefore makes it possible to rank projects according to their *a priori* attractiveness.

Figure 1.23 illustrates the case of four projects competing on an equity crowdfunding platform; the ICIp and the Affective Distance calculated for an individual I and each project makes it possible to determine an *a priori* order on the attraction of the four projects; the *a priori* choice vector is as follows:

$$(A_{\alpha 1}, A_{\alpha 2}, A_{\alpha 3}, A_{\alpha 4}) \qquad \text{with } \alpha_i \in \{1,..,4\}$$

In this example, $A_{\alpha 4}$ is the project that maximizes the intensity of the predicted investment choice; it is the most attractive project that should *a priori* (before he/she learns about the projects) choose the individual I, since it is the one that corresponds most to his/her preference structure (and minimizes the affective distance).

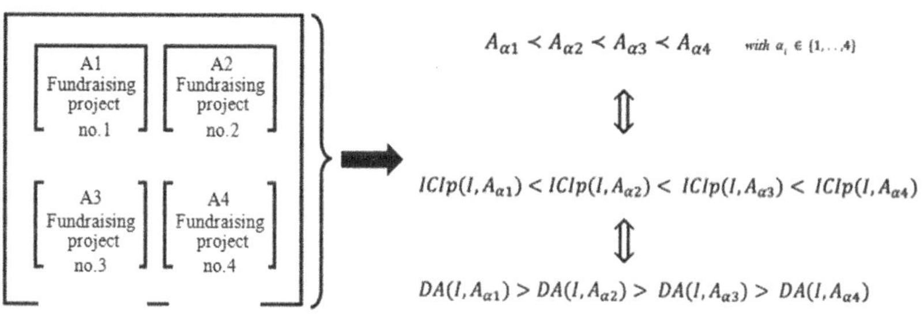

Figure 1.23. *Affective matching and order of projects*

1.3.4.5. *Choice of a method for calculating the "distance" between two vectors…*

While the theory of affective matching finds theoretical support in the P-O fit theory, the measure of the gap between the individual and the project (matching function), that we have defined, is consistent with the classical modes of operationalization of P-O fit.

Kristof (1996) discussed the methods of evaluating P-O fit as follows:

> A second popular method to assess the fit between person and organization is to reduce this measure to a single index reflecting the

degree of similarity between them. Researchers have generally used the bivariate congruence index of algebraic (X-Y), absolute (| X-Y |), or squared $(X\text{-}Y)^2$ difference. In the case of several variables, the profile similarity indices (PSI) such as the sum of the algebraic differences (D1), the sum of the absolute difference (| D |), the sum of the squared differences (D2), the Euclidean distance (D), or the correlation between two profiles (Q) are used.

1.3.4.5.1. ...to operationalize matching

The Spearman distance makes it possible to measure the similarity between two ordered vectors of a nominal variable by operating on the ranks of the modalities of the variable:

$$d_{ij} = \sum_{k=1}^{n} (x_{ik} - x_{jk})^2$$

For example[21], if we ask two people A and B for their preferred mode of transport, we can get for A: [Bus, Car, Train] and for B: [Car, Bus, Train].

If we take vector A as the row reference vector, we get rank (Bus) = 1, rank (Car) = 2 and rank (Train) = 3. The vector A is rewritten as [1,2,3], while vector B is written as [2,1,3] in terms of ranks. In this case, the Spearman distance is:

$$(1-2)^2 + (2-1)^2 + (3-3)^2 = 1 = 1 + 0 = 2.$$

In our opinion, this similarity measure does not take into account the importance of the position of the permutation in the vector, as whether it takes place at the head or at the tail of the vector does not modify the distance. For example, we previously calculated:

Distance ([**1,2**,3]; [**2,1**,3] = 2 with a permutation at the head

We obtain the same result, which is 2 with a permutation at the tail of the vector:

Distance ([1,**2,3**]; [1,**3,2**] = 2 with a permutation at the tail

But position matters; this becomes obvious if we take a more appropriate example such as the ATP ranking.

---

21 This example is taken from the blog of computer science professor Kardi Teknomo at the University of Ateneo de Manila (Available at: https://people.revoledu.com/kardi/tutorial/Similarity/SpearmanDistance.html).

Depending on whether the permutation impacts the top two players in the ranking or the players ranked 100th and 101st, respectively, the perception of the importance of changing the structure of the ranking will not be the same for observers. In the first case, the comments will say that the top of the hierarchy has changed, and in the second case, there will simply be no comment, as the event will be judged as unimportant.

Thus, it would be desirable for the similarity measure to calculate a lower distance in the second case (the ranking is barely changed, the rankings before and after permutation of rank remain close) to the first case (the ATP ranking underwent a subjectively greater change).

In the same spirit, within the framework of our research, we estimate that a prediction that fails at the tail of the vector of choice *a priori* but correctly predicts the first choices is more efficient, *mutatis mutandis*, that is, with the same number and permutation difference, than a prediction that would fail to predict the first choices but correctly predict the last choices.

We therefore propose a similarity measure, a variant of the Spearman distance, which takes into account the depth of the permutations.

DEFINITION 1.8.– In our research, the "distance" of two ordered vectors is calculated as *the average of the rank deviations of the* paired *components* of the vectors, *the deviations being weighted by the inverse of the position of the pair* in the two vectors, which is equal to the smallest rank of the components of the pair.

EXAMPLE 1.1.– The "distance" function must account for a greater proximity between Vector 1 and Vector 3, relative to Vector 1 and Vector 2:

Vector 1 = $(V_1 \leq V\mathbf{\underline{2}} \leq v3 \leq V_4 \leq V_5 \leq V_6)$ Rank 2 deviation of depth 2

Vector 2 = $(V_1 \leq V_4 \leq V_2 \leq V\mathbf{\underline{2}} \leq v5 \leq V_6)$

Vector 1 = $(V_1 \leq V_2 \leq V_3 \leq \mathbf{\underline{V_4}} \leq V_5 \leq V_6)$ Rank 2 deviation of depth 4

Vector 3 = $(V_1 \leq V_2 \leq V_3 \leq V_6 \leq V_5 \leq \mathbf{\underline{V_4}})$

General formulation of an *ad hoc* similarity measure for our research: let two ordered vectors $U(U_1 \leq \ldots \leq U_n)$ and $V(V_1 \leq \ldots \leq V_m)$ with $m \leq n$ *with* $(m, n) \in \mathbb{N}^* \times \mathbb{N}^*$ and U_i, $V_j \in \{\alpha_1, \ldots, \alpha_N\}$ N modalities of a nominal variable:

$$Distance'(U,V) := \sum_{i=1}^{n} |i - j| \times \frac{1}{n \times \min(i,j)}$$

with:

i = rank U_i in U or i;

j = rank V_j in V if ∃ V_j∈ V tq U_i= V_j;

else j = i.

Properties of the proposed similarity measure:

– the symmetry property (∀ (U,V), “Distance” (U,V) = “Distance” (V,U)), is direct and follows from the expression of “Distance” (U,V), which is written as a function of two symmetric functions (absolute value and min);

– concerning the separation property (∀ (U,V), “Distance” (U,V) = 0 ⇔ U = V):

- the implication (“Distance” (U,V) = 0 ⇒ U = V) is demonstrated by the contrapositive statement (i.e. U ≠V ⇒ “Distance” (U,V) ≠ 0). If U ≠V, then there exists at least one non-zero and strictly positive rank deviation ($|i-j_i|>0$) weighted by a quantity also strictly positive, therefore “Distance” (U,V) > 0,

- the reciprocal implication (U = V ⇒ “Distance” (U,V) = 0) is direct, since U=V means that the rank differences cancel out term by term ($|i-j_i|=|i-i|$).

We have not demonstrated the triangular inequality, which explains our use of quotation marks to mention this distance. At this point, it is safer to speak of a similarity measure.

If we return to the example of the mobility preferences of individuals A and B, with the Spearman distance, we had:

Distance ([**1,2**,3]; [**2,1**,3] = 2 = Distance ([1,**2,3**]; [1,**3,2**] = 2

With the similarity measure that we have defined, we get:

“Distance” ([**1,2**,3] ; [**2,1**,3] = |1-2|/1+|2-1|/1+|3-3|/0 = 2

“Distance” ([1,**2,3**] ; [1,**3,2**] = |1-1|/1+|2-3|/2+|3-2|/2 = 1

We get the desired result; this time the distance calculated with the two vectors having a permutation of depth 2 is less than that of two vectors having a permutation of depth 1.

The calculation of the matching function is a particular use case of this similarity function, since if the first operand is a preference order (similar to an ordered vector), the second operand is a value (promoted value or domain of activity).

2

Experimentation

2.1. Experimental protocol

Historically, psychology was the first discipline in the social sciences to use the experimental approach to study behavior induced by stimuli under highly controlled conditions. The origins of the experimental approach in economics can be traced back to the work of Thurstone (1931) who, on the recommendations of a friend and professor of psychology at the University of Chicago, applied the experimental approach to an economic question in order to give it empirical foundations. Thurstone sought to define the indifference curves representing individuals' preferences by using a simulation of choice between different combinations of goods (hats and shoes). The skepticism inspired by the artificial nature of the gains relating to participants' choices led economists to use actual financial incentives to concretize the consequences of choices and guarantee seriousness and motivation from participants.

Chamberlin (1948) and Smith (1962), two other precursors, opened the way for experimental economics a few years later. This emerging discipline experienced significant development thanks to the Theory of Games by Neumann and Morgenstern (1944), the formalism of which lends itself well to rigorous experimental protocols. The theory of expected utility was particularly tested and called into question by a succession of paradoxes (Allais paradox, Ellsberg paradox[1]), due to laboratory experiments.

More recently, the experimental approach, complementary to the theoretical and empirical approaches, gained recognition when the 2002 Nobel Prize in economics

---

Abbreviations within figures, tables and equations remain in the original French.

1 See Kast (2002).

was awarded to psychologist Daniel Kahneman and economist Vernon Smith, who represented the two streams of experimentation in economics.

The indisputable contribution of the experimental approach lies in the possibility of isolating the variables present and manipulating interest variables in a controlled environment corresponding to the *ceteris paribus* of economic reasoning, because of a device artificially reproducing a natural situation. Also, the subject covered by laboratory experimentation is on the understanding of causalities rather than correlations. The possible reproduction of experiences is another distinctive feature of this approach, which fits well with the approach of the progressive validation of theories by the accumulation of evidence or, conversely, by refuting using falsification, an epistemological approach advocated by Popper (Chalmers 1987). In addition, Broihanne *et al.* (2004) noted that the experimental method does not replace the analysis of field data, but can provide a beginning or an additional explanation on an observed or supposed phenomenon.

In management sciences, laboratory experimentation remains little used, except in the field of marketing (Lesage 2000). Lesage defines this approach as "factual observation under controlled factors". It consists of "reproducing a natural event in the laboratory[2] in order to facilitate its observation and to have easily reproducible data".

As part of our research, we decided to study, in the laboratory, the consequences of the choices of individual investors when exposed to information on fundraising campaigns of several projects, which were competing on a fictitious equity crowdfunding platform. Also, the affective reactions, which are at the heart of our explanatory model, are triggered and measured. Entrepreneurs' pitch videos act as stimuli; they are powerful inducers of emotions because they immerse the subject in a story that has its own dynamics and a complexity that makes the stimulus ecological, that is to say, close to real conditions (Gil 2009). Regarding the measurement of affective reactions, we have recourse to the Mehrabian and Russel (1974) scale, which collects, by self-assessment, the characteristics of the cognitive dimension of emotions: pleasure (or valence), defined on a pleasure-displeasure continuum relative to the subject's satisfaction and well-being and arousal, defined on a arousal-calm continuum that refers to the subject's degree of arousal.

In this first section, we first justify the use of a laboratory experiment and specify our objectives (section 2.1.1); then, we describe the process of recruiting participants (section 2.1.2), the experimental protocol (section 2.1.3) and the experimental design (section 2.1.4) carried out.

2 An experiment can also take place in a natural environment (Petit 2013).

2.1.1. *Rationale and objectives*

2.1.1.1. *Rationale*

In order to empirically compare the explanatory model using structural equations and the resulting individual predictive model, it was necessary to collect data. If at first we considered doing a survey with investors of an equity crowdfunding platform[3], we dropped this idea because the very objective of this research was not aligned with the interests of the platforms, as the latter wished to portray the image of a risky but reasoned investment.

Furthermore, the option of administering the questionnaire online and without control did not seem feasible, since its duration was approximately one hour, which presupposed seriousness and strong motivation on the part of the respondent. In addition, the participant is not supposed to have an exchange of any kind in our case, which this mode of data collection does not guarantee; hence, we have considered the option of a laboratory experiment or *in vivo* experimentation.

According to the criteria of Yin (2009), the characteristics of this research correspond to the experimental method because:

1) the research question here is of the "how: "How do equity crowdfunding investors choose their projects?";

2) this research requires monitoring behavior: as we have mentioned, it is important to ensure that participants do not have any outside communication and adhere to a reasonable amount of time to acquaint themselves with the information that the analysis is based on;

3) this research is centered on contemporary events.

The advantages of a laboratory experiment on a survey carried out by administering a questionnaire are multifold:

– monitoring compliance with the procedure: in our case observing sufficient time to analyze the business plans, watching pitch videos in their entirety and the absence of communication between participants;

– the experimental approach is indicated in the case of causal research, while survey techniques are indicated for correlational research. Indeed, only experimental

3 To this end, we participated in the 3rd edition of the Crowdfunding Festival on May 28, 2016, at ESCP Europe and developed contacts with several managers of equity crowdfunding platforms.

research guarantees compliance with the three conditions necessary for causality set by the book by Mill (1882):

- a concomitant variation in the explanatory and explained variables;
- the temporal ordering of events, and the evaluation of the causal variables precedes the evaluation of the explained variable;
- the absence of any other possible cause.

Moreover, as Lesage (2000) explained, laboratory experimentation traditionally has two objectives: (1) to test a theory and (2) to make it possible to identify regularities hidden by the complexity of reality.

This second objective concerns phenomena that are difficult to detect because they are masked by natural noise. When the researcher infers, by abduction, a hypothesis H as being the cause of a phenomenon, the demonstration of H may require a purification of reality using an experiment that will favor its perception. This is indeed the case with this research in which the natural noise that needs to be purified corresponds to all the social interactions that shape the investor's judgment and are a source of imitation.

Also, we chose to carry out our data collection using a role play type of controlled laboratory experiment, in which the participants had to achieve objectives while adhering to the prescribed rules.

2.1.1.2. *Objectives and nature of the experiment*

According to Petit (2013), an experiment aims to empirically test a theory, explore new knowledge, assist decision-making and even participate in the teaching of abstract concepts.

Our research is exploratory in nature, which is why this experiment contributes to the emergence of a phenomenon and the role of the affective dimension in the choice of individual investors in equity crowdfunding, by testing the hypotheses made, without being sufficient in itself to confirm the proposed theory.

From a practical point of view, the first objective of this data collection is to estimate the model of structural equations previously presented, as well as its extension, the individual predictive model. A joint sub-objective is to develop the Interest variable of the measurement model of the explanatory model.

The second objective is to implement design of the experiment, presented below, with the aim of manipulating the cognitive dimension of the choice to judge its effect on the model. Thus, the business plan, which the subjective evaluation of the perceived signal quality factor is based on, will be handled according to two modalities: a good quality business plan, rated BP+, and a degraded quality business plan, rated BP–.

Let us remember that this work falls within the field of behavioral finance, at the crossroads between finance and psychology, which is why the presented protocol departs from the usual requirements of experimental economics, and is more similar to the experiments of psycho-economists and psychologists. In particular, the financial incentive of this experimentation derogates from the principle that prevails in experimental economics, according to which subjects must receive a financial incentive proportional to their winnings in the game. This incentive modality is based on the following premise: only a financial incentive, the amount of which depends on the winnings in the game, guarantees the seriousness of the participant[4]. Moreover, this type of motivation is intended to constrain and guide the conduct of subjects in accordance with the hypothesis of instrumental rationality, i.e. behaving in an egoistic way with the sole horizon of maximizing their economic utility, or their profit.

According to Loewenstein (1999), if this artifice does not achieve its goal ("even with monetary rewards, subjects are likely to be powerfully influenced by motives other than profit maximization. Such motives include the desire to behave in an appropriate fashion, conform to the expectations of the experimenter, appear to be a smart (or at least not stupid), good person, a winner"), it is also not desirable: "even if experimenters were able to eliminate motives other than profit maximization from their experiments, it would not necessarily be a good thing as far as external validity is concerned. Profit maximization may be an important incentive in economic transactions, but it probably is not the most important".

Let us again look at these two points: (1) a financial incentive proportional to the winnings in the game guarantees the seriousness of subjects and (2) this type of incentive guarantees a behavior in accordance with *homo economicus*.

Regarding the first point, we adopt the point of view of experimental psychology which states that a modest flat-rate compensation is sufficient (from 5 to 10 euros for students), because an adequate level of motivation is guaranteed by the simple voluntary process of the subject's participation (Petit 2013).

The second point is decisive in our research, since, unlike the economic approach, we find ourselves within the framework of a complex rationality

4 A few dissonant voices among the most recognized economists in experimental economics recommend avoiding any dogmatism in terms of incentives; the motivation of participants does not necessarily have to happen through a monetary incentive (Eber and Willinger 2012).

(instrumental, axiological and affective). Consequently, forcing participants to adopt the behavior of maximizing their profit through monetary incentive would amount to artificially imposing a financial motivation on them, whereas in equity crowdfunding, financial and non-financial motivations are mixed. We have therefore defined a random incentive, independent of participants' choices, to approach the consequences of an actual investment in equity crowdfunding. In doing so, we abide by the recommendation of (Lesage 2000): "We must ensure that the subjects, although in a fictitious situation, have a reasonably 'realistic' behavior according to the hypotheses determined by the experiment. The researcher must determine the type of incentive that is most appropriate for his research objective".

The second major difference with experimental economics (we chose an ecological experiment) is approaching the real conditions of the choice rather than putting participants in front of decontextualized decisions applying to lotteries (or probability distributions). Indeed, we place ourselves in a context of uncertainty, that is to say a situation without (objective) probability allocated to the consequences of choices, which excludes any lottery and stylized formalization. On another note, we are specifically interested in the effects of presentation and context on investment choices through the elements of fundraising campaigns: pictures, videos and narration. Our approach is therefore similar to that of psycho-economists, who take the actual context into account in their experiments in order to capture the effects of presentation (Petit 2013). On this point, Loewenstein (1999), who is defined as a psycho-economist, recalled that one of the major discoveries of cognitive psychology was the influence of context on all forms of thought and problem solving. It should be noted all the same that we limit the context to that of an investor cut off from any social interaction, so that the choice observed results exclusively from their sole judgment.

2.1.2. *Constitution, sample size and recruitment procedure*

2.1.2.1. *Constitution*

While in absolute terms anyone can invest in an equity crowdfunding platform, in practice, the group of crowders who constitute the reference population for this research presents a very specific socioeconomic/demographic profile. However, we opted for an empirical sampling method, as we did not have a database of actual investors: the convenience sample. According to Gavard-Perret *et al.* (2013), this method should not be favored because, unlike probability sampling methods, it does not allow statistical extrapolation. However, its use is justified when the deadline for the investigation is very short and the budget is low, which was our case. In addition, an administrative constraint was imposed on us due to the financing of incentives from public funds: the participants could not be employed by the State, which limited our sample to the student population of the university.

Finally, students who volunteered to participate against payment made up the sample for this experiment, which is not without advantages: Eber and Willinger (2012) indicated that students have the advantage of being available, encouraged by modest sums, and motivated by curiosity and the desire to participate in research.

2.1.2.2. *Sample size*

The size of the sample had to make it possible to achieve the two previously defined objectives: (1a) estimation of the explanatory model by structural equation and of the associated individual predictive model, (1b) development of the Interest variable of the measurement model and (2) analysis of the results of the experimental design.

The size of the sample is closely linked to the statistical methods of data analysis; so, Box 2.1 specifies the methods of analysis chosen for the data.

(1a) Estimation of the structural equation model: the partial least squares (PLS) approach

Points no. 1, 2 and 4 of the five major reasons for using the PLS approach identified by Chin and Newsted (1999) are relevant to our research:

1) the objective of the research is more focused on predicting than validating the theory;

2) the phenomenon studied is relatively new or changing and the theoretical model or measurements are not well established;

3) the model is relatively complex, with a large number of indicators or latent variables;

4) it is essential to model the relationships between latent variables and their measurements in different ways (formative and reflective) or;

5) the conditions on the data relating to normal distribution, independence or sample size are not met.

(1b) Development of the measurement model: principal component analysis and PLS approach

The Situational Interest dimension of the Interest variable is constructed by combining the recommendations of Schiefele (2009) on the aroused situational interest scale of Yennek (2014).

Also, this subconstruct is developed according to a procedure adapted from the paradigm of Churchill (1979). Principal component analysis is used for the purification phase. The PLS approach is also used for confirmatory factor analysis.

(2) Analysis of the results of the experimental plan: T-test and PLS approach

The measurement of the effect of the Quality of the Business Plan factor on the Perceived Signal Quality variable results from a T-type analysis of variance.

A multigroup analysis using the PLS approach makes it possible to verify whether the Perceived Signal Quality has a significant impact on the parameters of the explanatory model.

Box 2.1. *Data analysis methods chosen for the three objectives of this data collection*

(1a) *Sample size for estimating the structural equation model*

Within the framework of the PLS approach adopted for estimating the structural equation model, Chin and Newsted (1999) provided an empirical rule to determine the size of the sample required:

> The number of observations must be greater than or equal to 10 times the number of indicators of the most complex formative variable, and/or 10 times the number of structural relations emanating from the central construct of the structural model.

In the case of this model, N = 10 × max (10.5) = 100 observations.

(1b) *Sample size for developing the measurement model*

For the phase of purification by principal component analysis, the standard recommendations require a number of observations corresponding to at least thrice the number of variables, with a minimum of 100 observations.

As specified in Box 2.1, the confirmatory analyses of constructs are also based on the PLS approach.

(2) *Sample size for analyzing the results of the experimental design*

For the T test, 30 individuals are often retained as the limit value (Labreuche 2010). Multigroup analysis is also carried out using the PLS approach.

Finally, a sample of at least 100 individuals is required for this experiment.

2.1.2.3. *Recruitment process*

In order to recruit the participants of this experiment, we drew up a communication plan in several phases via several channels. Information posters were made (available on request[5]) and were displayed on the information boards in the libraries at the University of Burgundy, as well as on information boards in other parts of the campus. A post on the Facebook profile of the university and emails to all students of the university from the general directorate of services of the University of Burgundy completed the plan.

At first, student volunteers were asked to pre-register on the event management platform Evento (a tool of the public interest group Renater). As the number of voluntary applicants was more than 100, we selected volunteers in the order of the arrival of responses to a confirmation email sent in the days leading up to the experiment.

We also launched a complementary and deliberately redundant communication campaign with IAE students, as this population has a useful characteristic (knowledge of management basics) for the Sophistication variable test, which acts as a moderating variable in the explanatory model. These students also have the advantage of adopting different behaviors than other students by being more selfish, and thus, more in line with the economic theory (Petit 2013), which paved the way for an interesting multigroup analysis between IAE students and other students.

Let us note that the information poster highlighted two points discussed in section 2.3 of this chapter:

– a random financial incentive;

– the scientific added value and originality of the experiment.

2.1.3. *Experimental protocol*

A laboratory experiment must be reproducible so that other experiments can falsify the results in accordance with Popper's verification criteria (Chalmers 1987) or, on the contrary, extend its external validity. The validation of a proposal is based on a logic of accumulating consistent observations in different contexts (Lesage 2000). This is why we detail the following conditions of this experiment, attach its material and describe the associated experiment design.

The experiment consisted of a simulation (or role play), in which the participants were placed in an ecological situation of choice, that is to say a situation close to reality. Nevertheless, according to Lesage (2000): "The interest of a model is judged

5 For details, contact via email: christian.goglin@gmail.com.

by its capacity to represent the chosen aspect of the real situation as well as by its aptitude to rule out all other unselected aspects. The key to success is to introduce the right simplifications".

Consequently, the real situation of the individual investor was artificially reproduced but limited to the object of study, i.e. the psychological dimension of a choice without social interaction. Also, any verbal or virtual communication between subjects was prohibited. The participants did not have discussion forums, messaging or any means of monitoring the real-time choices of other students, which made imitation impossible.

The experiment took place in the controlled environment of two classrooms at the University of Burgundy, organized in a laboratory. These rooms were equipped with microcomputers; data was collected by administering an electronic questionnaire. Four projects, each associated with an entrepreneur pitch video and a business plan, were submitted to the participants.

This experiment required developing an online questionnaire and material for a pseudo equity crowdfunding platform, reduced to two main elements: a website broadcasting entrepreneurs' pitch videos and business plans associated with the projects.

Let us now take a closer look at the development of this experimental material.

2.1.3.1. *Development of the online questionnaire*

The questionnaire for this study aggregates a series of questions relating to the indicators of the measurement model of the explanatory model, as well as to the moderating and control variables. All questions are closed-ended, given the objective of statistically processing the estimation of the subsequent structural equation model.

Particular attention has been paid to the wording of the questions, ensuring that the vocabulary is familiar and precise, the questions are short (no more than 20 words) and that there are no double questions or leading questions (Gavard-Perret *et al.* 2013). Apart from a 5-point Osgood scale used to measure affective reactions, the response modalities for each indicator of the latent variables are defined on a 5-point Likert scale, in which each level marks the respondent's degree of agreement according to a continuum ranging from 1 "strongly agree" to 5 "strongly disagree".

The choice of having five degrees for these interval scales results from a constraint of the Lime Survey online questionnaire implementation tool, which cannot be configured on this point. While this limitation initially brought our selection of this tool under scrutiny, the following reasons convinced us that this number was adequate:

– the main reason is the length of the questionnaire, which contains 235 items. However, even if all of the questions are not defined by an interval scale, the number of degrees is inseparable from the number of questions. Cognitive fatigue and the time constraint of the experiment did not suit a higher granularity of the scale;

– five degrees is well within the magical number seven plus or minus two range of Miller (1955), which is the consensus in the scientific community;

– a higher quantity would have run the risk of artificial precision, which is excluded only if the participants are interested, involved or put at risk by the subject of the study (Gavard-Perret *et al.* 2013);

– there is no consensus on the link between the number of degrees and the reliability of the scales, even if according to Cox (1980), increasing the number of degrees undoubtedly improves reliability slightly, but less than by resorting to other means.

The data collection questionnaire is organized into four parts. The first corresponds to the affective reactions measurement scale (Q1), and the second to investment choices (Q2). The third is the evaluation of the other variables of the model relative to each project (Q3, Q4, Q5, Q6), and the last makes it possible to collect the personality variables and structure of preferences; its questions are independent of the projects (Q7).

NOTE.– The entire questionnaire is available on request.

We organized a questionnaire evaluation pretest by administering it to four people, including two doctoral students from the laboratory, as well as two people with no particular knowledge on the topic of crowdfunding. It had a dual purpose:

– estimating the total duration of the questionnaire in order to determine the number of projects to be submitted over the duration of the experiment (one hour), three or four: these tests led us to retain the number of projects as four;

– reducing the instrumentation bias and more specifically, the poor formulation of questions: a question deemed ambiguous was reformulated.

We then administered the questionnaire using the free statistical survey software Lime Survey.

2.1.3.2. *Development of business plans*

The business plans drawn up are the result of a combination of the actual business plans of the projects selected for experimentation on the Wiseed.com financing platform; all of the information is laid out across three pages. The following sections are present in each business plan in order to facilitate comparative analysis:

– presentation;

– identity;

– values;

– vision;

– rewards;

– partnerships;

– use of funds;

– stages of development;

– exit strategy;

– competition;

– differentiating elements;

– financial forecasts;

– team.

For purposes of an experimental design, two business plans were developed for each project. The first, which is good quality and rated BP+, contains information from the real business plan; the second, which is poor quality and rated BP–, presents altered information with dissuasive financial forecasts, an unsuitable level of experience and educational qualification of the founders, etc.

NOTE.– Business plans are available on request.

2.1.3.3. *Selection of pitch videos and viewing platform*

Four projects were selected on the funding platform Wiseed.com, so that the corporate values conveyed by each of them (implicitly and explicitly in the business plan) maximize the variance of the Axiological Congruence variable of the explanatory model. To this end, they are distributed evenly over the Schwartz (1992) values circumplex. Figure 2.1 locates the four values chosen on this circumplex.

The keywords representative of the core values proposed by Schwartz are linked to the selected companies (available on request) on the Wiseed.com platform.

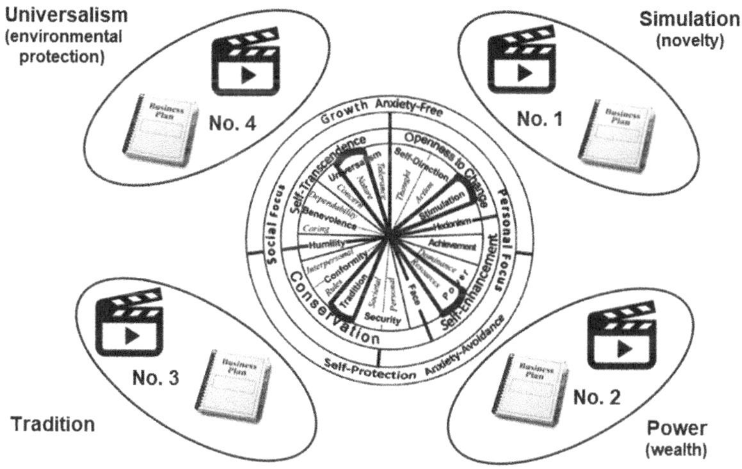

Figure 2.1. *Graphic representation of projects on the Schwartz value circumplex*

The four videos were not of the same duration; so, in order to not favor one project over another, a coherent clip of about one minute was selected for each of them.

Finally, an internet page was developed to integrate the four video clips of the project pitches.

2.1.4. *Experimental design*

The second objective of this experiment was to validate or refute the hypothesis linked to the secondary question of this research by an experimental design. This hypothesis, made explicit in the defended thesis, is that, within the framework of equity crowdfunding and in the absence of any social interaction, the choices of projects are overdetermined by the values and the affective reactions of the investor. In other words, the cognitive dimension of the choice, identified using the Perceived Signal Quality variable, has a non-significant or negligible effect (relative to the other variables of the model) on the explained variable, the Intensity of Investment Choice.

The estimation of the parameters of the structural equations model using the PLS approach makes it possible to test this hypothesis; nevertheless, it appeared useful for us to supplement this result by that of an experiment manipulating the determining factor of the subjective evaluation of the Perceived Signal Quality variable.

Also, we chose to implement a classic "after only" type of experimental design, the characteristics of which are listed in Box 2.2. This type of experimental design consists of randomly distributing the subjects of the sample into two groups (experimental group and control group); a treatment is applied to the experimental group only and the explained variable is subsequently measured for the two groups. Finally, the effect of the experiment is calculated using a difference of the means of the variable explained in the two groups (Gavard-Perret *et al.* 2013). This type of procedure is called "between-subject", since the behaviors of two different groups of subjects are compared.

The treatment applied to the experimental group results, in our case, from a manipulation of the Quality of the Business Plan factor. As a result, the following two groups were formed:

1) the experimental group (or tested sample), in which the students had to analyze a poor-quality business plan;

2) the control group (or control sample), in which the students had to analyze a normal business plan.

According to Lesage (2000), this type of experiment is also known as "within-experiment", as it measures the effect of a single explanatory variable in an otherwise identical environment (*ceteris paribus*).

It should be added that the experiment was repeated as each subject successively evaluated four projects (always using the same treatment); the total number of observations collected is therefore equal to 400 or 200 per group. In this way, the samples are of a sufficiently large size so that the selection bias inherent in a comparison of groups according to a between-subject procedure, is reduced (Eber and Willinger 2012).

The factor or explanatory variable is the Quality of the Business Plan.

The variable to be explained is the Perceived Signal Quality.

The treatment applied to the experimental group is exposing them to poor-quality business plans.

The external variables likely to influence the variable to be explained are the psychological traits of the subjects capable of influencing their perceptions.

The units tested are the individuals.

Box 2.2. *Characteristics of the experimental design*

The *internal validity* of an experiment ensures that the factors can be manipulated and that the external variables are controlled. In our case, the only factor that was manipulated directly was exposing the subjects to two separate treatments. External variables were controlled by the random assignment (randomized variables) of subjects to the experimental conditions. This type of procedure limits the risk of systematic error due to known and unknown external variables, by ensuring that they are distributed randomly among the treatments of the experiment (Gavard-Perret *et al.* 2013).

This experimental design operates in two stages; the first stage tests whether the Quality of the Business Plan has an effect on the Perceived Signal Quality, while the second stage focuses on the effect of the Perceived Signal Quality variable on the explanatory model by a multigroup analysis.

2.1.4.1. *First operating phase of the experimental design*

The causal relationship tested is:

Explained variable = Φ (Explanatory variable) or

Perceived signal quality = Φ (Quality of the business plan).

The Quality of the Business Plan factor takes two modalities on an ordinal scale: bad (BP–) or good (BP+), which corresponds to the two business plans developed for each project, mentioned above.

The subjects' perception of the business plan is subjective; it depends on their perceptions, which is why a pretest was carried out with two volunteer doctoral students. The purpose of this pretest was to carry out a preliminary study in order to test the manipulation of factors. This made it possible to ensure a sufficient *a priori* variability of the two modalities of the factor, which resulted in a significantly different evaluation. Thus, this pretest ensured differential treatment between the two groups.

The four projects, identified by their videos, are matched with business plans of both modalities, which form eight couples ($Video_i$, BP_j) with $i \in \{1..4\}$, $j \in \{-,+\}$.

Two groups, differentiated only by the Quality of the Business Plan variable, are defined and represented in Figure 2.2.

Video 1	Video 1	Video 2	Video 2	Video 3	Video 3	Video 4	Video 4
BP–	BP+	BP–	BP+	BP–	BP+	BP–	BP+

Table 2.1. *Alternatives of the experiment*

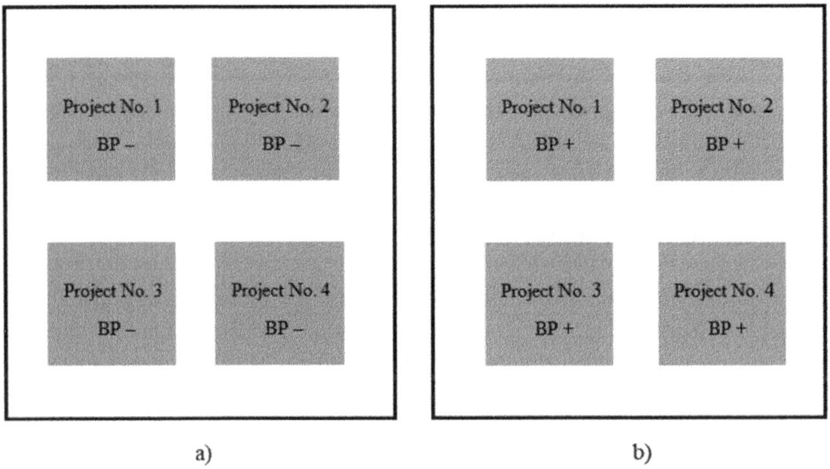

Figure 2.2. *Illustration of the two groups of the experimental design: a) tested sample; b) control sample*

The *selection effect*, which can arise when the characteristics of the participants in the experimental groups are different, was reduced by a random assignment process, in which each student was alternately assigned to room number one or two depending on the order of entry into room number one (room number two was adjacent).

2.1.4.2. *Second operating phase of the experimental design*

Secondly, a multigroup analysis made it possible to verify whether the Quality of the Business Plan had a significant impact on the parameters of the explanatory model.

2.1.5. *Conclusion*

In section 2.1, we started by justifying the use of laboratory experimentation for data collection by emphasizing the need to control the noise represented by real and virtual social interactions. This noise may mask the hypothesis of the determining role of the affective dimension in the choice of individual investors in equity crowdfunding.

We then specified the two main objectives of this experiment: (1) to have data to estimate the parameters of the structural equation model and (2) to execute a classic 1-factor experimental design – the quality of the business plan – in order to validate or refute the secondary hypothesis about the marginal role of the cognitive dimension in choice. The participant recruitment process was detailed; the experimental protocol was presented with the description of the related material: the questionnaire, business plans and pitch videos. Finally, the experimental design and its use were specified.

2.2. Carrying out the experimental procedure

2.2.1. *Conducting the experimental procedure*

The participants were instructed to be present in front of the experimentation room, with their student card, at least 15 minutes before the start of the session for the practical reasons of setting up. The planned duration of the experiment was one hour.

Upon entering, each participant was directed alternately to one of the two rooms, which corresponded, respectively, to the experimental and control group. Two experimenters, one per room, ensured that the procedure was carried out smoothly. The first experimenter was the author of this book and the second, a medical intern, received specific training prior to assist him.

Once the students settled down, general instructions regarding the anonymity of the questionnaire were communicated. It should also be added that the experiment took place under double anonymity, or double blind (anonymity of the participants and the experimenter), in order to limit the risk of the effect of induced demand, that is to say a situation in which the subjects seek to meet the supposed expectations of the experimenter or to oppose them (Petit 2013). It was also specified that there was neither a right or wrong answer, the latter being analyzed in groups and not individually, in order to reduce the anxiety bias relating to the conscious concern to be evaluated and the desire to obtain a positive evaluation from the evaluating body (Rosenberg 1965). In order to avoid any social interaction, students were asked to turn off their cell phones and it was clarified that discussions were not allowed during the session, including after finalizing the questionnaire.

The last important preliminary instruction, the terms of the distribution of incentives, was announced before the start of the experiment in accordance with good practices (Eber and Willinger 2012). In addition, participants were told that the random financial incentive in the form of a gift card was unrelated to the choices made during the experiment. Without this information, some students may have imagined a link between winning in the game and an actual reward, which would have distorted the motivations of the participant.

However, on the contrary, the following instruction was intended to give participants the complete freedom to imagine, through thought experience, the motivations that came naturally to them:

> You are simply asked to simulate a situation in which you have decided to invest the sum of €200 taken from your savings, for your own reasons, on an equity crowdfunding platform.
>
> So take a few seconds to ask yourself why you would want to invest in a startup.

A justification of the virtual amount of €200 is available on request.

A neutral definition of equity crowdfunding, taken from Wikipedia, was also read out so that the subjects had a minimal understanding of the objective of the experiment.

It should be noted that the objective of the research was not indicated in order to avoid the effect of contamination, which happens when a subject with this knowledge may not answer sincerely (Lesage 2000).

After this preparatory phase, the experiment opened with the screening of the four pitch video clips of the competing projects on the virtual platform. Each was immediately followed by a break dedicated to filling in the section of the questionnaire related to the measurement of affective reactions. In doing so, we complied with the recommendation of Lemoine and Plichon (2000) on the need for the immediate measurement of affective reactions after exposure to a stimulus in order to guarantee their reliability.

Then, a 12 minute business plan study time was granted to learn about the four business plans. This period of time corresponded to approximately one minute per page, which is sufficient time according to our pretests, and also in view of the average time required for the decision-making of actual investors[6].

NOTE.– The complete experimenter's guide is available on request.

At the end of this analysis time, the participants had to make their investment choice via the online questionnaire, the entire €200 (virtual sum) to be invested with the constraint of an allocation per project expressed as a multiple of €50: €0, €50, €100, €150 or €200.

A second choice was requested; it was a question of distributing, no longer the virtual sum of €200, but the entirety of the subject's personal savings, between the four projects in order to verify the effect of the amount to be invested on behavior. On this subject, economists speculate, and some argue, that anomalies revealed for small amounts could disappear when the stakes become high (Eber and Willinger 2012).

6 Skoglund and Bengtsson (2013) reported that 72% of the 390 true investors in ECF in their study chose their investment in less than 10 minutes.

After having communicated some precisions about the interpretation of the 5-point Likert scale, as well as on the choice of ordering the stacking of modalities for the preference hierarchies, the subjects filled in the rest of the questionnaire, grouping the items of the latent variables relating to each project, and then independent of the projects, linked to their preferences and their psychological profile, as well as to data relating to moderating and control variables.

The section of the questionnaire that deals with the evaluation of the variables of each project organizes the questions as follows:

1) questions relating to the Perceived Signal Quality (immediately after the allocation choices and reading the business plans);

2) questions relating to the Trust variable;

3) questions relating to affective variables: Interest and Familiarity.

This order respects the following logic: from cognitive variables to affective variables. Indeed, the Perceived Signal Quality variable is the cognitive variable of the model, Trust is a mixed cognitive/affective variable and the Interest and Familiarity variables are affective. The aim of this choice is to reduce a possible repercussion effect described by Bickart (1993), i.e. overestimation or underestimation, attributable to the participants' ignorance of the subject and combined with an overall evaluation (variables affective) preceding the evaluation of specific characteristics (cognitive variable). Moreover, asking the questions on affective variables before those on cognitive variables would have run the risk of an affective halo effect altering the judgment of the cognitive variable.

At the end of the experiment and after each participant had finalized their questionnaire, the students were thanked and paid by a random financial incentive in the form of a gift card of €10 or €20. Figure 2.3 shows the successive phases of the experimental procedure.

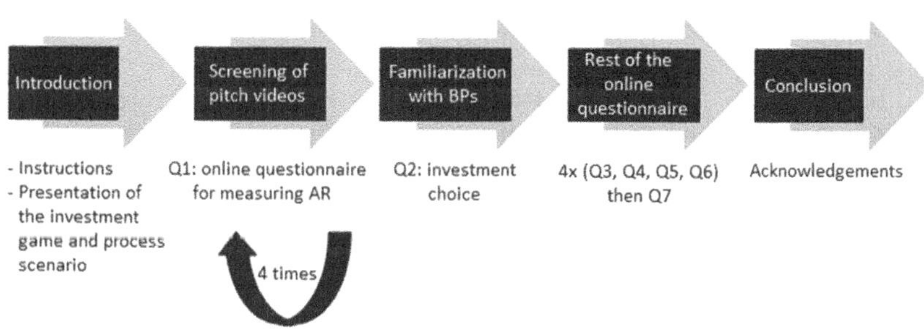

Figure 2.3. *Dynamics of the experimental procedure*

2.2.2. *Conclusion*

With control, the possibility of replicating the studies is an advantage of the experimental method over other empirical methods. This is why the sole purpose of this section was to describe, in more detail, the experimental procedure carried out. Thus, a possible faithful reproduction of this study, for example, with more representative participants such as actual investors, could increase the external validity of the results obtained or even falsify them in the future.

2.3. Validity and handling of biases

2.3.1. *Validity*

This laboratory experiment has a dual objective: to collect the data necessary for the estimation of a model by structural equations and to carry out an experimental design. It should be noted that the validity of the measurement model (outer model) of the model by structural equations will be dealt with in section 3.2.

2.3.1.1. *Internal validity*

According to Loewenstein (1999), the internal validity of a laboratory experiment refers to the level of trust that one can have in the conclusions drawn on the causality of the phenomena studied. The results obtained must be robust and replicable. From a practical point of view, it is a guarantee that the explained variable depends only on the variations of the manipulated factor. However, a certain number of biases or effects can harm this relationship, which is why we have tried to anticipate them in order to handle them preventively (see section 2.3.2).

2.3.1.2. *External validity*

External validity is the possible generalization of the results of an experiment; it is the question of parallelism, or to what extent the behaviors observed in the laboratory correspond to actual behaviors.

It should be noted that external validity and internal validity maintain a relationship of tension and even opposition (Schram 2005). This tension is explained by the remoteness of the real context (that is to say, reduction in external validity) induced by the process of improving internal validity, with the latter based on simplification and increased control of the context to "stick" to the theory. However, the latter is, by construction, an extremely simplified representation, for the social sciences, of the real world.

In our case, the ecological design of the experiment brings it closer, by certain features (the nature of the task and the nature of the environment), to the field experiments (Harrison and List 2004), which increases its external validity. However, the reconstituted context remains artificial due to the exclusion of any real or virtual social exchange, while these effects on behavior are verified and documented by numerous studies. But it is precisely this "noise" that we wanted to get rid of in order to isolate and reveal the effect of the affective dimension. Furthermore, the selection bias induced by the exclusive participation of students prohibits, in itself, any generalization. Also, the validity of the formulated hypotheses can only result from a progressive accumulation of concordant results by replicating the experiment in different contexts. At this stage, this experiment only makes it possible to establish the possibility of the studied phenomenon.

2.3.2. *Handling biases*

2.3.2.1. *Selection bias and financial incentive*

In order to reduce selection bias, we tried to attract students with a risk appetite, compared to students who would prefer a definite financial incentive. Also, the incentive consisted of a gift card with an expected amount of about €15 according to the following distributions:

– one in two chance of winning €10;

– one in two chance of winning €20.

The students plunged their hands blindly into an opaque bag containing 50 gift cards amounting to €10, and 50 gift cards amounting to €20.

2.3.2.2. *Selection bias and extrinsic motivations*

The information poster highlighted the scientific added value and the originality of the experiment with the aim of activating the Universalism and Stimulation values (Schwartz *et al.* 2012) of the students, and draining those who were sensitive to these messages.

2.3.2.3. *Cooperative or contradictory behavioral bias*

We choose not to reveal the objective of this research, without providing a misleading objective, as recommended by the deception principle applied by experimental psychologists, in order to avoid two problematic behaviors described by Weber and Cook (1972):

– cooperative behavior of a "good subject", where the participant wishes to please the researcher by validating their hypotheses;

– negative or contradictory behavior of the subject, opposite to the previous one, in which the participant tries to sabotage the experiment by responding to the contrary of what they think are the answers expected by the researcher.

We also did not reveal the nature of the treatment that they were exposed to; so, we conducted a blind, or even double-blind, experiment as previously mentioned.

2.3.2.4. *Instrumentation bias*

As mentioned above, a pretest aimed at limiting this bias was used, with the aim of ensuring that the questionnaire was properly understood by four people, including two doctoral students.

2.3.2.5. *First contamination bias*

This bias can arise when participants discuss the objective of the experiment amongst themselves. In our case, the two experimenters ensured compliance with the instructions, which prohibited any communication for the duration of the experiment.

2.3.2.6. *Second contamination bias*

The contamination of affective reactions is a phenomenon studied in the context of advertising clips. Poncin and Derbaix (2009) showed that contamination – the influence of an affective reaction on another subsequent affective reaction – occurs when an advertisement eliciting an emotion of low or medium intensity is immediately preceded by an advertisement eliciting a strong affective reaction with negative valence.

In our experiment, none of the four pitch videos were likely to elicit a strong negative emotional reaction. In addition, the four video clips were not linked together as is the case in an "advertising tunnel". Each video was separated from the next by some time for evaluating the emotional feelings of the participants via the online questionnaire; this interruption lasting approximately one minute separated each clip.

Also, for these two reasons, we consider that the contamination bias probably did not modify the evaluations of the affective reactions of the experiment.

2.3.2.7. *Bias related to researcher expectations*

The performance of participants can be influenced by the conscious and unconscious behavior of the experimenter/researcher, generally in the sense of validating the hypotheses being tested. For this reason, we limited interactions with subjects to the minimum: reading the instructions in the experimenter's guide, the formulation of which was as neutral as possible.

2.3.3. *Concluding remarks*

Section 2.3 describes the preventive treatments implemented within the framework of this laboratory experiment in order to attenuate the main biases likely to affect its internal validity.

2.4. Conclusion

This chapter allowed us to present the laboratory experiment selected for data collection. We justified the use of this empirical collection method by the need to control experimental conditions, like compliance with the procedure (given by the instruction), and specified the two objectives assigned to this experiment: to feed the explanatory model and to test our secondary hypothesis based on the marginal role of the cognitive dimension of choice, using an experimental design manipulating the quality of the business plan factor. Our position with respect to the experimental economy is explained, in particular with regard to the incentives, which determine motivations and orient behaviors, and the contextualization of the experiment, which is an important aspect in our case.

The experimental protocol, the material used, the experimental design and the procedure were detailed. We also presented the precautions taken to reduce the main biases, which were likely to harm the internal validity of this experiment.

Finally, we set out expectations in terms of external validity; the results obtained can only be interpreted in the context of the experiment, but nevertheless establish the possibility of the studied phenomenon. The validity of the hypotheses may gradually increase through the accumulation of evidence and convergent results.

3

Hypotheses Testing, Results and Discussion

This chapter presents our results and compares the two theoretical models formulated in Chapter 1 with empirical reality. After the description of the data prerequisites and the Partial Least Squares (PLS) approach (section 3.1), section 3.2 focuses on the validity of the measurement model, section 3.3 tests the "explanatory model" hypotheses by structural equations, section 3.4 presents the results of the experimental design and, finally, section 3.5 assesses the prediction quality of the "individual predictive model". The results are discussed as we proceed. The software mainly used for statistical data analysis is SmartPLS 3 (Ringle *et al.* 2015).

3.1. Data prerequisites and the PLS approach

3.1.1. *Statistical data of the sample*

Table 3.1 presents some statistical data concerning the sample of participants in the experiment.

These statistics indicate that the 100 subjects, all students at the University of Burgundy, were enrolled at the end of their undergraduate studies (on average), were predominantly female, were inexperienced in equity crowdfunding and that a quarter of them had been studying management for at least one year.

Abbreviations within figures, tables and equations remain in the original French.

Number of participants
100
Age
Average age of participants: 20 years and 10 months
Age variance: 2 years and 11 months
Minimum age: 17 years
Maximum age: 39 years
Gender
Percentage of male participants: 38%
Percentage of female participants: 62%
Sophistication
Percentage of participants enrolled at IAE (level is at or above second year of undergraduate degree): 25%
Experience
Percentage of participants who have already invested in equity crowdfunding: 4%

Table 3.1. *Statistical data of the sample*

3.1.2. *PLS-SEM*[1]

The choice of this statistical approach is explained in Chapter 2. Let us simply recall that our research is exploratory in nature and the PLS-SEM approach is entirely appropriate for the development of new theories or when the main objective of the research is explanation and prediction (Rigdon 2012).

This method of multivariate analysis of second-generation data is based on the explanation of the variance of dependent variables in a structural equation model (SEM). Specifically, the estimation of the coefficients of the SEM (or inner model) is done by maximizing the R^2 of the endogenous variables/constructs, carried out using linear iterative regressions. This approach is therefore based on variance, not covariances (a more detailed presentation is given in section 3.3.1).

1 PLS-SEM stands for Partial Least Squares-Structural Equation Modeling.

In addition, the PLS-SEM approach offers several useful advantages in our context:

– the covariation constraint regarding indicators of the same construct that prevails in the CB-SEM[2] method is avoided. This flexibility allows for the use of formative and single-indicator constructs and not just reflective ones in the model specification without causing an identification problem;

– there is no need for data to be distributed normally;

– the method is not binding in terms of measurement scale since it accepts equidistant ordinal scales or even binary data;

– the PLS-SEM approach is superior to the CB-SEM approach in regards to statistical power, in other words, it is more capable of reporting the significance of a truly meaningful relationship in the population (Hair *et al.* 2017). It should also be noted that the two methods converge for large samples (≥ 250 observations), as in our case (400 observations).

3.1.3. *Corrective reprocessing, transformation and adding control variables to the data file*

The questionnaire response file recovered from the online survey tool Lime Survey (version 2.65.0 + 170502) was, of course, not properly formatted for integration into the SmartPLS 3 application, so several reprocesses were required for its operation[3]. In addition, some data had to be corrected or provided with default values.

Finally, four specific questions to assess the attention of the participants in the experiment, disseminated in the questionnaire, required a logical calculation type of reprocessing. Similarly, a logical calculation reprocessing focuses on straight lining[4] control indicators, with one indicator per variable/construct of the model.

Details of the major reprocessing (fixes and control but no transformation to the SmartPLS 3 target format) are available on request.

2 CB-SEM stands for Covariance-Based Structural Equation Modeling.

3 For example, SmartPLS 3 does not accept any character strings in the input file.

4 Straight lining refers to an "online" entry, that is, an identical choice of answer for a large number of questions, characteristic of negligent participants.

3.1.4. *Sample size*

In Chapter 2, we determined the minimum sample size required for the PLS approach using the Chin and Newsted (1999) rule of thumb. In our case, this rule results in 100 observations. However, while we approached 100 subjects for our experiment, each carried out the successive evaluation of four projects which, in the end, resulted in a sample of 400 observations. This size is sufficient to ensure the robustness of the results, as it is significantly larger than the size of 212 observations recommended by Cohen (1992) for a statistical test power of 80%, at the threshold α of 1% for R^2 (≥ 0.1) of the endogenous constructs of the SEM and a model complexity of 10 maximum links pointing to a construct.

3.1.5. *Data review: completeness and data quality*

Before multivariate analysis of the data itself, it is necessary to ensure that there are several prerequisites for the quality and completeness (or comprehensiveness) of the data. This step is particularly recommended for primary data collected through questionnaires to be analyzed by SEM.

3.1.5.1. *Completeness: missing data*

When more than 15% of the data of an observation is missing, it must be deleted. In our case, the online questionnaire required filling out all the required fields; only two fields were optional (INTR1 and INTR2) because they were logically dependent on the previous questions[5]. A processing consisting of assigning a value to empty occurrences of these two fields is available on request. At the end of this processing, no data was missing.

3.1.5.2. *Quality: outliers*

Outliers can result from misrepresentation of open-ended questions, can significantly distort the results of the sample and must be identified. In our case, the file does not contain any outliers, as the questionnaire was closed, with the exception of the age entry field of the participants. The latter does not display clearly incorrect data.

3.1.5.3. *Quality: straight lining pattern data*

Visual analysis such as that of the straight lining phenomenon control indicators shows that participants did not negligently complete the questionnaire.

5 Indeed, these two fields assume that the subject has previously invested in the company concerned; otherwise, they are irrelevant.

3.1.5.4. *Quality: data distribution*

The PLS structural equation approach is non-parametric, does not require distribution of normally distributed data, or presuppose any hypothesis in this regard (Cassel *et al.* 1999). However, it is important to ensure that the data do not deviate significantly from a normal distribution. Indeed, data that are extremely far from a normal distribution increase the standard error obtained by the bootstrapping procedure (a resampling technique, explained later in the chapter), which decreases the likelihood that certain relationships will be considered significant (Hair *et al.* 2017).

While the Kolmogorov–Smirnov and Shapiro–Wilk tests are specified to test the normality of a distribution, they only allow for rejecting the null hypothesis of normality without assessing the relative distance of the distribution considered with a normal distribution. In this case, it is preferable to refer to the skewness shape parameters (asymmetry) and kurtosis (flattening), the rule of interpretation being that skewness or kurtosis greater than 1 in absolute value is far from a normal form of distribution.

The study of the asymmetry and flattening of the frequency distributions of the variables/indicators of the model reveals that two latent variables deviate significantly from a normal distribution:

– indicators of the Interest variable which, although symmetrical, have a flattened shape due to the juxtaposition of the four distributions (one per project) of heterogeneous frequencies in relation to the interests of the subjects of the experiment;

– the Familiarity variable presents indicators whose highly asymmetrical frequency distributions are peak-shaped, which is explained by two factors:

- because of the artificial conditions of the experiment, it made sense that the subjects were not related to the projects, i.e. not familiar with the startups involved or with any of their characteristics. As a result, responses to items are heavily focused on the "no" response option,

- indicators of this variable are initially coded on a 3-point ordinal scale, not 5, which increases the risk of pointiness (this scale is converted to a 5-point Likert scale for its operation).

It will therefore be necessary to keep in mind the risk of underestimating the significance of the effects of these two variables in the model (more specifically, the familiarity variable) induced by these data distributions that significantly deviate from normality.

3.1.6. *Indicator measurement scales: symmetry and equidistance*

The indicators associated with latent variables (not calculated, i.e. apart from the Congruence to the Base Values and Intensity of Investment Choice variables) of the explanatory model are all associated with 5-point Likert scales ("strongly agree" [note 1], "somewhat agree" [note 2], "neither agree nor disagree" [note 3], "somewhat disagree" [note 4] and "strongly disagree" [note 5]) with the exception of indicators of the Familiarity variable associated with a 3-point ordinal scale ("Yes" [note 1], "Undecided" [note 3] and "No" [note 5]).

Particular attention has been paid to the items on these scales so that they are symmetrical and have a formulation suggesting the equidistance of the points taken in pairs. This precaution allows for these measurement scales to be assimilated at interval scales. Therefore, indicators of latent variables can be used in a SEM (Hair *et al.* 2017).

3.2. Preliminary validity of the measurement model

The purpose of this section is the analysis of the psychometric qualities (reliability and validity) of the measurements of the model constructs. This step logically precedes the evaluation of the structural model (described in section 3.3) which is only possible if the measurement model is satisfactory.

After reviewing the associated variables, constructs and indicators and then mentioning the particular case of single-indicator variables, we will evaluate the quality of the measurement of reflective variables and then formative variables.

This section therefore focuses on the measurement model, also called the outer model, that connects the constructs (or unobservable latent variables) and the observable variables to their indicator(s) (which are themselves observable variables).

Let us remember that the constructs can be reflective or formative and are associated with one or more indicators; observable variables are single-indicator and are identified with their only indicator.

3.2.1. *Review of the measurement model*

The variable codes used throughout this chapter are listed in Table 3.2.

Construct or variable	Dimension	Code	Significance
Affective reaction	**Pleasure**	PLAI1	Unhappy/happy
		PLAI2	Upset/content
		PLAI3	Unsatisfied/satisfied
		PLAI4	Sad/cheerful
		PLAI5	Hopeless/optimistic
	Arousal	ACTI1	Without energy/full of energy
		ACTI2	Asleep/awake
		ACTI3	Unstimulated/stimulated
Perceived signal quality	**Management team**	EQUI1	The size of the management team is appropriate for this project
		EQUI2	Managers have complementary profiles
		EQUI3	Managers' degrees are appropriate for this project
		EQUI4	Managers' experience is appropriate for this project
	Business plan	PLAN1	I find this product/service innovative
		PLAN2	I think this market is growing
		PLAN3	I think competition does not prevent a newcomer from entering the market
		PLAN4	Financial prospects look good
Trust	**Benevolence**	BIENV1	I think this management team is committed to continuous improvement to develop its business
		BIENV2	I think this management team continuously seeks to improve the information given to its investors

Construct or variable		Dimension	Code	Significance
Trust		**Credibility**	CREDI1	The management team's involvement makes me feel safe
			CREDI2	I trust the commitment of the leaders
			CREDI3	Partnering with this management team is a guarantee
		Integrity	INTE1	The management team is sincere toward investors
			INTE2	The management team is honest with investors
			INTE3	The management team shows interest in investors
Interest	**Situational Interest**	**Affective implication**	AFFE1	I really appreciate this project
			AFFE2	I found this project to be stimulating
		Attention	ATTE1	This project caught my attention
			ATTE2	This project captivated me
		Curiosity	CURI1	This project aroused my curiosity
	Individual Interest	**Emotional valence**	EMO1	After a long period without contact with this domain, I look forward to having information related to it again
			EMO2	I prefer talking about my hobbies rather than this domain
			EMO3	When I am in a bookstore, I like to browse magazines related to this domain
		Intrinsic orientation	INTR1	With (COMPANY NAME), I am convinced that I have chosen an investment that corresponds to my personal preferences
			INTR2	I chose this investment first because of this interesting domain

Construct or variable		Dimension	Code	Significance
Interest	**Individual interest**	**Valence of the value**	VALE1	This domain has real personal value for me
			VALE2	Compared to the other subjects that matter to me (in connection with my hobbies), this domain is much less important to me
			VALE3	Acquiring new knowledge in this area is more important than acquiring new knowledge about my hobbies
			VALE4	Before I decided to invest, this domain was important to me
Familiarity		**Familiarity with company's attributes**	ATTR1	My hobbies or passions are related to the field of activity of the company
			ATTR2	I live in the city or region of this company
			ATTR3	I have already faced the problem solved by what this company offers
		Familiarity with the company	ENTR1	I have already invested in the company
			ENTR2	I know the products or services of this company
			ENTR3	I directly or indirectly know one or more founders of this company
Congruence to base values			CONGR AXIO	Measure of the congruence to base values, i.e. distance between participant values and the value associated with the evaluated project
Intensity of investment choice			MONT CASH	Amount invested in the project

Table 3.2. *Code of used variables*

It should be noted that the choice to group the two dimensions of interest (Individual Interest and Situational Interest) into a single construct is reasonable in light of their high (0.749) and statistically significant correlation at the 1% threshold (*p-value* = 0), shown in Figure 3.1.

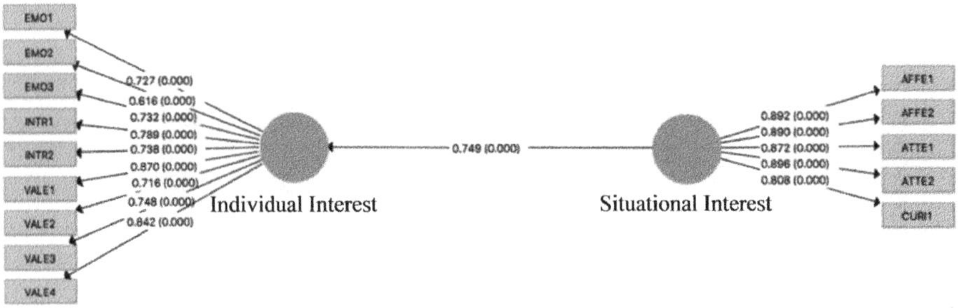

Figure 3.1. *Correlation linking the dimensions of Situational Interest and Individual Interest*

3.2.2. *Single-indicator variables*

According to Hair *et al.* (2017), single-indicator variables are perfectly appropriate for measuring observable variables, as is the case with the Intensity of Investment Choice variable, revealed by investment choices. Let us remember that, by definition, it is calculated as the ratio of the amount invested in the evaluated project over the initial allocation.

The Congruence to Base Values variable, also single-indicator, is a latent variable; however, as specified in Chapter 1, we have chosen not to develop an *ad hoc* measuring instrument, reflective or formative construct for this concept. Indeed, given the very nature of the concept we are studying, a congruence, we preferred to propose an original variable calculated as a "distance" (more exactly, a measure of similarity) between two points (vectors) in space: (1) the values of the individual and (2) the value carried by the concerned project (in this case, a vector with only one component). The measure relating to the values of the individual is based on a reliable and valid literature scale (Short Schwartz Value, Survey scale or SSVS) (Lindeman and Verkasalo 2005). The measurement of the second point in space (the value carried by the concerned project) was explicit in the business plans, in other words, it was observable. Let us add that, in addition to the benefit conferred by an adequacy between the nature of the concept (a congruence) and the method of measurement (a "distance"), this choice of modeling made it possible to avoid the subjectivity of the subjects for a delicate and abstract questioning of the type: "How important is the dominant value that I perceive for this project in my scale of personal values?" Also, for the individual to be able to answer this question, they would need to be capable of introspection to identify, label and order their values. Let us also remember that an activated value can induce behavior even when the activation takes place unconsciously (Chataigné 2014), which pleads in favor of indirect questioning. Finally, as the results of section 3.3 of this chapter show, the nomological validity of this latent variable is confirmed by links between measurements consistent with hypothetical links between constructs (see H2+ and H1+).

Finally, for these two variables (Intensity of Investment Choice and Congruence to Base Values), the correlation relationship linking the single-indicator variable to its indicator is always equal to 1, which means that they have the same value; there is therefore no measurement error between the true value and measurement: the measurement is the true value. Therefore, the psychometric evaluation criteria of validity and reliability are not applicable to single-indicator variables (Hair *et al.* 2017).

Let us also note that this property of absence of measurement error is shared by certain formative constructs (we will come back to this point later); however, single-indicator variables differ from formative constructs by the non-oriented relationship between variable and indicator (i.e. the single-indicator variable is neither formative nor reflective).

3.2.3. *Reflective variables*

Reflective measurements are characterized by a construct that exists by itself and whose indicators (or items) are observable reflections (Gavard-Perret *et al.* 2013). According to Jarvis *et al.* (2003), they differ from formative type measurements because of:

– the direction of causality between construct and measurement, this goes from construct to items;

– the interchangeability of indicators which must share a common theme;

– the covariation between indicators;

– the nomological network of indicators which must have the same antecedents and consequences.

Indicators are defined as linear functions of latent variables; consequently, a system of linear regressions corresponds to each reflective construct (see Figure 3.2 for an example).

The covariance between the indicators is attributable to their common cause, the latent variable *VL*. Indeed, in the affine equations of this regression system, the coefficients λ_i represent the slope of the line. When the ordinary least squares method is applied, these normalized coefficients are the correlations between indicators and the latent variable and are expressed depending on the variances and covariances of the explained variable (the indicator *Ii*) and the explanatory variable (the latent variable *VL*):

$$\lambda_i = \frac{Cov\ (I_i, VL)}{Var(VL)}$$

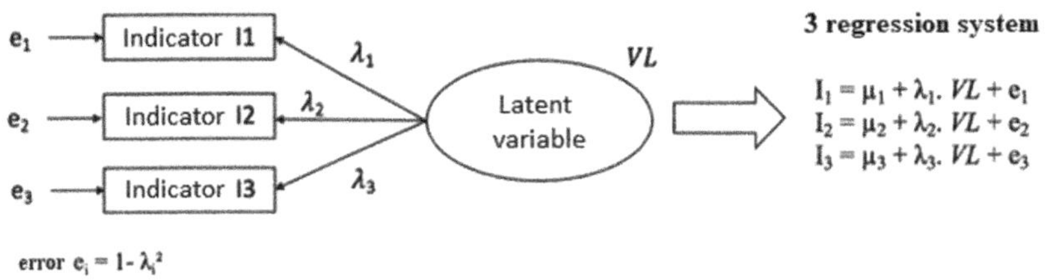

Figure 3.2. *Relationship between observable indicators and reflective latent variable, adapted from (Crié 2005)*

Squared, these coefficients are coefficients of determination (equivalent to the communality coefficients of the factorial analysis in principal components), which indicate the contribution of the latent variable to the indicator, that is to say, the proportion of variance in the manifest variable (indicator) that is predictable from the latent variable.

In Chapter 1, we specified an explanatory model integrating three latent reflective variables: Affective Reaction, Interest and Trust. The verification of reliability and validity proposed below is based on the calculation of several statistics compared with acceptance thresholds. Table 3.3 summarizes this approach.

Reliability		Cronbach's alpha
		Jöreskog's rho (composite reliability)
Validity	Convergent validity	Average Variance Extracted (AVE)
		Outer Loadings and Indicator Reliability
	Discriminant validity	Cross-loading
		Fornell–Lacker criterion
		Heterotrait–monotrait (HTMT) ratio

Table 3.3. *Steps for checking the psychometric quality of latent reflective variables*

3.2.3.1. *Psychometric quality of the measurement for the affective reaction, interest and trust constructs*

3.2.3.1.1. Reliability

Reliability, also known as internal consistency reliability, is the ability of a measurement to give statistically "consistent" results over time, that is, stable and consistent. For this, the random error must be low enough. This results in measurement scales whose items jointly measure the same concept but without redundancy.

The traditional criterion is Cronbach's alpha, defined by the following formula:

$$\alpha = \left(\frac{M}{M-1}\right).(1 - \frac{\sum_{i=1}^{M} S_i^2}{S_t^2})$$

where:

– M is the number of items or questions or indicators;

– S_i^2 is the variance of item i;

– S_t^2 is the total variance, i.e. the sum of all the coefficients of the variance-covariance matrix of the items.

Cronbach's alpha (Cronbach 1951) measures the part of the total variance of the construct explained by the indicators, and varies between 0 and 1. This estimate is conservative; it constitutes a low limit for the internal consistency. According to Nunnaly's criterion, a Cronbach's alpha greater than 0.60 is acceptable for basic research, while a value greater than 0.80 is acceptable for applied research. According to Hair *et al.* (2017), a value between 0.60 and 0.70 is acceptable for exploratory research, while a value between 0.70 and 0.90 is satisfactory for more advanced research.

A value greater than 0.95 is not desirable, as it means that all the indicators measure the same phenomenon, which is the case when several items in a questionnaire are redundant and represent the same question reformulated several times.

The SmartPLS 3 software calculates this coefficient for all variables; Figure 3.3 (bar graph) represents these coefficients, as well as an acceptability threshold of 0.70.

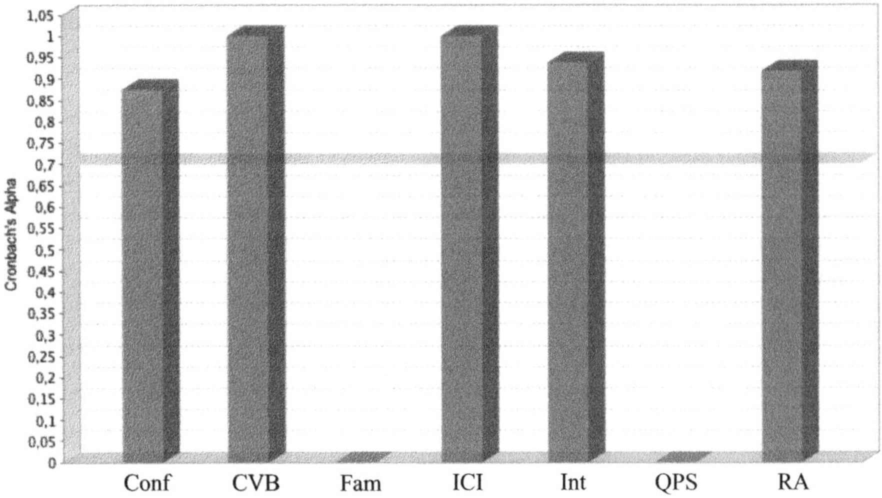

Conf: Trust; CVB: Congruence to base values; Fam: Familiarity; ICI: Intensity of investment choice; Int: Interest; QPS: Perceived signal quality; RA: Affective reaction.

Figure 3.3. *Cronbach's alpha coefficient for all model variables*

Let us note that this coefficient is not applicable to the single-item variables Congruence to Base Values and Intensity of Investment Choice, the value of which must not be interpreted. In addition, it is not calculated for the formative variables Familiarity and Perceived Signal Quality because it is irrelevant.

Among these data, Table 3.4 shows the values of the coefficients relating to the three reflective constructs.

	Cronbach's alpha
Affective reaction	0.918
Trust	0.876
Interest	0.938

Table 3.4. *Cronbach's alpha for the three reflective constructs of the explanatory model*

Interpretation: Cronbach's alpha reliability indicators are above the expected threshold of 0.70 for all three constructs, suggesting sufficient reliability.

However, as previously mentioned, Cronbach's alpha has certain drawbacks (Cortina 1993) such as an underestimation of reliability as well as a sensitivity to the number of items on the scale. In addition, Cronbach's alpha assumes equal indicators, that is to say, having the same coefficients (outer loadings), while the PLS-SEM approach calculates distinct coefficients.

A second coefficient offers an alternative for the evaluation of the reliability of internal consistency: the Jöreskog's rho (1971) or composite reliability.

The mathematical expression of Jöreskog's rho is as follows:

$$\rho_c = \frac{(\sum_{i=1}^{M} l_i)^2}{(\sum_{i=1}^{M} l_i)^2 + \sum_{i=1}^{M} var(e_i)}$$

where:

– l_i is the standardized coefficient (or outer loading) of the measure i (indicator) on the latent variable;

– M is the number of observed variables, that is, the number of indicators for the latent variable;

– e_i is the measurement error of indicator i ($e_i = 1 - l_i^2$).

Jöreskog's rho is based on the standardized coefficients connecting indicators and latent variables according to the *a priori* specification of the measurement model by structural equations; it is therefore a specific use of confirmatory factor analysis for the purpose of evaluating the internal consistency of constructs.

Like Cronbach's alpha, Jöreskog's rho varies between 0 and 1 and its interpretation in terms of thresholds is identical. This coefficient nevertheless presents an inverse bias to Cronbach's alpha, since it tends to overestimate the reliability. Finally, it is reasonable to assume that the actual reliability is framed by these two coefficients.

The SmartPLS 3 software calculates this coefficient for all the model variables; Figure 3.4 (bar graph) represents them.

The remarks made above about single-item variables and formative constructs also apply to this figure.

Among these data, Table 3.5 shows the values of the coefficients relating to the three reflective constructs.

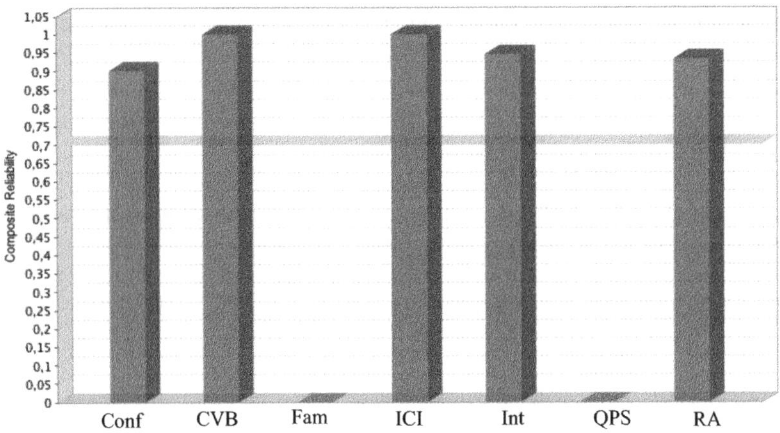

Conf: Trust; CVB: Congruence to base values; Fam: Familiarity; ICI: Intensity of investment choice; Int: Interest QPS: Perceived signal quality; RA: Affective reaction.

Figure 3.4. *Jöreskog's rho coefficient for all model variables (composite reliability)*

	Composite reliability
Affective reaction	0.933
Trust	0.902
Interest	0.946

Table 3.5. *Jöreskog's rho for the three reflective constructs of the explanatory model*

Interpretation: as expected, Jöreskog's rho is less conservative than Cronbach's alpha. In total, the reliability indicators Cronbach's alpha and Jöreskog's rho are above the expected threshold of 0.7 and remain below the threshold limit of 0.95, indicating excessive redundancy between measurements. These results suggest a sufficient reliability for these three reflective constructs, that is to say, a good internal coherence of the items, given that the questions are supposed to measure the same thing.

3.2.3.1.2. Validity

The trait validity (or construct validity) makes it possible to check whether the indicators represent the phenomenon, that is to say, the reflective construct to which they are attached. It breaks down into two distinct forms of validity: convergent validity and discriminant validity.

Convergent validity

Convergent validity ensures that indicators of the same phenomenon are positively correlated. Indeed, these indicators reflect the same construct; they must therefore share a high proportion of variance. The evaluation of convergent validity is based on two steps: (1) the rho of convergent validity or AVE for Average Variance Extracted and (2) the analysis of the coefficients (outer loadings) or equivalent, of their squared value, called indicator reliability.

Rho of the convergent validity or Average Variance Extracted (AVE)

The AVE is a measure defined as the average of the squares of the item loadings associated with a construct:

$$AVE = \frac{\sum_{i=1}^{M} l_i^2}{M}$$

It is interpreted as the proportion of the average variance of the indicators explained by the construct. In the same way that a minimum threshold of 50% is expected for the square of the loadings (indicator reliability) of each indicator, this same threshold applies to the AVE. Figure 3.5 shows the AVE of all the model variables.

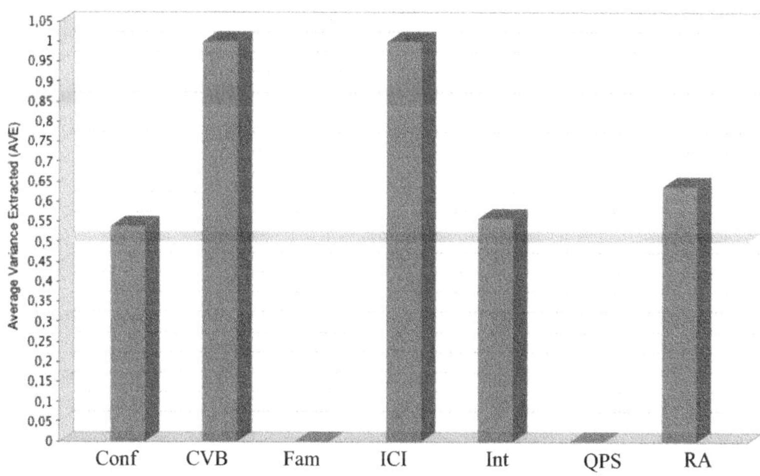

Conf: Trust; CVB: Congruence to base values; Fam: Familiarity; ICI: Intensity of investment choice; Int: Interest; QPS: Perceived signal quality; RA: Affective reaction.

Figure 3.5. *Rho of convergent validity (AVE) for all model variables*

	Average Variance Extracted (AVE)
Trust	0.539
Interest	0.558
Affective reaction	0.638

Table 3.6. *Rho of convergent validity (AVE) for the three reflective constructs of the explanatory model*

We find that the rho of convergent validity (AVEs) for the three reflective constructs are greater than the threshold of 0.5 and are therefore satisfactory.

Outer loadings and indicator reliability

The second stage of the convergent validity analysis is more detailed, since it proceeds indicator by indicator.

As previously indicated, the coefficients (outer loadings) of the indicators are calculated by linear regression; they are correlations between indicators and construct. Their value must be greater than 0.7 or, more precisely, 0.708 whose square is 0.5 or 50%. Indeed, the square of the outer loading (correlation) is a determination coefficient (similar to a commonality), which represents the part of the variance of the indicator explained by the construct. It is desirable that this part be substantial; the threshold of 50% is also retained (Hair *et al.* 2017). Let us note that while we choose to reason from the outer loadings, the indicator reliabilities (i.e. the squared outer loadings) are displayed below in a summary table on the quality of the reflective measurements.

The SmartPLS 3 software calculates the outer loadings; Table 3.7 shows the coefficients of the three reflective constructs.

Most loadings are above the threshold of 0.7. The loadings below the threshold, however, remain above 0.65, except for two indicators of the Trust construct (BIENV2 and INTE3) and one indicator of the Interest construct (EMO2) whose correlations are lower. Let us note that the weak correlation of the EMO2 indicator is possibly attributable to its inverted formulation, the first of its kind encountered in the questionnaire.

Indicators with loadings below the threshold of 0.40 should be automatically removed (Hair *et al.* 2011); those with loadings between 0.40 and 0.70 require more careful examination. They can only be deleted if this removal improves the reliability (Cronbach's alpha and Jöreskog's rho) and convergent validity (AVE) indicators beyond the minimum required thresholds. This condition is not sufficient, however, since the importance of the indicator for content validity must also be considered (Hair *et al.* 2017).

	Trust	Interest	Affective reaction
BIENV1	0.677		
BIENV2	0.546		
CREDI1	0.789		
CREDI2	0.840		
CREDI3	0.794		
INTE1	0.799		
INTE2	0.788		
INTE3	0.580		
AFFE1		0.867	
AFFE2		0.806	
ATTE1		0.783	
ATTE2		0.818	
CURI1		0.698	
EMO1		0.735	
EMO2		0.568	
EMO3		0.660	
INTR1		0.732	
INTR2		0.728	
VALE1		0.837	
VALE2		0.669	
VALE3		0.695	
VALE4		0.807	
PLAI1			0.853
PLAI2			0.865
PLAI3			0.859
PLAI4			0.807
PLAI5			0.845
ACTI1			0.741
ACTI2			0.653
ACTI3			0.744

Table 3.7. *Outer loadings of the three reflective constructs*

In our case, let us first check the impact of the removal of each loading indicator greater than 0.70 on Cronbach's alpha, Jöreskog's rho, and AVE. Table 3.8 shows these variations.

	Affective reaction	Interest	Trust	Cronbach's alpha variation	Jöreskog's rho variation	AVE variation
ACTI2	0.653			0	*0.002*	*0.035*
CURI1		0.698		– 0.003	– 0.002	*0.008*
EMO2		0.568		0	0	*0.02*
EMO3		0.66		– 0.002	– 0.002	*0.011*
VALE2		0.669		– 0.002	– 0.002	*0.011*
VALE3		0.695		– 0.003	– 0.002	*0.008*
BIENV1			0.677	– 0.012	– 0.006	*0.02*
BIENV2			0.546	0	*0.002*	*0.04*
INTE3			0.58	– 0.004	– 0.011	*0.033*

Table 3.8. *Variation in reliability and convergent validity indicators for removal of items with a correlation below the threshold of 0.70*

We find that removing two indicators (ACTI2 and BIENV2) improves Jöreskog's rho, while removing all indicators improves AVE. Nevertheless, the rule of eviction of indicators previously stated indicates that indicators whose loading is greater than or equal to 0.40, but strictly less than 0.70, are only removed if this action improves the reliability and convergent validity scores *beyond the required thresholds*. However, as we have seen, in our case, these thresholds are exceeded for all constructs. Consequently, and for the sake of content validity, we keep all the items of the measurement scales.

Discriminant validity

Discriminant validity ensures that the latent variables of a model are sufficiently distinct from each other; each one must only capture a phenomenon which is not represented by the others. The correlations should also not be too great between latent variables. Three approaches to discriminant validity are discussed: (1) cross-loadings, (2) the Fornell and Larcker (1981) criterion and (3) the approach by the heterotrait–monotrait (HTMT) ratio proposed by Henseler *et al.* (2015).

Cross-loadings

The first approach by cross-loadings postulates that the outer loading of a construct must be greater than the cross-loading (correlation) between this same indicator and the other constructs of the model. Table 3.9 compares the latent intravariable correlations with the latent intervariable correlations. For example, the first indicator BIENV1 of the Trust construct (the blue indicates that the indicators belong to the constructs) is equal to 0.677; this loading (correlation) is greater than the cross-loadings read on the same line: 0.372, 0.328, 0.263 and 0.396. The single-indicator variables do not appear, because their correlation is equal to 1 and cannot have any increase.

As we can see, the loadings are all greater than the cross-loadings, which suggests the discriminant validity of the latent variables.

	Trust	Interest	Affective reaction	Familiarity	Perceived signal quality
BIENV1	*0.677*	0.372	0.328	0.263	0.396
BIENV2	*0.546*	0.293	0.310	0.168	0.297
CREDI1	*0.789*	0.530	0.468	0.304	0.484
CREDI2	*0.840*	0.549	0.450	0.303	0.482
CREDI3	*0.794*	0.477	0.344	0.257	0.432
INTE1	*0.799*	0.443	0.402	0.320	0.378
INTE2	*0.788*	0.447	0.403	0.292	0.363
INTE3	*0.580*	0.276	0.244	0.209	0.247
AFFE1	0.639	*0.868*	0.626	0.505	0.458
AFFE2	0.549	*0.806*	0.547	0.425	0.414
ATTE1	0.402	*0.783*	0.505	0.365	0.370
ATTE2	0.514	*0.818*	0.526	0.406	0.409
CURI1	0.385	*0.698*	0.428	0.302	0.342
EMO1	0.405	*0.735*	0.472	0.472	0.329
EMO2	0.408	*0.568*	0.364	0.346	0.302
EMO3	0.292	*0.660*	0.382	0.401	0.216
INTR1	0.445	*0.732*	0.431	0.488	0.350
INTR2	0.443	*0.728*	0.449	0.411	0.323
VALE1	0.529	*0.837*	0.556	0.561	0.387
VALE2	0.344	*0.669*	0.403	0.371	0.260
VALE3	0.334	*0.695*	0.352	0.402	0.279

	Trust	Interest	Affective reaction	Familiarity	Perceived signal quality
VALE4	0.398	*0.807*	0.436	0.563	0.250
PLAI1	0.430	0.554	*0.853*	0.387	0.297
PLAI2	0.442	0.558	*0.865*	0.419	0.330
PLAI3	0.453	0.526	*0.859*	0.393	0.411
PLAI4	0.430	0.505	*0.807*	0.385	0.312
PLAI5	0.488	0.590	*0.845*	0.414	0.461
ACTI1	0.330	0.412	*0.741*	0.259	0.294
ACTI2	0.271	0.364	*0.653*	0.218	0.258
ACTI3	0.369	0.458	*0.744*	0.313	0.328
ATTR1	0.204	0.532	0.278	*0.670*	0.205
ATTR2	0.036	0.106	0.047	*0.152*	0.048
ATTR3	0.265	0.439	0.378	*0.744*	0.174
ENTR1	0.225	0.264	0.197	*0.463*	0.209
ENTR2	0.287	0.262	0.289	*0.690*	0.174
ENTR3	0.112	0.114	0.173	*0.271*	0.151
EQUI1	0.345	0.332	0.335	0.246	*0.643*
EQUI2	0.323	0.251	0.283	0.135	*0.601*
EQUI3	0.196	0.100	0.117	0.064	*0.364*
EQUI4	0.349	0.151	0.233	0.109	*0.649*
PLAN1	0.211	0.311	0.188	0.177	*0.392*
PLAN2	0.149	0.333	0.116	0.137	*0.277*
PLAN3	0.156	0.184	0.104	0.069	*0.290*
PLAN4	0.317	0.346	0.180	0.144	*0.591*

Table 3.9. *Loadings and cross-loadings of the latent variables of the model*

The Fornell–Larcker criterion

The principle of this method is that the construct must, on average, share more variance with its indicators than with the other constructs. In practice, the square root of the AVE of each construct must be greater than the greatest of the correlations of this construct with the other latent reflective variables (Hair *et al.* 2016).

The Fornell–Larcker table provided by SmartPLS (see Table 3.10) shows the squares of the AVEs on the diagonal and the interconstructed correlations below the diagonal.

	Trust	Interest	Affective reaction
Trust	*0.734*		
Interest	0.594	*0.747*	
Affective reaction	0.512	0.629	*0.799*

Table 3.10. *Fornell–Larcker table*

In our case, this second discriminant validity criterion is satisfied, since the squares of the AVEs are greater than the interconstructed correlations.

HTMT ratio method

Recent research has criticized the performance of the previous two criteria; for example, Henseler *et al.* (2015) showed that cross-loadings do not indicate a lack of discriminant validity when two constructs are perfectly correlated. The Fornell–Larcker criterion presents the same insufficiency when the loadings of indicators of a particular construct barely differ. According to Henseler and his colleagues, the HTMT ratio method addresses these shortcomings.

The HTMT ratio of two constructs is the quotient of the intertrait correlations over the intratrait correlations. More precisely, the numerator is calculated as the arithmetic mean of the correlations of the indicators of the constructs taken in pairs, while the denominator is the geometric mean of the means of the correlations of the indicators of each construct.

The higher this ratio and closer to 1, the less the discriminant validity is guaranteed. If the acceptable threshold is debated, Henseler *et al.* (2015) suggested a maximum threshold of 0.90 if the constructs are conceptually close and 0.85 for conceptually distinct constructs.

Figure 3.6 displays the HTMT ratios for the couples of model constructs.

The values of the HTMT ratios of the model's reflective variables are extracted in Table 3.11.

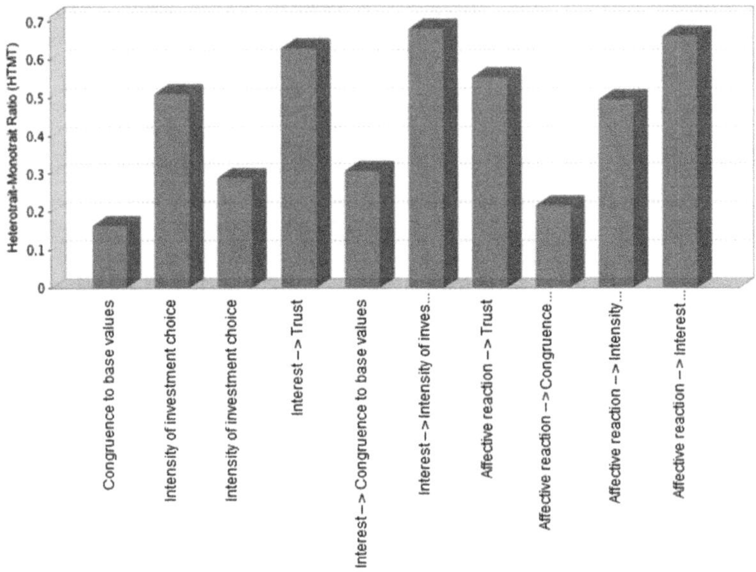

Figure 3.6. *Heterotrait–monotrait (HTMT) ratio*

	Trust	**Interest**
Interest	0.630	
Affective reaction	0.554	0.662

Table 3.11. *HTMT ratios of reflective variables*

We note that the relevant HTMT ratios are all well below the threshold of 0.85.

SmartPLS 3 also offers a statistical hypothesis test to ensure that the HTMT ratio is statistically significantly different from 1. To do this, knowing that the PLS-SEM approach does not presuppose a parametric law for the data, a bootstrapping algorithm by drawing random samples (configured at 5,000 in our case) constructs a distribution of HTMT ratios.

Table 3.12 shows the 95% trust intervals constructed by bootstrapping; none of them contains the value 1, which confirms the discriminant validity of the three formative constructs.

Finally, Table 3.13 presents a summary of the analysis of the psychometric quality of the reflective constructs.

	Original sample (O)	Sample mean (M)	Bias	2.5%	97.5%
Interest → Trust	0.643	0.643	0.001	*0.553*	*0.712*
Affective reaction → Trust	0.564	0.565	0.001	*0.475*	*0.647*
Affective reaction → Interest	0.662	0.661	– 0.001	*0.572*	*0.739*

Table 3.12. *Trust interval of HTMT ratios of reflective variables*

		Convergent validity			**Reliability**		**Discriminant validity**
Latent variables	**Indicators**	**Loadings**	**Indicator reliability**	**AVE**	**Composite reliability**	**Cronbach's alpha**	
		> 0.70	**> 0.50**	**> 0.50**	**0.70–0.95**	**0.70–0.95**	**HTMT trust interval does not include 1**
Trust	**BIENV1**	0.677	0.459	0.539	0.902	0.876	YES
	BIENV2	0.546	0.298				
	CREDI1	0.789	0.623				
	CREDI2	0.840	0.706				
	CREDI3	0.794	0.631				
	INTE1	0.799	0.639				
	INTE2	0.788	0.621				
	INTE3	0.580	0.336				
Interest	**EMO1**	0.735	0.540	0.558	0.946	0.938	YES
	EMO2	0.568	0.323				
	EMO3	0.660	0.435				
	INTR1	0.732	0.536				
	INTR2	0.728	0.531				
	VALE1	0.837	0.701				
	VALE2	0.669	0.447				
	VALE3	0.695	0.482				
	VALE4	0.807	0.652				
	CURI1	0.698	0.487				
	AFFE1	0.867	0.751				
	AFFE2	0.806	0.650				
	ATTE1	0.783	0.614				
	ATTE2	0.818	0.668				

Latent variables	Indicators	Convergent validity			Reliability		Discriminant validity
		Loadings	Indicator reliability	AVE	Composite reliability	Cronbach's alpha	
		> 0.70	**> 0.50**	**> 0.50**	**0.70–0.95**	**0.70–0.95**	**HTMT trust interval does not include 1**
Affective reaction	**ACTI1**	0.741	0.548	0.638	0.933	0.918	YES
	ACTI2	0.653	0.426				
	ACTI3	0.744	0.554				
	PLAI1	0.853	0.727				
	PLAI2	0.865	0.748				
	PLAI3	0.859	0.738				
	PLAI4	0.807	0.652				
	PLAI5	0.845	0.714				

Table 3.13. *Summary of the analysis of psychometric quality of reflective constructs*

In conclusion, the reliability and the convergent and discriminant validities are established for the three latent reflective variables of the model. Let us note, however, that several indicators have loadings below the required threshold of 0.70. Three indicators in particular (BIENV2, INTE3 and EMO2) are significantly below it. Nevertheless, in accordance with the procedure and recommendations of Hair *et al.* (2016), we are not removing them.

3.2.3.2. *Interest construct as a second-order variable: Individual Interest and Situational Interest*

So far in this chapter, we have considered the Interest construct as a single block of indicators. However, as Chapter 1 indicates, the Interest variable has two distinct dimensions: Individual Interest and Situational Interest. It is therefore possible to consider the Interest variable as a second-order variable, that is, a latent variable made up of several latent variables. In particular, the scale for measuring the dimension of Situational Interest is adapted from a scale borrowed from educational sciences (Yennek 2014), while respecting the recommendations of Schiefele (2009). The field of educational sciences is very different from that of finance; this incursion is explained by the importance of research work focused on the concept of interest in this field (Fenouillet 2016). So, strictly speaking, we did not develop a new reflective measure, in which case we would have conformed to Churchill's paradigm (1979), but started from a pre-existing scale. It nevertheless seems useful to us to make sure that the two forms of interest, taken as independent variables, satisfy the psychometric quality criteria of reliability (section 3.2.3.2.1) and validity (sections 3.2.3.2.2 and 3.2.3.2.3). We will also check whether the list of items on the Situational Interest measurement scale is well purified, that is to say, that the items form a single main component distinct from that formed by the indicators associated with the Individual Interest (focus of section 3.2.3.3).

3.2.3.2.1. Reliability

Let us note that, this time, we will capitalize on the explanations given above and will present the results in a more direct way. As Table 3.14 indicates, the two reliability indicators of Cronbach's alpha and Jöreskog's rho (composite reliability) are above the required threshold of 0.7 and are, therefore, satisfactory.

	Cronbach's alpha	**Composite reliability**
Individual Interest	0.905	0.923
Situational Interest	0.921	0.941

Table 3.14. *Reliability indicators for the Interest constructs*

3.2.3.2.2. Convergent validity

We establish the convergent validity in two steps: by the AVE and by analysis of the loadings.

AVE

Table 3.15 shows that the rho of convergent validity (AVEs) of the two Interest constructs are greater than the threshold of 0.5.

	Average Variance Extracted (AVE)
Individual Interest	0.573
Situational Interest	0.761

Table 3.15. *Average Variance Extracted (AVE)*

Loadings analysis

The analysis of the loadings (Table 3.16) indicates that only the EMO2 indicator (associated with the Individual Interest variable) is below the threshold of 0.70. Its removal deteriorates Cronbach's alpha (which decreases to 0.904), has no effect on the composite reliability (which remains constant at 0.923), but significantly improves the AVE (which increases to 0.601). Nevertheless, the value of the AVE was already above the minimum threshold; therefore, in accordance with the recommendations of Hair *et al.* (2017), we keep this indicator.

	Individual Interest	**Situational Interest**
EMO1	0.716	0.923
EMO2	0.622	0.941
EMO3	0.734	
INTR1	0.793	
INTR2	0.736	
VALE1	0.869	
VALE2	0.722	
VALE3	0.75	
VALE4	0.839	
CURI1		0.813
AFFE1		0.888
AFFE2		0.889
ATTE1		0.874
ATTE2		0.896

Table 3.16. *Loadings of Individual Interest and Situational Interest constructs*

3.2.3.2.3. Discriminant validity

We establish the discriminant validity in three steps: the analysis of loadings and cross-loadings, the Fornell–Larcker criterion and the HTMT ratio.

Analysis of loadings and cross-loadings

The analysis of the cross-loadings (see Table 3.17) shows that the loadings of the two Interest constructs are greater than their cross-loadings with the other latent variables.

	Individual Interest	Situational Interest	Trust	Familiarity	Perceived signal quality	Affective reaction
EMO1	*0.716*	0.651	0.405	0.472	0.329	0.472
EMO2	*0.622*	0.422	0.408	0.346	0.302	0.364
EMO3	*0.734*	0.483	0.292	0.401	0.216	0.382
INTR1	*0.793*	0.525	0.445	0.488	0.350	0.431
INTR2	*0.736*	0.589	0.443	0.411	0.323	0.449
VALE1	*0.869*	0.664	0.529	0.561	0.387	0.556
VALE2	*0.722*	0.496	0.344	0.371	0.260	0.403
VALE3	*0.750*	0.537	0.334	0.402	0.279	0.352
VALE4	*0.839*	0.643	0.398	0.563	0.250	0.436
AFFE1	0.743	*0.888*	0.639	0.505	0.458	0.626
AFFE2	0.647	*0.889*	0.549	0.425	0.414	0.547
ATTE1	0.627	*0.874*	0.402	0.365	0.370	0.505
ATTE2	0.665	*0.96*	0.514	0.406	0.409	0.526
CURI1	0.541	*0.13*	0.385	0.302	0.342	0.428

Table 3.17. *Loadings and cross-loadings of the Interest variables and other variables of the model*

Fornell–Larcker criterion

The Fornell–Larcker table (see Table 3.18) reveals that this second criterion of discriminant validity is satisfied, since the squares of the AVEs (located on the diagonal of the table) are greater than the interconstructed correlations (located under the diagonal).

	Trust	Individual Interest	Situational Interest	Affective reaction
Trust	*0.734*			
Individual Interest	0.531	*0.757*		
Situational Interest	0.576	0.743	*0.872*	
Affective reaction	0.512	0.568	0.607	*0.799*

Table 3.18. *Fornell–Larcker table*

HTMT ratio

As shown in Table 3.19, the relevant HTMT ratios (in italics) are all below the threshold of 0.85.

	Trust	**Congruence to base values**	**Intensity of investment choice**	**Individual Interest**	**Situational Interest**
Congruence to base values	0.164				
Intensity of investment choice	0.510	0.289			
Individual Interest	*0.583*	*0.311*	*0.635*		
Situational Interest	*0.793*	*0.2616*	*0.662*	*0.805*	
Affective reaction	0.554	0.216	0.495	*0.612*	*0.651*

Table 3.19. *HTMT ratios of reflective variables*

As shown in Table 3.20, the 95% trust intervals do not contain the value 1.

	Original sample (O)	**Sample mean (M)**	**Bias**	**2.5%**	**97.5%**
Individual Interest → Trust	0.583	0.583	0.000	*0.492*	*0.664*
Situational Interest → Trust	0.618	0.619	0.000	*0.523*	*0.699*
Situational Interest → Individual Interest	0.805	0.805	0.000	*0.749*	*0.848*
Affective reaction → Trust	0.554	0.555	0.001	*0.455*	*0.639*
Affective reaction → Individual Interest	0.612	0.614	0.002	*0.515*	*0.696*
Affective reaction → Situational Interest	0.651	0.652	0.001	*0.567*	*0.725*

Table 3.20. *Trust interval of HTMT ratios of reflective variables*

Finally, Table 3.21 presents a synthesis of the analysis of the psychometric quality of the reflective constructs of Individual and Situational Interest.

Latent variables	Indicators	Convergent validity			Reliability		Convergent validity
		Loadings	Indicator reliability	AVE	Composite reliability	Cronbach's alpha	
		> 0.70	> 0.50	> 0.50	0.70–0.95	0.70–0.95	HTMT trust interval does not include 1
	EMO1	0.716	0.513				
	EMO2	0.622	0.387				
	EMO3	0.734	0.539				
	INTR1	0.793	0.629				
Individual Interest	INTR2	0.736	0.542	0.573	0.923	0.905	YES
	VALE1	0.869	0.755				
	VALE2	0.722	0.522				
	VALE3	0.750	0.563				
	VALE4	0.839	0.704				
	CURI1	0.813	0.660				
	AFFE1	0.888	0.788				
Situational Interest	AFFE2	0.889	0.791	0.761	0.941	0.921	YES
	ATTE1	0.874	0.763				
	ATTE2	0.896	0.802				

Table 3.21. *Summary of the analysis of the psychometric quality of the Interest constructs*

In conclusion, reliability, convergent validity and discriminant validity are established for the two dimensions of Interest.

3.2.3.3. *Principal component analysis and confirmatory factor analysis of the Interest variable*

In this section, we first make sure that the items of the Situational Interest scale do share a common meaning and form a single principal component, thanks to a principal component analysis or PCA (section 3.2.3.3.1); we then confirm the model for measuring Situational Interest by confirmatory factor analysis (section 3.2.3.3.2); in a third step, we perform a PCA on the Interest variable taken as a whole to ensure that its two dimensions (Situational Interest and Individual Interest) indeed represent distinct concepts (section 3.2.3.3.3).

3.2.3.3.1. PCA result for Situational Interest variable

Principal component analysis is a multivariate technique that aims at database reduction by extracting a minimum number of factors from variables, so that the factors are expressed as a linear combination of these initial variables and restore the greatest quantity of variances of the variables thus summarized. This technique is called interdependence, as the variables are neither identified as dependent or independent; it offers a tool for understanding the structures underlying the collected data. For these reasons, it is generally considered to be exploratory in nature (Gavard-Perret *et al.* 2013).

It is, nevertheless, possible to use it in a confirmatory approach; this is the case when the researcher has certain theoretical *a priori* and wishes to confirm a documented factor structure. We agree with this scenario, since our objective is to confirm the Situational Interest dimension of the Interest variable, defined according to a construct already validated in educational sciences, adapted to the context of investment in equity crowdfunding, and modified by integrating the recommendations of Schiefele (2009).

Our objective is also not to reduce a large number of variables, but to confirm that the five variables (items) defined in Chapter 1 are factorizable into a single factor. Let us note that the nature of these items (5-point Likert scales), comparable to continuous variables (Bentler and Chou 1987), allows for recourse to PCA. The size of our sample (400 observations) is also clearly greater than the minimum required size; in fact, Hair *et al.* (2010) suggested a ratio of 10 subjects per variable, i.e. 50 (= 5*10) subjects in our case.

The analysis is done in two stages, first by checking the conditions of application, then by determining the number of factors of the factorial solution[6]. It should be noted that the results used for the analysis come from the SPSS 21 software.

Verification of application conditions

This first step answers the following question: is the data factorizable?

The synthesis of variables into factors assumes that the variables are sufficiently related to each other, the study of correlations between variables provides a first answer (interitem correlations); however, in order to determine whether correlated

6 The factorial solution is defined by the selected factors.

variables are sufficiently correlated, we will use two standard criteria: the KMO (Kaiser–Mayer–Olkin) index and Bartlett's test of sphericity.

Interitem correlations

This prerequisite makes it possible to ensure minimum correlations between the five items of the Situational Interest measure. The correlation between two variables measures the strength of the link that exists between them; for an affine relationship, the correlation coefficient is linear and is calculated by linear regression. Taken in absolute value, it varies between 0 (independent variables) and 1 (perfectly correlated variables). For interpretation, correlations greater than 0.5 in absolute value suggest possible groupings, that is to say, factorizations. Table 3.22 displays the correlation coefficients calculated on the five Situational Interest indicators: all are clearly greater than 0.5.

		Correlation matrix				
		CURI1	**ATTE1**	**ATTE2**	**AFFE1**	**AFFE2**
Correlation	CURI1	1.000	0.753	0.696	0.609	0.649
	ATTE1	0.753	1.000	0.747	0.712	0.705
	ATTE2	0.696	0.747	1.000	0.743	0.764
	AFFE1	0.609	0.712	0.743	1.000	0.822
	AFFE2	0.649	0.705	0.764	0.822	1.000

Table 3.22. *Correlation matrix of Situational Interest indicators*

KMO index

This measure provides a global view of the quality of interitem correlations. The index varies between 0 and 1; it increases with the size of the sample, the significance of interitem correlations and the number of variables, and decreases with the number of factors. Deemed unacceptable if it is less than 0.5, the closer it is to 1, the better it is (Kaiser and Rice 1974).

The KMO index calculated in our case can be read in Table 3.23; its value, 0.869, is "meritorious" in the words of Kaiser and Rice, that is to say, very good.

Bartlett's test of sphericity

This hypotheses test admits, for null hypothesis H_0, the hypothesis of a matrix of the correlation coefficients of the indicators equal to the identity matrix, corresponding to perfectly independent variables. If the null hypothesis is rejected (at 5% risk in our case, that is to say if $p < 0.05$), then the correlation matrix is significantly different from the identity matrix, in other words, some item correlation coefficients are significantly different from 0.

In our case, Table 3.23 shows a zero probability (significance = 0) of rejecting the null hypothesis H_0 (at 5% risk), while the latter is true (type 1 risk). The correlations are therefore not all equal to zero and we can continue the analysis.

KMO index and Bartlett's test		
Kaiser–Meyer–Olkin index for measuring sampling quality		0.869
Bartlett's test of sphericity	Chi-square approx.	1597.345
	DOF	10
	Significance	0.000

Table 3.23. *KMO index and Bartlett's test on Situational Interest indicators*

Finally, given the correlation coefficients, the KMO index and Bartlett's test of significance, we conclude that it is possible to factorize the Situational Interest items.

Determining the number of factors of the factorial solution

The approaches used to determine the number of factors retained are based on the percentage of variance returned by the chosen factorial solution. We will successively analyze the Kaiser criterion, the percentage of returned variance and then the Cattell criterion; we will also observe the quality of the factorial solution chosen for each indicator.

Kaiser's criterion

In most statistical software (in particular, in SPSS), the indicators are standardized variables (in order to erase the effects of scales with different numbers of levels). Each variable also contributes to the total variance of the measure up to the quantity 1/k if the measure has k indicators. The eigenvalue (VP) of a factor is defined as the ratio between the variance that it returns (VR) and the fraction 1/k; we have:

$$VP = \frac{VR}{\frac{1}{k}}$$

However, it seems natural that a factor, which synthesizes (by linear combination) the information contained in several variables, restores more variance (VR) than that contributed by each of its variables (1/k), i.e. VR > 1/k or VP > 1.

Based on this observation, Kaiser (1960) proposed retaining only the eigenvalue factors greater than 1.

In our case, Table 3.24 indicates that only the first factor satisfies this criterion with an eigenvalue = 3.882; this factor alone restores 3.882/5 ≅ 77.64% of the variance.

Percentage of returned variance

This criterion proposes determining the factorial solution according to a minimum threshold of returned variance. In social sciences, the 60% threshold is reasonable (Gavard-Perret *et al.* 2013). In our case, the first component (factor) returns 77.643% of the total information contained in the data (see Table 3.24), which is satisfactory.

Cattell criterion

The graph (histogram) of the eigenvalues obtained from PCA draws a decreasing curve, which can be analyzed in terms of the marginal variance returned by each factor. The Cattell (1966) criterion (or scree test) proposes retaining only the factors which precede the "break" of the curve, the shape of which flattens out afterwards, because the marginal variance returned by the factors located after the break (including that located on the break) is negligible, and harms the simplicity of the factorial solution sought. In our case, the scree plot in Figure 3.7 indicates a break located on the second factor, so only the first factor should be retained.

Total variance explained						
Component	**Initial eigenvalues**			**Sums extracted from the square of the loading**		
	Total	**% of variance**	**% cumulated**	**Total**	**% of variance**	**% cumulated**
1	3.882	77.643	77.643	3.882	77.643	77.643
2	0.466	9.327	86.970			
3	0.245	4.893	91.863			
4	0.238	4.760	96.623			
5	0.169	3.377	100.000			

Extraction method: principal component analysis.

Table 3.24. *Eigenvalues and total variance explained by the factorial solution*

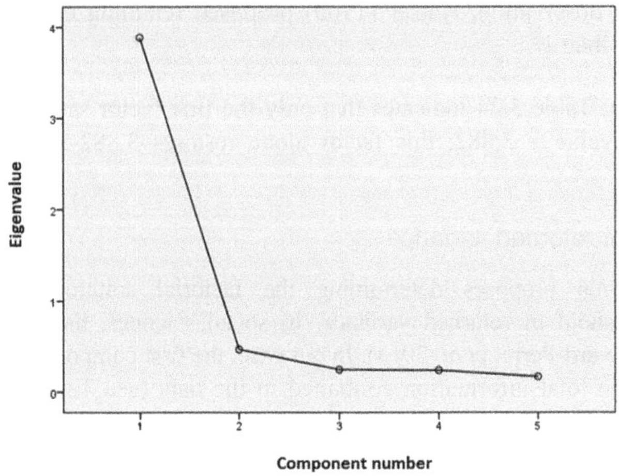

Figure 3.7. *Scree plot of eigenvalues*

Quality of the factorial solution retained for each indicator

Therefore, a factorial solution with only one factor is retained; let us now look at the impact of this solution (of a single factor) on each indicator of the latent variable in terms of commonality and correlation.

Quality of representation

Table 3.25 shows the commonalities of each indicator of the Situational Interest construct relative to the factor selected. These commonalities represent the percentage of the variance of each initial indicator returned by the single-factor solution. In our case, all the commonalities are greater than the minimum threshold of 0.5. All the variables (indicators) are therefore correctly represented, in other words, the representation of the variables by the single factor is of good quality.

Quality of representation		
	Initial	**Extraction**
CURI1	1.000	0.701
ATTE1	1.000	0.790
ATTE2	1.000	0.807
AFFE1	1.000	0.781
AFFE2	1.000	0.803

Table 3.25. *Commonality of each indicator with the factorial solution*

Component matrix

Table 3.26 presents the correlations (or loadings or even saturations) of the indicators (initial variables) with the single factor selected. In our case, each variable shows a high correlation (since a correlation becomes significant beyond 0.30, in absolute value) with the factor; the latter is therefore strongly representative of all the indicators of the Situational Interest construct.

Component matrix	
	Component
	1
ATTE2	0.898
AFFE2	0.896
ATTE1	0.889
AFFE1	0.884
CURI1	0.838

Table 3.26. *Loading of each indicator with the factorial solution*

In conclusion, this analysis by PCA of the indicators of the Situational Interest dimension of the latent variable of Interest confirms that the five indicators (AFFE1, AFFE2, ATTE1, ATTE2 and CURI1) form one and the same main component and measure the same phenomenon.

3.2.3.3.2. Confirmatory factor analysis of Situational Interest

Section 3.2.3.3.1 allowed us to establish that the items of the latent reflective variable of Situational Interest measured the same phenomenon. In this section, we want to check whether this measurement model is empirically acceptable (Gavard-Perret *et al.* 2013). To do this, we perform a confirmatory factor analysis to ensure that the data fit sufficiently well with the theoretical model. More precisely, it is a question of comparing the theoretical and empirical variance-covariance matrices of the variables of the following SEM (Figure 3.8).

While the most commonly used estimation method is maximum likelihood, this requires that the data meet the condition of multivariate normality. However, we saw in the data prerequisites of this chapter that several indicators of the latent variable of Interest, in particular, some indicators of the Situational Interest dimension (indicators AFFE1 and AFFE2), presented flattened frequency distributions (kurtosis < -1) that are significantly different from that of a normal distribution. This means that the associated marginal distributions are not normal and hence the multidimensional joint law cannot be normal. In the event that the multivariate normality condition is not satisfied, it is possible to resort to other estimation methods. We choose

Browne's (1984) Asymptotically Distribution Free (ADF) method. We are implementing this estimation method under the free software R, dedicated to statistics. The lavaan package for latent variable analysis offers a routine for model estimation by structural equations (SEM), the function CFA (confirmatory factor analysis) admitting a parameter specifying the estimation method chosen. When this parameter takes the WLS value (Weighted Least Squares), then the estimation is executed with the ADF method. Figure 3.9 shows the results of this confirmatory analysis.

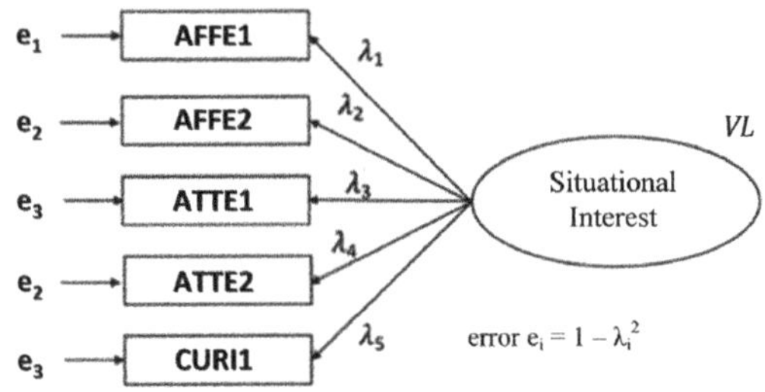

Figure 3.8. *Model by structural equations of the Situational Interest variable*

```
lavaan (0.5-23.1097) converged normally after  17 iterations

  Number of observations                           400

  Estimator                                        WLS
  Minimum Function Test Statistic               29.696
  Degrees of freedom                                 5
  P-value (Chi-square)                           0.000

Model test baseline model:

  Minimum Function Test Statistic              382.642
  Degrees of freedom                                10
  P-value                                        0.000

User model versus baseline model:

  Comparative Fit Index (CFI)                    0.934
  Tucker-Lewis Index (TLI)                       0.867

Root Mean Square Error of Approximation:

  RMSEA                                          0.111
  90 Percent Confidence Interval          0.075  0.151
  P-value RMSEA <= 0.05                          0.004

Standardized Root Mean Square Residual:

  SRMR                                           0.051

Parameter Estimates:

  Information                                 Expected
  Standard Errors                             Standard

Latent Variables:
                   Estimate  Std.Err  z-value  P(>|z|)   Std.lv  Std.all
  INTS =~
    CURI1             1.000                               1.030    0.817
    ATTE1             1.107    0.052   21.451    0.000    1.141    0.877
    ATTE2             1.091    0.051   21.382    0.000    1.124    0.882
    AFFE1             1.206    0.056   21.458    0.000    1.242    0.897
    AFFE2             1.141    0.052   21.745    0.000    1.175    0.907
```

Figure 3.9. *Results of the Asymptotically Distribution Free (ADF) approach under R*

We are interested in the fit between the theoretical and empirical variance-covariance matrices. While several fit indicators exist, in the case of an estimate performed with the ADF method, Browne pointed out that most of the usual fit tests used under the multivariate normality hypothesis should not be used when this estimate is not met, especially in the case of a flattened data distribution. For the ADF method, Hu and Bentler (1998) recommended the use of the Standardized Root Mean Square Residual (SRMR) fit indicator, supplemented by one of the indices: TLI, BL89, RNI or CFI, provided the sample size is sufficient, as in our case (400 observations). The SRMR is an absolute measure of adjustment defined as the standardized difference between observed correlations and predicted correlations. As with any absolute measure, a value of zero indicates a perfect fit, while a value below 0.08 is generally considered a good fit (Hu and Bentler 1998). In our case, the SRMR index is 0.051; its value is satisfactory. In accordance with Hu and Bentler's recommendation, we supplement this information with the Comparative Fit Index (CFI). This CFI is an incremental measure; a value below 0.90 indicates a poor fit, a value between 0.90 and 0.95 is satisfactory and a value above 0.95 indicates a good fit. In our case, the CFI is 0.934, which indicates a satisfactory fit. In light of these two fit indices, we conclude that the confirmatory analysis of the Situational Interest dimension measurement model of the latent reflective variable of Interest is satisfactory.

3.2.3.3.3. PCA result on all items of the Interest variable

The purpose of this section is to ensure that the two dimensions (Situational Interest and Individual Interest) of Interest represent distinct concepts. To do this, we will use a PCA, which should extract two factors, each combining indicators of the two Interest dimensions. In section 3.2.3.3.1, we detailed the PCA technique; therefore, in this section, we will go directly to the gist of the results. We will also respect the same presentation structure and begin by checking application conditions before determining the number of factors in the factorial solution.

Verification of application conditions

Once again, the size of our sample (400 observations) is significantly larger than the minimum required size of 10 subjects per variable/indicator, or 140 (= 14*10) subjects, in our case. The synthesis of variables into factors assumes that the variables are sufficiently related to each other; the study of correlations between variables provides a preliminary answer. However, in order to determine whether correlated variables are sufficiently correlated, we will use two standard criteria: the KMO index and Bartlett's test of sphericity.

Correlation		EMO1	EMO2	EMO3	VALE1	VALE2	VALE3	VALE4	INTR1	INTR2	CURI1	ATTE1	ATTE2	AFFE1	AFFE2
	EMO1	1	0.345	0.521	0.565	0.376	0.49	0.6	0.483	0.461	0.525	0.536	0.592	0.56	0.536
	EMO2	0.345	1	0.43	0.504	0.478	0.51	0.412	0.36	0.288	0.318	0.324	0.325	0.426	0.374
	EMO3	0.521	0.43	1	0.567	0.472	0.54	0.57	0.453	0.397	0.419	0.414	0.423	0.442	0.388
	VALE1	0.565	0.504	0.567	1	0.611	0.613	0.763	0.624	0.554	0.474	0.543	0.537	0.696	0.571
	VALE2	0.376	0.478	0.472	0.611	1	0.513	0.536	0.501	0.444	0.345	0.391	0.394	0.495	0.452
	VALE3	0.49	0.51	0.54	0.613	0.513	1	0.622	0.49	0.426	0.421	0.472	0.485	0.521	0.481
	VALE4	0.6	0.412	0.57	0.763	0.536	0.622	1	0.638	0.585	0.454	0.572	0.558	0.64	0.555
	INTR1	0.483	0.36	0.453	0.624	0.501	0.49	0.638	1	0.727	0.357	0.445	0.517	0.587	0.481
	INTR2	0.461	0.288	0.397	0.554	0.444	0.426	0.585	0.727	1	0.424	0.503	0.524	0.578	0.531
	CURI1	0.525	0.318	0.419	0.474	0.345	0.421	0.454	0.357	0.424	1	0.753	0.696	0.609	0.649
	ATTE1	0.536	0.324	0.414	0.543	0.391	0.472	0.572	0.445	0.503	0.753	1	0.747	0.712	0.705
	ATTE2	0.592	0.325	0.423	0.537	0.394	0.485	0.558	0.517	0.524	0.696	0.747	1	0.743	0.764
	AFFE1	0.56	0.426	0.442	0.696	0.495	0.521	0.64	0.587	0.578	0.609	0.712	0.743	1	0.822
	AFFE2	0.536	0.374	0.388	0.571	0.452	0.481	0.555	0.481	0.531	0.649	0.705	0.764	0.822	1

Table 3.27. *Correlation matrix of indicators of the latent variable of interest*

Interitem correlations

Table 3.27 shows that all the variables are at least slightly correlated. In addition, a majority of values are above 0.5, which is a possible factoring index.

KMO index

The KMO index calculated on the variables of the Interest construct can be read in Table 3.28; its value of 0.936 is described as "wonderful" in the words of Kaiser and Rice (1974).

Bartlett's test of sphericity

Bartlett's test of sphericity calculated on the variables of the Interest construct indicates (see Table 3.28) a zero probability (significance = 0) of rejecting the null hypothesis H_0 (at 5% risk), while the latter is true (type 1 risk). The correlations are therefore not all equal to zero and we can continue the analysis. Finally, given the correlation coefficients, the KMO index and Bartlett's test of significance, we conclude that it is possible to factorize the indicators of the Interest construct.

KMO index and Bartlett's test		
Kaiser–Meyer–Olkin index for measuring sampling quality		0.936
Bartlett's test of sphericity	Chi-square approx.	3986.340
	DOF	91
	Significance	0.000

Table 3.28. *KMO index and Bartlett's test on the indicators of the Interest variable*

Determining the number of factors of the factorial solution

As before, we will successively analyze Kaiser's criterion, the percentage of variance returned, and then the Cattell criterion. We will then observe the quality of the factorial solution chosen and the matrix of the components and conclude with a rotation for the identification of factors.

Kaiser's criterion

Table 3.29 indicates that two factors meet the Kaiser test with an eigenvalue greater than the unit; the first factor is predominant, with an explained variance percentage close to 56%.

Percentage of returned variance

Table 3.29 indicates that a factorial solution combining the two factors with an eigenvalue greater than 1 allows for exceeding the required threshold of 60% of the total explained variance with a cumulative variance of 65.42%.

Component	Initial eigenvalues			Sums extracted from the square of the loading		
	Total	% of variance	% cumulated	Total	% of variance	% cumulated
1	7.828	55.914	55.914	7.828	55.914	55.914
2	1.331	9.504	65.419	1.331	9.504	65.419
3	0.893	6.382	71.801			
4	0.693	4.951	76.752			
5	0.501	3.58	80.332			
6	0.48	3.431	83.763			
7	0.441	3.153	86.916			
8	0.391	2.792	89.709			
9	0.368	2.63	92.338			
10	0.271	1.936	94.274			
11	0.25	1.788	96.062			
12	0.21	1.502	97.563			
13	0.198	1.417	98.98			
14	0.143	1.02	100			

Table 3.29. *Eigenvalues and total variance explained by the factorial solution*

Cattell criterion

The scree plot in Figure 3.10 indicates a break on the second factor so only one factor should be retained, if there is enough total variance left on its own. However, this is not the case (it returns 55.91% for a required threshold of 60%).

Finally, the analysis of the three criteria shows that the factorial solution must retain two factors.

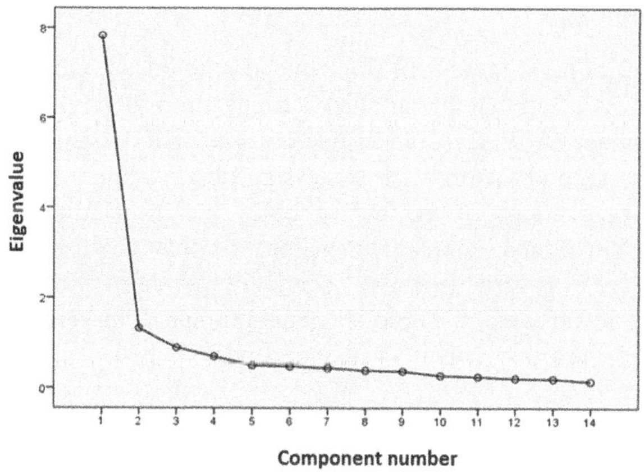

Figure 3.10. *Scree plot of eigenvalues*

Quality of the factorial solution and component matrix

Quality of representation

The commonality coefficients presented in Table 3.30 are above the threshold of 0.5, with the exception of the EMO2 variable for which 47% of its variance is returned by both factors, which, nevertheless, remains very close to the threshold. The representation of variables by this two-factor factorial solution has an overall good quality.

Quality of representation		
	Initial	**Extraction**
EMO1	1.000	0.534
EMO2	1.000	0.470
EMO3	1.000	0.539
VALE1	1.000	0.749
VALE2	1.000	0.584
VALE3	1.000	0.605
VALE4	1.000	0.713
INTR1	1.000	0.589
INTR2	1.000	0.514
CURI1	1.000	0.715
ATTE1	1.000	0.790
ATTE2	1.000	0.808
AFFE1	1.000	0.777
AFFE2	1.000	0.772

Table 3.30. *Commonality coefficients of each indicator with the factorial solution*

Component matrix

Both Table 3.31 and Figure 3.11 show the correlations of indicators with the two factors selected. We find that all variables saturate strongly on the first factor, while only a few variables (AFFE2, ATTE2, ATTE1 and CURI1) saturate jointly on both the first and the second factors with some significant weights (i.e. 0.3 in absolute value) with a negative sign. These four variables of significant and negative weight belong to the Situational Interest dimension; all that is missing is the AFFE1 variable. However, this variable is also negatively correlated with the second factor, although with a lower weight. These elements prompt us to perform a VARIMAX rotation that preserves orthogonality (i.e. independence) between factors.

Component matrix		
	Component	
	1	2
AFFE1	0.857	– 0.208
VALE1	0.828	0.251
VALE4	0.819	0.204
AFFE2	0.807	– 0.348
ATTE2	0.806	– 0.398
ATTE1	0.787	– 0.413
INTR1	0.734	0.224
EMO1	0.729	– 0.052
VALE3	0.721	0.291
CURI1	0.718	– 0.446
INTR2	0.715	0.048
EMO3	0.664	0.312
VALE2	0.662	0.382
EMO2	0.565	0.388

Table 3.31. *Loading of each indicator with the factorial solution*

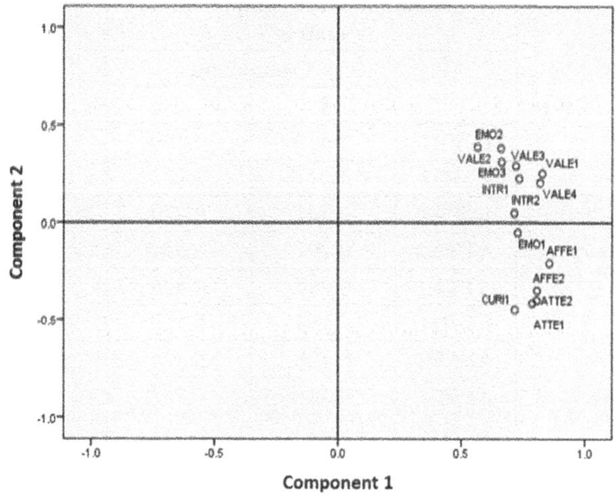

Figure 3.11. *Plot of components in the factorial plane*

Rotation for factor identification

Table 3.32 and Figure 3.12 show the correlations of indicators with the two factors selected after the VARIMAX rotation[7]. This time, we find that the variables are much better distributed on the different factors. In particular, the five variables of the Situational Interest subconstruct are detached by their particularly significant weight (i.e. 0.7) on factor 2 and lower weight on factor 1.

Thus, the Individual Interest dimension is recognizable in factor 1 and the Situational Interest dimension is recognizable in factor 2.

Rotation of the component matrix		
	Component	
	1	2
VALE1	*0.765*	0.406
VALE2	*0.739*	0.196
VALE4	*0.725*	0.433
VALE3	*0.717*	0.302
EMO3	*0.691*	0.247

7 Let us note that an OBLIMIN rotation would have been possible insofar as the two interest dimensions are correlated; however, the VARIMAX rotation is sufficient in order to draw conclusions.

Rotation of the component matrix		
	Component	
	1	2
INTR1	*0.678*	0.359
EMO2	*0.674*	0.123
INTR2	*0.541*	0.470
ATTE2	0.291	*0.851*
ATTE1	0.267	*0.848*
CURI1	0.194	*0.823*
AFFE2	0.326	*0.816*
AFFE1	0.461	*0.751*
EMO1	*0.480*	0.551

Table 3.32. *Loading of each indicator with the factorial solution after VARIMAX rotation*

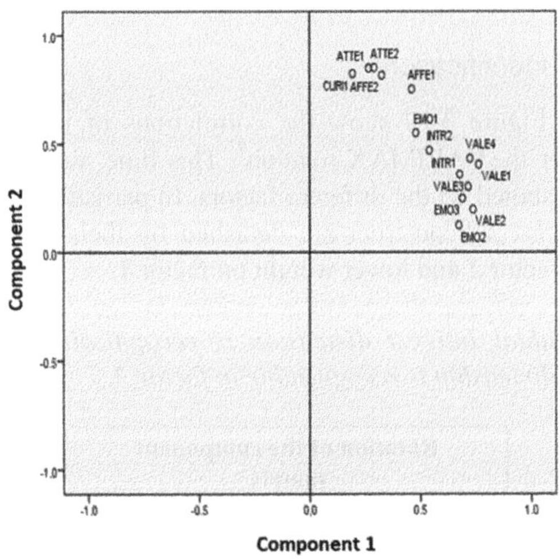

Figure 3.12. *Plot of components in the factorial plane after VARIMAX rotation*

3.2.4. *Formative variables*

Formative measures are defined by the measurable indicators that constitute them. The composite or index construct does not exist by itself, it is formed by its indicators (Gavard-Perret *et al.* 2013). According to Jarvis *et al.* (2003), formative constructs differ from reflective measures because of:

– the direction of causality between construct and measure, this goes from items to construct;

– the lack of interchangeability of the indicators, which should not share a common theme and cannot be eliminated without changing the conceptual domain of the construct;

– the lack of a need for indicators to covariate;

– the nomological network of indicators, which do not necessarily have to have the same antecedents and consequents.

The latent formative variable is a weighted linear function of its measurements (see Figure 3.13); there is no measurement error. Specifically, there is no measurement error with the formative construct associated with "composite indicators", while a measurement error must be specified when the formative construct is associated with "causative indicators". While the formative latent variables associated with causative indicators are commonly used in the *covariance* structure analysis approach, in the PLS-SEM approach, the only formative latent variables considered are those associated with composite indicators. The latter perfectly "form" the construct; in other words, the R^2 of the linear regression of the latent formative variable on its indicators is 1 (Rigdon 2012). The composite variable is also considered an approximation of the measured concept, which is a reasonable assumption in the social sciences.

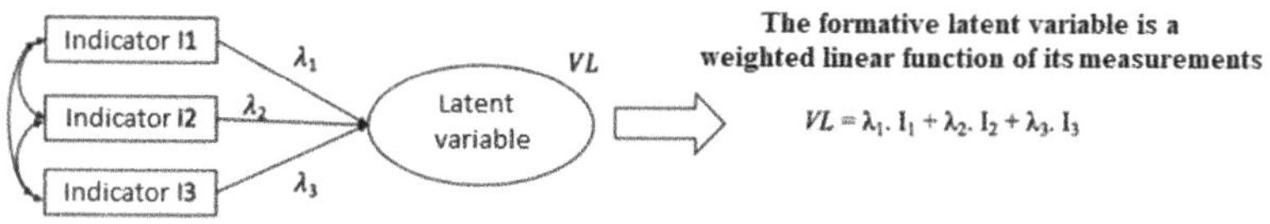

Figure 3.13. *Relationship between observable indicators and latent formative variable, adapted from (Crié 2005)*

In Chapter 1, we specified an explanatory model incorporating two formative latent variables: Perceived Signal Quality and Familiarity. Below, we study the quality of these two constructs (section 3.2.4.1). It is also possible to treat the Interest variable as formative and as a second-order variable, which we will do in section 3.2.4.2. The quality check stages of the formative constructs differ significantly from those of reflective constructs. Many researchers misuse the criteria for evaluating reflective measures for formative measures when they are not transferable (Hair *et al.* 2012). Indeed, indicators of formative measures are supposed to represent the causes independent of the constructs and are therefore not necessarily correlated. Moreover, the indicators of the formative constructs do not, by hypothesis, have a measurement error (Diamantopoulos 2006); these two points imply that the study of reliability is irrelevant. In addition, the converging and discriminant validity do not make sense in the context of formative constructs (Vinzi *et al.* 2010).

The following approach, based on the recommendations of Hair *et al.* (2017), is based on the calculation of several indicators; Table 3.33 gives a summarized view. It also assumes that the validity of the content is established beforehand, i.e. the facets of the construct be captured by the construct (see the specification of the variables in Chapter 1).

Quality of formative measures	Convergent validity	Redundancy analysis
	Collinearities check	Variance Inflation Factor (VIF)
	Significance and relevance of indicators	Relative weight analysis and significance test

Table 3.33. *Steps to verify the psychometric quality of formative latent variables*

3.2.4.1. *Perceived signal quality and familiarity constructs*

In this section, we study the quality of the Perceived Signal Quality (section 3.2.4.1.1) and Familiarity (section 3.2.4.1.2) constructs.

3.2.4.1.1. Perceived signal quality construct

As indicated above, we will successively analyze the convergent validity, the control of collinearities, then the significance and relevance of the indicators.

Convergent validity

Convergent validity is based on the importance of the correlation of the formative construct with a reflective measure of the same construct from the literature, which must be high. This analysis is also known as "redundancy analysis", since the same information, that of the concept, is supposed to be represented by the two constructs of different natures. More precisely, the formative construct must be used as an exogenous explanatory variable of the reflective construct; the correlation must be sufficiently strong (greater than 0.70).

This approach requires including items relating to the equivalent reflective construct in the initial questionnaire, at the risk of making it longer. However, the number of questions is not without consequences on the fatigue of subjects and the response rate. An alternative consists of inserting a global question summarizing the essence of the formative construct (Hair *et al.* 2017). Although single-item constructs are not generally recommended (Diamantopoulos *et al.* 2012), their role for the redundancy analysis is different; it is not a matter of capturing the entire content of the formative construct but its salient elements.

In our case, we introduced a question (item VALI2) that was supposed to encompass the two subdimensions of the formative construct Perceived Signal Quality: the "business plan" and "management team" dimensions:

> VALI2: "I consider that the information relating to the business plan and the management team of this company is a quality signal".

Figure 3.14 shows the results of the estimation of the coefficients of the model by using structural equations, in which the formative construct Perceived Signal Quality explains the single-item construct (of validation) identified in item VALI2.

The coefficient linking the two constructs is 0.489, which is below the minimum required threshold of 0.70. The weakness of this coefficient can potentially be explained by the difficulty that the subjects could have had (most of whom were inexperienced in management) in producing the summarizing assessment requested. Although this criterion is not met, it is not a showstopper because:

– we used a single-item construct and not a reliable and valid reflective construct from the literature;

– in the specification of the explanatory model, the choice of a formative construct as a proxy for the Perceived Signal Quality was primarily based on the desire to form an index from items adapted to the specific context of investment in equity crowdfunding. To do this, we identified the relevant items (taken from the literature) with regard to an analysis of lexicometric content. Also, the content validity criterion (i.e. "do the selected items compose an index that correctly approximates the studied concept?") dominates a convergence towards a *reliable and valid equivalent* reflective construct, which cannot exist given the singularity of the proposed formative construct. Furthermore, this last remark also explains, in addition to the advantage already explained of a choice that does not weigh down the questionnaire, the decision to resort to a single-item construct.

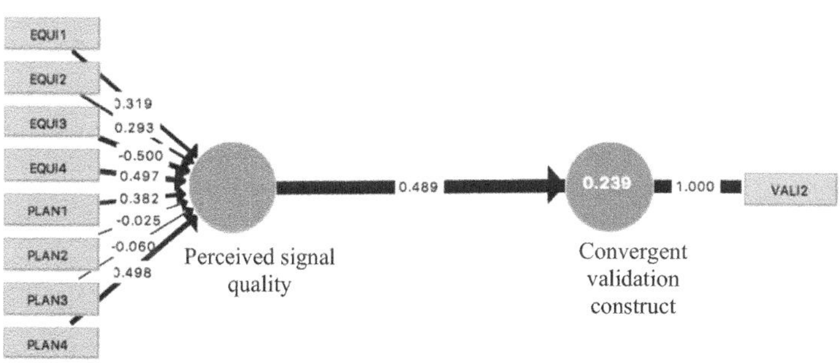

Figure 3.14. *Redundancy analysis of the Perceived Signal Quality*

Collinearities check

Unlike reflective constructs, the indicators of latent formative variables should not be too redundant, because they are supposed to represent the different complementary facets of a concept. Moreover, a formative construct is expressed as a linear combination of its indicators; however, the algorithm for estimating the parameters of the model by structural equations PLS-SEM proceeds by iterations of linear regressions, successively on the structural model (or inner model) and measurement model (or outer model). Thus, the condition of application of non-multicollinearity explanatory variables which prevail for a linear regression (Gavard-Perret *et al.* 2013), applies to the indicators of the formative constructs. Technically, it involves successively regressing each indicator of the formative construct on the other indicators. The complement to 1 of the determination coefficient is the unexplained part of the variance of the indicator considered by the other indicators. This quantity ($1 - R^2$), called "Tolerance" (TOL), must not be too low (i.e. $1 - R^2 > 0.20$). With the Variance Inflation Factor (VIF) being defined as the inverse of "Tolerance", an equivalent condition is given by the inequality: VIF < 5.

As shown in Table 3.34, the VIFs of the eight indicators of the Perceived Signal Quality construct are below the critical threshold of 5, which means that less than 80% of the variance of each indicator is explained by the other seven indicators.

Indicator	VIF
EQUI1	1.165
EQUI2	1.550
EQUI3	1.913
EQUI4	1.760
PLAN1	1.337
PLAN2	1.459
PLAN3	1.189
PLAN4	1.682

Table 3.34. *Variance Inflation Factor of indicators of the Perceived Signal Quality construct*

Significance and relevance of indicators

The third criterion for evaluating the indicators of formative constructs and their relevance is based on the analysis of the external coefficients (outer weight). These are calculated by multiple linear regressions (converging iterative process) and are *in fine* the regression coefficients associated with the indicators explaining the formative latent. As we previously mentioned, the PLS-SEM approach only considers composite constructs (made up of composite indicators) explained at 100% by their indicators (R^2 of regression = 1). In addition, the values of the external coefficients are standardized, which makes it possible to compare them, as well as an interpretation of the relative contribution of the indicators.

It should also be noted that the external coefficients are generally of a lower value than the loadings of the reflective constructs, which is explained by the decreasing relationship between the maximum value of an indicator and the number n of indicators that belong to the same formative construct; this value is $\frac{1}{\sqrt{n}}$ (on the assumption that the indicators are not correlated). Also, a question arises regarding the real contribution of each external coefficient (potentially small if n is large). In other words, is the coefficient considered significant? More precisely, is it significantly different from 0?

As we have indicated, the PLS-SEM approach does not require normally distributed data, which is why the significance tests are based on a bootstrapping procedure.

Hair *et al.* (2017) specified that the bootstrapping procedure consists of generating a large number of samples from the sample of initial observations. In our case, 5,000 samples of a size of 400 observations are generated[8], constructed by random selection (with replacement) from the initial sample of observations. For each of these 5,000 samples, an estimation of the parameters (internal, between constructs AND external, between constructs and indicators: loadings and external coefficients) of the model is carried out by using the PLS-SEM algorithm. Thus, each parameter can be associated with a frequency distribution, whose standard deviation (standard error) can be reasonably interpreted as an approximation of the standard deviation of the parameter for the population.

Consequently, the statistical test of significance of the external coefficients is based on a Student's *t*-test, whose *t*-test statistic follows a Student's law with N degree of freedom, with N = number of observations – number of indicators of the formative construct – 1. In our case N= 400 – 8 – 1 = 391. Since this figure is much greater than 30, Student's law can be approximated by a normal or theoretical t law. Therefore, a coefficient is significant at (standard threshold α = 5% in two-tailed test), if the empirical t is greater than 1.96, a value which corresponds to the 97th percentile and a half of the normal distribution of the theoretical t.

8 In the remainder of the chapter, we systematically adopted a parameterization of 5,000 samples recommended by the authors, with the (mentioned) exceptions attributable to the failure of the procedure.

In other words, the external coefficient is significant at the 5% threshold if its *p*-value is less than 5%. The *p*-value is the probability associated with the type 1 risk or α risk, that is to say the risk of rejecting the hypothesis H_0 (the external parameter is zero), while H_0 is true.

In practice, the empirical t is calculated as the ratio of the external coefficient estimated from the initial sample (Original Sample column [O]), to the standard error of this coefficient calculated from the distribution resulting from the bootstrapping procedure (Standard Deviation column [STDEV]).

Finally, an estimated parameter "Original Sample (O)" is significant at the 5% threshold if:

$$\frac{\text{Original Sample (O)}}{\text{Standard Deviation (STDEV)}} = T\ Statistics\left(\left|\frac{O}{STDEV}\right|\right) > 1.96$$

$$\Leftrightarrow PValues \leq 0.05$$

In the remainder of this chapter, we will determine the significance of an estimated coefficient based on this second condition. Nevertheless, we will systematically record the confidence interval to 95% $[a_{2.5\%}, b_{97.5\%}]$, built according to the bootstrapping distribution, which must not contain the value 0 for H_0 to be rejected. In fact, this interval provides additional information on the stability of the estimated parameter, since the latter decreases when the size of the interval increases.

The interval $[a_{2.5\%}, b_{97.5\%}]$ is calculated by the percentile method, in our case, the 5,000 estimated parameters are ordered; (a) 2.5% is the 125th largest value (125 = 2.5%*5,000) and (b) 97.5% is the 4,875th largest value (4,875 = 97.5%*5,000)[9].

Coming back to the significance of the indicators of the latent variable Perceived Signal Quality, Table 3.35 summarizes the results obtained by bootstrapping with the SmartPLS 3 software.

Three indicators PLAN1, PLAN2 and PLAN3 present non-significant external coefficients (*p*-value > 0.05). In this case, Hair *et al.* (2017) proposed a decision tree to determine whether to delete the offending indicators.

In the event of insignificant external coefficients, it is advisable to consider the importance of the outer loading of the indicator, as this represents the absolute

9 To be exact, we have chosen to adjust the bounds of the 95% trust interval by the BCa bias correction (short for Bias-Corrected and accelerated) of Efron (1987), in accordance with the authors' recommendation.

contribution (and not relative to that of the other indicators of the construct) of the indicator to the construct. The outer loading is calculated by linear regression, as we explained above for reflective constructs. If the outer loading is greater than 0.5, then the indicator must be kept; otherwise, it is a question of checking if the outer loading is significant. Finally, if it is not significant, it is strongly recommended to delete the indicator, unless it is based on solid theoretical foundations or its deletion would alter the content of the construct, that is to say, does not affect its content validity.

As Table 3.35 shows, the loadings of the PLAN1, PLAN2 and PLAN3 indicators are significant (p-value $\leq$ 0.05); these three indicators respectively represent product-service innovation, growth and intensity of competition in the market which the company is positioned in. So, these are three important elements of the business plan. However, the literature on the selection of projects in venture capital points to the importance of the business plan as a selection criterion (Desbrières and Broye 2000). Also, given the significance of the loadings (although their value is less than 0.5) of the solid theoretical bases, and also in order to not alter the content of this construct, we choose to keep these three indicators. Regarding the relevance of the parameters, the analysis of the relative weights indicates that the EQUI1, EQUI3, EQUI4 and PLAN4 indicators are the indicators that are contributing the most to this index.

For the Perceived Quality of the management team dimension of the construct, the main contributing indicator is EQUI4 (external coefficient = 0.576), i.e. the adequacy of the managers' experience, followed by the size of the team, EQUI1 (0.479). Surprisingly, a negative weight is associated with EQUI3 (– 0.412), indicating that the perceived signal quality decreases with the adequacy of the level of qualification of the managers in the project. A return to the questionnaire reveals that the EQUI3 question is not inverted and its understanding is easy: "Managers' degrees are appropriate for this project". Analysis of the raw data and then of the various stages of processing of the data file did not reveal any handling error. This result is counterintuitive and contradicts the theory; it is possibly explained by the design of the poor quality business plans (BP–), in which the level of qualification was deliberately inappropriate to the complexity of the projects carried out.

For the Perceived Quality of the business plan dimension, PLAN4, i.e. the indicator relating to the financial perspectives, is the only one that is significant with an external coefficient of 0.401.

Finally, the weight of the Perceived Quality of the management team subdimension is overall significantly greater than that of the business plan dimension.

Weights								
Perceived Signal Quality (QPS)	**Original sample (O)**	**Sample mean (M)**	**Standard deviation (STDEV)**	**T statistics (|O/STDEV|)**	***p*-values**	**Bias**	**2.5%**	**97.5%**
EQUI1 → QPS	0.479	0.466	0.103	4.665	0.000	– 0.012	0.287	0.696
EQUI2 → QPS	0.286	0.279	0.112	2.557	0.011	– 0.007	0.065	0.500
EQUI3 → QPS	– 0.412	– 0.400	0.129	3.196	0.001	0.012	– 0.672	– 0.172
EQUI4 → QPS	0.576	0.557	0.125	4.618	0.000	– 0.019	0.336	0.821
PLAN1 → QPS	0.108	0.104	0.093	1.170	0.242	– 0.004	– 0.070	0.294
PLAN2 → QPS	– 0.021	– 0.019	0.114	0.184	0.854	0.002	– 0.256	0.194
PLAN3 → QPS	0.076	0.077	0.104	0.733	0.464	0.001	– 0.134	0.269
PLAN4 → QPS	0.401	0.387	0.105	3.805	0.000	– 0.014	0.202	0.621
Loadings								
EQUI2 → QPS	0.601	0.580	0.089	6.743	0.000	– 0.021	0.431	0.765
PLAN1 → QPS	0.392	0.377	0.096	4.084	0.000	– 0.015	0.203	0.566
PLAN2 → QPS	0.277	0.268	0.118	2.358	0.018	– 0.009	0.049	0.505
PLAN3 → QPS	0.290	0.278	0.106	2.723	0.006	– 0.012	0.072	0.491

Table 3.35. *Estimation and significance of external coefficients (weights) and loadings of the Perceived Signal Quality formative construct*

3.2.4.1.2. Familiarity construct

Convergent validity

This time, concerning the redundancy analysis of the Familiarity formative construct, we varied the questionnaire by inserting two additional items (and not just one as for the Perceived Signal Quality construct) to define an *ad hoc* reflective construct. This approach is inspired by that of Sarstedt *et al.* (2013) and Diamantopoulos and Winklhofer (2001). The two related questions were intended to capture the two dimensions of the construct – familiarity with the company and familiarity with the attributes of the company, respectively:

– VALI3: "I directly or indirectly know this company";

– VALI4: "A context element (attribute) of this company is familiar to me".

Figure 3.15 shows the results of the estimation of the coefficients of the model by using structural equations, in which the Familiarity formative construct explains the *ad hoc* reflective construct defined by the items VALI3 and VALI4.

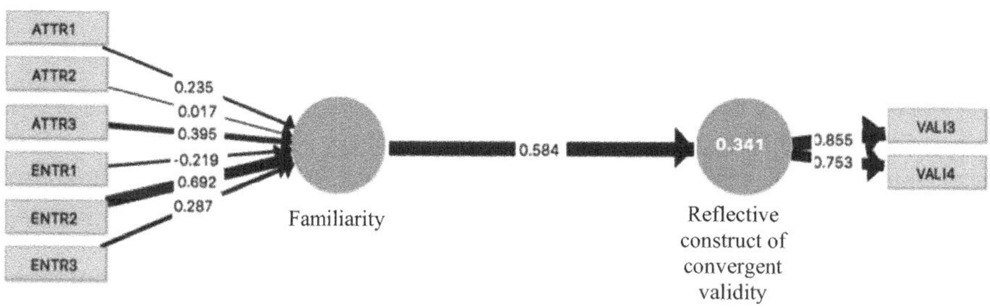

Figure 3.15. *Redundancy analysis of the familiarity variable*

The coefficient linking the two constructs is 0.584, which is again below the required threshold of 0.70. This time, the weakness of this coefficient can potentially be explained by the difficulty that the subjects had in answering relatively abstract questions. The remark made above (section 3.2.4.1.1) about the Perceived Signal Quality construct on this subject also applies to the Familiarity latent variable.

Collinearities check

As shown in Table 3.36, the VIF of the six indicators of the Familiarity construct is below the critical threshold of 5, which indicates that less than 80% of the variance of each indicator is explained by the other five indicators.

Indicators	VIF
ATTR1	1.196
ATTR2	1.012
ATTR3	1.251
ENTR1	1.452
ENTR2	1.240
ENTR3	1.348

Table 3.36. *Variance Inflation Factor of the indicators of the familiarity construct*

Significance and relevance of indicators

Table 3.37 gives the estimates and the *p*-values of the outer weights of the Familiarity construct. Three indicators (ATTR2, ENTR1 and ENTR3) are not significant at the 5% threshold. Moreover, their respective loadings are less than 0.5. However, the loadings of ENTR1 and ENTR3 are significant, while the loading of the ATTR2 indicator is not.

According to the decision tree proposed by Hair *et al.* (2017) summarized above, the indicators ENTR1, ENTR3 and ATTR2 are likely to be deleted unless their exclusion adversely affects the validity of the construct, or if the indicators are based on solid theoretical foundations.

Indicators ATTR2 and ENTR3 represent familiarity with the region or city of the financing company, and familiarity with one of its founders, respectively. Their lack of significance can be explained by the representativeness of the sample, an artificial crowd of investors disconnected from the projects. Conversely, in Chapter 1 (on modeling), the study on qualitative material by lexicometry focused on a sample made up of real investors in equity crowdfunding. The analysis highlighted the relative importance of these two indicators, thus corroborating the literature, for example with Agrawal *et al.* (2015) for the geographic region and Mollick (2013) and Wechsler (2013) for friends and family. The ENTR1 indicator represents having already invested in a project. Again, the artificiality of the sample may explain the lack of significance of the external coefficient. However, its loading is close to 0.5, which indicates a non-negligible absolute contribution to the construct; moreover, the loading is significant; finally, the concordance analysis carried out on the declarations of actual investors revealed the relevance of a previous first investment in the project. For these reasons, we keep the formative construct of Familiarity as it is. Let us add that this choice has no impact on the rest of the analysis, as according to Hair *et al.* (2017), removing insignificant indicators has virtually no effect on the estimation of parameters.

Familiarity	Original sample (O)	Sample mean (M)	Standard deviation (STDEV)	T statistics (|O/STDEV|)	*p*-values	Bias	2.5%	97.5%
Weights								
ATTR1 → Familiarity	0.440	0.430	0.102	4.321	0.000	– 0.011	0.246	0.638
ATTR2 → Familiarity	0.052	0.055	0.086	0.604	0.546	0.003	– 0.109	0.224
ATTR3 → Familiarity	0.424	0.411	0.104	4.077	0.000	– 0.013	0.220	0.625
ENTR1 → Familiarity	0.090	0.093	0.119	0.755	0.450	0.003	– 0.136	0.325
ENTR2 → Familiarity	0.486	0.476	0.105	4.642	0.000	– 0.010	0.283	0.695
ENTR3 → Familiarity	0.015	0.012	0.121	0.124	0.901	– 0.003	– 0.213	0.256
Loadings								
ATTR2 → Familiarity	0.152	0.151	0.106	1.428	0.153	– 0.001	– 0.066	0.350
ENTR1 → Familiarity	0.463	0.455	0.095	4.895	0.000	– 0.008	0.283	0.645
ENTR3 → Familiarity	0.271	0.266	0.106	2.559	0.011	– 0.005	0.068	0.481

Table 3.37. *Estimation and significance of external coefficients and loadings of the Familiarity formative construct*

Concerning the Familiarity with company attributes subdimension, the ATTR1 and ATTR3 indicators indicate high weights (0.440 and 0.424, respectively), signifying a considerable relative contribution to the index. The ATTR1 indicator, either having hobbies or a passion related to the company's field of activity, has the most weight ahead of ATTR3, which relates to having been confronted with the problem solved by the company being funded.

Concerning the Familiarity with the company subdimension, the ENTR2 indicator has the largest relative contribution (0.486) to the index. ENTR2 is knowledge of the company's products or services. Finally, the Familiarity with company attributes dimension generally dominates the Familiarity with the company dimension.

3.2.4.2. *Interest construct as a second-order (formative) variable*

Transforming the Interest variable (initially specified as reflective) into a second-order (formative) variable aims to identify the relative contribution of the two interest dimensions: Individual Interest and Situational Interest. This transformation is "manual" in SmartPLS 3; it involves associating the scores of each dimension (scores obtained by the estimation of the model modified so that the two dimensions are distinct reflective variables, see section 3.2.3.2) with a new indicator, which is itself attached to a new formative variable of interest. The Interest variable resulting from this operation is therefore made up of two indicators: INT_IND for the Individual Interest dimension and INT_SIT for Situational Interest. The analysis of the psychometric quality of this variable respects the steps seen above for the formative constructs.

3.2.4.2.1. Convergent validity

No questionnaire item was provided to test the convergent validity of the Interest construct as a secondary formative variable, because this control is not relevant. Indeed, as we have recalled, the Interest construct is initially defined as reflective; it only becomes formative artificially by the transformation mentioned above, and so it is not useful to correlate it with an equivalent reflective construct.

3.2.4.2.2. Collinearities check

As shown in Table 3.38, the VIF of the two indicators of Interest does not present excessive collinearity and is less than 5, the threshold. Note that this VIF of 2.229 corresponds to an R^2 of 55% and is therefore consistent with the correlation of 0.749, corresponding to an R^2 of 56% in Figure 3.1.

Indicator	VIF
INT_IND	2.229
INT_SIT	2.229

Table 3.38. *Variance Inflation Factor of the indicators of the interest construct*

3.2.4.2.3. Significance and relevance of indicators

The two indicators are significant; the analysis of their relative weights indicates that *the Situational Interest dimension (weight of 0.60) dominates the Individual Interest dimension (weight of 0.47)*.

This result is consistent with an average (0.794) of the loadings of the items linked to the Situational Interest dimension of the Interest reflective variable, greater than that (0.715) of the loadings of the items in the Individual Interest dimension (see Table 3.7).

Let us remember that *Situational Interest is made up of three subdimensions: curiosity, attention and affective involvement.*

Weights					
Interest	**Original sample (O)**	**Sample mean (M)**	**Standard deviation (STDEV)**	**T statistics (|O/STDEV|)**	***p*-values**
INT_IND → Interest	0.470	0.470	0.081	5.769	0.000
INT_SIT → Interest	0.600	0.599	0.079	7.590	0.000
Interest	***Bias***	**2.5%**	**97.5%**	**Significance ($p < 0.05$)**	
INT_IND → Interest	–0.000	0.305	0.622	Yes	
INT_SIT → Interest	–0.001	0.446	0.754	Yes	

Table 3.39. *Estimation and significance of the external coefficients of the Interest formative construct*

3.2.5. *Conclusion*

The objective of section 3.2 was to check the quality of the measurement model, a preliminary step in the analysis of the structural model, which is the main subject of section 3.3. The section begins with the study of the data prerequisites: the data, collected by experimentation, is complete, without aberrant data and without a straight lining type pattern. Some items (Interest and Familiarity variables) present data distributions whose shape deviates from normality, which does not prevent the use of the PLS-SEM approach, but can lead to an underestimation of the effects linked to these two variables.

Single-item variables are identified with their unique item; they naturally have no measurement error and do not require any particular analysis.

The quality of the measurement of reflective variables is deduced from the analysis of reliability and convergent, and then discriminant validities. The three reflective variables of the model – Affective Reaction, Interest and Trust – are reliable (Cronbach's alpha and Jöreskog's rho are above the thresholds) and convergent validity is established. We note that three indicators show mediocre loadings; nevertheless, they are kept in accordance with the exclusion rule adopted. The discriminant validity of the constructs is established.

The study then focuses on the Interest variable, which groups together two dimensions (Individual Interest and Situational Interest) which were brought together due to a sufficient correlation, but were separated into two distinct constructs in order to study their separate psychometric qualities. The two reflective constructs representative of the two dimensions are reliable and valid measurements. We also perform a preliminary PCA to ensure that the measurement items of the Situational Interest dimension represent the same concept and form a single principal component, which is the case. We also carry out a second PCA on all of the items in the Interest construct in order to check their natural grouping into two distinct concepts. These checks seemed necessary to us because, while the Situational Interest dimension is not developed *ex nihilo*, it is transposed from a distant field of literature: the sciences of education. In addition, as section 3.3 shows, the Interest variable is the main explanatory variable of the structural model, which warrants increased attention.

The remainder of the section focuses on the quality of the measurement of the two formative constructs (Perceived Signal Quality and Familiarity). This is determined in three stages: convergent validity, checking for collinearities and significance/relevance of the indicators. Convergent validity was not established, which can be explained by the use of *ad hoc* validation constructs, not borrowed from the literature due to too great singularity (desired to stick to the context) of the two formative constructs. The collinearity condition is technically necessary for the continuation of the analysis; it is satisfied for both constructs.

The significance and relevance of the indicators reveal several items whose external coefficients are insignificant, but are nevertheless kept in accordance with the exclusion procedure adopted. In any case, keeping them has practically no effect on the estimation of the structural parameters and does not influence the analysis in section 3.3. Moreover, an analysis of the model for measuring the Interest variable seen as formative, and made up of two indicators deduced from its two dimensions, reveals the dominance of the Situational Interest dimension over the Individual Interest dimension.

Finally, the results obtained demonstrate a measurement model whose quality is satisfactory, which allows us to consider an analysis of the structural model in section 3.3.

3.3. Estimation of the explanatory model by structural equations

After ensuring the quality of the measurement model in section 3.2, we focus on the evaluation and analysis of the structural model in this section. First, we briefly present the PLS-SEM approach (section 3.3.1), then revise the structural model (section 3.3.2) before proceeding to its evaluation (section 3.3.3), and the analysis of mediators (section 3.3.4), moderators (section 3.3.5) and control variables (section 3.3.6).

3.3.1. *PLS-SEM approach*

We begin this section with a synthetic presentation of the PLS-SEM approach and its underlying mechanisms. The PLS-SEM approach is one of the two dominant approaches for estimating SEMs. It is an alternative to the covariance analysis approach. These two approaches, qualified as second-generation methods, offer the means to estimate theoretical relational models describing simultaneous dependency relationship patterns. These diagrams are broken down into a measurement model and structural model. The measurement model links the indicators (observable or manifest variables) to latent variables or constructs. The structural model causally links the latent variables. Within the framework of the estimation of theoretical relational models, the main contribution of these methods is to allow for a simultaneous estimation of several dependency relations.

Originally, the PLS regression technique was developed by Wold and his colleagues (e.g. Wold 1985) with the aim of describing the links between sets of dependent and independent variables for complex input–output systems. The PLS method is based on the application of PLS regressions to the estimation of SEMs.

The central idea of the PLS-SEM algorithm is to estimate the coefficients of the SEMs by maximizing the explained variance of the dependent constructs or maximizing the R^2, which also amounts to maximizing the covariance between the explanatory variable and explained variable (Lacroux 2011). We can also say that the estimation is based on the minimization of the unexplained variance.

Technically, the algorithm takes as input, the matrix of indicators of latent variables (reflective and/or formative) of all the observations of the sample. The unknowns of the algorithm are the scores of the latent variables, the coefficients of the measurement model (loadings and outer weights) linking indicators and latent variables, as well as the coefficients of the structural model (path coefficient) linking endogenous (explained) latent variables and exogenous (explanatory) latent variables. Known elements are used to determine unknown elements. The PLS algorithm essentially consists of a sequence of regressions in terms of vectors of weight, following the PLS and minimizing the residual variances under a constraint of a "fixed point". The estimation process is therefore carried out by regression of the latent variables with their respective indicators and regression of the latent variables between them. More precisely, the algorithm breaks down into two stages, the first of which is iterative and is subdivided into four stages: (1) the scores of the latent variables are estimated from their respective indicators and their coefficients (weights and loadings), initialized in weight equal for the first iteration; (2) the internal weights (path coefficients) connecting the latent variables are calculated in order to maximize the R^2 of the score of the explained latent variable; (3) the scores of the latent variables are recalculated using the internal weights from the previous step; and (4) the external weights (weights and loadings) are recalculated according to the scores of their respective latent variables. These four steps are played iteratively until the results stabilize, i.e. when the changes between the outer weights of two successive iterations are below a threshold or a maximum number of iterations is achieved. Finally, the second step of the algorithm consists of estimating the coefficients of the model (outer weights, outer loadings and path coefficients) by simple or multiple regressions (Henseler *et al.* 2012).

It is important to note that the PLS-SEM approach is centered on the prediction of the dependent variables and not on the confirmation of the model, as the method based on the analysis of covariances and the technique of the maximum likelihood does it. It is therefore more suitable for exploratory research, in which the theory or constructs are not stabilized, rather than for testing proven theories.

Given the statistical objective (of maximizing the explained variance) of the PLS-SEM approach, the quality of a model is judged by its ability to correctly predict the explained variables, and not by the quality of the fit of the tested model to empirical data. The evaluation of the structural model is therefore based on the predictive relevance of the latent variables, that is to say, on their nomological validity (Fernandes 2012).

Also, the concept of fit that prevails with the analysis of the covariance approach is not completely transferable to the PLS-SEM approach. In fact, in the method based on the analysis of covariances, the fit defines a measure of the difference between the covariance matrix of the theoretical model and that resulting from the data. However, the analysis of the covariance approach estimates the parameters of the models by minimizing the differences between the theoretical and empirical covariance matrices by minimizing the fit.

Therefore, the latter is a natural measure of the quality of a model. Let us also note that most of the fit indices used with the method based on the analysis of covariances are based on the analysis of covariations between indicators, and are therefore based on a presupposition of reflective constructs, whereas with the PLS-SEM approach, constructs can be reflective and formative (Lacroux 2011).

Again, the PLS-SEM approach does not have the same objective (of minimizing the difference between theoretical and empirical covariance matrices); so, it is reasonable to say that a model fits (taken in a different meaning) the data if the dependent variables observed (manifest) or approximated (latent), are "close" to the variables predicted by the model, that is to say, if the specific statistical objective of this method is achieved (Hair *et al.* 2017).

3.3.2. *Revision of the structural model*

Figure 3.16 makes it possible to recall the structural model developed in Chapter 1, studied in this section.

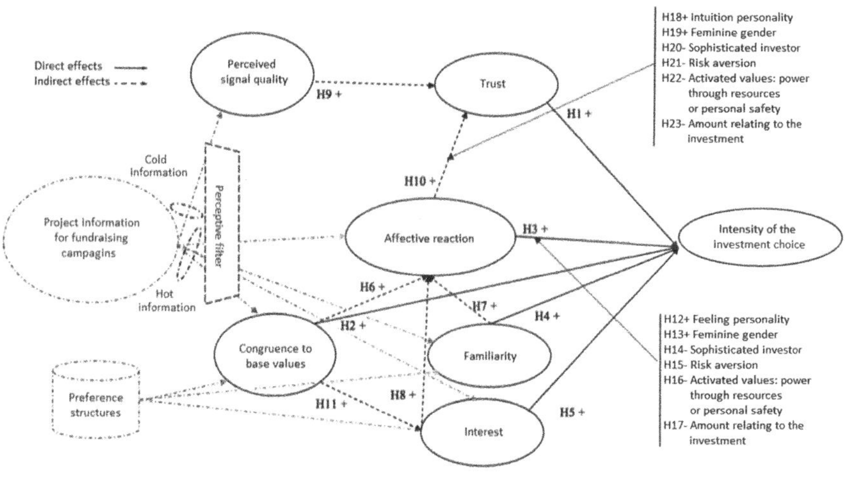

Figure 3.16. *Structural model and hypotheses*

3.3.3. *Structural model*

In this section, we evaluate the structural model for the first time with the "Cash Case" (section 3.3.3.1), which was estimated according to the choices of the initial allocation of the cash amount of €200 by the subjects of the experiment. Then, we evaluate the model in a comparative way with the "Percent Case" (section 3.3.3.2) estimated according to the relative allocation choices (expressed as a percentage of the subject's total wealth).

The "Cash Case" is the main case because the average individual investor does not invest all of their assets in an equity crowdfunding type of investment.

This is why the "Cash Case" serves as a benchmark for the comparative analysis of the "Percent Case", which is a borderline case (the investor invests all of their assets) whose purpose is to judge the effect of the amount allocated on the coefficients and R^2 of the model, beyond the moderating effects H17 and H23 studied in section 3.2.

3.3.3.1. *"Cash Case"*

The evaluation of the explanatory structural model in the "Cash Case" follows the six-step procedure described in Figure 3.17.

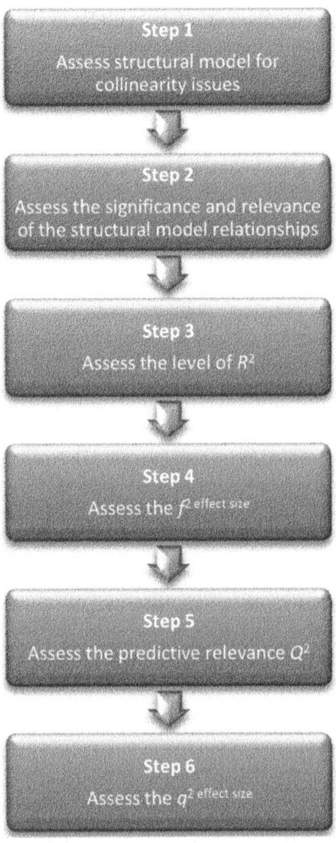

Figure 3.17. *Structural model evaluation procedure of Hair* et al. *(2017)*

Thus, we will successively evaluate: the collinearities (section 3.3.3.1.1), the significance and relevance of coefficients (section 3.3.3.1.2), the R^2 (section 3.3.3.1.3), the predictive contribution of the variables or Cohen's f^2 (section 3.3.3.1.4), the predictive quality Q^2 (section 3.3.3.1.5) and the q^2 effect size.

Before going into the details of the evaluation of the structural model, Figure 3.18 represents the reader with a global and graphical view of the result of the PLS-SEM algorithm in the "Cash Case". The R^2 of the explained variables (endogenous) can be identified within the oval-shaped latent variables (e.g. 0.479 for the Intensity of Investment Choice variable). The path coefficients of the structural model link the latent variables (e.g. 0.140 between the Trust and Intensity of Investment Choice variables). The coefficients of the measurement model (loadings and weights) are located on the arrows connecting the constructs and indicators (e.g. 0.677 for the loading connecting the indicator BIENV1 to the Trust construct).

3.3.3.1.1. Collinearity assessment

As in the procedure for evaluating the quality of the formative constructs, a preliminary step to check the collinearities is necessary in order to estimate the path coefficients, as these result from multiple linear regressions (or a single one in the case of the Interest variable, but this one is not concerned) of the endogenous variables of the model on their explanatory antecedents.

The possible multicollinearities of the antecedent constructs are checked by the VIF indicator, which has already been presented.

The VIF collinearity indicators shown in Table 3.40 are below the threshold of 5, which indicates that the collinearities between predictors of endogenous variables are not problematic.

	Trust	Intensity of Investment Choice	Interest	Affective Reaction
Trust		1.626		
Congruence to Base Values		1.115	1	1.114
Familiarity		1.549		1.524
Interest		2.412		1.558
Perceived Signal Quality	1.222			
Affective Reaction	1.222	1.768		

Table 3.40. *VIF collinearity indicators of the explanatory constructs of the structural model*

3.3.3.1.2. Significance and relevance of the coefficients

The significance of the coefficients of the structural model are checked first; only the significant coefficients are subjected to a relevance analysis.

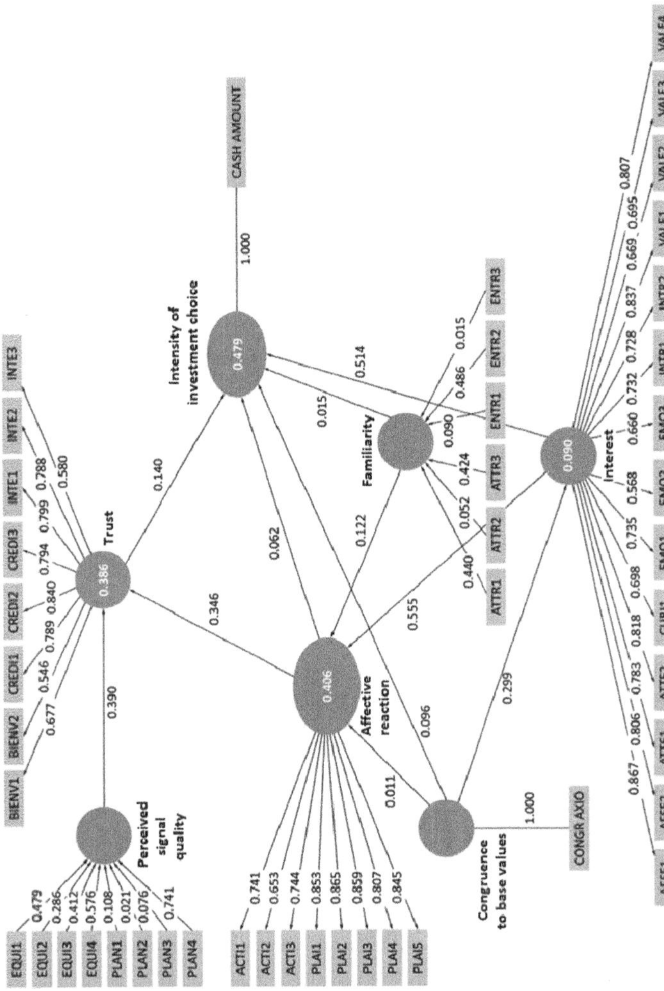

Figure 3.18. R^2 *of the endogenous latent variables and estimated coefficients of the measurement and structural models ("cash case")*

Significance of coefficients

The coefficients between constructs resulting from the PLS algorithm are standardized, included in the interval [– 1, +1]; a value close to 1 (– 1, respectively) signifies a strong positive (negative, respectively) relationship. A value close to 0 indicates a weak relationship; the significance depends on the standard error, calculated by the bootstrapping procedure. We systematically applied a bootstrapping setting of 5,000 samples and set the significance level at 5%, as is customary in management science. The results can be read using the *p*-value. If this is less than 5%, then the coefficient is significant, which amounts to rejecting the null hypothesis.

Table 3.41 aggregates the results of the tests of the 11 hypotheses in the structural model; the far-right column indicates the accepted ("Yes" value) and rejected ("No" value) hypotheses. In addition, two graphical representations (Figures 3.19 and 3.20) make it possible to visualize the impact of the rejected hypotheses on the original structural model.

Hypo-thesis	Relationship	Original sample (O)	Sample mean (M)	Standard deviation (STDEV)	T statistics (|O/STDEV|)	*p*-values	Significance ($p < 0.05$)
H1	Trust → Intensity of Investment Choice	0.140	0.141	0.048	2.907	0.004	Yes
H2	Congruence to Base Values → Intensity of Investment Choice	0.096	0.093	0.047	2.032	0.042	Yes
H3	Affective Reaction → Intensity of Investment Choice	0.062	0.057	0.053	1.164	0.245	No
H4	Familiarity → Intensity of Investment Choice	0.015	0.032	0.057	0.263	0.793	No
H5	Interest → Intensity of Investment Choice	0.514	0.509	0.058	8.853	0.000	Yes
H6	Congruence to Base Values → Affective Reaction	0.011	0.010	0.051	0.222	0.824	No
H7	Familiarity → Affective Reaction	0.122	0.131	0.062	1.965	0.049	Yes
H8	Interest → Affective Reaction	0.555	0.554	0.054	10.355	0.000	Yes
H9	Perceived Signal Quality → Trust	0.390	0.412	0.055	7.115	0.000	Yes
H10	Affective Reaction → Trust	0.346	0.339	0.047	7.302	0.000	Yes
H11	Congruence to Base Values → Interest	0.299	0.300	0.052	5.804	0.000	Yes

Table 3.41. *Accepted and rejected hypotheses*

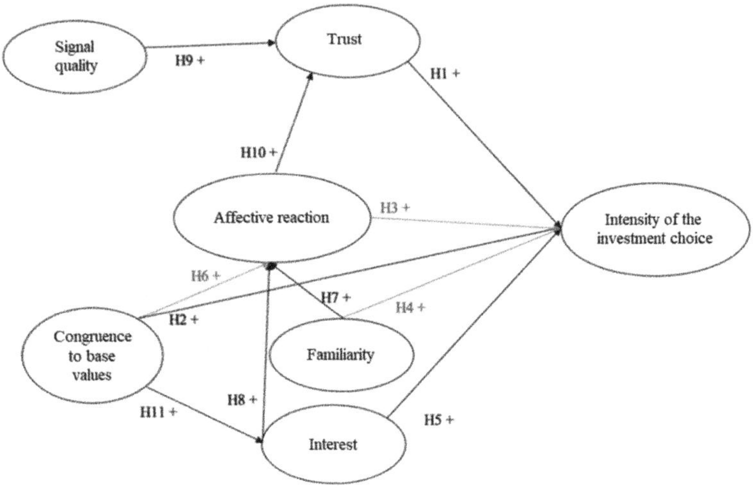

Figure 3.19. *Graphic representation of rejected hypotheses (in red). For a color version of this figure, see www.iste.co.uk/goglin/investment2.zip*

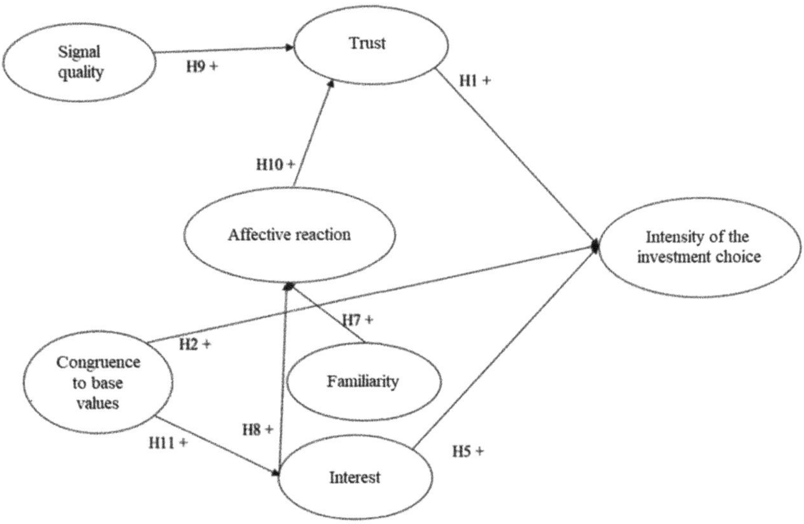

Figure 3.20. *Graphic representation of validated hypotheses*

Relevance of coefficients

The analysis of the relevance of the coefficients consists of studying the relative weights of the coefficients. A coefficient can be significant, but of low weight relative to another significant coefficient explaining the same construct. The interpretation of the coefficients is identical to that which prevails for linear regression analyses: the change of one unit of the exogenous (explanatory) construct modifies the endogenous (explained) construct in proportion to the size of the coefficient connecting them (everything otherwise equal). In addition, the total effects, taking into account all the indirect effects (via the mediating variables), must be analyzed, as they are the ones that really indicate the importance of an explanatory variable (Hair *et al.* 2017).

Table 3.42 shows the coefficients of the direct paths between the constructs of the structural model. We see that:

– the Intensity of Investment Choice is first determined by Interest, then by Trust, Congruence to Base Values, Affective Reaction and finally, marginally, by Familiarity. Interest overdetermines the Intensity of Investment Choice given the relative weights of the coefficients;

– Trust is first determined by the Perceived Signal Quality and then by the Affective Reaction, this double determination is fairly balanced;

– Interest is determined by Congruence to Base Values;

– the Affective Reaction is first determined by Interest, then significantly weaker, by Familiarity and finally, marginally, by Congruence to Base Values.

	Trust	Congruence to Base Values	Familiarity	Intensity of Investment Choice	Interest	Perceived Signal Quality	Affective Reaction
Trust				0.140			
Congruence to Base Values				0.096	0.299		0.011
Familiarity				0.015			0.122
Intensity of Investment Choice							
Interest				0.514			0.555
Perceived Signal Quality	0.390						
Affective Reaction	0.346			0.062			

Table 3.42. *Coefficients of direct paths*

Tables 3.43 and 3.44 are intermediate tables, necessary for the calculation of the total effects presented in Table 3.45.

	Specific indirect effects
Congruence to Base Values → Affective Reaction → Trust	0.004
Familiarity → Affective Reaction → Trust	0.042
Congruence to Base Values → Interest → Affective Reaction → Trust	0.057
Perceived Signal Quality → Trust → Intensity of Investment Choice	0.055
Congruence to Base Values → Affective Reaction → Trust → Intensity of Investment Choice	0.001
Familiarity → Affective Reaction → Trust → Intensity of Investment Choice	0.006
Congruence to Base Values → Interest → Affective Reaction → Trust → Intensity of Investment Choice	0.008
Congruence to Base Values → Interest → Intensity of Investment Choice	0.154
Congruence to Base Values → Affective Reaction → Intensity of Investment Choice	0.001
Familiarity → Affective Reaction → Intensity of Investment Choice	0.008
Congruence to Base Values → Interest → Affective Reaction → Intensity of Investment Choice	0.010
Congruence to Base Values → Interest → Affective Reaction	0.166

Table 3.43. *Specific indirect effects*

	Trust	Intensity of Investment Choice	Affective Reaction
Congruence to Base Values	0.061	0.173	0.166
Familiarity	0.042	0.013	
Interest	0.192	0.061	
Perceived Signal Quality		0.055	
Affective Reaction		0.048	

Table 3.44. *Cumulative indirect effects*

	Trust	Intensity of Investment Choice	Interest	Affective Reaction
Trust		0.140		
Congruence to Base Values	0.061	0.269	0.299	0.177
Familiarity	0.042	0.028		0.122
Interest	0.192	0.575		0.555
Perceived Signal Quality	0.390	0.055		
Affective Reaction	0.346	0.110		

Table 3.45. *Total effects*

Let us consider the case of the total effect of the Congruence to Base values variable on the Intensity of Investment Choice. This total coefficient is 0.269 (Table 3.45). Let us find this result.

This total effect breaks down into direct effects (Table 3.42) and cumulative indirect effects (Table 3.44). We have:

> Total effect = Direct effects + Cumulative indirect effects = 0.096 + 0.173 = 0.269

with Cumulative indirect effects = $\sum Specific\ indirect\ effects$ (Table 3.43).

We have:

> Cumulative indirect effects = 0.173 = $\sum Specific\ indirect\ effects$ = sum of the coefficients in Table 3.43 associated with the paths linking the Congruence to Base Values variable to the Intensity of Investment Choice variable, regardless of the number of intermediate mediating variables = 0.001 + 0.008 + 0.154 + 0.01

Specific indirect effects:

> Congruence to base values → Affective reaction → Trust → Intensity of investment choice = 0.001
>
> Congruence to base values → Interest → Affective reaction → Trust → Intensity of investment choice = 0.008
>
> Congruence to base values → Interest → Intensity of investment choice = 0.154
>
> Congruence to base values → Interest → Affective reaction → Intensity of investment choice = 0.01

The analysis of the total effects (Table 3.45) shows that:

– the two main exogenous determinants of the Intensity of Investment Choice are Interest and Congruence to Base Values, with Trust in third position, and the impact of the Perceived Signal Quality clearly down;

– the Affective Reaction is overdetermined by Interest, then to a lesser extent by Congruence to base values and finally, by Familiarity;

– Trust is first determined by the Perceived Signal Quality, then by Affective Reaction and finally by Interest. The relative balance of weights associated with the Perceived Signal Quality and the Affective Reaction make Trust a mixed variable, both affective and cognitive.

Moreover, among the exogenous variables (Perceived Signal Quality, Congruence to Base Values and Familiarity), Congruence to Base Values clearly dominates the other two variables by the importance of its effect on the Intensity of Investment Choice.

The impact of indirect paths substantially affects the effects of the following variables:

– Congruence to Base Values:

- impact on Trust through the mediation of Interest and Affective Reaction,

- strong impact on the Intensity of Investment Choice, mainly via the Interest variable,

- strong impact on Affective Reaction via the Interest variable;

– Familiarity: an effect of Familiarity on Trust via Interest appears (not significant at the 5% threshold);

– Interest: an effect of Interest on Trust via Affective Reaction appears;

– Affective Reaction: the effect of Interest on the Intensity of Investment Choice is substantially increased by its indirect effect on Trust.

3.3.3.1.3. R^2 evaluation

The determination coefficient[10] or R^2 is a measure of the predictive quality of the model equal to the square of the linear correlation coefficient of the real and

10 It will not be based on the *R*2 adjusted by the size of the sample and by the number of exogenous constructs, as this coefficient is only useful for comparing models, the objective being to identify the most frugal model, that is to say that which offers the best explanatory power/number of exogenous constructs.

predicted variables. The R^2 represents the combined effect of the exogenous latent variables, that is to say, the amount of variance of the endogenous construct explained by all the exogenous constructs that are related to it. This coefficient is between 0 and 1; values close to 1 indicate a high level of predictive accuracy.

According to Hair *et al.* (2011), R^2 can be interpreted as follows: substantial effect for a coefficient of 0.75, moderate effect for a coefficient of 0.50 and weak effect for a coefficient of 0.25.

In our case, Table 3.46 shows that the percentage of variance explained by the exogenous variables is moderate for the Intensity of Investment Choice variable, intermediate, between low and moderate, for the Trust and Affective Reaction variables and finally, low for the Interest variable.

	***R* square**
Trust	0.386
Intensity of Investment Choice	0.479
Interest	0.09
Affective Reaction	0.406

Table 3.46. *Determination coefficients of explained variables*

3.3.3.1.4. Evaluation of the predictive contribution of variables: Cohenf's f^2

The effect size or Cohen's (2009) f^2 is a complementary indicator when evaluating the predictive contribution of endogenous variables antecedents. When a variable is explained by several antecedents, it is interesting to measure, for each of them, the importance of its contribution in the explanation of the endogenous variable. In practice, it involves removing the evaluated exogenous variable, calculating the R^2 without the variable, and appreciating the relative variation of the determination coefficient by the following formula:

$$f^2 = \frac{R^2_{included} - R^2_{excluded}}{1 - R^2_{included}}$$

In this expression, $R^2_{included}$ includes the evaluated exogenous variable, while $R^2_{excluded}$ excludes it.

According to Cohen, an f^2 of 0.02, 0.15 and 0.35 indicates a weak, medium and large effect, respectively.

In our case, Table 3.47 presents Cohen's f^2 of the exogenous variables of the model. We see that:

– trust has a weak effect on the Intensity of Investment Choice;

– congruence to Base Values has an intermediate level effect, between low and medium, on the Interest variable, but has no effect on the Intensity of Investment Choice and the Affective Reaction;

– Familiarity has no effect on the Intensity of Investment Choice and Affective Reaction;

– Interest has an intermediate level effect, between medium and high, on the Intensity of Investment Choice and a large effect on the Affective Reaction;

– the Perceived Signal Quality has an intermediate and significant effect on Trust;

– Affective Reaction has an intermediate effect on Trust, but has no effect on the Intensity of Investment Choice.

	Trust	Intensity of Investment Choice	Interest	Affective Reaction
Trust		0.023		
Congruence to Base Values		0.016	0.098	0
Familiarity		0		0.016
Interest		0.21		0.333
Perceived Signal Quality	0.202			
Affective Reaction	0.159	0.004		

Table 3.47. *Effect size: Cohen's f^2*

3.3.3.1.5. Assessment of the predictive quality: Q^2

The Q^2 of Geisser (1974) and Stone (1974) is an indicator for measuring the predictive quality of endogenous reflective or single-item variables, complementary to R^2. Its objective is to measure the quality of prediction of the values observed by the modeling of an endogenous variable. The procedure for calculating this measurement is as follows.

Let us suppose an endogenous reflective variable Y for which one wishes to evaluate the predictive quality of the modeling. We set a distance D (a natural number) such that N is not a multiple of D, with N the size of the sample (D is generally between 5 and 10). This figure D is used in a so-called blindfolding procedure to remove the values of the indicators of the endogenous variable, according to a systematic pattern. For example, if D = 5, then one indicator out of 5 is deleted, i.e. 20% of the information. The deleted indicators are then treated as missing data and are, for example, initialized to the average value of the remaining indicators (mean value replacement processing).

The score ($\hat{Y}$) of the endogenous variable is then calculated, not directly from its measurement model, but from the scores of its antecedents and the coefficients (path coefficients) linking it to its antecedents, calculated by the PLS algorithm during a run that takes into account the $\frac{100}{D}$% deleted data. Finally, the deleted indicators are estimated from the $\hat{Y}$ and the loadings (the indicator is expressed as the product of the score and the loading). The prediction error depends on the difference between the real known value of the deleted indicator and the value of the indicator estimated according to the procedure described. The indicator Q^2 aggregates the prediction errors calculated for the endogenous variable according to a number of iterations (depending on D), which makes it possible for all the indicators to be deleted. This procedure is said to be of the cross-validated type, since the validation of the predictive quality is based on the structural model and the measurement model (Hair *et al.* 2017).

In practice, a strictly positive Q^2 suggests the good predictive quality of the model for a given endogenous construct, while a zero or negative value indicates insufficient predictive quality.

In our case, the distance 7 (intermediate between 5 and 10) is chosen for the blindfolding procedure because the number of observations, 400, is not a multiple of 7.

The results of predictive relevance of the endogenous reflective variables of the model are shown in Table 3.48. We note that the Q^2 are all strictly positive, which provides support for the predictive quality of the model.

	SSO	SSE	Q^2 (= 1 – SSE/SSO)
Trust	161,600.000	131,280.535	0.188
Congruence to Base Values	20,200.000	20,200.000	
Familiarity	121,200.000	121,200.000	
Intensity of Investment Choice	20,200.000	11,067.427	0.452
Interest	282,800.000	269,858.328	0.046
Perceived Signal Quality	161,600.000	161,600.000	
Affective Reaction	161,600.000	123,197.457	0.238

Table 3.48. *Predictive relevance: Q^2*

3.3.3.1.6. Evaluation of the size effect: q^2

The size effect q^2 is to Q^2 what f^2 is to R^2; the approach and the calculation formula are identical. The q^2 makes it possible to measure the relative predictive contribution (within the meaning of Q^2) of one of the explanatory variables of an endogenous construct. This indicator is calculated as follows:

$$q^2 = \frac{Q^2_{included} - Q^2_{excluded}}{1 - Q^2_{included}}$$

In this expression, $Q^2_{included}$ includes the explanatory variable evaluated, while $Q^2_{excluded}$ excludes it.

In our case, Table 3.49 provides the indicators q^2 calculated for all antecedents (column) of endogenous variables (row). Table 3.49 is an interim table for calculating $Q^2_{excluded}$. For example: 0.129 = Q^2 (Trust) with Perceived Signal Quality being excluded.

In Table 3.50, the relative predictive contribution of the Perceived Signal Quality explanatory variable on the Trust endogenous construct is calculated as follows:

$$0.07 \approx \frac{0.188 - 0.129}{1 - 0.188}$$

with $Q^2_{included}$ = 0.188 taken from Table 3.48.

	Trust	Intensity of Investment Choice	Interest	Affective Reaction
Trust		0.447		
Congruence to Base Values		0.449	0	0.238
Familiarity		0.453		0.232
Interest		0.344		0.12
Perceived Signal Quality	0.129			
Affective Reaction	0.138	0.452		

Table 3.49. *Indicator Q^2 of the calculated endogenous variables by excluding a causal variable*

	Trust	Intensity of Investment Choice	Interest	Affective Reaction
Trust		0.01		
Congruence to Base Values		0.01	0.05	0.00
Familiarity		0.00		0.01
Interest		0.20		0.15
Perceived Signal Quality	0.07			
Affective Reaction	0.06	0.00		

Table 3.50. *Indicator q^2 of endogenous variables*

The practical interpretation of q^2 is as follows: a value of 0.02, 0.15 and 0.35 indicates a weak, medium and large effect, respectively.

Also, Table 3.50 shows that:

– the predictive quality of the Trust variable on the Intensity of Investment Choice and Affective Reaction variables is practically zero;

– the predictive quality of Congruence to Base Values on the Interest variable is low; it is zero on the Intensity of Investment Choice and Affective Reaction variables;

– the predictive quality of the Familiarity variable on the Intensity of Investment Choice and Affective Reaction variables is zero, practically zero (respectively);

– the predictive quality of the Interest variable on the Intensity of Investment Choice variable is intermediate, between medium and high, and medium for the Affective Reaction;

– the predictive quality of the Perceived Signal Quality on the Trust variable is intermediate, between low and medium;

– the predictive quality of the Affective Reaction on Trust is intermediate, between low and medium, and is null on the Intensity of Investment Choice variable.

3.3.3.2. *Percent Case*

Let us remember that the "Percent Case" is a borderline case in which the investor invests all of their assets in equity crowdfunding. The objective is to judge the effect of the amount allocated on the coefficients and R^2 of the model in comparison with the "Cash Case". Two effects are particularly interesting, because they correspond to the moderation hypotheses H17 and H23 and are studied in section 3.3.5.2.

We now evaluate the structural model estimated with the "Percent Case" data according to the procedure previously seen, but partially focusing on the evaluation of the collinearities (section 3.3.3.2.1), then on the comparison of the total effects (section 3.3.3.2.2), R^2 (section 3.3.3.2.3) and Cohen's f^2 (section 3.3.3.2.4) with the model estimated from the "Cash Case" data.

First, Figure 3.21 represents a global and graphical view of the result of the PLS-SEM algorithm in the "Percent Case".

3.3.3.2.1. Collinearity assessment

The VIF collinearity indicators shown in Table 3.51 are below the threshold of 5, which indicates that the collinearities between predictors of endogenous variables are not problematic.

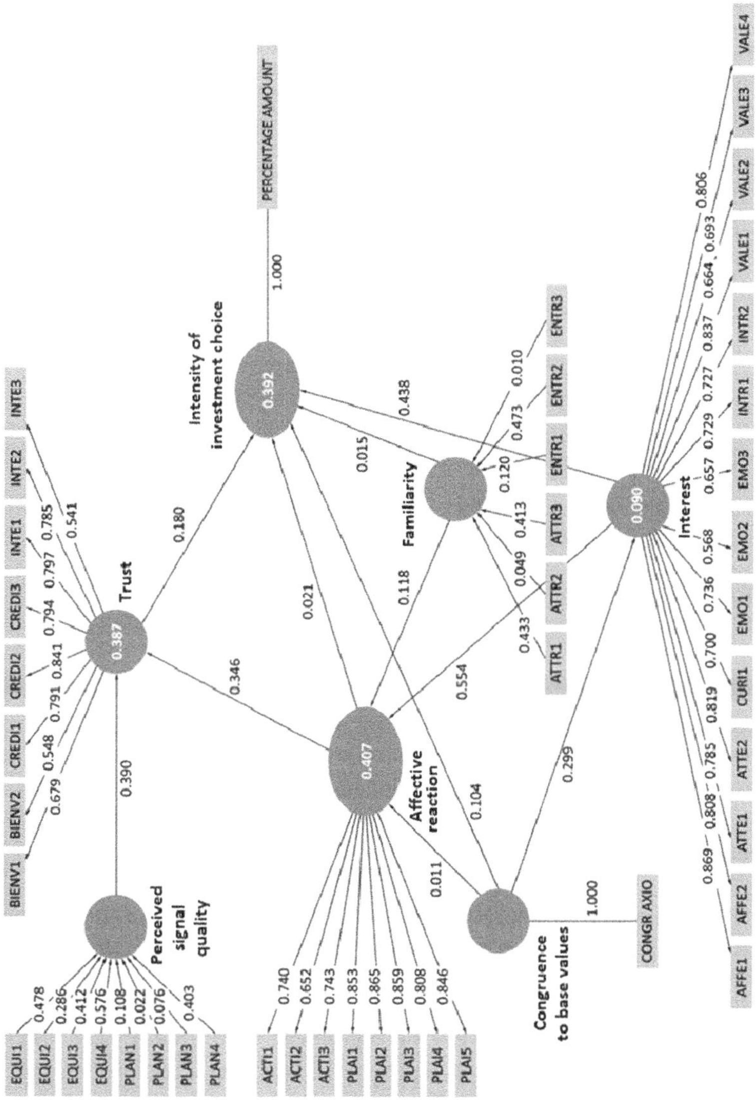

Figure 3.21. *R^2 of the endogenous latent variables and estimated coefficients of the measurement and structural models ("Percent Case")*

	Trust	Intensity of Investment Choice	Interest	Affective Reaction
Trust		1.629		
Congruence to Base Values		1.115	1	1.113
Familiarity		1.548		1.524
Interest		2.422		1.559
Perceived Signal Quality	1.222			
Affective Reaction	1.222	1.77		

Table 3.51. *VIF collinearity indicators of the explanatory constructs of the structural model*

3.3.3.2.2. Relevance of coefficients: comparative analysis

Table 3.52 compares the total effects (resulting from the addition of cumulative direct and indirect effects) of the model variables.

It will be compared to Table 3.45. The most salient comparative results are as follows.

Compared to the "Cash Case", the effect of Trust on the Intensity of Investment Choice increases in impact (going from 0.14 to 0.18); it is the same with the Perceived Signal Quality variable (going from 0.055 to 0.07), while, conversely, the weight of the coefficients of the two antecedents Interest and Affective Reaction (moderation hypothesis H17-) reduces, going from 0.575 to 0.485 and from 0.110 to 0.083, respectively.

This translates into a less affective (reduction of the effect of Interest and Affective Reaction) and more rational decision (increase of the effect of the Perceived Signal Quality variable).

These results seem logical, and can be interpreted as a greater need for the rationalization of the investment choice, due to how much is at stake: investing all of one's savings or €200 does not represent the same risk.

	Trust	Intensity of Investment Choice	Interest	Affective Reaction
Trust		0.180		
Congruence to Base Values	0.062	0.254	0.300	0.179
Familiarity	0.041	0.025		0.118
Interest	0.193	0.485		0.558
Perceived Signal Quality	0.390	0.070		
Affective Reaction	0.346	0.083		

Table 3.52. *Total effects ("Percent Case")*

3.3.3.2.3. R^2 evaluation

Compared to the estimated model of the "Cash Case" (see Table 3.46), the estimated model of the "Percent Case" sees a reduction of the explanatory power of exogenous variables on the Intensity of Investment Choice construct, which goes from 47.9% to 39.2%, i.e. a relative reduction of 18% (see Table 3.53). The other determination coefficients are stable.

This result is normal as the model is specified for describing the reality of the investment in equity crowdfunding. However, the "Cash Case" is precisely calibrated to ecologically replicate (apart from the removal of social interactions) real conditions, in particular, for the perception of the invested amount. It is probable that the other psychological variables would have appeared if we had specified the "Percent Case", if it existed (as it is an implausible borderline case).

	***R* square**
Trust	0.387
Intensity of Investment Choice	0.392
Interest	0.09
Affective Reaction	0.407

Table 3.53. *Determination coefficient of explained variables ("Percent Case")*

3.3.3.2.4. Evaluation of the predictive contribution of variables (Cohenf's f^2)

Compared to the estimated model in the "Cash Case" (see Table 3.47), we can note a considerable reduction in the impact of the effect of the Interest variable on the Intensity of Investment Choice, which goes from 0.21 down to 0.13 (a relative reduction of 38%) and is no more than a medium effect (see Table 3.54). This result converges with that of section 3.3.3.2.2 on the total effects compared.

	Trust	Intensity of Investment Choice	Interest	Affective Reaction
Trust		0.033		
Congruence to Base Values		0.017	0.099	0
Familiarity		0		0.015
Interest		0.131		0.337
Perceived Signal Quality	0.203			
Affective Reaction	0.16	0		

Table 3.54. *Effect size: Cohen's^2 ("Percent Case")*

3.3.4. *Mediators*

A mediation appears when a variable (called a mediating variable) comes between two constructs linked in a causal relationship. In this case, a change in the exogenous variable leads to a change in the mediating variable, which in turn leads to a change in the endogenous variable. In order to determine nature of the mediations at play, we have applied the procedure recommended by Zhao *et al.* (2010) whose procedure is described in Figure 3.22. This decision tree describes the steps for identifying the nature of a mediation in the case of a simple mediation of two constructs Y_1 and Y_3 (linked by the path coefficient p_3; let us note that $Y_1 \rightarrow Y_3 = p_3$) by a tertiary construct Y_2 (such as: $Y_1 \rightarrow Y_2 = p_1$ and $Y_2 \rightarrow Y_3 = p_2$).

Five cases are possible: (1) there is no effect, neither direct nor indirect; (2) only the direct effect is significant; (3) only the indirect effect is significant (4) there is a competitive mediation (opposite effect) with the direct effect and (5) there is a complementary mediation (same sign effect) with the direct effect. The analysis concerns the significance of the path coefficients p_3 of the direct path and that of the indirect path: $p_1.p_2$.

For the more complex mediation cases which appear in our model, Hair and his colleagues recommended considering all the simultaneous mediations before applying the procedure by Zhao *et al.* (2010), completed by a test of the total effect of the indirect mediations (total indirect effects). Let us also note that it is necessary to carry out a sampling procedure by bootstrapping in order to construct a frequency distribution and then derive the necessary standard error from it in the Student's *t*-test of significance of coefficients. According to the standard recommendations of Hair *et al.* (2017), we have set a bootstrapping of 5,000 samples in the SmartPLS software and have obtained, for a calibrated model in the "Cash Case", the direct, specific, total indirect and total coefficients, with their significance shown in Table 3.55.

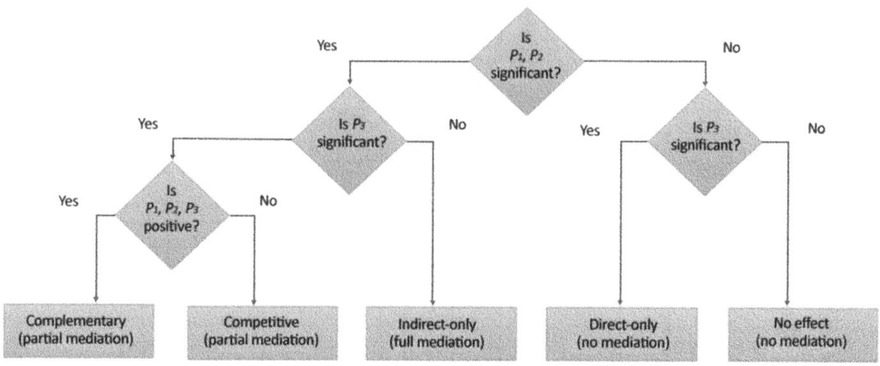

Figure 3.22. *Mediation analysis procedure, adapted from Zhao* et al. *(2010)*

In sections 3.3.4.1 to 3.3.4.5 below, we have compared the results obtained concerning the nature of the mediations of the structural model; we used the data from Table 3.55 and the procedure by Zhao *et al.* (2010).

For Figures 3.23–3.27:

– the causality paths of specific indirect effects and total indirect effects, which only accept one specific indirect effect, are indicated in italics;

– for better readability, each mediation path has a distinct color;

– the significant coefficients at the threshold of 5% are green, others are red.

Path coefficients

	Original sample (O)	Sample mean (M)	Standard deviation (STDEV)	T statistics (|O/STDEV|)	*p*-values	Significance ($p < 0.05$)
Trust → Intensity of Investment Choice	0.140	0.141	0.048	2.907	0.004	Yes
Congruence to Base Values → Intensity of Investment Choice	0.096	0.093	0.047	2.032	0.042	Yes
Congruence to Base Values → Interest	0.299	0.300	0.052	5.804	0.000	Yes
Congruence to Base Values → Affective Reaction	0.011	0.010	0.051	0.222	0.824	No
Familiarity → Intensity of Investment Choice	0.015	0.032	0.057	0.263	0.793	No
Familiarity → Affective Reaction	0.122	0.131	0.062	1.965	0.049	Yes
Interest → Intensity of Investment Choice	0.514	0.509	0.058	8.853	0.000	Yes
Interest → Affective Reaction	0.555	0.554	0.054	10.355	0.000	Yes
Perceived Signal Quality → Trust	0.390	0.412	0.055	7.115	0.000	Yes
Affective Reaction → Trust	0.346	0.339	0.047	7.302	0.000	Yes
Affective Reaction → Intensity of Investment Choice	0.062	0.057	0.053	1.164	0.245	No

Total indirect effects

	Original sample (O)	Sample mean (M)	Standard deviation (STDEV)	T statistics (|O/STDEV|)	p-values	Significance ($p < 0.05$)
Congruence to Base Values → Trust	0.061	0.06	0.022	2.757	0.006	Yes
Congruence to Base Values → Intensity of Investment Choice	0.173	0.171	0.033	5.205	0	Yes
Congruence to Base Values → Affective Reaction	0.166	0.166	0.034	4.875	0	Yes
Familiarity → Trust	0.042	0.044	0.022	1.897	0.058	No
Familiarity → Intensity of Investment Choice	0.013	0.014	0.01	1.321	0.186	No
Interest → Trust	0.192	0.188	0.034	5.686	0	Yes
Interest → Intensity of Investment Choice	0.061	0.058	0.03	2.057	0.04	Yes
Perceived signal quality → Intensity of Investment Choice	0.055	0.058	0.022	2.524	0.012	Yes
Affective reaction → Intensity of Investment Choice	0.048	0.048	0.017	2.77	0.006	Yes

Specific indirect effects						
	Original sample (O)	Sample mean (M)	Standard deviation (STDEV)	T statistics (|O/STDEV|)	*p*-values	Significance ($p < 0.05$)
Congruence to Base Values → Affective Reaction → Trust	0.004	0.003	0.017	0.224	0.823	No
Familiarity → Affective Reaction → Trust	0.042	0.044	0.022	1.897	0.058	No
Congruence to Base Values → Interest → Affective Reaction → Trust	0.057	0.057	0.015	3.86	0	Yes
Perceived Signal Quality → Trust → Intensity of Investment Choice	0.055	0.058	0.022	2.524	0.012	Yes
Congruence to Base Values → Affective Reaction → Trust → Intensity of Investment Choice	0.001	0	0.003	0.211	0.833	No
Familiarity → Affective Reaction → Trust → Intensity of Investment Choice	0.006	0.006	0.004	1.483	0.138	No
Congruence to Base Values → Interest → Affective Reaction → Trust → Intensity of Investment Choice	0.008	0.008	0.003	2.404	0.016	Yes
Congruence to Base Values → Interest → Intensity of Investment Choice	0.154	0.153	0.032	4.777	0	Yes
Congruence to Base Values → Affective Reaction → Intensity of Investment Choice	0.001	0	0.004	0.175	0.861	No
Familiarity → Affective Reaction → Intensity of Investment Choice	0.008	0.008	0.008	0.89	0.374	No
Congruence to Base Values → Interest → Affective Reaction → Intensity of Investment Choice	0.01	0.009	0.009	1.114	0.265	No
Congruence to Base Values → Interest → Affective Reaction	0.166	0.166	0.034	4.875	0	Yes

Total effects

	Original sample (O)	Sample mean (M)	Standard deviation (STDEV)	T statistics (|O/STDEV|)	*p*-values	Significance ($p < 0.05$)
Trust → Intensity of Investment Choice	0.14	0.141	0.048	2.907	0.004	Yes
Congruence to Base Values → Trust	0.061	0.06	0.022	2.757	0.006	Yes
Congruence to Base Values → Intensity of Investment Choice	0.269	0.263	0.053	5.051	0	Yes
Congruence to Base Values → Interest	0.299	0.3	0.052	5.804	0	Yes
Congruence to Base Values → Affective Reaction	0.177	0.176	0.057	3.089	0.002	Yes
Familiarity → Trust	0.042	0.044	0.022	1.897	0.058	No
Familiarity → Intensity of Investment Choice	0.028	0.046	0.056	0.511	0.609	No
Familiarity → Affective Reaction	0.122	0.131	0.062	1.965	0.049	Yes
Interest → Trust	0.192	0.188	0.034	5.686	0	Yes
Interest → Intensity of Investment Choice	0.575	0.567	0.049	11.72	0	Yes
Interest → Affective Reaction	0.555	0.554	0.054	10.355	0	Yes
Perceived Signal Quality → Trust	0.39	0.412	0.055	7.115	0	Yes
Perceived Signal Quality → Intensity of Investment Choice	0.055	0.058	0.022	2.524	0.012	Yes
Affective Reaction → Trust	0.346	0.339	0.047	7.302	0	Yes
Affective Reaction → Intensity of Investment Choice	0.11	0.104	0.052	2.11	0.035	Yes

Table 3.55. *Direct, specific, total indirect and total coefficients with their significance*

3.3.4.1. *Effects of Affective Reaction on the Intensity of Investment Choice*

Figure 3.23 shows an indirect-only mediation: Affective Reaction has a significant and positive indirect effect on the Intensity of Investment Choice by the mediation of the Trust variable.

Affective reaction → Trust → Intensity of Investment Choice 0.048

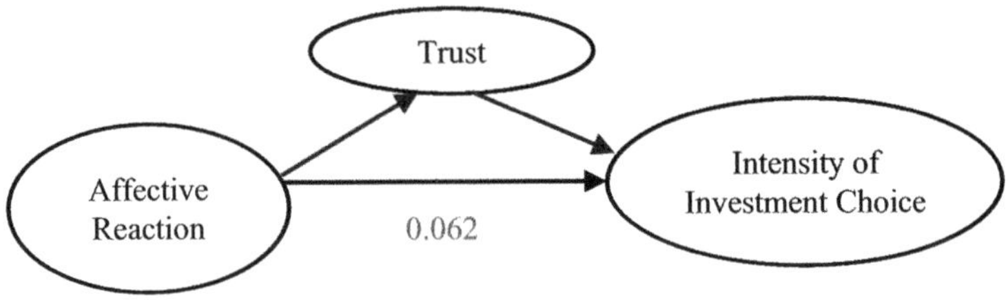

Figure 3.23. *Effect of Affective Reaction on the Intensity of Investment Choice. For a color version of this figure, see www.iste.co.uk/goglin/investment2.zip*

3.3.4.2. *Effects of the Congruence to Base Values on Affective Reaction*

Figure 3.24 shows an indirect-only mediation: the Congruence to Base Value has a significant and positive indirect effect on the Affective Reaction by the mediation of the Interest variable.

Congruence to Base Values → Interest → Affective Reaction 0.166

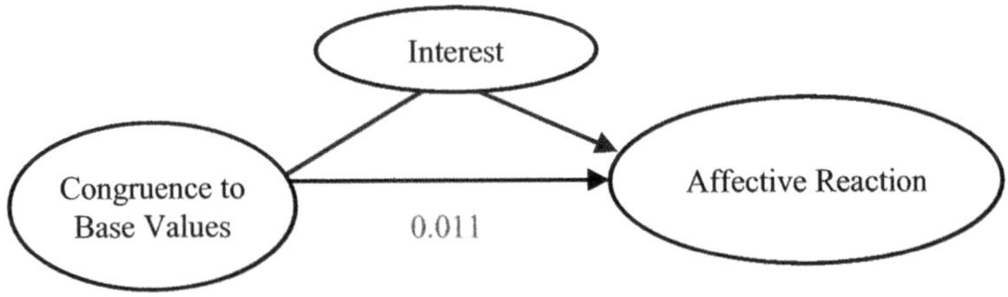

Figure 3.24. *Effect of Congruence to Base Values on Affective Reaction. For a color version of this figure, see www.iste.co.uk/goglin/investment2.zip*

3.3.4.3. *Effects of Interest on the Intensity of Investment Choice*

Figure 3.25 shows a complementary partial mediation: the total indirect effect of Interest on the Intensity of Investment Choice is significant with a coefficient of 0.061, but it remains relatively marginal.

This effect is divided into specific indirect effects. As they are not directly calculated by the SmartPLS, we calculated them manually (see Table 3.56). To do this, we extracted the path coefficient samples from the direct paths from bootstrapping and imported them into Excel, in order to deduce path coefficients of the specific indirect paths (per product) and calculate the standard deviation to deduce the empirical t-value as well as the p-value.

	Original sample (O)	Sample mean (M)	Standard error (STERR)	T statistics (|O/STERR|)	p-values
Interest → Intensity of Investment Choice via Affective Reaction	0.034	0.033	0.029	1.176	0.240
Interest → Intensity of Investment Choice via Affective Reaction and Trust	0.027	0.026	0.010	2.689	0.007

Table 3.56. *Indirect specific effect of Interest on the Intensity of Investment Choice*

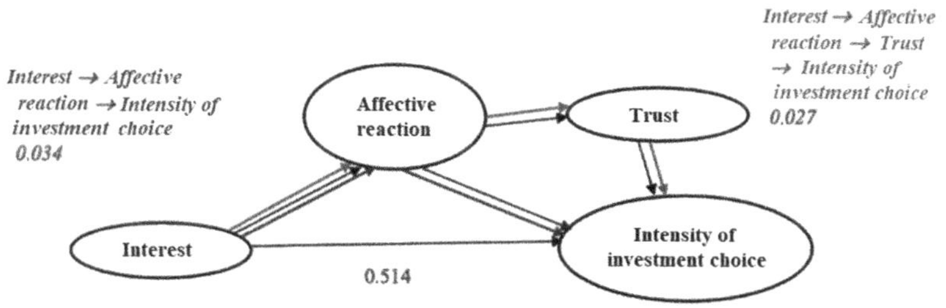

Figure 3.25. *Effects of Interest on the Intensity of Investment Choice. For a color version of this figure, see www.iste.co.uk/goglin/investment2.zip*

3.3.4.4. *Effects of Familiarity on the Intensity of Investment Choice*

Figure 3.26 shows that Familiarity has no effect on the Intensity of Investment Choice (no effect, no mediation): Familiarity has no significant direct or indirect effect on the Intensity of Investment Choice.

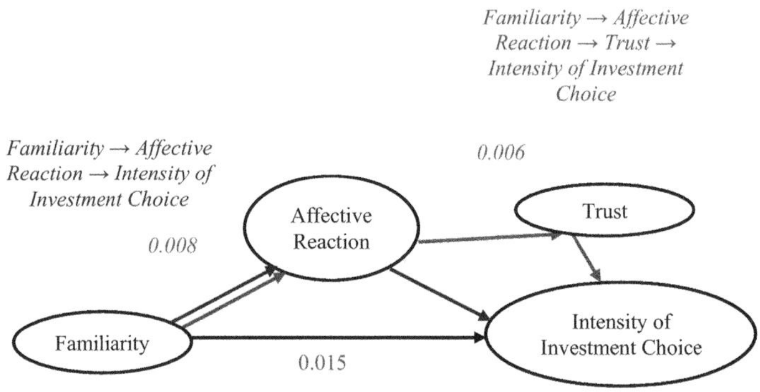

Figure 3.26. *Effects of Familiarity on the Intensity of Investment Choice. For a color version of this figure, see www.iste.co.uk/goglin/investment2.zip*

3.3.4.5. *Effects of Congruence to Base Values on the Intensity of Investment Choice*

Figure 3.27 shows a complementary partial mediation: the Congruence to Base Values has significant direct effect, as well as a positive and significant total indirect effect on the Intensity of Investment Choice, due to the effect of the double mediation of Interest, Affective Reaction and Trust on one hand, and the mediation of the Interest variable on the other; these two mediations are complementary. Mediation by Interest explains the gist of the effect of Congruence to Base Values on the Intensity of Investment Choice.

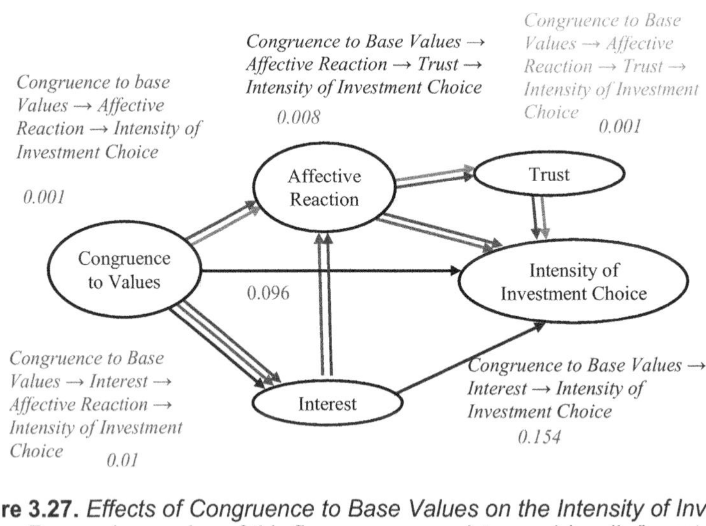

Figure 3.27. *Effects of Congruence to Base Values on the Intensity of Investment Choice. For a color version of this figure, see www.iste.co.uk/goglin/investment2.zip*

3.3.5. *Invariance and moderators*

3.3.5.1. *Invariance*

When we proceed to multigroup analysis, it is necessary to ensure measurement invariance. When this is established, the model estimation differences between the groups are real and do not result in the difference in the interpretation of latent constructs between groups; the validity of the analysis is thus ensured.

Henseler *et al.* (2016) proposed a procedure aiming to establish measurement invariance for the PLS-SEM approach. This procedure, measurement invariance of composite models or MICOM, is divided into three steps:

– step 1 establishes the configuration invariance. This is verified if the constructs are identical (i.e. have the same indicators) and if the processing and setting of algorithms are similar for the analyzed groups. Also, this evaluation is based on inspecting the model's configuration and settings, but does not involve a statistical test. In our research, configuration invariance is established from the outset for what concerns constructs; the settings are also always identical with one exception, which we will point out below (see H14 and H20). Steps 2 and 3 of the MICOM procedure are carried out using SmartPLS 3 software;

– step 2 is carried out only if step 1 establishes the configuration invariance. This second step establishes, through a statistical test, the compositional invariance, which guarantees that the scores of the constructs are not appreciably different between the groups, despite possibly different coefficients. For this step, SmartPLS 3 uses a non-parametric permutation test to determine if a composite has a correlation of its score significantly lower than unity for the compared groups A and B. Otherwise, the composite does not differ significantly between the two groups and the compositional invariance is established;

– step 3 is carried out only if step 2 establishes the compositional invariance. This third step establishes, through a statistical test, the invariance of the means and variations of the constructs. When compositional invariance and, consequently, configuration invariance are established, then partial invariance is established. Furthermore, when the invariance of the means and variances is established, the total invariance is established. Only partial invariance is necessary to ensure the validity of the intergroup comparison of the parameters of the structural model.

Also, below, we will study the compositional invariance of the pairs of classes (Male/Female), (Sensing/Intuition) and (Thinking/Feeling) in order to ensure that the multigroup analyses, relating to hypotheses H12, H13, H18 and H19, carried out in section 3.3.5.2.1 are valid. It should be noted that we cannot apply the MICOM measure to the groups underlying hypotheses H14, H17, H20 and H23; we will come back to this later.

In our case, as shown in Tables 3.57, 3.58 and 3.59, the correlations, between the pairs of classes concerned, of the scores of constructs are not significantly lower than unity (at the 5% threshold).

The partial measurement invariance is therefore established.

	Original correlation	Correlation permutation mean	5.0%	Permutation *p*-values	Significance ($p < 0.05$)
Trust	0.994	0.998	0.994	0.063	No
Congruence to Base Values	1.000	1.000	1.000		
Familiarity	0.979	0.890	0.766	0.971	No
Intensity of Investment Choice	1.000	1.000	1.000	0.999	No
Interest	1.000	0.999	0.998	0.908	No
Perceived Signal Quality	0.763	0.860	0.737	0.083	No
Affective Reaction	0.999	0.999	0.997	0.507	No

Table 3.57. *Compositional invariance of the female/male classes*

	Original correlation	Correlation permutation jean	5.0%	Permutation *p*-values	Significance ($p < 0.05$)
Trust	0.999	0.998	0.995	0.606	No
Congruence to Base Values	1.000	1.000	1.000		
Familiarity	0.929	0.899	0.788	0.654	No
Intensity of Investment Choice	1.000	1.000	1.000	1.000	No
Interest	0.999	0.999	0.998	0.190	No
Perceived Signal Quality	0.865	0.869	0.759	0.419	No
Affective Reaction	1.000	0.999	0.997	0.580	No

Table 3.58. *Compositional invariance of sensing/intuition classes*

	Original correlation	Correlation permutation mean	5.0%	Permutation p-values	Significance ($p < 0.05$)
Trust	0.996	0.998	0.995	0.077	No
Congruence to Base Values	1.000	1.000	1.000		
Familiarity	0.883	0.908	0.811	0.270	No
Intensity of Investment Choice	1.000	1.000	1.000	0.096	No
Interest	0.999	0.999	0.999	0.537	No
Perceived Signal Quality	0.880	0.861	0.741	0.566	No
Affective Reaction	0.999	0.999	0.997	0.315	No

Table 3.59. *Compositional invariance of thinking/feeling classes*

3.3.5.2. *Moderators*

Moderation describes a situation in which the relationship binding two variables (or constructs) is not constant but depends on a third variable (or construct) called a moderating variable. This moderating variable changes the strength, or even the direction, of the relationship.

For example, for a sample subgroup (characterized by "Female" gender), a positive causal relationship may be stronger than in the complementary subgroup (characterized by "Male" gender). Also, moderation is a form of data heterogeneity. Moderation can only concern a specific relationship of a model, or concern the whole model. In our case, we have specified a list of moderating hypotheses (H12–H23) concerning only a specific causal relationship of the structural model

Moderators can take two forms: class moderators and continuous moderators. Class moderators depend on a categorical variable, often dichotomous; we will analyze these moderating variables in section 3.3.5.2.1 using a multigroup analysis or the Student's t-test. Continuous moderators are continuous variables, or continuous constructs, measured by scales with sufficient points; we will analyze these moderating variables in section 3.3.5.2.2 using the two-stage approach.

Table 3.60 presents the distribution of the moderators of the explanatory model by type (class moderation or continuous moderation) and associates one or more hypotheses with each moderator, as well as the method used for its analysis.

Moderations					
Class moderation			**Continuous moderation**		
Moderator	**Hypotheses**	**Method**	**Moderator**	**Hypotheses**	**Method**
Relative amount	H17, H23	Student's *t*-test	Risk aversion	H15, H21	Two-stage approach
Personality (feeling/thinking)	H12	Multigroup analysis	Power	H16, H22	Two-stage approach
Personality (intuition/sensing)	H18	Multigroup analysis			
Gender (male/female)	H13, H19	Multigroup analysis			
Sophistication (Iae_oui/Iae_non)	H14, H20	Student's *t*-test			

Table 3.60. *Classification of moderators, hypotheses and methods of the explanatory model*

3.3.5.2.1. Class moderators

The analysis of categorical-type class moderators (dichotomous in our case) consists of comparing the coefficients of the structural model estimated at each subgroup (of the classes in our case). The significance of the difference of a given parameter, corresponding to a moderation hypothesis, is then studied.

To do this, we use two methods: multigroup analysis or Student's *t*-test. We used multigroup analysis when possible, as it is consistent with the PLS approach by being non-parametric (therefore, it does not make assumptions about the data distributions), and is less prone to type 1 errors than parametric testing (Sarstedt *et al.* 2011); moreover, it is carried out using SmartPLS 3 software. The method used for multigroup analyzes is the PLS multi-group analysis (PLS-MGA, Henseler 2010), which compares all the bootstrapping occurrences of the estimated parameter studied for group 1 with all the bootstrapping occurrences of the same parameter for the group 2. The principle is as follows: the number of positive differences in the quantity $(p^i_{group2} - p^j_{group1})$ between occurrences of the parameter for the two groups with i and $j \in$ [1, number of observations of the bootstrapping]), divided by the total number of comparisons (=[number of observations of bootstrapping]^2) indicates the probability that the parameter of group 2 is greater than the parameter of group 1 in the population.

The Student's *t*-test on the comparison of means is conventionally preceded by an *F*-test on the equality of standard errors between the two classes:

$$F = (\text{Standard error group 1})^2/(\text{Standard error group 2})^2$$

The result of this first test determines the formula used for the variance of the difference in means. The significance of the parameter difference between the compared groups is then determined by comparing the empirical t, equal to the ratio of the difference of the means, to the variance of the difference of the means, to the theoretical t at the 5% threshold, i.e. 1.95. Finally, if empirical > 1.95, then the parameter difference is significant.

H17 and H23: moderation by the size of the invested amount

Testing hypotheses H17 and H23 consists of comparing the same group of subjects twice, the latter having invested in cash (€200) and then a percentage of their assets. Therefore, the two groups are not subgroups of the sample defined by the modalities of a moderating variable; we could not perform multigroup analyses and invariance tests relying on SmartPLS.

Also, in order to test the two hypotheses H17 and H23 of moderation by the size of the invested amount, we successively used the F and then the Student's *t*-test, in an Excel sheet[11], the standard errors come from a sampling procedure of 5,000-sample *bootstrapping*. The consequent size of the sample allows for a Student's *t*-test, as it is robust to the normality hypothesis, thanks to the central limit theorem, for sufficiently large samples. It should be noted that we are not doing a paired-sample *t*-test because the parameter samples from the two groups being compared come from a random sampling procedure, so they are not paired.

HYPOTHESIS 17 (H17).– *Moderation of H3. The larger the amount invested with respect to the investor's wealth, the more the positive relationship between the Affective Reaction and the Intensity of Investment Choice is mitigated.*

Hypothesis H17 is rejected because the difference in the parameters is not significant (Table 3.61).

11 The calculation of the test of difference of the standard errors is as follows: =SI(INVERSE.LOI.F.DROITE(0,05;Taille_Groupe1-1;Taille_Groupe2-1)>=MAX(Erreur_Standard_Groupe1^2;Erreur_Standard_Groupe2^2)/MIN(Erreur_Standard_Groupe1^2;Erreur_Standard_Groupe2^2); "Equivalentes"; "Différentes") The calculation of the test of difference of the parameters is as follows: =SI(ABS(Différence)>1,95; "Différence significative"; "Différence non significative") with Différence =SI(Erreurs_Standards_Différentes; (Param_Groupe1-Param_Groupe2)/(RACINE(((Taille_Groupe1-1)^2/(Taille_Groupe1+Taille_Groupe2-2))*Erreur_Standard_Groupe1^2+((Taille_Groupe1-1)^2/(Taille_Groupe1+Taille_Groupe2-2))*Erreur_Standard_Groupe2^2)*RACINE((1/Taille_Groupe1)+(1/Taille_Groupe2)));(Param_Groupe1-Param_Groupe2)/RACINE(Erreur_Standard_Groupe1^2+Erreur_Standard_Groupe2^2)).

	Sample size	Parameter	Standard error	
Group 1	5,000	0.062	0.053	
Group 2	5,000	0.0210	0.059	
	Difference test Standard errors		1.239	Different
	Parameter difference test		0.517	Insignificant difference

Table 3.61. *F- and student's t-tests for H17*

HYPOTHESIS 23 (H23).– *Moderation of H10. The larger the amount invested, with respect to the investor's wealth, the more the positive relationship between the Affective Reaction and Trust is mitigated.*

Hypothesis H23 is rejected because the difference in the parameters is not significant (Table 3.62).

	Sample size	Parameter	Standard error	
Group 1	5,000	0.3456	0.048	
Group 2	5,000	0.3459	0.047	
	Difference test Standard errors		1.043	Equivalent
	Parameter difference test		– 0.004	Insignificant difference

Table 3.62. *F- and student's t-tests for H23*

H12: moderation by personality (feeling/thinking)

HYPOTHESIS 12 (H12).– *Moderation of H3. The more the investor has a Feeling-oriented personality type (Thinking/Feeling axis) in the MBTI model, the more the positive relationship between the Affective Reaction and the Intensity of Investment Choice will be reinforced.*

Table 3.63, result of the PLS-MGA procedure (configured with a bootstrapping of 5,000 samples), shows no significant difference between the two groups at the 5% threshold for the parameter Affective Reaction → Intensity of Investment Choice.

Hypothesis H12 is rejected. It should, however, be noted that the effect of Affective Reaction on Trust is significantly different between the two groups; the effect is greater for the Feeling than for the Thinking subjects, which is quite intuitive.

Feeling (F)/thinking (T)	Path coefficients original (F)	Path coefficients original (T)	Path coefficients mean (F)	Path coefficients mean (T)	STDEV (F)	STDEV (T)	t-values (F)	t-values (T)
Trust → Intensity of Investment Choice	0.109	0.154	0.110	0.156	0.076	0.064	1.437	2.408
Congruence to Base Values → Intensity of Investment Choice	0.069	0.113	0.063	0.109	0.068	0.068	1.016	1.665
Congruence to Base Values → Interest	0.287	0.317	0.289	0.318	0.076	0.071	3.776	4.449
Congruence to Base Values → Affective Reaction	0.041	– 0.025	0.038	– 0.031	0.068	0.070	0.600	0.361
Familiarity → Intensity of Investment Choice	– 0.062	0.125	– 0.025	0.143	0.094	0.073	0.667	1.709
Familiarity → Affective Reaction	0.097	0.161	0.114	0.176	0.091	0.091	1.067	1.774
Interest → Intensity of Investment Choice	0.567	0.461	0.552	0.458	0.095	0.076	5.963	6.088
Interest → Affective Reaction	0.603	0.510	0.598	0.511	0.071	0.079	8.438	6.480
Perceived Signal Quality → Trust	0.337	0.503	0.373	0.539	0.077	0.056	4.396	8.991
Affective Reaction → Trust	0.432	0.241	0.419	0.232	0.063	0.062	6.797	3.850
Affective Reaction → Intensity of Investment Choice	0.071	0.046	0.067	0.038	0.080	0.068	0.888	0.686

Feeling (F)/thinking (T)	*p*-values (F)	*p*-values (T)	2.5% (F)	97.5% (F)	2.5% (T)	97.5% (T)	Path coefficients-diff (|F – T|)	*p*-values (F vs. T)	Significance ($p < 0.05$)
Trust → Intensity of Investment Choice	0.151	0.016	– 0.040	0.257	0.024	0.277	0.045	0.674	FALSE
Congruence to Base Values → Intensity of Investment Choice	0.310	0.096	– 0.061	0.200	– 0.011	0.251	0.045	0.676	FALSE
Congruence to Base Values → Interest	0.000	0.000	0.128	0.429	0.164	0.443	0.030	0.612	FALSE
Congruence to Base Values → Affective Reaction	0.548	0.718	– 0.089	0.177	– 0.154	0.120	0.066	0.250	FALSE
Familiarity → Intensity of Investment Choice	0.505	0.087	– 0.278	0.083	– 0.038	0.249	0.187	0.942	FALSE
Familiarity → Affective Reaction	0.286	0.076	– 0.118	0.247	– 0.052	0.313	0.064	0.689	FALSE
Interest → Intensity of Investment Choice	0.000	0.000	0.396	0.769	0.310	0.606	0.105	0.193	FALSE
Interest → Affective Reaction	0.000	0.000	0.467	0.745	0.355	0.667	0.093	0.192	FALSE
Perceived Signal Quality → Trust	0.000	0.000	0.176	0.457	0.333	0.578	0.166	0.958	FALSE
Affective Reaction → Trust	0.000	0.000	0.309	0.552	0.130	0.375	0.191	0.019	TRUE
Affective Reaction → Intensity of Investment Choice	0.375	0.493	– 0.088	0.223	– 0.075	0.194	0.025	0.403	FALSE

Table 3.63. *Results of the multigroup analysis of moderation by personality (feeling/thinking)*

Intuition (I)/sensing (S)	Path coefficients original (I)	Path coefficients original (S)	Path coefficients mean (I)	Path coefficients mean (S)	STDEV (I)	STDEV (S)	*t*-values (I)	*t*-values (S)
Trust → Intensity of Investment Choice	0.078	0.220	0.080	0.216	0.072	0.064	1.081	3.459
Congruence to Base Values → Intensity of Investment Choice	0.087	0.100	0.082	0.096	0.069	0.063	1.262	1.577
Congruence to Base Values → Interest	0.380	0.223	0.381	0.223	0.064	0.082	5.896	2.724
Congruence to Base Values → Affective Reaction	−0.116	0.113	−0.121	0.111	0.056	0.076	2.067	1.479
Familiarity → Intensity of Investment Choice	0.023	0.023	0.040	0.050	0.094	0.080	0.242	0.281
Familiarity → Affective Reaction	0.146	0.129	0.166	0.146	0.080	0.098	1.824	1.316
Interest → Intensity of Investment Choice	0.556	0.470	0.554	0.464	0.090	0.079	6.184	5.928
Interest → Affective Reaction	0.610	0.509	0.605	0.506	0.064	0.085	9.465	5.989
Perceived Signal Quality → Trust	0.411	0.402	0.446	0.443	0.070	0.072	5.876	5.574
Affective Reaction → Trust	0.361	0.341	0.351	0.330	0.058	0.070	6.194	4.845
Affective Reaction → Intensity of Investment Choice	0.032	0.078	0.025	0.072	0.064	0.077	0.502	1.007

Intuition (I)/ sensing (S)	*p*-values (I)	*p*-values (S)	2.5% (I)	97.5% (I)	2.5% (S)	97.5% (S)	Path coefficients diff (|I – S|)	*p*-values (I vs. S)	Significance ($p < 0.05$)
Trust → Intensity of Investment Choice	0.280	0.001	– 0.061	0.223	0.097	0.349	0.143	0.930	FALSE
Congruence to Base Values → Intensity of Investment Choice	0.207	0.115	– 0.040	0.227	– 0.024	0.225	0.013	0.555	FALSE
Congruence to Base Values → Interest	0.000	0.006	0.246	0.499	0.058	0.376	0.157	0.065	FALSE
Congruence to Base Values → Affective Reaction	0.039	0.139	– 0.220	– 0.000	– 0.033	0.263	0.229	0.992	FALSE
Familiarity → Intensity of Investment Choice	0.808	0.779	– 0.187	0.181	– 0.176	0.155	0.000	0.498	FALSE
Familiarity → Affective Reaction	0.068	0.188	– 0.034	0.281	– 0.096	0.292	0.017	0.448	FALSE
Interest → Intensity of Investment Choice	0.000	0.000	0.372	0.726	0.326	0.638	0.085	0.234	FALSE
Interest → Affective Reaction	0.000	0.000	0.484	0.733	0.341	0.672	0.101	0.172	FALSE
Perceived Signal Quality → Trust	0.000	0.000	0.226	0.516	0.211	0.501	0.009	0.464	FALSE
Affective Reaction → Trust	0.000	0.000	0.254	0.481	0.217	0.492	0.020	0.411	FALSE
Affective Reaction → Intensity of Investment Choice	0.616	0.314	– 0.089	0.160	– 0.070	0.234	0.045	0.674	FALSE

Table 3.64. *Results of the multigroup analysis of moderation by personality (intuition/sensing)*

Male (H)/female (F)	Path coefficients original (F)	Path coefficients original (H)	Path coefficients mean (F)	Path coefficients mean (H)	STDEV (F)	STDEV (H)	*t*-values (F)	*t*-values (H)
Trust → Intensity of Investment Choice	0.154	0.130	0.147	0.136	0.070	0.071	2.195	1.836
Congruence to Base Values → Intensity of Investment Choice	0.065	0.131	0.056	0.131	0.059	0.075	1.105	1.756
Congruence to Base Values → Interest	0.291	0.334	0.292	0.332	0.066	0.084	4.385	3.976
Congruence to Base Values → Affective Reaction	0.011	0.036	0.008	0.034	0.064	0.078	0.172	0.454
Familiarity → Intensity of Investment Choice	−0.009	0.101	0.018	0.124	0.077	0.082	0.117	1.227
Familiarity → Affective Reaction	0.082	0.185	0.095	0.195	0.081	0.109	1.003	1.705
Interest → Intensity of Investment Choice	0.500	0.515	0.496	0.509	0.075	0.084	6.688	6.146
Interest → Affective Reaction	0.595	0.479	0.591	0.483	0.065	0.089	9.137	5.354
Perceived Signal Quality → Trust	0.382	0.462	0.412	0.513	0.075	0.059	5.079	7.894
Affective Reaction → Trust	0.393	0.316	0.382	0.312	0.061	0.062	6.424	5.104
Affective Reaction → Intensity of Investment Choice	0.062	0.063	0.058	0.054	0.068	0.073	0.905	0.868

Male (H)/female (F)	*p*-values (F)	*p*-values (H)	2.5% (F)	97.5% (F)	2.5% (H)	97.5% (H)	Path coefficients-diff (|H – F|)	*p*-values (H vs. F)	Significance ($p < 0.05$)
Trust → Intensity of Investment Choice	0.028	0.066	0.013	0.286	– 0.008	0.266	0.023	0.595	FALSE
Congruence to Base Values → Intensity of Investment Choice	0.269	0.079	– 0.048	0.182	– 0.008	0.285	0.066	0.245	FALSE
Congruence to Base Values → Interest	0.000	0.000	0.158	0.416	0.154	0.486	0.042	0.340	FALSE
Congruence to Base Values → Affective Reaction	0.864	0.650	– 0.114	0.138	– 0.116	0.188	0.025	0.405	FALSE
Familiarity → Intensity of Investment Choice	0.907	0.220	– 0.214	0.112	– 0.103	0.233	0.110	0.164	FALSE
Familiarity → Affective Reaction	0.316	0.088	– 0.099	0.223	– 0.107	0.356	0.104	0.211	FALSE
Interest → Intensity of Investment Choice	0.000	0.000	0.365	0.657	0.346	0.672	0.016	0.436	FALSE
Interest → Affective Reaction	0.000	0.000	0.467	0.725	0.282	0.634	0.116	0.854	FALSE
Perceived Signal Quality → Trust	0.000	0.000	0.211	0.503	0.272	0.527	0.080	0.204	FALSE
Affective Reaction → Trust	0.000	0.000	0.277	0.514	0.196	0.439	0.077	0.813	FALSE
Affective Reaction → Intensity of Investment Choice	0.366	0.385	– 0.073	0.193	– 0.068	0.220	0.002	0.495	FALSE

Table 3.65. *Results of the multigroup analysis of moderation by gender (male/female)*

H18: moderation by personality (intuition/sensing)

HYPOTHESIS 18 (H18).– *Moderation of H10. The more the investor has an Intuition-oriented personality type (Sensing/Intuition axis) in the MBTI model, the more the positive relationship between the Affective Reaction and Trust is amplified.*

Table 3.64, which shows the results of the PLS-MGA procedure (configured with a bootstrapping of 5,000 samples), shows no significant difference at the 5% threshold between the two groups. Hypothesis H18 is rejected.

H13 and H19: moderation by gender (male/female)

HYPOTHESIS 13 (H13).– *Moderation of H3. If the investor is female, the positive relationship between Affective Response and Intensity of Investment Choice is strengthened.*

HYPOTHESIS 19 (H19).– *Moderation of H10. If the investor is female, the positive relationship between Affective Response and Trust is strengthened.*

Table 3.65, which shows the results of the PLS-MGA procedure (configured with a *bootstrapping* of 5,000 samples), shows no significant difference at the 5% threshold between the two groups. *Hypotheses H13 and H19 are rejected.*

H14 and H20: moderation by sophistication (Iae_oui/Iae_non)

HYPOTHESIS 14 (H14).– *Moderation of H3. If the investor is sophisticated, the positive relationship between the Affective Reaction and the Intensity of Investment Choice is mitigated.*

HYPOTHESIS 20 (H20).– *Moderation of H10. If the investor is sophisticated, the positive relationship between the Affective Reaction and Trust is mitigated.*

These two hypotheses could not be tested by the PLS-MGA procedure, as the mean path coefficients of the Iae_oui group were not available, whatever the setting. Also, in order to test these two hypotheses, we successively used *F*- and Student's *t*-tests

It should be noted that for the preparation of the results that follow (H14 and H20), the bootstrapping procedure used to find the standard error was set with 5,000 samples for the Iae_non group, but with only 250 samples for the Iae_oui group. This limiting choice of parameterization considerably reduces the validity of these results because the condition of configuration invariance is not respected.

Hypothesis H14 is rejected because the difference in the parameters is not significant (Table 3.66).

	Sample size	Parameter	Standard error	
Group 1	5,000	– 0.0600	0.104	
Group 2	250	0.0990	0.053	
	Difference test Standard errors		3.850	Different
	Parameter difference test		– 0.305	Insignificant difference

Table 3.66. *F- and student's t-tests for H14*

Hypothesis H20 is rejected because the difference in the parameters is not significant (Table 3.67).

	Sample size	Parameter	Standard error	
Group 1	5,000	0.3530	0.079	
Group 2	250	0.3610	0.047	
	Difference test Standard errors		2.825	Different
	Parameter difference test		– 0.019	Insignificant difference

Table 3.67. *F- and student's t-tests for H20*

3.3.5.2.2. Continuous moderators

Concerning continuous moderators, we will model the interaction term (product of the explanatory exogenous variable and of the moderator) by the two-stage approach of Chin *et al.* (2003). This approach has the advantage of being applied to exogenous constructs and to formative moderators as well as reflective constructs; moreover, its use is recommended by Hair *et al.* (2017) when the objective is to reveal the significance of the moderating effect, which is our case.

Let us consider the case of a causal relationship between an explanatory exogenous variable (X) and an explained endogenous variable (Y); this relationship is moderated by a moderating variable (M). As its name suggests, the two-stage approach breaks down into two stages:

– *stage 1*: the structural model is enriched with the moderating variable (M), which is only integrated as an additional explanatory variable of the explained variable (Y). The PLS algorithm is run to calculate the scores of the three latent variables: Score(X), Score(Y) and Score(M);

– *stage 2*: the previous structural model is enriched by an interaction term (product of X and M) defined as a single-item construct, whose item equals the product of Score(X) and Score(M). All other latent variables in the model are transformed into single-item constructs, the latter being equal to the score of the concerned construct calculated in step 1.

This model is estimated by the PLS algorithm; the p_{xm} parameter of the interaction term (XM) expresses the magnitude of the moderator interaction effect on the p_{xy} parameter connecting X to Y. More precisely, it is interpreted as the variation of p_{xy} when M increases or decreases by one standard deviation. Let us add that p_{xy} is not the parameter measuring the strength of the relationship linking X to Y in the original model, i.e. without the presence of the moderating variable. The coefficient p_{xy} represents the strength of the relationship linking X to Y when the moderating variable is present but equal to its mean (zero when this has already been normalized).

Finally, it is useful to complete the analysis by the f^2 (see predictive contribution in section 3.3.3.1.4) in order to measure the importance of the contribution of the interaction effect to R^2, i.e. the explanation of the endogenous variable Y. Note that the interpretation of f^2 for the interaction term differs from the general case, according to Kenny (2015); the values 0.005, 0.001 and 0.025 correspond to weak, medium and large effects, respectively.

H15 and H21: moderation through Risk Aversion (continuous moderator)

HYPOTHESIS 15 (H15).– *Moderation* of *H3.*

In order to test the moderating effect of Risk Aversion, the two Risk Aversion indicators are combined into a single indicator (AVER) resulting from the sum of the items proposed by Nivoix (2008) (variables AVER1 and AVER2 in the questionnaire). The AVER variable can take values ranging from 2 to 10.

As indicated previously, we adopt the two-stage approach, with the objective being to verify the significance of the moderating effect (interaction term). Figure 3.28 represents the enriched SEM of the moderating variable with its joint effects: the direct effect on the explained variable and the effect of the interaction term.

Table 3.68 shows the significance results of the moderating effect for a bootstrapping of 5,000 samples.

The moderating effect of Risk Aversion on the relationship between Affective Reaction and Intensity of Investment Choice (i.e. the effect of the interaction term "Affective Reaction * Risk Aversion") is not significant.

There is also no significant direct effect of the Risk Aversion variable on the Intensity of Investment Choice.

Hypothesis H15 is rejected.

	Original sample (O)	Sample mean (M)	Standard deviation (STDEV)	T statistics (|O/STDEV|)	*p*-values	Significance ($p < 0.05$)
Risk Aversion → Intensity of Investment Choice	0.034	0.035	0.044	0.771	0.441	No
Affective Reaction → Intensity of Investment Choice	0.058	0.053	0.053	1.077	0.281	No
Affective Reaction * Risk Aversion → Intensity of Investment Choice	0.007	0.006	0.040	0.164	0.870	No

Table 3.68. *Significance of the effect of the interaction term "Affective Reaction * Risk Aversion" on the Intensity of Investment Choice*

HYPOTHESIS 21 (H21).– Moderation of *H10. The more risk-averse the investor, the more the positive relationship between the Affective Reaction and Trust is mitigated.*

Table 3.69 shows the significance results of the moderating effect for a *bootstrapping* of 5,000 samples.

The moderating effect of Risk Aversion on the relationship between Affective Reaction and Trust (i.e. the effect of the interaction term "Affective Reaction * Risk Aversion") is significant. There is no significant direct effect of the Risk Aversion variable on Trust.

Hypothesis H21 is confirmed.

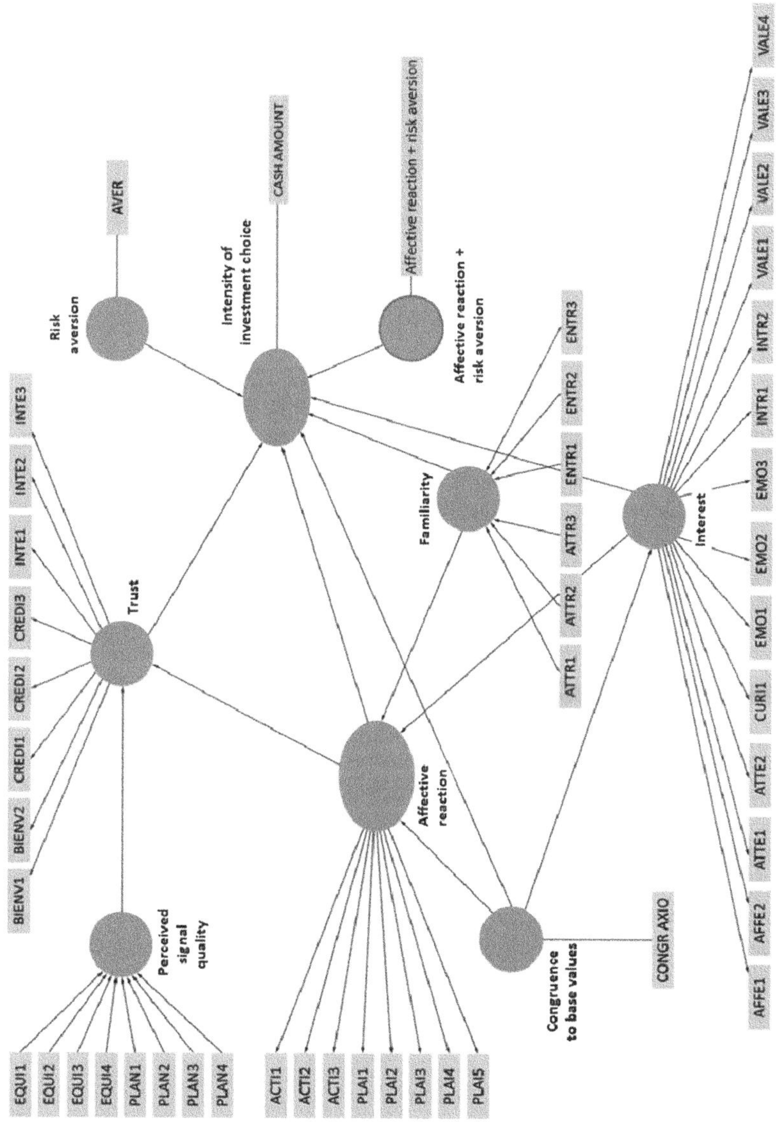

Figure 3.28. *Structural model integrating the Risk Aversion moderator*

	Original sample (O)	Simple mean (M)	Standard deviation (STDEV)	T statistics (|O/STDEV|)	*p*-values	Significance ($p < 0.05$)
Risk Aversion → Trust	– 0.076	– 0.074	0.048	1.571	0.116	No
Affective Reaction → Trust	0.347	0.341	0.047	7.427	0.000	No
Affective Reaction * Risk Aversion → Trust	0.100	0.097	0.048	2.104	0.035	Yes

Table 3.69. *Significance of the effect of the interaction term "Affective Reaction * Risk Aversion" on Trust*

Figure 3.29 makes it possible to interpret this result.

The relationship between Affective Reaction and Trust is 0.347 for an average value of the Risk Aversion variable. When the Risk Aversion variable increases by one standard deviation, this relationship = 0.347 + 0.1 = 0.447. When the Risk Aversion variable decreases by one standard deviation, this relationship = 0.347 – 0.1 = 0.247.

The direction of the effect is the reverse of that expected.

The greater the Risk Aversion, the stronger the relationship between Affective Reaction and Trust. This surprising result may find an explanation in the composition of the sample. This was made up of more female participants, who are both more risk averse than men, but also more prone to making decisions on emotional grounds. In other words, the initial moderation hypothesis H21 may be gender dependent.

Evaluation of the predictive value of the interaction term "Affective Reaction * Risk Aversion" on Trust by measuring the effect size of f^2 = 0.016, which corresponds to an intermediate effect between average effect and large effect but closer to the large effect range.

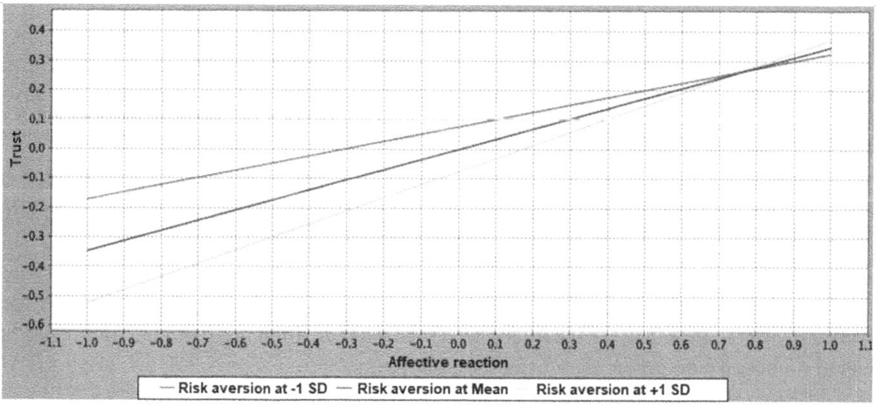

Figure 3.29. *Effect of the interaction term "Affective Reaction *. For a color version of this figure, see www.iste.co.uk/goglin/investment2.zip*

H16 and H22: moderation by the activated Power value (initially binary moderator transformed into continuous moderator)

The moderator defined by the Power base value, separating the group that chose this value as the first value from the complementary group, was too small, with seven observations, to carry out a multigroup analysis using the PLS-MGA method.

Nevertheless, it seems interesting to us to present the model estimated for these two groups, because if we cannot statistically evaluate the significance of the differences, the differences in parameters are significant, which offers avenues for future research.

Figure 3.30 estimates the structural model for participants who chose "Power" as the first value, while Figure 3.31 estimates the structural model based on responses from other subjects.

We first of all note that:

– hypothesis H16 does not seem to be verified with similar parameters in the two groups – 0.054 against + 0.052);

– hypothesis H22 does not seem to be verified with equally close parameters (0.343 and 0.337).

On the other hand, the following effects are notably different:

– the effect of Trust on the Intensity of Investment Choice dominates that of the Interest on the Intensity of Investment Choice in the group of participants who chose the Power value as the first value;

– the effect of the Perceived Signal Quality on Trust dominates that of Affective Reaction on Trust in the group of participants who chose the Power value as the first value.

These observations seem natural insofar as participants promoting Power (through the acquisition of wealth) should rationalize their investment more and be based on cognitive, rather than affective, elements.

In order to overcome this statistical analysis problem, we created a second Power variable that is no longer binary but metric, taking values from 1 to 10 depending on the rank of this value for the participant. Thus, it became possible to test hypotheses H16 and H22 by the interaction effect (continuous indicator) on the sample of 400 participants.

HYPOTHESIS 16 (H16).– *Moderation of H3. The higher the Power value is ranked in the investor's hierarchy of values, the more the positive relationship between the Affective Reaction and the Intensity of Investment Choice is mitigated.*

Table 3.70 shows the significance results of the moderating effect for a bootstrapping of 5,000 observations.

The moderating effect of the Power moderating variable on the relationship between Affective Reaction and Intensity of Investment Choice (i.e. the effect of the interaction term "Affective Reaction * Power") is significant. There is no significant direct effect of the Power variable on the Intensity of Investment Choice.

	Original sample (O)	Sample mean (M)	Standard deviation (STDEV)	T statistics (|O/STDEV|)	*p*-values	Significance ($p < 0.05$)
Power → Intensity of Investment Choice	0.036	0.037	0.042	0.849	0.396	No
Affective Reaction → Intensity of Investment Choice	0.063	0.061	0.052	1.207	0.228	No
Affective Reaction * Power → Intensity of Investment Choice	0.100	0.100	0.038	2.639	0.008	Yes

Table 3.70. *Significance of the effect of the interaction term "Affective Reaction * Power" on the Intensity of Investment Choice*

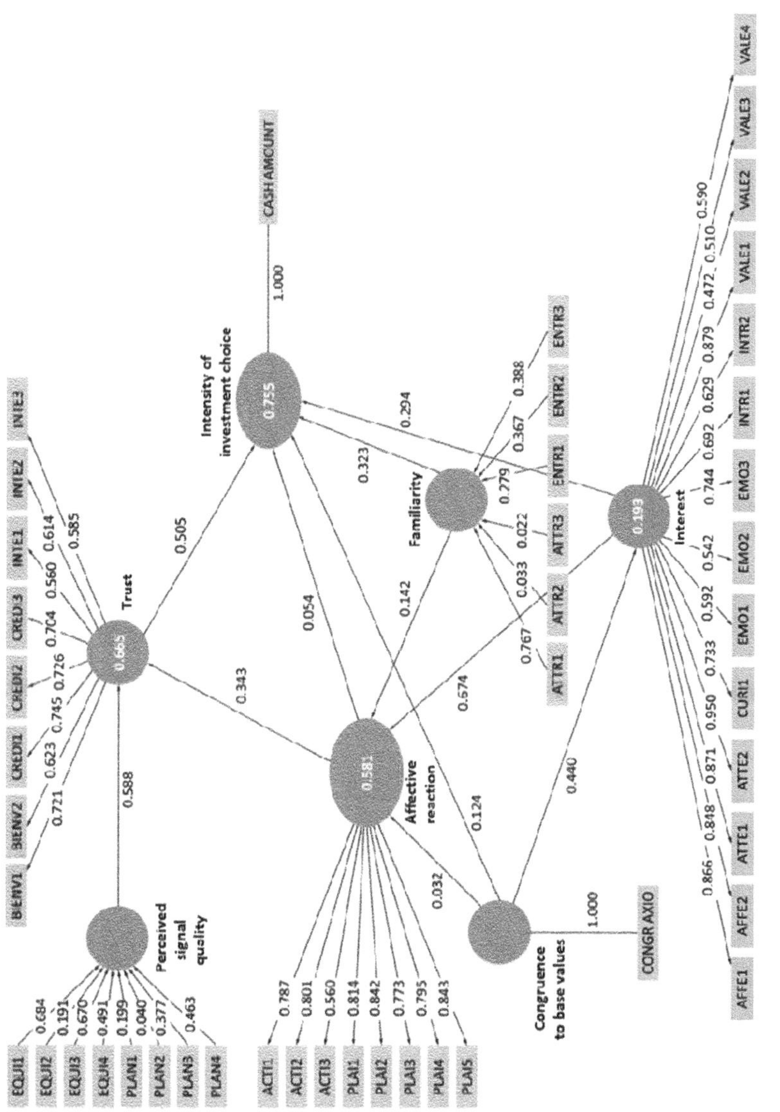

Figure 3.30. *Estimation of the structural model for participants who chose the Power value as the first value*

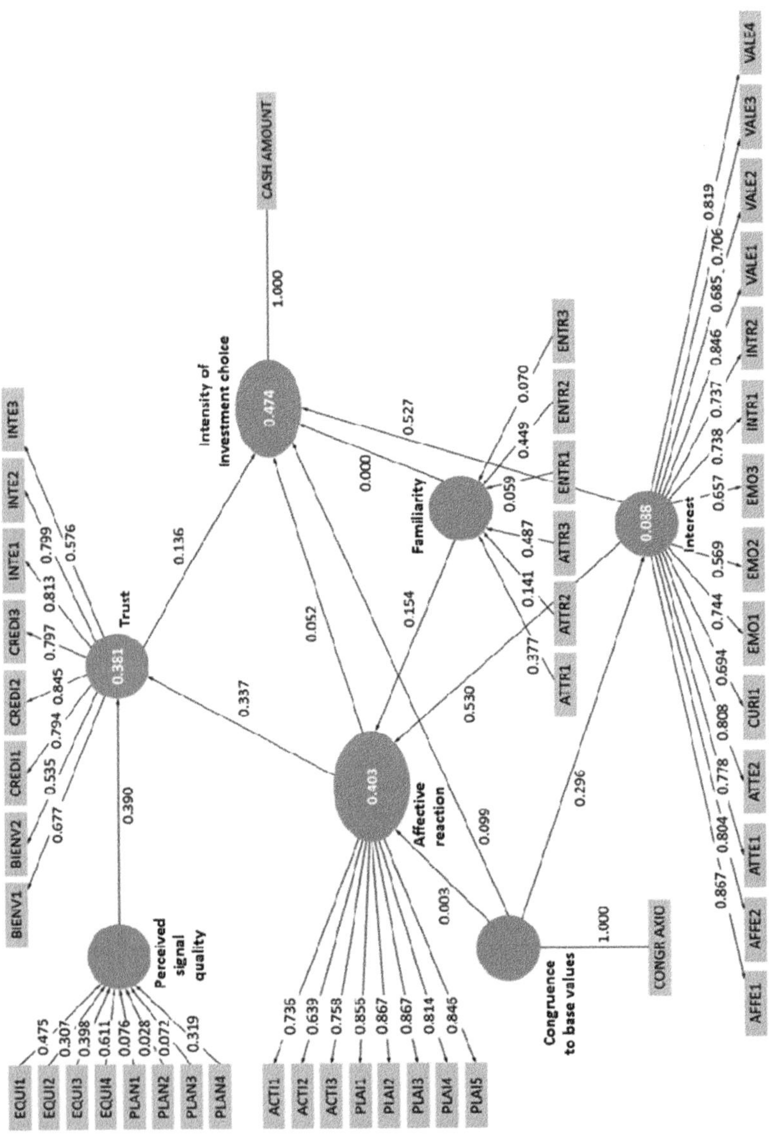

Figure 3.31. *Estimation of the structural model for participants who did not choose the Power value as the first value*

Hypothesis H16 is confirmed.

Figure 3.32 makes it possible to interpret this result. The relationship between Affective Reaction and Intensity of Investment Choice is 0.063 for an average value of the Power variable. When the Power variable increases by one standard deviation, this relationship = 0.063 + 0.1 = 0.163. When the Power variable decreases by one standard deviation, this relationship = 0.063 – 0.1 = – 0.037.

The greater the activated Power value, the stronger the relationship between Affective Reaction and Intensity of Investment Choice, which can be interpreted as follows: people for whom power (material and financial) is important make more decisions based on the affect.

Ultimately, we can see that:

– the direction of the effect is the reverse of that expected;

– the Power variable moderates an insignificant relationship between Affective Reaction and Intensity of Investment Choice.

The evaluation of the predictive value of the interaction term "Affective Reaction * Power" on the Intensity of Investment Choice by Cohen's f^2 = 0.018, which corresponds to an intermediate effect, between the average effect and a large effect but closer to the large effect boundary.

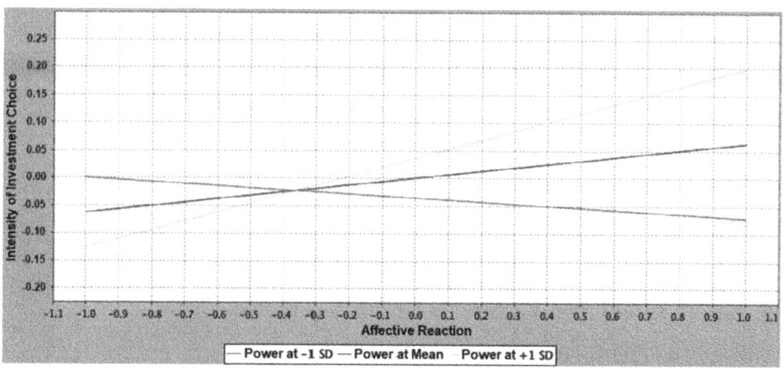

Figure 3.32. *Effect of the interaction term "Affective Reaction * Power" on the Intensity of Investment Choice. For a color version of this figure, see www.iste.co.uk/goglin/investment2.zip*

HYPOTHESIS 22 (H22).– *Moderation of H10. The higher the Power value is ranked in the investor's hierarchy of values, the more the positive relationship between the Affective Reaction and Trust is mitigated.*

Table 3.71 shows the significance results of the moderating effect for a bootstrapping of 5,000 observations.

The moderating effect of the moderating variable Power on the relationship between Affective Reaction and Trust (i.e. the effect of the interaction term "Affective Reaction * Power") is significant. There is no significant direct effect of the Power variable on Trust.

	Original sample (O)	**Sample mean (M)**	**Standard deviation (STDEV)**	**T statistics (|O/STDEV|)**	***p*-values**	**Significance ($p < 0.05$)**
Affective Reaction * Power → Trust	–0.116	–0.111	0.046	2.535	0.011	Yes
Power → Trust	0.048	0.047	0.042	1.125	0.260	No
Affective Reaction → Trust	0.341	0.336	0.046	7.346	0.000	Yes

Table 3.71. *Significance of the effect of the interaction term "Affective Reaction * Power" on Trust*

Hypothesis H22 is confirmed.

Figure 3.33 makes it possible to interpret this result. The relationship between Affective Reaction and Trust is 0.341 for an average value of the Power variable. When the Power variable increases by one standard deviation, this relationship = 0.341 – 0.116 = 0.225. When the Power variable decreases by one standard deviation, this relationship = 0.341 + 0.116 = 0.457.

The higher the activated Power value, the weaker the relationship between Affective Reaction and Trust.

The evaluation of the predictive value of the interaction term "Affective Reaction * Power" on Trust by Cohen's f^2 = 0.021 which, according to Kenny (2016), corresponds to a practically large effect.

At the end of this study of moderating variables, we summarize our results in Table 3.72.

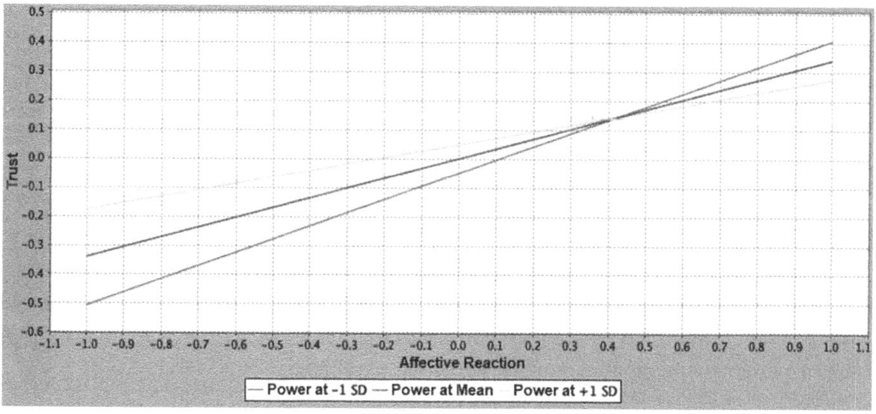

Figure 3.33. *Effect of the interaction term "Affective Reaction * Power" on Trust. For a color version of this figure, see www.iste.co.uk/goglin/investment2.zip*

Accepted hypotheses	H16, H21, H22
Rejected hypotheses	H12, H13, H14, H15, H17, H18, H19, H20, H23

Table 3.72. *Accepted and rejected moderation hypotheses*

Let us just recall that:

– in H16, the moderator moderates an insignificant relationship and the effect is the opposite of that expected;

– in H21, the effect is the reverse of that expected.

3.3.6. *Control variables*

In Chapter 1, we defined two control variables for the structural model: age and having already invested in equity crowdfunding. Regarding age, it should be noted that the standard deviation of this variable is low in our sample: 2.89 years. The effect of age is therefore difficult to assess in this study. Regarding the second control variable, only four participants had already invested in equity crowdfunding before the experiment.

The process of analyzing the effect of control variables in SmartPLS is explained by Dr. Jan-Michael Becker, one of the developers of the SmartPLS software and co-author of specialized articles on the PLS-SEM approach:

> Just have an arrow from your control variable (e.g., age) to all constructs that you want age be controlled for[12].
>
> You just add the data to your data file and model it as a single-indicator in PLS. You include a path from that single-indicator construct to your dependent construct in the path model to control for the influence of that variable[13].

In accordance with this recommendation, we have defined two control variables ("Age" and "Already invested in ECF") as explanations of the four endogenous variables (see Figure 3.34); we then estimated the model by a bootstrapping of 5,000 draws in order to check the significance of the parameters.

The results of the parameter estimation and of the bootstrapping, shown in Table 3.73, indicate parameters close to 0 and insignificant at the 5% threshold.

	Original sample (O)	**Sample mean (M)**	**Standard deviation (STDEV)**	**T statistics (|O/STDEV|)**	***p*-values**	**Significance ($p < 0.05$)**
Already invested in ECF → Trust	0.005	0.006	0.041	0.114	0.909	No
Already invested in ECF → Intensity of Investment Choice	0.015	0.014	0.028	0.531	0.596	No
Already Invested in ECF → Interest	– 0.033	– 0.032	0.040	0.810	0.418	No
Already Invested in ECF → Affective Reaction	– 0.012	– 0.011	0.040	0.303	0.762	No
Age → Trust	– 0.083	– 0.079	0.045	1.848	0.065	No
Age → Intensity of Investment Choice	– 0.009	– 0.006	0.051	0.170	0.865	No
Age → Interest	0.042	0.044	0.052	0.807	0.420	No
Age → Affective Reaction	0.009	0.007	0.042	0.211	0.833	No

Table 3.73. *Significance test of the effects of control variables*

12 http://forum.smartpls.com/viewtopic.php?f=12&t=3944.

13 http://forum.smartpls.com/viewtopic.php?f=12&t=16017.

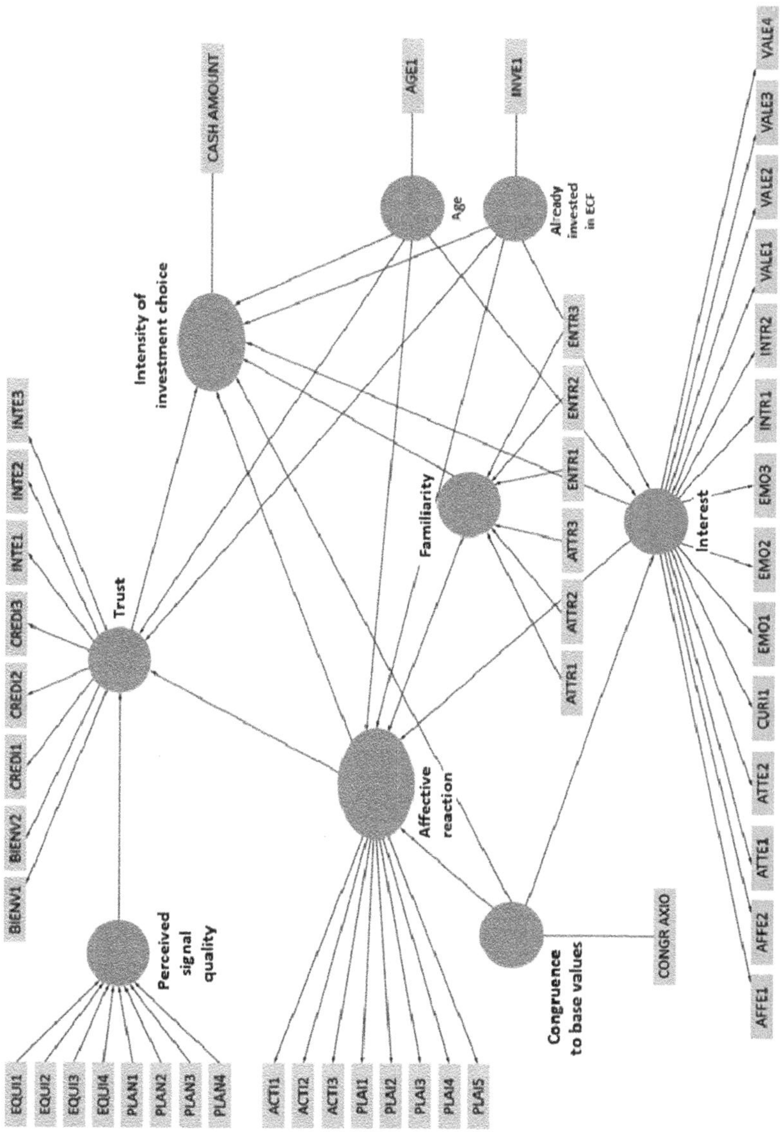

Figure 3.34. *Specification of the control variables in the model*

3.3.7. *Conclusion*

This section focuses on the evaluation and analysis of the structural model. After briefly presenting the specifics of the PLS-SEM approach, we evaluated the structural model. This does not present any particular collinearities. The model parameters are significant with the exception of three, relating to hypotheses H3, H4 and H6 and corresponding to the causal links linking the Affective Reaction to the Intensity of Investment Choice, Familiarity to the Intensity of Investment Choice and Congruence to Base Values to Affective Reaction, respectively.

The analysis of the total effects shows that the two main determinants of the Intensity of Investment Choice are Interest and Congruence to Base Values. The impact of the Perceived Signal Quality is clearly weaker, which legitimizes the individual predictive model. Let us recall that the analysis of the measurement model gives greater weight to the Situational Interest dimension, which includes Curiosity, Attention and Affective Involvement. These results are supported by the indicators f^2 and q^2. In addition, the variance of the main endogenous variable, the Intensity of Investment Choice, is shown at nearly 48% by the model, with the evaluation of the predictive quality of the model by Q^2 being satisfactory.

The "Percent Case" corresponding to the model estimated according to investment choices as a percentage of the subjects' total wealth sees a difference in the parameters, reflecting a decision that is less affective (decrease in the effect of Interest and Affective Reaction) and more rational (increased effect of the Perceived Signal Quality variable).

The study of mediators highlights the role of the Interest variable. Mediation by Interest explains, in particular, the main part of the effect of Congruence to Base Values on the Intensity of Investment Choice.

The study of moderators invalidates most of the hypotheses. Three moderating variables have a significant effect; nevertheless, among these, two hypotheses have an empirical effect opposite to that expected (H16 and H21), and only hypothesis 22 is truly confirmed.

Ultimately, we can see that the control variables have no significant effect.

3.4. Experimental design

Let us briefly recall the objective of this experimental design (detailed in Chapter 2). The aim is to bring a complementary response element to the analysis by structural equations, on the secondary question of this research. It has to do with the cognitive and analytical dimension of the choice, represented by the Perceived Signal Quality variable in the model and postulates that this variable has a negligible effect, relative to the other affective variables, on the explained variable: Intensity of Investment Choice.

The total sample of subjects is split into two groups, one experimental group having benefited from the "treatment", exposure to degraded business plans, while the second group, the control group, was exposed to the original business plans.

The treatment consisted of manipulating the Quality of the Business Plan factor according to two modalities of an ordinal scale: bad (BP–) or good (BP+).

This experimental design is used in two stages. The first stage consists of ensuring the effect of the Quality of the Business Plan factor on the Perceived Signal Quality (section 3.4.1). The second stage is centered on the effect of the Perceived Signal Quality variable on the variable of the explanatory model that depends on it (the Trust variable) and the one that indirectly depends on it (the Intensity of Investment Choice variable) through the mediation of the Trust variable using multigroup analysis (section 3.4.2).

3.4.1. *Impact of the Quality of the Business Plan on the Perceived Signal Quality*

This involves verifying whether the Quality of the Business Plan is a significant factor that explains the dependent Perceived Signal Quality variable.

The Quality of the Business Plan is a dichotomous categorical variable that takes two modalities:

– "2" for the group of subjects subject to the BP+ business plan;

– "5" for the group of subjects subject to the BP– business plan.

The Perceived Signal Quality is a continuous quantitative variable, calculated as the average of the indicators of the composite formative latent variable, weighted by its outer weights; the latter results from the algorithm of the PLS-SEM approach in the "Cash Case", i.e. the case where the model is estimated relative to asset allocations in cash (versus as a percentage of the total wealth).

We have, for i varying from 1 to 100 (100 = number of subjects) and j varying from 1 to 4 (4 = number of cash allocation choices per subject):

Perceived Signal Quality (individual i, choice j) =

PLAN1(i,j)*0.108284157313197 +

PLAN2(i,j)* –0.0209974202530764 +

PLAN3(i,j)*0.0759900741620221 +

PLAN4(i,j) *0.401325323909841 +

EQUI1(i,j)*0.478613987411354 +

EQUI2(i,j)*0.286492348991311 +

EQUI3(i,j)* –0.41208205445248 +

EQUI4(i,j)*0.576472124661253

We therefore have $100 \times 4 = 400$ observations for the Perceived Signal Quality variable.

We seek to establish a link between two variables – a dichotomous categorical variable and a continuous quantitative variable. Student's test or the *t*-test for independent (or unpaired) samples is suitable to establish the significance of such a link, provided that certain conditions are verified. Indeed, the *t*-test offers a means of comparing the means of two groups, the question being whether their difference is large (statistically significant) enough that it cannot be due to chance.

3.4.1.1. *Conditions for applying the* t-*test*

Four conditions are necessary for the application of the *t*-test – (C1) the groups are independent, (C2) the normality of the explained variable, (C3) the variances of the groups are equal (homogeneity of the variance or homoscedasticity) and (C4) a sufficient number of observations are available.

3.4.1.1.1. (C1) Independence of groups

This condition states that the same observations cannot belong to both groups. In our case, the two groups are composed of different individuals (between subject experiment) and, since the observations depend on the individuals (the Perceived Signal Quality (i,j) depends on the individual i and their choice j), the condition of independence is therefore naturally satisfied.

3.4.1.1.2. (C2) Normality of the explained variable Perceived Signal Quality

Let us check if for the two groups, the shape parameters, i.e. the Skewness (asymmetry) and Kurtosis (flattening) moments, do not exceed 1 in absolute value, which will indicate a form of frequency distribution reasonably similar to that of a normal distribution:

BP+ group (modality 2): Skewness = – 0.275714419 and Kurtosis = – 0.048462383

BP– group (modality 5): Skewness = – 0.281446421 and Kurtosis = 0.061298697

The explained variable Perceived Signal Quality presents a frequency distribution sufficiently close to that of a normal distribution for the two groups.

3.4.1.1.3. (C3) Homogeneity of variance

We test this condition below using Levene's test, automatically performed with Student's *t*-test under SPSS and whose null hypothesis is the homogeneity of variances.

3.4.1.1.4. (C4) Sufficient number of observations for analysis

This condition is satisfied (see section 2.1.2.2 of Chapter 2).

3.4.1.2. t-*test results*

Below are the results of the *t*-test produced by the SPSS software on the categorical explanatory variable (Group variable with two modalities, 2 for BP+ and 5 for BP–) and the continuous variable explained (Perceived Signal Quality). We will comment on them as we go.

	Group statistics				
	Group	**N**	**Mean**	**Standard deviation**	**Standard error of the mean**
Perceived quality	5	196	*5.38370883568*	1.061329362776	0.075809240198
	2	196	*5.83848271287*	0.892654505581	0.063761036113

Table 3.74. *Descriptive statistics of BP+ and BP– groups*

The descriptive statistics above indicate that, on average, the participants of the BP+ group logically assessed the Perceived Signal Quality of the business plans in their possession higher (with an average of 5.84) than that of participants in the BP– group (with an average of 5.38).

		Testing of independent samples		
		Levene's test for equal variances		*t*-test for equal means
		F	Sig.	*T*
Perceived quality	Equal variance hypothesis	4.729	*0.030*	– 4.591
	Unequal variance hypothesis			*– 4.591*

Table 3.75. *Homogeneity test of the variances of the BP+ and BP– groups*

The test for homogeneity of variances is significant ($p = 0.03 < 0.05$). We reject the null hypothesis: the variances are significantly different; the homoscedasticity hypothesis is not satisfied. However, this result is not a showstopper. In this case, the *t* statistic should be corrected using a combined variance rather than the individual variances of the two groups. The corrected Student's *t* is readable in the second line of the SPSS results.

		Testing of independent samples		
		t-test for equal means		
		DOF	Sig. (bilateral)	Mean difference
Perceived quality	Equal variance hypothesis	390	0.000	– 0.454773877189
	Unequal variance hypothesis	378.873	*0.000*	– 0.454773877189

Table 3.76. *Corrected Student's* t*-test*

		Testing of independent samples		
		t-test for equal means		
		Standard error difference	At 95% confidence interval of the difference	
			Lower	Higher
Perceived quality	Equal variance hypothesis	0.099058117414	– 0.649528607621	– 0.260019146757
	Unequal variance hypothesis	0.099058117414	– 0.649546412948	– 0.260001341430

Table 3.77. *Corrected Student's* t*-test, second part*

Finally, the *t*-test is significant at the 5% threshold (0.000 < 0.05); the means of two groups are therefore significantly different.

In order to assess the strength of the relationship linking the Quality of the Business Plan to the Perceived Signal Quality, we calculate the eta-squared magnitude index (η^2) defined by the formula:

$$\eta^2 = \frac{t^2}{t^2 + (N_1 + N_2 - 2)}$$

$$\eta^2 = \frac{-4.591^2}{-4.591 + (196 + 196 - 2)} \approx 0.05$$

According to Cohen (2009), an eta-square around 0.06 corresponds to a moderate effect.

Finally, participants who studied an original business plan of good quality (BP+) rated an average Perceived Signal Quality of 5.84, higher than the average Perceived Signal Quality of 5.38, associated with participants who studied a poor-quality business plan (BP–). These means are significantly different ($p \leq 0.001$). The strength of this relationship is moderate, as evidenced by an eta-square of 0.05.

In other words, the Quality of the Business Plan variable has a significant effect of average strength on the Perceived Signal Quality variable; we can continue the analysis by studying the impact of the Perceived Signal Quality on the estimated parameters of the structural model by proceeding to a multigroup analysis.

3.4.2. *Effect of the business plan on the parameters estimated by multigroup analysis*

In this section, we compare the direct effect of the Perceived Signal Quality variable on Trust as well as its indirect effect on the Intensity of Investment Choice through the mediation of the Trust variable for the two groups BP+ and BP–, in order to check whether these effects differ significantly from one group to another. We rely on a multigroup analysis, similar to those already carried out in section 3.3.5.2.1 for the analysis of class moderators. Table 3.78 shows the results of the multigroup analysis (in the PLS-MGA method) for the BP+ and BP– groups, though with a bootstrapping setting of only 500 samples. Indeed, a better parameterization was not possible, with the path coefficients of the BP– group being no longer available beyond the threshold of 500 samples.

Nevertheless, the results indicate that:

– the effect of the Perceived Signal Quality on Trust is logically greater in the BP+ group, with a coefficient of 0.453, against a coefficient of 0.359 for the BP– group;

– the effect of Trust on the Intensity of Investment Choice is greater in the BP– group, with a coefficient of 0.141, against a coefficient of 0.103 for the BP+ group. This result is explained by the effect of Affective Reaction on Trust, which is higher in the BP– group, with a coefficient of 0.397, against only 0.232 for the BP+ group.

We will not elaborate further on the interpretation of these results, as the *p*-value does not indicate any significant parameter difference at the 5% level between the two groups.

The measurement invariance check, carried out in the previous multigroup analyses and aimed at ensuring that the differences in the structural coefficients between groups are not attributable to differences in perception of the measurement model between groups, is not relevant within the framework of this experimental design since, by the *design* of the experiment, the measurement data of the Perceived Signal Quality variable perceived is not identical.

3.4.3. *Conclusion*

In this section, we seek to provide additional answers to the secondary question of this work on the negligible role of cognition and deliberative judgment in the choice of investment in equity crowdfunding.

To do this, the *design* of our experimental model subdivided the total sample of subjects of the experiment into two subgroups, the first receiving a "treatment", that is to say, an exposure to poor quality business plans, the second receiving the original business plans.

The business plan is the sole source of information determining the cognitive and analytical variable Perceived Signal Quality. The first step of this section attempts to check whether the Perceived Quality of the Business Plan variable significantly depends on the Quality of the Business Plan.

The results of analysis by Student's *t*-test demonstrate a significant effect of average strength.

BP+/BP–	Path coefficients original (BP+)	Path coefficients original (BP–)	Path coefficients mean (BP+)	Path coefficients mean (BP–)	STDEV (BP+)	STDEV (BP–)	*t*-values (BP+)	*t*-values (BP–)
Trust → Intensity of Investment Choice	0.103	0.141	0.109	0.140	0.082	0.056	1.259	2.529
Congruence to Base Values → Intensity of Investment Choice	0.068	0.100	0.067	0.095	0.077	0.062	0.888	1.616
Congruence to Base Values → Interest	0.205	0.354	0.207	0.359	0.082	0.071	2.505	4.993
Congruence to Base Values → Affective Reaction	−0.010	0.017	−0.019	0.020	0.079	0.066	0.129	0.265
Familiarity → Intensity of Investment Choice	0.022	0.035	0.054	0.059	0.109	0.068	0.201	0.522
Familiarity → Affective Reaction	0.006	0.223	0.023	0.230	0.112	0.079	0.056	2.805
Interest → Intensity of Investment Choice	0.596	0.464	0.578	0.459	0.113	0.070	5.285	6.667
Interest → Affective Reaction	0.622	0.505	0.620	0.507	0.074	0.066	8.412	7.620
Perceived Signal Quality → Trust	0.453	0.359	0.493	0.398	0.080	0.074	5.630	4.832
Affective Reaction → Trust	0.232	0.397	0.229	0.383	0.079	0.063	2.947	6.270
Affective Reaction → Intensity of Investment Choice	−0.114	0.154	−0.109	0.148	0.083	0.070	1.375	2.185

BP+/BP–	*p*-values (BP+)	*p*-values (BP–)	2.5% (BP+)	97.5% (BP+)	2.5% (BP–)	97.5% (BP–)	Path coefficients-diff (|BP+ – BP-)	*p*-values (BP+ vs. BP–)	Significance ($p < 0.05$)
Trust → Intensity of Investment Choice	0.209	0.012	– 0.079	0.250	0.041	0.263	0.038	0.645	FALSE
Congruence to Base Values → Intensity of Investment Choice	0.375	0.107	– 0.075	0.207	– 0.007	0.230	0.032	0.626	FALSE
Congruence to Base Values → Interest	0.013	0.000	0.015	0.341	0.200	0.481	0.149	0.917	FALSE
Congruence to Base Values → Affective Reaction	0.897	0.791	– 0.152	0.155	– 0.122	0.150	0.028	0.610	FALSE
Familiarity → Intensity of Investment Choice	0.840	0.602	– 0.229	0.196	– 0.111	0.142	0.014	0.538	FALSE
Familiarity → Affective Reaction	0.955	0.005	– 0.284	0.185	0.040	0.372	0.216	0.948	FALSE
Interest → Intensity of Investment Choice	0.000	0.000	0.387	0.835	0.331	0.591	0.133	0.161	FALSE
Interest → Affective Reaction	0.000	0.000	0.480	0.753	0.355	0.632	0.117	0.120	FALSE
Perceived Signal Quality → Trust	0.000	0.000	0.294	0.581	0.113	0.455	0.094	0.197	FALSE
Affective Reaction → Trust	0.003	0.000	0.086	0.388	0.283	0.522	0.164	0.946	FALSE
Affective Reaction → Intensity of Investment Choice	0.170	0.029	– 0.283	0.026	0.027	0.302	0.268	0.994	FALSE

Table 3.78. *Multigroup analysis for BP+ and BP– groups*

The question that follows is to determine whether the subjects who received a good quality business plan relied more on this information to make their investment choices. The second part of this section answers this question by means of a multigroup analysis relating to the BP+ and BP– groups and focusing on the direct and indirect effects of the Perceived Signal Quality variable. These effects are not significant at the 5% threshold.

This leads us to conclude that *the subjects do not rely significantly on business plans to make their choices*. In other words, the choice depends little on the analytical judgment; the cognitive aspect is a marginal determinant of the choice, in accordance with the results of the analysis of the SEM by the PLS-SEM approach.

3.5. Results of the individual predictive model

3.5.1. *Reminder of the model*

The individual predictive model, previously introduced in the modeling chapter, is intended to predict the choices of an individual whose preference structure is known. This preferably individualized structure sets the parameters of the individual model, deriving directly from the structural model, simplified by hypothesis, and from which the estimated coefficients are recovered from the data of the experiment.

The individual predictive model constitutes an implementation of the affective matching theory, applied to the specific case of investment in equity crowdfunding[14].

3.5.1.1. *Determining the* a priori *order of projects*

The order of the projects chosen *a priori* is predicted by the "affective distance" between each competing project and the decision-maker (investor). Affective Distance is defined as the inverse of the predicted Intensity of Investment Choice. The predicted Intensity of Investment Choice is calculated as a linear combination of the *a priori* congruence variables: Interest and Congruence to Base Values[15]. The coefficients of the equation come directly from the estimate of the explanatory model. The two *a priori* congruence variables are calculated by the first step of the matching, i.e. the function that takes as parameters two declarative preference structures (the first for Interest and the second for Congruence to Base Values) as

14 The Excel model implementation sheet is available on request.

15 The Familiarity construct is excluded because it has no significant effect on the Intensity of Investment Choice.

well as the value and the area of activity associated with the evaluated project. Let us illustrate the determination of the *a priori* order of projects with an example.

Let us take the case of two competing projects *A* and *B* for an investor *I*.

The affective matching theory states that certain projects correspond to us more; these will naturally be our preference before any evaluative judgment. Under certain conditions, the project that suits us the most, that is to say the most attractive, will be chosen. Investor *I* will choose project *A* or *B* that corresponds to them the most. In the case of equity crowdfunding, our study made it possible to identify two non-evaluative affective correspondence variables: the values (Congruence to Base Values variable) and the interests (Interest variable).

Investor *I* should therefore choose the project (*A* or *B*) that best corresponds to their values and interests; this correspondence being all the stronger as the affective distance is weak. Equivalently, this correspondence is all the stronger the greater the predicted Intensity of Investment Choice, since, by definition, the affective distance is the inverse of the predicted Intensity of Investment Choice.

Therefore:

> *A* is preferred to *B* denoted A > B ⇔ BICIp(I,A)> ICIp(I,B) ⇔ CDA(I,A)< DA(I,B)
>
> *A* is preferred to *B* if and only if the predicted Intensity of Investment Choice (ICIp) calculated for the individual *I* and the project *A* is strictly greater than the predicted Intensity of Investment Choice calculated for the individual *I* and project *B*

or:

> *A* is preferred to *B* if and only if the Affective Distance (DA) calculated for individual *I* and project *A* is strictly less than the Affective Distance calculated for individual *I* and project *B*

We have the relationship:

$$DA(I,X) := \frac{1}{ICIp(I,X)}$$

and:

$$ICIp(I,X) = \alpha.CVB(I,X) + \beta\,.Int(I,X)$$

that we write in a simpler manner:

$$ICIp = \alpha . CVB + \beta . Int \qquad [3.1]$$

with $\alpha, \beta \in \mathcal{R}$, the coefficients of the linear equation, *CVB* and *Int* $\in [0,1]$, the *a priori* congruence variables for the values (*CVB*) and Interest (*Int*).

It should be recalled that this equation derives directly from the linear regressions of the structural model, obtained using the PLS-SEM approach, and formatted by factorization (see equation [3.2]) to express the Intensity of Investment Choice depending on the affective variables (Congruence to Base Values = *CVB*, Familiarity = *Fam* and Interest = *Int*) and the cognitive variable (Perceived Signal Quality = *QS*):

$$ICI = A . QS + B' . CVB + \Gamma . Fam + \Delta . Int + \varepsilon_6 \qquad [3.2]$$

The transition from equations [3.2] to [3.1] is not mathematically formal; therefore, equation [3.1] must be considered as an approximation or *proxy* of equation [3.2]. This approximation results from:

– the elimination of the residual regression error;

– the removal of the effect of the Familiarity variable, which is not significant;

– the removal of the effect of the Perceived Signal Quality variable which, although significant, is marginal compared to the effects of Congruence to Base Values and Interest in terms of cumulative effects, as the results of section 3.3 show. *Moreover, this eviction stems from the hypothesis of affective matching, which is closely linked to the thesis that we defend: "In the context of equity crowdfunding, that is to say, that of an investment in a situation of uncertainty in which the persuasive advertising tool is used, the choice of the investor is overdetermined by the affect and their values, their deliberative judgment being only an antecedent to marginal causal power".*

Considering the coefficients α and β from the PLS-SEM algorithm, equation [3.1] becomes:

$$ICIp = 0.096 . CVB + 0.514 . Int \qquad [3.3]$$

The *a priori* congruence structure, defined as the set of *a priori* congruence variables {*CVB, Int*} results from the first step of the matching procedure between the data explicitly communicated to the investor (*X*) and their preference structure (*I*).

The data explicitly communicated to the investor, relevant to the two constructs Congruence to Base Values and Interest, are:

– the *value* promoted by the company, indicated in the business plan;

– the *field of activity* of the company, indicated in the business plan.

Values: the four values associated with the projects competing in the experiment are: “Universalism”, “Stimulation”, “Power” and “Tradition”.

Field of activity: let us remember that the field of activity is the object to which eight of the nine items of the Individual Interest construct relate. In the experiment, the four fields of activity associated with the projects are: “fair trade”, “new technological uses”, “the medical field” and “traditional remedies or recipes”.

The investor preference structure is taken from questions no. 23 of the questionnaire for preferences on securities and no. 25 of the questionnaire for preferences in terms of interest in fields of activity.

For example, individual *I* can have the following preference structure.

For values:

> Autonomy > Stimulation > Universalism > Safety > Benevolence > Achievement > Power > Tradition > Hedonism > Compliance

In other words, the autonomy value is their most important value; then comes the stimulation value and so on up to the compliance value.

For the field of activity:

> Fair trade > Medical field > Traditional remedies or recipes > New technological uses

In other words, the fair trade field is the one which presents the most interest for the individual *I*, followed by the medical field and so on until finally the field of new technological uses.

Let us now assume that project *A* is the company Ethiquable for which the associated value is “Universalism” and the associated field of activity is “fair trade”. The matching has all the necessary parameters for calculating the *a priori* congruence values: *CVB*, *Int*:

> CVB_A = matching of value (Individual, Project) = *matching* of value (*I*, ETHIQUABLE)

= matching of value (*preference structure for the values of I*, value promoted by the company ETHIQUABLE)

= matching of value ("Autonomy > Stimulation > Universalism > Safety > Benevolence > Achievement > Power > Tradition > Hedonism > Compliance", "Universalism")

Int, the second *a priori* congruence variable, is calculated in the same way.

Int_A = matching of interest for the field of activity (Individual, Project)
= matching of interest for the field of activity (*I*, ETHIQUABLE)

= matching of interest for the field of activity (*preference structure for the field of activity of I*, field of activity of the company ETHIQUABLE)

= matching of interest for the field of activity ("Fair trade > Medical field > Traditional remedies and recipes > New technological uses", "Fair trade")

The matching function calculates the *a priori* congruence values like the *reverse of the result* of the measurement of similarity between two ordered vectors, defined in Chapter 1.

However, we are in the particular case where one of the two vectors is of dimension 1 (because only one value and one field of activity are associated with each project). Therefore, the *a priori* congruence values *CVB* and *Int* are calculated with the help of a simple formula, equivalent to the reverse of the similarity measurement and specified in Box 3.1 for the *CVB* variable.

Hypotheses (Ha and Hb)

Ha: we take the axiological preference structure of the individual *I*, from the questionnaire, i.e. the ordered list V1≤ V2≤…≤V10 with k ranks; k in [1,10].

Hb: to each startup i in the investment scenario is associated a unique value Vi.

The Congruence to Base Values variable CVB is calculated in the simple case (one single value associated with the startup) depending on the rank r of Vi in the ordered list and of k, total rank number of the following, according to the formula:

$$Similarity = 1 - \frac{(k+1)-r}{k} = \frac{k-(k+1)+r}{k} = \frac{r-1}{k}$$

and:

CVB=1/Similarity

(=k+1 if Similarity =0)

Examples: let us say there are 4 values V1, V2, V3, V4 ordered as follows for a subject having filled the SSVS:

V2>V1=V4>V3 with k = 3

– Let us say there is a startup to which the value V1 is associated. The rank r of this value is 2 and the Congruence to Base Values = 1 – [(*k*+*1*) – *r*]/*k* = 1 – [(3+1) – 2]/3 =1 – 2/3 = 1/3 (medium congruence).

– Let us say there is another startup to which the value V2 is associated. Its rank r is 1 and the Congruence to Base Values = 1 – [(*k*+1) – *r*]/*k* = 1 – [(3+1) – 1]/3 =3/3=1 – 1 = 0 (maximum congruence, minimal similarity).

– Finally, let us say there is a startup to which the value V3 is associated. Its rank r is 3 and the Congruence to Base Values = 1 – [(*k*+1) – *r*]/*k* = 1 – [(3+1) – 3]/3 =1 – 1/3 = 2/3 (minimal congruence, maximum similarity).

Box 3.1. *Computational method for the CVB variable*

The same formula is applied to determine the *Int* variable; we can come back to our example to describe the chosen implementation in Excel. We note that, in this implementation, the formulae used are different; this is in order to normalize the congruence (i.e. the maximum congruence is 1):

A is preferred to B i.e. $A \succ B$

$\Leftrightarrow$ BICIp (I, A)> ICIp (I, B)

$\Leftrightarrow$ CIp $(\mathrm{I}, CVB_A + 0.514\,.Int_A > 0.096.\,CVB_B + 0.514\,.Int_B$

CVB_A = SI (ESTNA(=RECHERCHEH(“UNIVERSALISM”;ORDRE_DES_VALEURS;2;FAUX));1/10;(11-RECHERCHEH(“UNIVERSALISM”; TABLEAU; FAUX))/10) = 0.8

With ORDRE_DES_VALEURS = (see Table 3.79).

Autonomy	Stimulation	Universalism	Safety	Benevolence
1	2	3	4	5
Achievement	**Power**	**Tradition**	**Hedonism**	
6	7	8	9	

Table 3.79. *Order of preference for values of the individual*

Int_A= 1/RECHERCHEH("Fair trade";ORDRE_DES_DOMAINES_D_INTERET; 2;FAUX) = 1

With ORDRE_DES_DOMAINES_D_INTERET = (see Table 3.80).

Fair trade	Medical field	Traditional remedies and recipes	New technological uses
1	2	3	4

Table 3.80. *Order of preference of fields of interest of the individual*

We get:

$$ICIp(I, A) = 0.096.0.8 + 0.514 . 1 = 0.59$$

Let us now assume that project *B* is the company Mamie & Co whose associated value is "Tradition" and associated field of activity is "Traditional remedies and recipes".

By adopting the same approach as with company *A*, we get:

$$ICIp(I, B) = 0.096.0.3 + 0.514 . 1/3 = 0.20$$

Finally, $ICIp(I, A) = 0.59 > ICIp(I, B) = 0.20 \Leftrightarrow= A > B$.

Given the preferences of individual *I* and the characteristics of projects *A* and *B*, individual *I* has an *a priori* preference for project *A*.

The same method makes it possible to naturally order n projects. In the experiment carried out, n is 4; the method determines a "quartet", i.e. a dimension-4 ordered vector called the *a priori* choice vector.

The Intensity of Investment Choice values of each project are ordered for the individual:

$$ICIp(I, A_{\alpha1}) > ICIp(I, A_{\alpha2}) > ICIp(I, A_{\alpha3}) > ICIp(I, A_{\alpha4})$$

$$\Leftrightarrow A_{\alpha1} \succ A_{\alpha2} \succ A_{\alpha3} \succ A_{\alpha4} \quad \text{with } \alpha_i \in \{1,..,4\}$$

This determines the *a priori* choice vector:

$$(A_{\alpha1}, A_{\alpha2}, A_{\alpha3}, A_{\alpha4}) \quad \text{with } \alpha_i \in \{1,..,4\}$$

It is now a matter of measuring the prediction quality, i.e. getting a measurement of the error that separates the *a priori* "quartet" and the *a posteriori* quartet, which is the one chosen by the individual after assessment.

It is thus a matter of comparing the *a priori* choice vector:

$$(A_{\alpha1}, A_{\alpha2}, A_{\alpha3}, A_{\alpha4}) \quad \text{with } \alpha_i \in \{1,..,4\}$$

with the *a posteriori* choice vector:

$$(A_{\alpha'1}, A_{\alpha'2}, A_{\alpha'3}, A_{\alpha'4}) \quad \text{with } \alpha'_i \in \{1,..,4\}$$

Section 3.5.1.2 describes the chosen method for calculating this error measurement defining the *a priori* prediction quality.

3.5.1.2. A priori *prediction quality*

The *a priori* prediction quality is quantified for measuring the prediction error of the vector chosen by the individual *I* (*a posteriori* vector) by the predicted vector (*a priori* vector).

With the previously seen notations, we write:

$$\text{Prediction error} = \text{Similarity } (a\ priori \text{ vector; } a\ posteriori \text{ vector})$$

$$=$$

$$\text{Similarity } ((A_{\alpha1}, A_{\alpha2}, A_{\alpha3}, A_{\alpha4});\ (A_{\alpha'1}, A_{\alpha'2}, A_{\alpha'3}, A_{\alpha'4}))$$

This error measurement is calculated thanks to the vectorial similarity measurement already used (in a simplified and normalized version) depending on the matching of the calculation of the *a priori* congruence structure.

This vectorial similarity measurement (see the reminder below) operates on two ordered vectors: the *a priori* choice vector and the *a posteriori* choice vector; it is 0 if the two vectors are identical, and increases with:

– distance between the ranks of the components of a permutation;

– the closeness of the rank of the permutation, defined by the rank of the component with the lowest rank.

Here is a reminder of the formula for the vectorial similarity measurement.

Let us say there are two ordered vectors $U(U_1 \leq \ldots \leq U_n)$ and $V(V_1 \leq \ldots \leq V_m)$ such that $m \leq n$ with $(m, n) \in \mathbb{N}^* \times \mathbb{N}^*$ et U_i, $V_j \in \{\alpha_1,\ldots,\alpha_N\}$ N modalities of a nominal variable:

$$\textit{Similarity measurement}\,(U,V) := \sum_{i=1}^{n} |i - j_i| \times \frac{1}{n \times \min(i, j_i)}$$

with:

i = rang (i.e. “rank”) U_i in U or i;

j_i = rang V_j in V if $\exists\, V_j \in V$ tq $U_i = V_j$;

j = i otherwise.

In the case of the experiment, the *a priori* and *a posteriori* vectors are to be compared with the “quartet”; the implementation of this similarity measurement in Excel is given below. Let us note that the 1/n coefficient of the formula is not applied, as it is not necessary for the comparison that we will later do from these similarity measures. In the interests of clarity, the Excel functions below appear in the original French: SI(), ET(), OU(). These correspond to IF(), AND(), OR() in English.

Similarity measurement (*a posteriori* vector, *a priori* vector) =

SUM (VECTEUR_DE_SIMILARITE_PAR_COMPOSANTE)

With VECTEUR_DE_SIMILARITE_PAR_COMPOSANTE=

ABS(RANG_A_POSTERIORI_1 - RANG_A_PRIORI_1)/MIN(RANG_A_POSTERIORI_1; RANG_A_PRIORI_1)

ABS(RANG_A_POSTERIORI_2 - RANG_A_PRIORI_2)/MIN(RANG_A_POSTERIORI_2; RANG_A_PRIORI_2)

ABS(RANG_A_POSTERIORI_3 - RANG_A_PRIORI_3)/MIN(RANG_A_POSTERIORI_3; RANG_A_PRIORI_3)

ABS(RANG_A_POSTERIORI_4 - RANG_A_PRIORI_4)/MIN(RANG_A_POSTERIORI_4; RANG_A_PRIORI_4)

Let us now detail the similarity measurement for component 1:

ABS(RANG_A_POSTERIORI_1 - RANG_A_PRIORI_1)/MIN(RANG_A_POSTERIORI_1; RANG_A_PRIORI_1)

It depends on the parameters RANG_A_POSTERIORI_1 and RANG_A_ PRIORI_1.

The parameter RANG_A_POSTERIORI_i (for i ranging from 1 to 4) determines the rank (also ranging from 1 to 4) of the no. 1 component depending on the cash amounts invested by the individual I in the four projects.

Component no. 1 = ETHIQUABLE

Component no. 2 = HEXAPAY

Component no. 3 = MAMIE & CO

Component no. 4 = STEMCIS

RANG_A_POSTERIORI_1 =

SI(ET($MI_{ETHIQUABLE}$>=$MI_{HEXAPAY}$;$MI_{ETHIQUABLE}$>=$MI_{MAMIE\ \&\ CO}$;$MI_{ETHIQUABLE}$>=$MI_{STEMCIS}$);1;

SI(OU(ET($MI_{ETHIQUABLE}$>=$MI_{HEXAPAY}$;$MI_{ETHIQUABLE}$>=$MI_{MAMIE\ \&\ CO}$);ET($MI_{ETHIQUABLE}$>=$MI_{HEXAPAY}$;$MI_{ETHIQUABLE}$>=$MI_{STEMCIS}$);ET($MI_{ETHIQUABLE}$>=$MI_{MAMIE\ \&\ CO}$;$MI_{ETHIQUABLE}$>=MISTEMCIS));2;
SI(OU($MI_{ETHIQUABLE}$>=$MI_{HEXAPAY}$;$MI_{ETHIQUABLE}$>=$MI_{MAMIE\ \&\ CO}$;$MI_{ETHIQUABLE}$>=$MI_{STEMCIS}$);3;4)))

RANG_A_POSTERIORI_2 =

SI(ET($MI_{HEXAPAY}$>=$MI_{ETHIQUABLE}$;$MI_{HEXAPAY}$>=$MI_{MAMIE\ \&\ CO}$;$MI_{HEXAPAY}$>=$MI_{STEMCIS}$);1;

SI(OU(ET($MI_{HEXAPAY}$>=$MI_{ETHIQUABLE}$;$MI_{HEXAPAY}$>=$MI_{MAMIE\ \&\ CO}$);ET($MI_{HEXAPAY}$>=$MI_{ETHIQUABLE}$;$MI_{HEXAPAY}$>=$MI_{STEMCIS}$);ET($MI_{HEXAPAY}$>=$MI_{MAMIE\ \&}$

$_{CO}$;$MI_{HEXAPAY}$>=$MI_{STEMCIS}$));2;SI(OU($MI_{HEXAPAY}$>=$MI_{ETHIQUABLE}$;$MI_{HEXAPAY}$>=$MI_{MAMIE \& CO}$;$MI_{HEXAPAY}$>=$MI_{STEMCIS}$);3;4)))

RANG_A_POSTERIORI_3 =

SI(ET($MI_{MAMIE \& CO}$>=$MI_{ETHIQUABLE}$;$MI_{MAMIE \& CO}$>=$MI_{HEXAPAY}$;$MI_{MAMIE \& CO}$>=$MI_{STEMCIS}$);1;

SI(OU(ET($MI_{MAMIE \& CO}$>=$MI_{ETHIQUABLE}$;$MI_{MAMIE \& CO}$>=$MI_{HEXAPAY}$);ET($MI_{MAMIE \& CO}$>=$MI_{ETHIQUABLE}$;$MI_{MAMIE \& CO}$>=$MI_{STEMCIS}$);ET($MI_{MAMIE \& CO}$>=$MI_{HEXAPAY}$;$MI_{MAMIE \& CO}$>=$MI_{STEMCIS}$));2;SI(OU($MI_{MAMIE \& CO}$>=$MI_{ETHIQUABLE}$;$MI_{MAMIE \& CO}$>=$MI_{HEXAPAY}$;MI_{MAMIE} & CO>=$MI_{STEMCIS}$);3;4)))

RANG_A_POSTERIORI_4 =

SI(ET($MI_{STEMCIS}$>=$MI_{ETHIQUABLE}$;$MI_{STEMCIS}$>=$MI_{HEXAPAY}$;$MI_{STEMCIS}$>=$MI_{MAMIE \& CO}$);1;
SI(OU(ET($MI_{STEMCIS}$>=$MI_{ETHIQUABLE}$;$MI_{STEMCIS}$>=$MI_{HEXAPAY}$);ET($MI_{STEMCIS}$>=$MI_{ETHIQUABLE}$;$MI_{STEMCIS}$>=$MI_{MAMIE \& CO}$);ET($MI_{STEMCIS}$>=$MI_{HEXAPAY}$;$MI_{STEMCIS}$>=$MI_{MAMIE \& CO}$));2;SI(OU($MI_{STEMCIS}$>=$MI_{ETHIQUABLE}$;$MI_{STEMCIS}$>=$MI_{HEXAPAY}$;$MI_{STEMCIS}$>=$MI_{MAMIE \& CO}$);3;4)))

With MI_{PROJET} = cash amount invested in the PROJET project.

The parameter RANG_A_PRIORI_j (for j ranging from 1 to f) determines the rank (also ranging from 1 to 4) of the component no. j depending on the predicted ICI for the four projects and the individual configured by the preference structure.

Component no. 1 = ETHIQUABLE

Component no. 2 = HEXAPAY

Component no. 3 = MAMIE & CO

Component no. 4 = STEMCIS

RANG_A_PRIORI_1=SI(ET($ICI_{(ETHIQUABLE, I)}$ >=$ICI_{(HEXAPAY, I)}$;$ICI_{(ETHIQUABLE, I)}$ >=$ICI_{(MAMIE \& CO, I)}$;$ICI_{(ETHIQUABLE, I)}$ >=$ICI_{(STEMCIS, I)}$);1;SI(OU(ET($ICI_{(ETHIQUABLE, I)}$ >=ICI(HEXAPAY, I);$ICI_{(ETHIQUABLE, I)}$ >=$ICI_{(MAMIE \& CO, I)}$);ET($ICI_{(ETHIQUABLE, I)}$ >=$ICI_{(HEXAPAY, I)}$;$ICI_{(ETHIQUABLE, I)}$ >=$ICI_{(STEMCIS, I)}$);ET($ICI_{(ETHIQUABLE, I)}$ >=$ICI_{(MAMIE \& CO, I)}$;$ICI_{(ETHIQUABLE, I)}$ >$ICI_{(STEMCIS, I)}$));2; SI(OU($ICI_{(ETHIQUABLE, I)}$ >=$ICI_{(HEXAPAY, I)}$;$ICI_{(ETHIQUABLE, I)}$ >=$ICI_{(MAMIE \& CO, I)}$;$ICI_{(ETHIQUABLE, I)}$ >=$ICI_{(STEMCIS, I)}$);3;4)))

RANG_A_PRIORI_2=SI(ET($ICI_{(HEXAPAY, I)}$>=$ICI_{(ETHIQUABLE, I)}$;$ICI_{(HEXAPAY, I)}$>=$ICI_{(MAMIE \& CO, I)}$;$ICI_{(HEXAPAY, I)}$>=$ICI_{(STEMCIS, I)}$);1;SI(OU(ET($ICI_{(HEXAPAY, I)}$>=$ICI_{(ETHIQUABLE, I)}$;$ICI_{(HEXAPAY, I)}$>=$ICI_{(MAMIE \& CO, I)}$);ET($ICI_{(HEXAPAY, I)}$>=$ICI_{(ETHIQUABLE, I)}$;$ICI_{(HEXAPAY, I)}$>=ICI(STEMCIS, I));ET($_{ICI(HEXAPAY, I)}$>=$ICI_{(MAMIE \& CO, I)}$;$ICI_{(HEXAPAY, I)}$>=$ICI_{(STEMCIS, I)}$));2;SI(OU($ICI_{(HEXAPAY, I)}$>=$ICI_{(ETHIQUABLE, I)}$;$ICI_{(HEXAPAY, I)}$>=$ICI_{(MAMIE \& CO, I)}$;$ICI_{(HEXAPAY, I)}$>=$ICI_{(STEMCIS, I)}$);3;4)))

RANG_A_PRIORI_3=SI(ET($ICI_{(MAMIE \& CO, I)}$>=$ICI_{(ETHIQUABLE, I)}$;$ICI_{(MAMIE \& CO, I)}$>=$ICI_{(HEXAPAY, I)}$;$ICI_{(MAMIE \& CO, I)}$>=$ICI_{(STEMCIS, I)}$);1;SI(OU(ET($ICI_{(MAMIE \& CO, I)}$>=$ICI_{(ETHIQUABLE, I)}$;$ICI_{(MAMIE \& CO, I)}$>=$ICI_{(HEXAPAY, I)}$);ET($ICI_{(MAMIE \& CO, I)}$>=$ICI_{(ETHIQUABLE, I)}$;$ICI_{(MAMIE \& CO, I)}$>=$ICI_{(STEMCIS, I)}$);ET($ICI_{(MAMIE \& CO, I)}$>=$ICI_{(HEXAPAY, I)}$;$ICI_{(MAMIE \& CO, I)}$>=$ICI_{(STEMCIS, I)}$));2;SI(OU($ICI_{(MAMIE \& CO, I)}$>=$ICI_{(ETHIQUABLE, I)}$;$ICI_{(MAMIE \& CO, I)}$>=$ICI_{(HEXAPAY, I)}$;$ICI_{(MAMIE \& CO, I)}$ >=$ICI_{(STEMCIS, I)}$);3;4)))

RANG_A_PRIORI_4=SI(ET($ICI_{(STEMCIS, I)}$>=$ICI_{(ETHIQUABLE, I)}$;$ICI_{(STEMCIS, I)}$>=$ICI_{(HEXAPAY, I)}$;$ICI_{(STEMCIS, I)}$>=$ICI_{(MAMIE \& CO, I)}$);1;SI(OU(ET($ICI_{(STEMCIS, I)}$>=$ICI_{(ETHIQUABLE, I)}$;$ICI_{(STEMCIS, I)}$>=$ICI_{(HEXAPAY, I)}$);ET($ICI_{(STEMCIS, I)}$>=$ICI_{(ETHIQUABLE, I)}$;$ICI_{(STEMCIS, I)}$>=$ICI_{(MAMIE \& CO, I)}$);ET($ICI_{(STEMCIS, I)}$>=$ICI_{(HEXAPAY, I)}$;$ICI_{(STEMCIS, I)}$>=$ICI_{(MAMIE \& CO, I)}$));2;SI(OU($ICI_{(STEMCIS, I)}$>=$ICI_{(ETHIQUABLE, I)}$;$ICI_{(STEMCIS, I)}$>=$ICI_{(HEXAPAY, I)}$;$ICI_{(STEMCIS, I)}$>=$ICI_{(MAMIE \& CO, I)}$);3;4)))

With

$ICI_{(ETHIQUABLE, I)} = 0.096*CVB_{ETHIQUABLE} + 0.514*Int_{ETHIQUABLE}$

$ICI_{(HEXAPAY, I)} = 0.096*CVB_{HEXAPAY} + 0.514*Int_{HEXAPAY}$

$ICI_{(MAMIE \& CO, I)} = 0.096*CVB_{MAMIE \& CO} + 0.514*Int_{MAMIE \& CO}$

$ICI_{(STEMCIS, I)} = 0.096*CVB_{STEMCIS} + 0.514*Int_{STEMCIS}$

The *a priori* CVB_{Projet} and Int_{Projet} congruence variables with Project ∈ {ETHIQUABLE, HEXAPAY, MAMIE & CO, STEMCIS} are calculated according to the modalities in section 3.5.1.1.

3.5.2. *Results of the individual predictive model*

In section 3.5.1, we presented a possible implementation of affective matching theory for the case of equity crowdfunding investment. We first discussed the method for determining *a priori* preferences on projects and then a measure of the prediction quality of *a priori* choices for an individual who had previously revealed their preference structure.

We now present the results obtained with the individual predictive model on the experiment data. The rate of exact predictions of preferred projects for all 100 subjects in the sample is first compared (section 3.5.2.1). We then compare the error measures of affective matching predictions with those of random draws (section 3.5.2.3). Finally, we show how the affective matching theory can provide a complementary response element to the central question of this research.

3.5.2.1. *Rate of exact predictions of the preferred project of each subject in the sample*

We first define the preferred project as the one that obtained the maximum invested amount. It should be recalled that the questionnaire initially asked the subjects of the experiment to break down all of the €200 of initial virtual allocation (in increments of €50) on the four competing projects of the equity crowdfunding platform.

Second, they were asked to break down virtually all of their personal assets over the four projects by 25% of their assets.

This double allocation made it possible to define two preferred projects, a "preferred cash project" for the choice of cash investment and a "preferred percent project" for the relative investment choice (in percentage).

In practice, for each of the 100 subjects of the experiment, we compared "the preferred cash project" with the preferred project predicted by affective matching. We renewed the operation with the "preferred percent project".

Finally, *affective matching* (configured with *a priori* preferences on values and fields of activity, revealed by the subjects) *made it possible to correctly predict the preferred project in 55% of cases in the configuration of investments in cash amounts* and in 53% of cases in the configuration of investments in relative amounts (percentage).

Let us determine the probability of getting a score as high or higher than 55% of the correct prediction on the entire sample of participants with a uniform distribution (four-sided balanced dice, one for each project). Probability of doing at least as well as the prediction, result of affective matching with chance:

$$\text{Probability} = \sum_{i=55}^{100} C_{100}^{i} \left(\frac{1}{4}\right)^{i} \left(\frac{3}{4}\right)^{100-i}$$

$$= 0.000000015\%$$

or 15 chances out of 1 billion.

In other words, the result of the prediction of the preferred project (cash case) obtained by affective matching is immeasurably better than that given by chance.

3.5.2.2. *Relative quality of prediction: error measures compared between prediction and random selection*

In section 3.5.2.1, we looked at the quality of the prediction of the preferred project revealed by the individual predictive model. In this section, we take it a step further by focusing on the quality of the prediction of the *a priori* vector (a quarter in our case).

To do this, we take as a benchmark a random vector each component of which follows a uniform law.

We then measure for each individual i, the prediction error $\varepsilon_{prédit(i)}$ of the *a priori* (predicted) vector with respect to the *a posteriori* vector, determined by the effective choices of this same subject i.

We also measure for each individual i, the error $\varepsilon_{Aléa(i)}$ of “prediction” of the random vector compared to the *a posteriori* vector, determined by the effective choices of this same subject.

We can therefore write:

$$\varepsilon_{prédit(i)} = Similarity\ (a\ priori\ \text{vector};\ a\ posteriori\ \text{vector})$$

and:

$$\varepsilon_{Aléa(i)} = Similarity\ (\text{random vector};\ a\ posteriori\ \text{vector})$$

These two quantities are calculated according to the indications seen above in section 3.5.1.2.

Figure 3.35 shows the difference $\varepsilon_{Aléa(i)} - \varepsilon_{prédit(i)}$ on the y-axis; the x-axis indicates the number of the individual (from 1 to 100). In this figure (which relates to a particular set of draws), *the average gain of the predicted quartet on the random quartet is 18%*, calculated as the average for the 100 individuals of the following percentage:

$$Percentage\ of\ relative\ gain(predicted, Random, i) = \frac{\varepsilon_{Aléa(i)} - \varepsilon_{Prédit(i)}}{\varepsilon_{Aléa(i)}}$$

In other words, the measure of the similarity error of the predicted vector with the *a posteriori* vector is 18% less than the measure of the similarity error of the random vector with the *a posteriori* (see Figure 3.35). *Predicted vectors are more similar to a posteriori vectors than random vectors.*

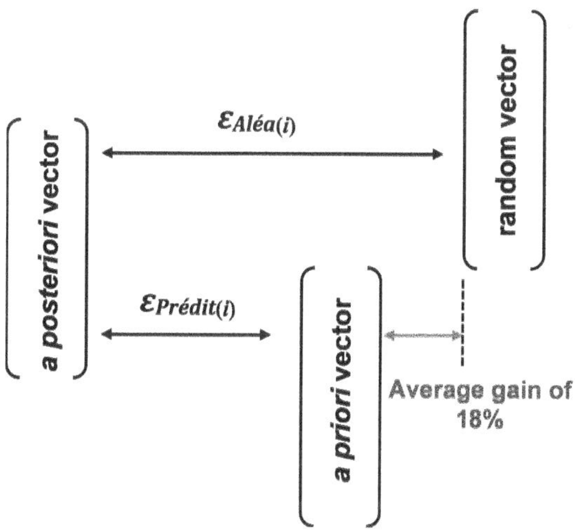

Figure 3.35. *Relative gain of the prediction error over the random error. For a color version of this figure, see www.iste.co.uk/goglin/investment2.zip*

This result is visually reflected in Figure 3.36 by a curve positioned above the x-axis, on average.

The prediction "beats" the chance, which is natural given the additional information (on the preferences of the individual used as parameter) of the matching function. It can also be concluded that *individuals make choices in accordance with their preferences* (in terms of values and interest in the fields of activity).

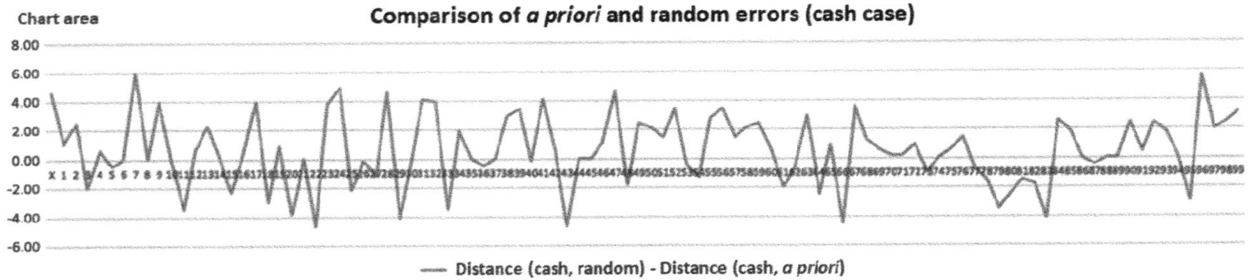

Figure 3.36. *Graphical representation of the difference between predicted errors and random errors. For a color version of this figure, see www.iste.co.uk/goglin/investment2.zip*

3.5.2.3. *Affective matching theory: affective and cognitive dimensions of the investment choice in equity crowdfunding*

The central question of this research concerns the domination of the affective dimension over the cognitive dimension of individual investors' investment choice in equity crowdfunding. The results of the estimation of the explanatory model using the PLS approach validated this initial conjecture with a marginal effect (cumulative indirect effect) of the perceived signal quality (cognitive variable) compared to the effects of the affective evaluation variables of Congruence to Base Values and Interest.

In this section, we express this affective/cognitive dualism thanks to the affective distance concept of affective matching theory.

Let us remember that the affective matching theory makes the hypothesis of the superiority of the affect over cognition under certain conditions. Figure 3.37 represents a point cloud. Each point in the plane is associated with a chosen project, that is to say, a project in which the individual investor has actually invested (orange) and an unselected project (blue). The projects have an "Affective distance" and a "Perceived signal quality" as coordinates. The affective matching theory predicts that the projects that best match the individual are chosen independently of any deliberative judgment. In other words, projects that minimize Affective Distance (and maximize the Intensity of Investment Choice) are selected by the investor, regardless of the associated Perceived Signal Quality. These projects draw an "affective boundary".

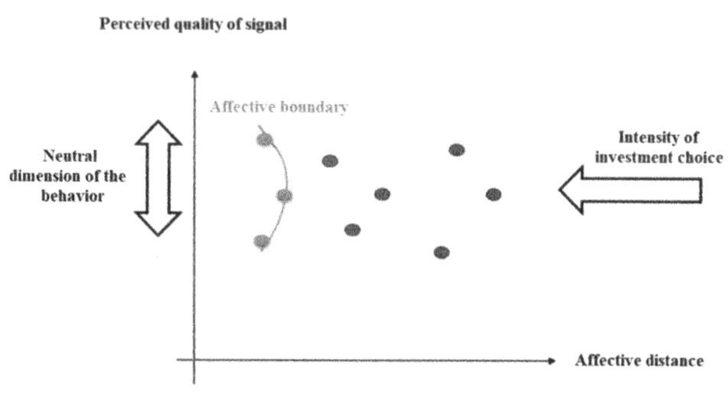

Figure 3.37. *Affective boundary of chosen projects. For a color version of this figure, see www.iste.co.uk/goglin/investment2.zip*

Figure 3.38 represents the 400 observations, each associated with a couple (individual, project), projected in the plane (X, Y) such that X is the Affective Distance calculated for the couple (individual, project) and Y is the Perceived Signal

Quality calculated for this observation. Observations in orange indicate that the subject has invested in the project (in cash or in percentage); otherwise, observations are blue.

For X, the Affective Distance is calculated according to the modalities specified in section 3.5.1.1.

For Y, the Perceived Signal Quality is calculated by the score of the external coefficients (outer weights) determined by the PLS-SEM method (see Table 3.35):

$$Y= 0.108*PLAN1(i,j)-0.021* PLAN2(i,j)+0.076* PLAN3(i,j)+0.401* PLAN4(i,j)+0.479*EQUI1(i,j)+0.286*EQUI2(i,j)-0.412*EQUI3(i,j)+0.576*EQUI4(i,j)$$

with i ranging from 1 to 100 (the subject) and j ranging from 1 to 4 (the project).

The results (see Figure 3.38) are not as sharp as theory predicts. However, while an affective line does not emerge clearly from the diagram, we still visually note a concentration of orange observations located on the left (value on the x-axis less than 2), i.e. for the projects that correspond the most to the subject by minimizing the Affective Distance.

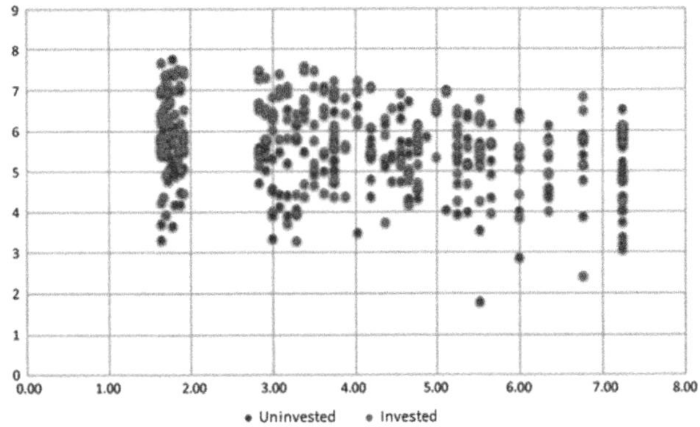

Figure 3.38. *Chosen and non-chosen projects projected on the affective and cognitive axes (X = Affective Distance; Y = Perceived Signal Quality). For a color version of this figure, see www.iste.co.uk/goglin/investment2.zip*

Let us study this result in more detail by separating the case of investments in cash (section 3.5.2.3.1) from the case of relative investments, i.e. as a percentage of assets (section 3.5.2.3.2).

3.5.2.3.1. Cash investment case

The two cases are not visually distinguishable (see Figures 3.39 and 3.41), which is explained by a certain constancy in the choices of investors, whether the amount invested is marginal ("Cash Case") or large ("Percent Case"). This phenomenon is captured by the insignificant moderation hypotheses H17 and H23 (see section 3.3.5.2.1).

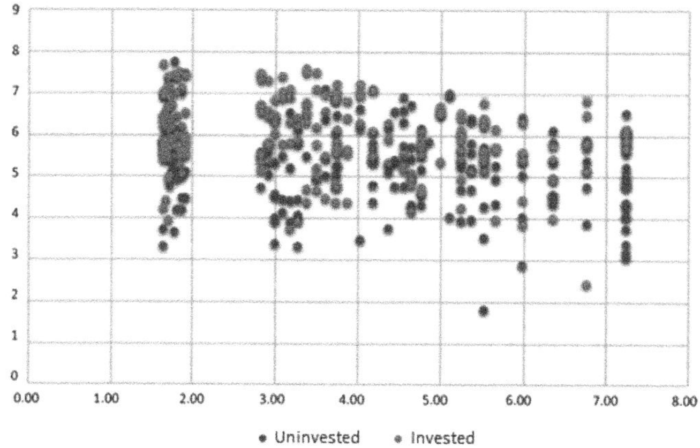

Figure 3.39. *Chosen and non-chosen projects projected on the affective and cognitive axes ("Cash Case") (X = Affective Distance; Y = Perceived Signal Quality). For a color version of this figure, see www.iste.co.uk/goglin/investment2.zip*

The aggregated results are interesting, if we calculate the "blue" observation (i.e. uninvested) mean of coordinates (X = average of Affective Distance of blue observations, Y = average of Perceived Signal Quality of blue observations) and we proceed in the same way to calculate an orange observation (i.e. invested) mean, obtain the following results:

Average Affective Distance (uninvested/blue) = 4.49

Perceived Signal Quality (uninvested/blue) = 5.18

Average Affective Distance (invested/orange) = 3.54

Perceived Signal Quality (invested/orange) = 5.94

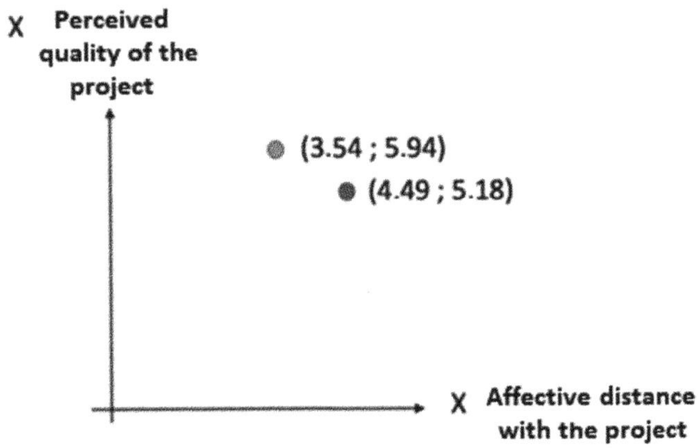

Figure 3.40. *Average invested (orange) and uninvested (blue) projects. For a color version of this figure, see www.iste.co.uk/goglin/investment2.zip*

Delta Affective Distance = Average Affective Distance (invested) – Average Affective Distance (uninvested) = – 0.95 < 0

Delta Perceived Signal Quality = Perceived Signal Quality (invested) – Perceived Signal Quality (uninvested) = 0.76 > 0

Figure 3.40 shows that, on average, the participants invested in projects that were more affectively close (negative "Affective Distance" Delta) *and exhibiting better "Perceived Signal Quality"* (positive "Perceived Signal Quality" Delta).

3.5.2.3.2. Relative investment case

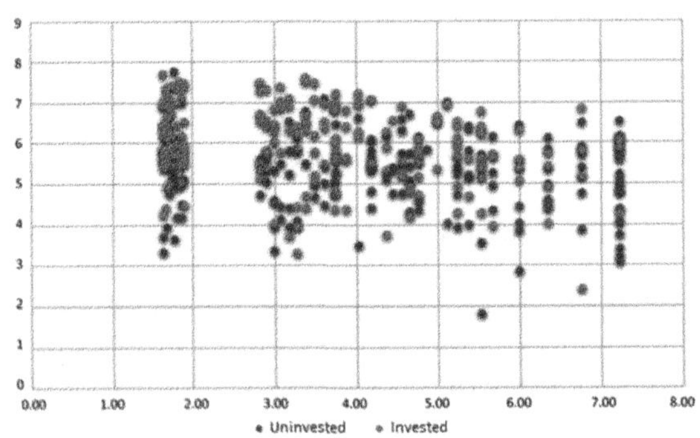

Figure 3.41. *Chosen and non-chosen projects projected on the affective and cognitive axes ("Percent Case") (X = Affective Distance; Y = Perceived Signal Quality). For a color version of this figure, see www.iste.co.uk/goglin/investment2.zip*

The results calculated on the relative investment choices (as a percentage of the subjects' assets) are similar to those obtained in the "Cash Case". We note, however, an increase (in absolute value) of the "Affective Distance Delta", which goes from – 0.95 to – 1.01, while at the same time the "Perceived Signal Quality Delta" decreases slightly, which indicates that the subjects favored more affectively related projects, whereas the challenge was to (virtually) invest all of their assets. This result is counterintuitive, as we could expect more reasoned choices based more on the perceived quality of the projects:

Average Affective Distance (uninvested/blue) = 4.51

Perceived Signal Quality (uninvested/blue) = 5.20

Average Affective Distance (invested/orange) = 3.50

Perceived Signal Quality (invested/orange) = 5.94

Delta Affective Distance = Average Affective Distance (invested) – Average Affective Distance (uninvested) = – 1.01 < 0

Delta Perceived Signal Quality = Perceived Signal Quality (invested) – Perceived Signal Quality (uninvested) = 0.74 > 0

3.5.3. *Conclusion*

This section began by discussing an implementation of affective matching theory. The method of determining the preferred projects and then a measure of the quality of the predictions of the individual predictive model were presented.

The result of the individual predictive model applied to the data resulting from the experiment was then presented.

First of all, we find that the affective matching theory *correctly predicted the subjects' preferred project in 55% of cases* in the configuration of investments in cash amounts, which is a very good score, considering the probabilities of occurrence of such a result with a random prediction.

Second, we show that the prediction *a priori* vector by *the individual predictive model does better than chance*, based on a comparison of the predicted error and the random error.

Finally, we represent the cloud of projects chosen and not chosen by the subjects of the experiment in a plan with x-axis X = Affective Distance and y-axis Y = Perceived Signal Quality. The aggregated results show that if we compare the average project chosen/invested in and the average project not chosen/uninvested in, then the average chosen project has a better Perceived Signal Quality and a lower Affective Distance than the average project not chosen, which indicates that *investors choose the projects that they consider the most sound as well as those that they prefer. Moreover, in the case of the investment of the total assets, the affective dimension is more marked than in the case of a small investment, which testifies to a form of instrumental irrationality*.

3.6. Conclusion

This third and final chapter compares the two theoretical models formulated in Chapter 1 (explanatory model and individual predictive model) with empirical reality. Section 3.3 is devoted to the analysis of the explanatory model; section 3.5 focuses on the presentation and analysis of the individual predictive model. The two models are, however, closely linked, since the individual predictive model is derived directly from the explanatory model.

Section 3.2 shows that the constructs of the measurement model of the explanatory SEM have a satisfactory psychometric quality for analyzing the structural model. In addition, with the Interest construct being central in the remainder of the analysis, let us specify that the analysis of its measurement model gives *a preponderant weight to the Situational Interest dimension, which combines Curiosity, Attention and Affective Involvement*.

Section 3.3 assesses the structural model of the explanatory model. It reveals *the two main determinants of the Intensity of Investment Choice, namely, Interest and Congruence to Base Values, while the impact of the Perceived Signal Quality has a relatively marginal total effect*. This result legitimizes the specification of the individual predictive model, which removes this cognitive variable. The study of mediators again highlights the determining role of the Interest variable, the mediation of which explains the majority of the effect of Congruence to Base Values on the Intensity of Investment Choice.

Section 3.4 analyzes the results of the experimental design. These results show that while the Quality of the Business Plan has a significant effect on the Perceived Signal Quality, it has no significant effect on the coefficients of the explanatory model. This leads us to the following conclusion: "*Subjects do not rely significantly on business plans to make their investment choices*", which is in line with the results of section 3.3.

Section 3.5 presents the implementation of the original affective matching theory: the method of determining the preferred projects and then a measure of the prediction quality of the individual predictive model are presented. We then show that *affective matching correctly predicts subjects' preferred project in 55% of cases*. In addition, the prediction of the *a priori* vector by the individual predictive model does better than chance. Finally, a representation of the projects chosen and not chosen by the subjects of the experiment, with an x-axis X = Affective Distance and y-axis Y = Perceived Signal Quality, shows that if we compare the average project chosen/invested in and the average project not chosen/uninvested in, then the average project chosen has a better Perceived Signal Quality and a lower Affective Distance than the average project not chosen. In other words, *investors, on average, choose the projects they prefer and consider to be very sound. In addition, the affective dimension of the choice is amplified in the case of relative investment (as a percentage of the subjects' assets), which is paradoxical and supports the idea of an (instrumental) irrationality of the subjects.*

Conclusion

The purpose of this exploratory research was to understand, explain and predict the behavior of investors in equity crowdfunding by focusing on the affective and axiological dimensions of the investment choice. Because of a corpus of qualitative data, we were able to adopt a back-and-forth approach between theory and data. Using this abductive/deductive/inductive approach, we developed an explanatory model that we estimated empirically by collecting data through laboratory experiment. Below, we first present our theoretical, methodological and managerial contributions (section C.1); we continue with the limits encountered at each major stage of this research (section C.2); and finally, we list the research avenues envisaged (section C.3).

C.1. Contributions

This first section presents our contributions to the theoretical, methodological and managerial aspects.

C.1.1. *Theoretical contribution*

C.1.1.1. *An increased understanding of the relative weight of the rational and emotional determinants of the choice between several investment opportunities in a situation of uncertainty*

Is the equity crowdfunding investor a cold, emotionless calculator looking for the project that presents the best quality signals? Is he/she only driven by a pure financial motivation to maximize utility, that is to say profit?

In the field of entrepreneurial finance, research on equity crowdfunding with an interest in the investment choice focuses on the asymmetry of information that the investor faces. Signal theory responds quite naturally to this dangerous situation. Also, signals can take several forms: relevant information from the business plan (financial forecasts, market positioning and patents) or entrepreneur profile (Ahlers *et al.* 2015), decisions of other investors (Lin *et al.* 2013; Freedman and Jin 2014), private information (on the competence of the entrepreneur) that one has if one comes under the friends and family category (Agrawal *et al.* 2015), campaign dynamics or the rate of completion of fundraisers (Agrawal *et al.* 2014; Hornuf and Schwienbacher 2015b), etc. All this information allows the investor to either have a basis for their analysis, if they are competent, or, if they are not, to replicate the choices of others by imitation. Ultimately, the choice is treated as rational, cognitive and oriented toward a goal: maximizing the profit.

We do not dispute that a fraction of equity crowdfunding investors exclusively or primarily seek profit or at least a tax benefit. We also do not dispute the results established on the links between real or virtual social interactions and investment choices.

However, we have explained how this mode of investment presents singular characteristics that call for other theoretical frameworks in connection with the affect to refine its understanding. The synthetic transversal framework that we have chosen essentially intersects with the fields of finance, psychology, marketing and HRM.

We are not alone in this theoretical approach, since a small number of works in entrepreneurship have recently started a movement toward explanations integrating the affective dimension of choice. These studies focus on the phenomenon of emotional contagion, the impact of entrepreneurs' pitch videos, and the effects of storytelling and persuasion on investors (Milovac *et al.* 2015; Wuillaume *et al.* 2016; Allison *et al.* 2017; Davis *et al.* 2017; Wuillaume *et al.*, 2017). We are part of the lineage of this work, but we position ourselves in the field of entrepreneurial finance.

For these reasons, we have chosen to focus on the identification and appreciation of the importance of the affective determinants of investors' choice as an object of research, while circumscribing the context of the choice by eliminating real and virtual social interactions, in order to highlight the studied phenomenon.

Finally, at the end of this work, we are able to answer the two questions selected for our problem.

The main question was to determine to what extent values and affective reactions determine the choices of equity crowdfunding investors. The empirical estimation of our explanatory model on a sample resulting from a laboratory experiment carried out on 100 subjects reveals that the values have a considerable significant effect and come in second place in terms of influence on behavior. Then, taken in isolation, affective reactions are significant, but their impact is not as significant as that of values. *An affective variable, Interest, surpasses all explanatory variables by the importance of its effect on the investment choice.* For this variable, the Situational Interest dimension, defined by the Curiosity, Attention and Affective Involvement subdimensions, has a greater weight than the Individual Interest dimension defined by the Valence of value and the Emotional Valence subdimension.

The cognitive variable of the model weighs little and is in the fifth position among the explanatory variables by the weight of its effect. Compared to all the affective variables, it becomes negligible, which provides an answer to the second question of this research: the affective dimension of choice dominates the cognitive dimension, at least in the context of our experiment. In addition, the results of the experiment are convergent and show that the subjects do not significantly rely on business plans to make their investment choices. These conclusions legitimize the specification of the individual predictive model, which removes the cognitive variable from the explanatory model.

The results of the individual predictive model support the analysis of the explanatory model as well as that of the experimental design. *The participants, on average, subscribed to the capital of projects that they preferred* (i.e. which corresponded to them most in terms of interest and values) and were judged on average to be of better quality; but paradoxically, in the case of relative investment (as a percentage of the subjects' wealth), the affective effect was amplified along with a simultaneous reduction in cognitive effect, which supports the idea of an (instrumental) irrationality of subjects.

C.1.1.2. *Proposal of an original affective matching theory between the information perceived by the investor and the latter's preference structure*

According to Pare and Rédis (2011), the hypotheses of traditional finance are not necessarily capable of fully understanding the field of entrepreneurial finance, because it has specificities, both in the entrepreneurial and financial dimensions. Our proposal is a possible answer to their call for a theoretical renewal.

The main idea of this doctoral work lies in proposing an original theory aimed at understanding and comprehending the investor's choice in a situation of uncertainty. This reading grid aims to complete the signal theory (Akerlof 1970; Spence 1973) mentioned to explain the choices of investors facing a strong information asymmetry.

As we explain in our work, this reading prism, which is a part of the paradigm of the efficiency of financial markets, probably does not fully explain investors' choices, particularly the choices of those who engage in equity crowdfunding with non-financial motivations and who therefore move away from the *homo economicus* prototype.

The theory we propose is, in a way, the projection of the organizational attraction theory in entrepreneurial finance. Organizational attraction is an individual's affective attitude toward an organization considered particularly desirable, combined with the motivation to enter into a contractual relationship with it (Aiman-Smith *et al.* 2001; Lis 2012). Borrowed from HRM, this theory is based on an affective and holistic approach rather than a cognitive and evaluative one; it is based on the P-O Fit theory, which explains an individual's attractiveness for an organization by a congruence of values and standards (Chatman 1989; Kristof 1996; Chapman *et al.* 2005). Finally, the P-O Fit theory can itself be based on the fundamental hypothesis shared by cognitive consistency theories such as Festinger's (1957) cognitive dissonance theory as well as on the psychology of values (Rokeach 1973; Schwartz 2006).

The affective matching theory is based on a congruence or correspondence of values, and more broadly on a correspondence between the characteristics of the project and the psychological preferences of the individual; these preferences include values as well as other dimensions specific to the context of equity crowdfunding, and it is for this reason that an *ad hoc* theory seemed necessary to us. This theory can be defined as follows: in the context of equity crowdfunding, certain entrepreneurial projects suit us more; they are naturally more attractive, regardless of any subjective evaluation. The correspondence between an investor and a project concerns two dimensions[1]: the values implicitly or explicitly promoted by the entrepreneurial team and the interest in the field of activity of the project. This almost immediate preference is an affective determinant of the investor's choice, which, under certain conditions related to the importance of the stakes, the nature of the motivations, the sophistication, the experience and the available time of the individual investor, dominates the effects of a subsequent cognitive assessment.

1 A third dimension, familiarity with the project, was not chosen because of the lack of significance of its effect on the investment choice. We nevertheless believe that this result is attributable to the artificial conditions of the experiment.

C.1.2. *Methodological contribution*

C.1.2.1. *Modeling individual investor behavior by designing an algorithm for calculating an affective distance between investor and project*

The exploratory approach of this work aimed primarily at developing a positive theory reflecting the role of the affect in investors' choice in equity crowdfunding. This is why, first, we developed an explanatory model that we estimated empirically on a sample of individuals. The estimated coefficients coincided with our expectations: the cognitive variable of the model, the Perceived Signal Quality, had a negligible effect with regard to the affective variables.

We therefore developed an individual predictive model by truncating the equation of the explanatory model (by removing the Perceived Signal Quality variable) and by resorting to additional information: the preference structure of each investor, or the data from the ordered lists of the 10 basic values and the fields of activity of the projects classified according to the interest given to them.

Because of an original matching procedure or algorithm, the individual explanatory model calculates an affective distance between an individual and 1 or n projects. It is then possible to order these affective distances in order to ultimately define an ordinal relationship between the competing projects, with information summarized in the *a priori* choice vector.

Applying this procedure to the subjects of the experiment gave an encouraging result, since it made it possible to correctly predict 55% of the first choices of the 100 subjects of the experiment. Moreover, the *a priori* choice vector predicted the *a posteriori* choice vector better than that by chance with a relative gain of 18% over a sequence of 50 draws – a result calculated because of the similarity measure that we proposed.

It should be noted first of all that the development of an individual predictive model meets the expectations of Mangot (2013), who defined the future of behavioral finance in three points: *personalization*, *learning* and *modeling*.

Then, we chose to place ourselves within the context of uncertainty, i.e. a universe where the consequences are not probabilized (objectively) without looking at the decision theory, whereas it would have been possible, essentially because of our main objective, which is explanatory and exploratory and not normative. However, as Kast (2002) pointed out: "One of the aims of the decision theory is to provide the means to build quantified descriptions of problems as well as criteria, which would allow for solutions to be found".

But, *the individual predictive model offers a means to quantify the affective distance between an individual and a project, with the choice criterion being defined by the optimum of the matching procedure that matches the individual with the project that corresponds to them the most.* This feature does not apply to the consequences of choices; so, it is not a utility. Matching is defined by the difference between certain characteristics of a project and those of an individual, and is based on interactionist theoretical foundations (the P-O Fit theory) and the cognitive consistency hypothesis. Thus, this model, based on an optimization, depending on affective preferences, implements a hedonic version of utility (without formally being a utility) close to that of the precursors of economic theory. In fact, the project that corresponds to us (result of affective matching) and attracts us the most is also the one that generates the most positive affective reactions. We therefore arrive at a conclusion similar to that of Slovic *et al.* (2002) on the experiential system (that is to say the intuitive system or system (1): "Ironically, the perception and integration of affective feelings, within the experiential system, appears to be the kind of high-level maximization process postulated by economic theories since the days of Jeremy Bentham. These feelings form the neural and psychological substrate of utility".

Then, the question of the possibly normative dimension of this work arises. Can an investor be recommended to choose the project that best matches his/her preferences regardless of the assessment of its quality? In other words, in a choice criterion, can we take as objective function – the one that is maximized – a function that results from an empirical approach and not from an axiomatic one?

In the foreword to Billot's (1987) book, the economist Claude Ponsard answered this question. For this researcher, optimization and explanation are not separate. A normative model is always based on the optimization of an objective function that necessarily results from an explanation. "It is our knowledge of reality that leads us to declare that such and such a choice is better than another".

From our point of view, a function resulting from an empirical explanatory approach may or may not act as an objective function. Indeed, if this function describes a behavioral bias prejudicial to the interests of the individual, what sense would a recommendation based on the maximization of this function, i.e. the bias, have? Also, we agree with Howard (1988), for whom a normative model makes sense only if it compensates for human deficiencies:

> The idea of the normative model is essential when we are not satisfied with our functioning. As we know that we are subject to optical illusions, we believe in our measuring instruments rather than our perceptions. [...] In view of all the shortcomings so easily demonstrated in human decision-making, who would want to rely on

unaided judgment to resolve a complex and important decision-making problem?

In the case that interests us, we distinguish between two alternatives: either the main motivation of the investor is financial, and in this case, it does not seem appropriate to base an investment recommendation on the basis of his/her preferences without taking into account the quality of the project, even subjectively, or his/her main motivation is non-financial, and in this case, such a recommendation becomes possible and even desirable because it is aligned with the individual's preferences, which corresponds to the definition of a good decision according to Howard (1988). "A good decision is an action we take that is logically compatible with the alternatives we perceive, the information we have, the preferences we feel".

C.1.2.2. *Designing an original similarity measure*

The individual predictive model (or matching procedure) associates a numerical value with each (investor, project) couple: the predicted Intensity of Investment Choice (or attraction). This number is calculated without the investor knowing about the project (therefore without evaluation) on the basis of the characteristics of the project and of the individual. It therefore becomes possible to order the most attractive projects, *a priori*, for the investor. If the latter faces n competing projects, then this algorithm results in an ordered vector with n components or an *a priori* choice vector. The question that arises next is that of the quality of the prediction, measured by the prediction error between the *a priori* choice vector and the chosen vector (or the *a posteriori* choice vector), determined by the evaluation of the n projects by the investor. In order to calculate this error measure, we have proposed an original calculation, of the vector similarity measure kind, that is based on two rules:

1) the measure of similarity, and therefore of the error, is all the smaller as the rank of each component is close, i.e. the component rank permutation is small. This rule is analogous to that which determines the Spearman distance;

2) the measure of similarity, and therefore of the error, is all the lower as the rank of the permutation, defined by the rank of the component of the smallest rank, is large.

Because of this tool, we were able to measure the relative gain of the proposed prediction over a random prediction, which validates the added value of the individual predictive model.

Let us add that this similarity measure can find an application in any problem, including perceptual measure, involving the comparison of ordered (hierarchical) data (or objects) structure for which the importance of the data (or objects) is in decreasing order.

Let us consider, for example, the ATP ranking of the 20 best world players taken on two successive dates t_1 and t_2 (with $t_2 > t_1$). Let us assume that the only difference occurring in the interval $t_2 - t_1$ is the permutation of the world no. 2 with the world no. 5 (case A), or else that the only difference is the permutation of the world no. 17 with the world no. 20 (case B); then, the proposed measure will calculate a greater distance in case A than in case B. This result corresponds to the natural intuition of a more considerable change that took place in case A because the top of the hierarchy is modified.

C.1.3. *Managerial contribution*

C.1.3.1. *For investors and the AMF*

Our work highlights the importance of values and interest in the project as determinants of the investment choice. The low impact on the decision of the quality of the project, assessed on the basis of the business plan, is a second striking result. In this case, the affective dimension takes precedence over the cognitive dimension, judging by the relative weights of the effects of the variables of our explanatory model.

This result raises the question of the conscious or unconscious risks taken by the investor, in particular if his/her objective is underpinned by a financial motivation, in which case the latter should conform to the theory of rational choice. But whatever the motivation, including an altruistic one, a judgment altered by an affective bias can lead at best to disillusion, at worst to substantial and damaging financial losses.

It is not necessary to go back to the classical philosophers who, from Plato to Kant, vigorously criticized passions, which are bad in themselves and from which one would have to free oneself in order to live a good life to understand the link between risk and affective decision.

In the field of neuroscience, Bechara and Damasio (2005) are at the origin of the somatic marker theory and defend the role of emotions as a guide for a good decision. However, they warned of a risk, revealed by an experiment in which the subject, subjected to a strong emotional inducer, did not make the best choices during the tasks they were subjected to.

Regarding his dual system 1 and system 2 decision-making model, Kahneman (2003) warned of decisions made in an affective way, i.e. those where system 1 takes precedence over reason, as nothing indicates that their choice is relevant. Indeed, Kahneman explained affective reasoning using the concept of accessibility of memorized information. Information is all the more accessible when it is associated with intense emotional states; however, there is no reason why the most accessible information should be relevant for decision-making. In this regard, Slovic (2001) mentioned the case of decisions with far-reaching consequences for which the risk perception is reduced. He illustrated his point with the emblematic case of cigarettes. It is not unreasonable to draw the analogy with the distant exit horizons (5–8 years) of an equity crowdfunding investment.

Work on affectivity heuristics shows that the perception of risks is negatively correlated with the expected benefits, when making a decision about a positively perceived object (Fischhoff *et al.* 1978). Thus, in finance, Ganzach (2000) showed that the familiarity of financial analysts with an asset altered their perception of the risk/reward ratio. According to Slovic *et al.* (2002), affect heuristics could induce erroneous decisions through the intrinsic limits of the experiential system, but, moreover, the affective could be manipulated.

Advertising and marketing professionals deliberately manipulate our affective reactions by using persuasion to influence our attitudes and behaviors.

According to Epstein (1994b), persuasive advertising is not only effective, but above all it carries more weight than rational discourse, *a fortiori* if the emotion inducer is an image or a video, as demonstrated by the results obtained during experiments associating images and preferences of travel destinations (Slovic *et al.* 1991).

In this book, we reported the impact, on decision-making, of persuasion via a video pitch professionally marketed by crowdfunding platforms and entrepreneurial teams.

In view of the risks associated with affective decisions, combined with our results on the likely importance of the affective dimension in the choice of investment in equity crowdfunding, it seems essential to us to at least inform and warn the individual investor in equity crowdfunding on the existence of this specific risk.

A current of law has also taken up the behavioral approach of investor behavior to come up with regulations aimed at correcting the biases that have been brought to light (Wetzer 2008). One possible way to protect the investor from his/her own biases could be through the nudge (Thaler and Sustein 2012), which is simply offering a default choice that most individuals adopt.

For France, it is up to the *Autorité des marchés financiers* (AMF), the financial institution and administrative authority, whose mission is in particular to safeguard the information of investors, to take charge of this work to protect investors.

We submit four proposals of gradual intensity:

– including a warning about this affective bias in the information to investors;

– inserting a legal notice in video pitches, as this is the most powerful emotional inducer;

– imposing a minimum diversification for investments whose amounts related to the financial capacity of the investor exceed a threshold;

– imposing exposure limits proportional to the level of income/or wealth, inspired by the American JOBS Act (title 3).

C.1.3.2. *For companies considering equity crowdfunding*

In addition to the financial aspect, books on crowdfunding highlight the importance of the information provided by the crowd of contributors to entrepreneurs. Advice, contacts and feedback are all sources of improvement, and even validation of the market offer (Bessière and Stéphany 2015). The crowd promotes the chances of success of the project and participates in its cognitive governance, i.e. in value creation by building skills that encourage innovation and the emergence of new opportunities (Charreaux 2011). Consequently, encouraging the commitment of these future shareholders becomes strategic. Specifically, the commitment to the achievement of the objectives of the firm is one of the three dimensions of the concept of commitment to an organization (Meyer and Allen 1991), which is explained by the P-O Fit, i.e. the congruence between the values and standards of the individual with those of an organization that we are already mobilizing to provide a theoretical basis for the proposed affective matching theory.

This reasoning, like the results of our work, reveals the importance of the role of values in the choice of projects. Let us remember that in our explanatory model, the Congruence to Base Values variable is the second most important by the total effects (cumulative direct and indirect effects) after the Interest variable in explaining the Intensity of Investment Choice.

Finally, these theoretical and empirical elements encourage us to recommend to entrepreneurs who wish to develop an advantageous cognitive governance *to attract investors aligned with their values, as they will be involved and, therefore, committed.*

An explicit communication of the project's values via the video pitch and the business plan seems to us an effective way of achieving this goal.

C.1.3.3. *For platforms*

C.1.3.3.1. Meeting the legal requirement for suitability testing more thoroughly

The CIP (investment advisor) or PSI (investment service provider) regulations require legal obligation on platforms to advise on personalized investments consistent with the profile of investors. This is given by the suitability test, defined by the MiFID II Directive No. 2014/65/UE of May 15, 2014, and administered by means of a questionnaire. Currently, the required information is related to the investment objectives, the customer or prospect's knowledge and experience in investing in the type of product or service offered, his/her financial situation and his/her tolerance for losses. As Wetzer (2008) notes, "it would not be difficult to enrich this questionnaire with a section with certain psychological aspects for investment advice relevant to both financial objectives and the psychological profile of the investor". Specifically, these additional questions could relate to the investor's preferred structure defined by the investor's hierarchy of values and preferences for a summarized list of sectors of activity in the economy.

Therefore, the individual predictive algorithm would determine the emotional proximity of the recommended projects, i.e. the level of a project's suitability with the psychological profile of the investor.

C.1.3.3.2. Meeting the legal requirement for personalized advice more thoroughly

The purpose of the suitability test is to enable platforms to provide relevant personalized investment advice for clients and prospects. As mentioned in the first chapter of Volume 1, the AMF doctrine grants the status of investment advice to mailings in numbers, provided they are accompanied by a recommendation, opinion and value judgment on a transaction opportunity. In other words, the personalized advice can be the same for the entire client and prospect file of a platform, which is quite paradoxical.

As we mentioned in the previous point, the individual predictive algorithm offers the possibility of quantifying the suitability of the psychological profile of the investor, reduced to his/her preferred structure, with a project requiring funding. This information could also be used to define and then transmit a selection of companies requiring funding that correspond to the idiosyncratic character of each individual. Thus, investment advice would be truly individualized.

This type of application is in line with personalized behavioral finance which, according to Mangot (2013), corresponds to the future evolution of this field of research. Moreover, as this author reports, behavioral finance has already found concrete opportunities in wealth management in which its results are used to improve customer relations with behavioral questions that give information about the financial personality of clients.

It should be noted that it is possible to go further in terms of automation. For example, the definition of the psychological profile of individuals could be inferred in a non-declarative manner from the digital double of the client whose contours are defined by all the data left by the customer when he/she surfs the Internet, especially on social networks. Junghans (2016) discussed the power of Big Data in predicting consumer behavior, but pointed out that the limit of these technologies is in predicting the future based on the past and the calculation of probabilities without being able to anticipate trends.

Automated and customized investment advice, or a *robot-advisor*, is another possible application of the individual predictive algorithm. These online wealth management tools offer financially competitive solutions to manage household savings in a fully or partially automated manner and in accordance with passive or active management strategies in relation to an investor profile. Also, it would be possible to automatically allocate a fraction of the capital of the "wealth objective" compartment of Shefrin and Statman's (2000) behavioral portfolio to subscriptions for shares in equity crowdfunding. This automatic allocation with diversification and growth objectives would have the advantage of being simple.

However, this mechanism would short-circuit the discovery and selection phase of the projects by the investor, even though it is a real hedonic experience in which, similar to a consumer, it enjoys the control conferred by the platform to make its choices. According to Ryu and Kim (2014), this dimension of autonomy is a source of intrinsic motivation (Deci and Ryan 1985) that is pervasive in crowdfunding platforms.

C.1.3.3.3. Preference structure and market segmentation

For individual investors, registered on a platform to which they would agree to reveal their preferred structure by declarative means, in order to, for example, benefit from targeted notifications about new projects that correspond to them, the collected information would establish a market segmentation, i.e. a classification.

Let us remember that the preference structure is the data for each investor of three orderly (hierarchical) lists, one for congruence to base values, the second for interest in the field of activity and the third for familiarity with the field of activity.

Because of the similarity measure proposed in our book, it becomes possible to classify investors of a platform according to a standard hierarchical (bottom-up or top-down) method to create investor typologies on the basis of proximity of psychological profile in relation to one, two or these three variables (ordered list).

Seven different segmentations can be considered:

– segmentation to one variable: (1) (congruence to base values) or (2) (interest), or (3) (familiarity);

– segmentation to two variables: (4) (congruence to base values, interest) or (5) (congruence to base values, familiarity) or (6) (interest, familiarity);

– segmentation to three variables: (7) (congruence to base values, interest, familiarity).

For example, a classification by the (congruence to base values, interest) pair would bring together all investors from a platform close to both their values and their interest in the different areas of activity of the funded projects.

One possible application, after using quantitative data with these classes, like the total amount of invested funds, would be to comparatively analyze these market segments to learn from them about the types of projects that can generate the most subscriptions, etc.

C.1.3.3.4. Possibility of implementing a market place with automatic matching system for unlisted assets

In financial markets, asset prices make it possible for transactions to be automated, for example, for order-driven markets, the automation of order matching based on the type of order ("limit order", "best limit order", etc.), and quantities and prices, except for the order in the market that favors speedy performance and does not depend on prices.

Also, this matching associates a purchase order with one or more sales orders for a given stock, resulting from a prior selection by the investor or his/her representant (asset management company, CGPI (independent financial adviser), etc.). This preselection is usually based on a passive management strategy (replication of a market index) or an active picking management strategy (based on fundamental and technical analysis), generally algorithm-automated.

In the world of unlisted assets (private equity) and especially for equity crowdfunding, the stages of stock selection (projects) and order matching are confused to the extent that the individual investor operates in a primary market. Selection is necessarily active, as financing startups are not listed and do not belong to any index.

The individual predictive model offers the possibility of an automated and active asset management for unlisted assets, *relevant to selection situations with a wide range of projects in competition*. This type of configuration is expected to develop in the future, for example, with aggregation platforms or unlisted securities like Alternativa[2].

In addition, an automated selection will be essential if, as the equity crowdfunding profession expects, a portion of UCITS OPCVM (investment company) assets becomes eligible for unlisted securities. This regulatory development is part of the list of proposals of the *Financement Participatif France* association of July 2017, to divert the savings of French people toward the real economy via unit-linked life insurance contracts and savings plans.

Another development could justify this type of mechanism: the PACTE Bill (Action Plan for Business Growth and Transformation) allows crowdfunding-financed securities eligible for the PEA-PME tax envelope.

C.2. Limitations

This section presents the limitations of this research and discusses the limits related to the chronological milestones of this research: literature review, qualitative study, laboratory experimentation and quantitative study.

C.2.1. *Limitations related to literature review*

This book is exploratory in nature. Based on an intuitive conjecture about the likely role of the affect in the decision-making of equity crowdfunding investors, a first literature review in the field of entrepreneurial finance (included in Chapter 1 of Volume 1) convinced us of the existence of a gap between the reasons given for reporting project choices by investors, centered on the cognitive dimension of choice and cognitive/affective dualism that we think is more relevant, as it potentially has greater explanatory power.

The intellectual path of this research naturally took us off the beaten track of finance. Also, the second phase of our literature review (see Chapter 2 of Volume 1) has seen the scope of the fields of knowledge explored and expanded, first to the disciplines of management sciences and then beyond, drawing from sources of the social sciences with cognitive psychology and social psychology.

---

2 Alternativa, a company liquidated in 2017, offered an alternative stock exchange for unlisted SMEs: https://www.boursorama.com/bourse/actualites/alternativa-une-solution-de-crowdfunding-equity-alternative-a-euronext-alternext-et-le-marche-libre-df35be927770fe9fa3516c2075560b4e.

The proposed modeling is the result of this cross-cutting theoretical research. The integrative approach that prevailed has led to a summarized model whose variables are transposed to finance from fields more or less distant.

Therefore, a weakness of the theoretical stage, a corollary of this cross-cutting and synthetic approach, relates to the lack of depth granted to some constructs that deserve an effort centered on finer operationalization. This is particularly the case for the Interest variable Interest, because it is transposed from cognitive psychology applied to the education sciences as well as because our book reveals its importance. Aware of this point, we however believe that our abductive approach to enriching the constructs by field work has partially alleviated this gap.

Similarly, while the transversality of this book has made it possible to produce an original theory (the affective matching theory), it requires further investigation both in its formulation and for its theoretical anchoring.

A second legitimate criticism can be made about the seemingly unbalanced nature of our explanatory model. It has only one variable representative of the cognitive dimension (Perceived Signal Quality) against four variables for the affective dimension (Axiological Congruence, Interest, Familiarity, and Affective Reaction), with the Trust variable being of a mixed nature. Does this asymmetrical modeling not introduce a bias?

First of all, as the purpose of our research is focused on explaining choices by their affective dimension, it was natural to identify the variables that we thought were relevant in this regard. Second, it seems to us that when one or more variables are added to a model, statistical analysis reveals their importance and, if necessary, their uselessness.

C.2.2. *Limitations related to the qualitative study*

C.2.2.1. *Limitations related to data*

The public qualitative corpus collected on the Wiseed.com platform is substantial, as it includes 3,020 mini-narratives of investors testifying to the reasons for their choice of project.

This convenience sample has advantages and drawbacks. The advantages include:

– data availability;

– a sample that includes actual investors, which favors external validity;

– the size of the corpus, which is large enough to use lexicometric tools and of course meet the data saturation criterion;

– answers given via an online questionnaire without communication with an interviewer, eliminating the Pygmalion effect[3] by which an experimenter influences a subject interviewed or not.

As for the drawbacks:

– short answers (19 words on average), which is probably related to the lack of motivation of investors to explain their decision-making reasons in depth. It should be noted, in this regard, that one-on-one interviews would provide more comprehensive answers;

– data from a single platform.

This last point, in our view, represents the main limitation related to the nature of the data. Indeed, Wiseed.com is the main French player by the volumes collected for crowdfunding. It is also a generalist platform; however, a significant proportion of the proposed projects are part of the sustainable development theme and especially the environment. At the time of writing, the distribution of funded projects into the four possible categories – environment, health, digital and food – is, respectively, 62, 19, 35 and 19 projects. Therefore, are these data not a biased representation of reality that distorts the internal validity of this work?

We recognize that this over-representation of eco-friendly projects may have influenced our judgment of the weight of non-financial motivations in investor choice and reinforced our belief *a priori* in a more affective than cognitive investment. However, we are convinced that this is a question of degree because even when reduced to the subset of the projects of the "health" and "digital" classes of the platform, i.e. projects furthest from the concept of sustainable development, the analysis of verbatim attests to the relevance of the variables of the model.

C.2.2.2. *Data processing limitations*

Skimming and manual thematic content analyses were performed by a single researcher, which is detrimental to the reliability of the results. The contradictory intersubjectivity would have made it possible to lean more toward objectivity and thus improve the internal validity of the results. Nevertheless, carrying out lexicometric routines (lexical intensity, co-occurrence and concordances) may have limited this risk due to the objective nature of these tools.

3 See Trouilloud and Sarrazin (2003).

Finally, while we have not triangulated by crossing several sources of information, our approach of going back and forth between fieldwork and theory has allowed us to corroborate the results resulting from abductive inferences.

C.2.3. *Limitations related to laboratory experiments*

In Chapter 2 of this volume, we outlined the treatments applied to the main biases of this experiment. Despite our desire to reduce these effects through an appropriate protocol, our research continued in a constrained framework (by time, means, etc.), which inevitably led to certain limitations.

C.2.3.1. *Capturing affective reactions*

Regarding the measurement of affective reactions, we used a self-reported questionnaire immediately after exposure to the stimulus: entrepreneurs' pitch videos.

There are limitations to this easy-to-implement method. First, the results obtained are purely subjective; second, Derbaix and Poncin (2005) mentioned the difficulty of certain subjects in the face of questions of introspection or retrospection.

The means of capturing affective reactions, especially emotions, are multifold: measurement of vocal expressions, measurement of facial expressions, psychobiological measures (electrical skin conductivity, pupil dilation, heart rate, electrical activity of muscles, measurement of alpha waves or blood flow in the brain, etc.).

In this regard, only a multimethod approach would improve the reliability of the measurement.

C.2.3.2. *Selection bias and familiarity variable*

A consequence of the selection bias induced by the composition of our sample is, from our point of view, the weak effect of the Familiarity variable of the model.

Indeed, there is an abundance of literature in entrepreneurial finance about the role of friends and family in initiating the funding of a project. The social environment of entrepreneurs is naturally subject to the familiarity bias, whereas in the artificial framework of our experiment, students were perfectly disconnected from the entrepreneurs of the four competing projects. We also believe that this work underestimates the importance of this variable, especially in the dimension of proximity to entrepreneurs. In addition, the data from the indicators of the formative

Familiarity construct showed distributions significantly far removed from the normal distribution, which mechanically underestimated the significance of causal relationships by the PLS-SEM approach.

C.2.3.3. *Selection bias and gender*

The lack of representativeness of the sample was highlighted in Chapter 2 of this volume. The group of participants was made up of a proportion of female students (62%) significantly higher than that of male students (38%). However, if we consider the case of the Wiseed.com platform, the study by Hervé *et al.* (2016) indicated that 93% of investors were men and that their behavior differed from those of female investors, the latter having a preference for less risky assets in accordance with their level of risk aversion.

However, in our research, the conducted multigroup analysis did not reveal a significant difference (at the 5% threshold) between students for the model hypotheses, without consideration for the effects of control and moderating variables, including risk aversion, which is not tested in multigroup analysis.

C.2.3.4. *Selection bias and financial incentive*

We chose an incentive in the form of a lottery with a one-in-two chance of winning a €10 card and a one-in-two chance of winning a €20 card. However, this distribution of probability is much more favorable than prevailing in the real world of venture capital. Thus, the risk aversion profile of participants is probably not as risk loving as that of real investors.

This limitation is explained by our desire to attract enough subjects for the sample size to allow for statistical processing.

C.2.3.5. *Role playing bias, actual motivations and artificial motivations*

We have no doubt about the conscientiousness and involvement of almost all the participants in the experiment because of their attitude during the session as well as, more objectively, thanks to four control questions scattered in the questionnaire (only four out of 100 participants were wrong in one of the four questions) or by the automatic verification of absence of straight lining (identical answers to all the questions) in the answers to the question.

Nevertheless, we ask ourselves about the limitation of role playing in which the motivations were imagined and not real. To what extent would students have made the same choices if they had really had to invest 200 euros, let alone all their savings?

The solution of experimental economists to this problem is clear; the consequences must be real and the gains proportional to the results in the experiment. As we explained specifically in Chapter 2 of this volume, this type of protocol setting was not aligned with our hypothesis of (instrumental, axiological and "affective") the rationality of investors, as the subjects would have been artificially oriented toward utilitarian-type behaviors aligned with a strictly instrumental rationality.

Three points, however, suggest that the simulation has generated behaviors that are faithful to those that would have prevailed in reality:

1) after the session, during a brief informal chat with some students, we mentioned that they had chosen one project instead of another, as it presented, in their eyes, a better potential in terms of future profits, and thus their choice was not simply because of their preference;

2) IAE students (similar to sophisticated investors in the experiment) made less affective-driven investments than the others (see moderation of the effect of the Affective Reaction on the Intensity of Investment Choice by moderating variable Sophistication);

3) the students choosing the Power Through the Acquisition of Wealth value as the first value characterizing them also made a notably more cognitive choice than the other participants.

C.2.3.6. *Effect of contamination*

In order to avoid the effect of contamination, by which subjects informed of the objective of a study may not answer sincerely, we did not reveal the purpose of the experiment. Nevertheless, the design of the questionnaire could make it possible to guess its objective insofar as many questions were related to the subject of affect.

C.2.3.7. *Limited external validity calling for further research*

As with any laboratory experiment of this type, the external validity of our experiment is limited to the framework and the conditions that prevailed for its realization. We cannot claim any generalization of these results. In fact, on the one hand, our sample is not representative of the real crowd of investors in equity crowdfunding and, on the other hand, the context for carrying out the tasks was artificial (role play, absence of real or virtual interactions, etc.) by construction and by virtue of the protocol implemented. Nevertheless, the conclusions obtained make it possible for us to present the possibility of the phenomenon. New research will make it possible, on the basis of an accumulation, to gradually validate these initial results.

C.2.4. *Limitations related to the quantitative study*

While the PLS approach has many advantages, it also has some disadvantages as follows:

– the method does not offer a fit index to the data, which hinders the comparison of models. On this point, we should remember that this research is exploratory in nature;

– the consistency problem: the PLS approach does not take into account the measurement errors for the estimation of the coefficients, which become asymptotically correct with large samples, and the consequence is an underestimation of the structural relationships and an overestimation of the loadings of the indicators. In our case, the number of points in the sample (400) was high, which limits this problem.

C.3. Research paths

This section discusses the five avenues of research envisaged as a result of this work: the transposition of the model to other objects of finance, business angels and socially responsible investment (SRI) (sections C.3.1 and C.3.2); the proposal of a formal multicriteria normative model integrating matching in the expectation of utility (section C.3.3); improving the modeling because of affective computing (section C.3.4); and reflecting on the link between ethics and affective matching theory (section C.3.5).

C.3.1. *Adaptation and transposition of the model to the case of BAs*

While research on the factors explaining the selection of projects (screening) by business angels emphasizes the cognitive dimension of choice by adopting the analytical frameworks of agency and information theories, the role of non-financial motivations like the pleasure of accompanying a creator or interpersonal affinity (Mason and Stark 2004) like the role of intuition (Ola 2016) seems to bridge with our research.

Intuition, in particular, is based on experience and on the affect (Coget *et al.* 2009); so, it seems to us that the explanatory model of our work could be adapted to the case of business angels.

This seems to make sense insofar as business angels are associated with equity crowdfunding fundraising by syndication, or even participate in fundraising directly, without special status. However, the specificities of investment by business angels relative to investment in equity crowdfunding are multifold: the amount involved, sophistication, due diligence, direct and hands on relationship, etc.

Also, *we plan to use the concept of personal attraction* (Michinov 2001) instead of the concept of organizational attractiveness to adapt the affective matching theory to the case of business angels.

C.3.2. *Adaptation and transposition of the model to the case of SRI and ethical finance*

SRI investment and ethical finance have similarities with equity crowdfunding on at least two points: (1) the role of extra-financial incentives in investment choices; and (2) the importance of values. For this reason, we believe that it would be relevant to apply our model to this segment of finance.

C.3.2.1. *Role of extra-financial incentives in investment choices*

While the role of non-financial incentives in the choices of equity crowdfunding investors is still debated, a presumption (see Chapter 1 of Volume 1, section 1.2.1.2) seems to attest to their importance.

In ethical finance as in SRI, the role of non-financial motivations in the selection of securities or projects is attested by the literature. For example, in a comparative study of ethical and unethical investors, Lewis (2001) showed that the motivations of all participants were both financial and non-financial. There is no *homo economicus*; in particular, ethical investors are torn between their need for security, which pushes them to invest in standard funds, and their guilt, a feeling that encourages them to invest in ethical funds.

Impact investing has the same characteristic; according to Bugg-Levine and Emerson (2011), the investor pursues a profit objective while aiming for social and environmental impact goals. The concept of blended value is the indivisible combination of three elements – economic, social and environmental – to which intrinsic and extrinsic motivations correspond.

C.3.2.2. *Importance of values*

A classification of SRI investors reveals the heterogeneity of this population. Lavison (2011) mentioned the two main classes of SRI investors:

– value-seeking people are part of a classic approach to maximizing risk-adjusted returns, with ESG (environmental, social and governance) information being only a complementary indicator revealing the quality of securities;

– the value-based people are altruistic and ready to give up profitability in order to increase collective well-being, meaning that they base their choices on values independently of the traditional tools of financial analysis.

Kinder (2005), who is behind the term "value-based investors", also underlined the need for consistency of investors between their investments and their values, which is reminiscent of the Congruence to Base Values variable of our explanatory model. The author also specifies that the value-based investor is part of a long-term approach through a buy-and-hold strategy, which constitutes another similarity with the equity crowdfunding investor in, as the latter is captive and cannot expect an exit for several years.

In ethical finance, Lewis (2001) noted that the investment made is in accordance with the morals and values of the investor; moreover the purpose of the investment is to change things. The main difference between ethical and unethical investors is that the former transform their beliefs into acts and thus maintain consistency between their financial investments and their lifestyle. Once again, we note that *consistency, more global this time, characterizes ethical investors, which echoes the affective matching theory proposed in our work.*

C.3.2.3. *Possible relevant reading grid*

Déjean (2002) believed that research on SRI has no theoretical foundations and by default confronts the SRI investor with the rational agent; the biases observed do not mean that the latter is irrational but that the contours of his/her rationality need to be established.

Due to the reconciliation we suggest between equity crowdfunding and SRI/ethical investment, we believe that it would be relevant to apply our model to these assets classes. In addition, the affective matching theory has its roots in the I-O Fit theory according to which individuals are more attracted to organizations whose norms and values are congruent with theirs (Chatman 1989; Kristof 1996; Chapman *et al.* 2005), which fits with the value-based investor approach.

Finally, the logic of maximizing an attraction (by matching different preferences) of our individual predictive model, close to a Benthamian utility insofar as it is associated with an increase in well-being, echoes the assertion of Lavison (2011) for whom "the agents [value-based and value-seeking of SRI] all maximize their utility, but the sources of satisfaction of different individuals are not identical".

C.3.3. *Defining a multicriteria normative model as an extension of expected utility*

If transposing this research to SRI bears fruit, it would then be interesting to *think about modeling an optimal decision, the result of a multicriteria objective function. The first criterion would be the expected utility and the second the matching criterion.* The weightings of these two dimensions would make it possible to represent the three classes of investors according to Lavison's (2011) typology of SRI investors: altruistic, value-based and value-seeking.

Operational research offers tools adapted to this type of problem, like multicriteria decision support (Roy 1985) that would allow the rational choice theory to be extended from the agent driven by an instrumental rationality to an agent driven by a more complex rationality. This extension would be distinguished from economic decision models derived from expected utility integrating morality and social considerations in the utility function (Lopes 2005), as it would not be solely utilitarian. Indeed, in the objective function that we would propose, the term representing matching, i.e. the adequacy of a project with the values and affective preferences of the investor, is not a utility but an attraction resulting from a congruence. However, the limit of this type of decision-making tool would be to restrict the universe of possible investment securities with the corollary of reduced risk diversification.

C.3.4. *Refining the modeling using affective AI for a dynamic discrete-time simulation model*

The predictive individual model makes it possible to predict, using matching at an instant *t*, the project preferences of an investor whose congruence structure is known *a priori*. The chosen project is one that minimizes Affective Distance or maximizes its Congruence, or the predicted Intensity of Investment Choice or even attraction.

It would be interesting to verify the learning effect of the investor over time, based on a history of real investors, as theory teaches us that experience reduces most behavioral biases (Mangot 2008). Consequently, the learning effect should be manifested by an increasingly rational choice, in other words by an Affective Distance from choices that increases over time. In accordance with the somatic markers theory of Bechara and Damasio (2005), a positive or negative exit would be considered as an event promoting learning, generating pleasure or unpleasure and modifying the respective weights of the affective and cognitive dimensions resulting from the dynamics of the previous choices. A total loss of capital would, for example, be a highly unpleasant event, remembered during a subsequent investment, which would have the effect of orienting the investor toward further reflection and analysis in order to avoid the risk experiencing this feeling of discomfort again.

Affective computing is a branch of artificial intelligence that aims to model emotions and design systems capable of recognizing, synthesizing and expressing emotions. In this field, a stream focused on modeling emotional processes aims in particular to (1) model the subprocesses triggering emotions; and (2) model the subprocesses that influence cognitive processes (Ochs 2007). To a certain extent, our explanatory model relates to this field of research, as we borrow from appraisal theory for the generation of affective reactions in the same way[4] that affective computing does to model subprocesses triggering emotions.

The second point mentioned – modeling the subprocesses that influence cognitive processes – finds applications in reinforcement learning techniques. Salichs and Malfaz (2012), for example, proposed implementing a learning program in which emotions reinforce the memorization of favorable actions to guide subsequent choices: "Emotions [...] provide the means by which the robot can learn from past emotional experiences and modify its behavior accordingly".

Ochs (2007) said that in this type of algorithm:

> [...] *emotions* are used as a *heuristic for selecting an action*, memorizing, and finding information, or choosing a reasoning strategy. These models are particularly intended [...] for agents evolving in *an uncertain environment*, capable of having *several goals simultaneously* and *limited resources*.

Starting from the similarity between the contexts of application of this type of program with those with which the equity crowdfunding investor faces (decision with an affective dimension, situation of uncertainty, multiplicity of goals and limited resources), it seems to us that a simulation using an affective computing algorithm, transposed to the case of equity crowdfunding and calibrated on a sample of individuals, would make it possible to better understand the dynamics of investor choices and to study more particularly the hypothesis of reinforcement learning.

C.3.5. *Thoughts on the ethical dimension linked to the perspective of affective matching*

It seems useful to us to take a step back to think more about the ethical dimension that can possibly be attributed to investments in equity crowdfunding.

Indeed, equity crowdfunding investors seem to share a common trait with ethical finance investors: they are driven by financial and non-financial motivations (Akili-Goglin 2018).

---

4 It should be noted all the same that our approach to emotions is continuous, whereas it is generally discreet in the field of affective computing.

Moreover, according to Lelart (2014): "Ethical finance, which is really ethical, is defined by its destination: to whom will the money be loaned, what will it be used for? [...] Ethical finance is now that which is oriented towards certain companies, certain activities".

This definition highlights the ethical dimension of equity crowdfunding, which gives the individual investor the possibility of choosing the destination and use of their savings. The affective matching theory is in fact a prism in which *the investor directs their savings by aligning the characteristics of the chosen project with their goals and preferences. In doing so, consciously or not, they participate in the transformation of reality by selecting an entrepreneurial team that they commission to achieve their own objectives.* This approach can be opposed to that of the *homo economicus* of traditional finance who consciously maximizes their profit, without wishing to impact reality in a precise direction. However, through their choices of financial allocation, the *homo economicus* modifies the world by contributing to the transformation operated by the blind forces (that is to say without orientation) of economic capitalism. They commission managers, *a priori* capable of generating profit, whatever their vision of the world, including if it is in opposition to their values.

References

Ackert, L.F. and Church, B.K. (2006). Firm image and individual investment decisions. *Journal of Behavioral Finance*, 7(3), 155–167.

Agrawal, A., Catalini, C., Goldfarb, A. (2011). The geography of crowdfunding. Working document, NBER, Cambridge.

Agrawal, A., Catalini, C., Goldfarb, A. (2014). Some simple economics of crowdfunding. *Innovation Policy and the Economy*, 14(1), 63–97.

Agrawal, A., Catalini, C., Goldfarb, A. (2015). Crowdfunding: Geography, social networks, and the timing of investment decisions. *Journal of Economics & Management Strategy*, 24(2), 253–274.

Agrawal, A., Catalini, C., Goldfarb, A. (2016). Are syndicates the killer app of equity crowdfunding? *California Management Review*, 58(2), 111–124.

Ahlers, G.K.C., Cumming, D., Günther, C., Schweizer, D. (2015). Signaling in equity crowdfunding. *Entrepreneurship Theory and Practice*, 39(4), 955–980.

Aiman-Smith, L., Bauer, T.N., Cable, D.M. (2001). Are you attracted? Do you intend to pursue? A recruiting policy-capturing study. *Journal of Business and Psychology*, 16(2), 219–237.

Aïte, A.A. (2013). Processus émotionnels et cognitifs dans le développement des capacités de prise de décision sous ambiguïté. PhD Thesis, Paris 5, Paris.

Akerlof, G.A. (1970). The market for "lemons": Quality uncertainty and the market mechanism. *Quarterly Journal of Economics*, 84(3), 488–500.

Akili-Goglin, C. (2018). Financer les jeunes entreprises innovantes. *Centraliens*, 657.

Alba, J.W. and Hutchinson, J.W. (1987). Dimensions of consumer expertise. *Journal of Consumer Research*, 13(4), 411–454.

Allais, M. (1953). Le comportement de l'homme rationnel devant le risque : critique des postulats et axiomes de l'École américaine. *Econometrica*, 21(4), 503–546.

Allison, T.H., Davis, B.C., Webb, J.W., Short, J.C. (2017). Persuasion in crowd-funding: An elaboration likelihood model of crowdfunding performance. *Journal of Business Venturing*, 32(6), 707–725.

Andrieu, G. and Groh, P. (2018). Specialist versus generalist investors: Trading off support quality, investment horizon and control rights. *European Economic Review*, 101, 459–478.

Arrow, K.J. (1974). *The Limits of Organization*. W.W. Norton & Company, New York.

Ashforth, B.E. and Mael, F. (1989). Social identity theory and the organization. *Academy of Management Review*, 14(1), 20–39.

Aspara, J. and Tikkanen, H. (2011). Individuals' affect-based motivations to invest in stocks: Beyond expected financial returns and risks. *Journal of Behavioral Finance*, 12(2), 78–89.

Aspara, J., Olkkonen, R., Tikkanen, H., Moisander, J. (2008). A theory of affective self-affinity: Definitions and application to a company and its business. *AMS Review*, 12(3), 40.

Aurifeille, J.-M. (1991). Proposition d'une méthode de mesure du halo affectif en marketing. *Recherche et application en marketing*, 6(4), 59–77.

Baker, H.K. and Nofsinger, J.R. (2010). *Behavioral Finance: Investors, Corporations, and Markets*. John Wiley & Sons, New York.

Baker, W., Hutchinson, J.W., Moore, D., Nedungadi, P. (1986). Brand familiarity and advertising: Effects on the evoked set and brand preference. *ACR North American Advances*, 13, 637–642.

Baker, M., Pan, X., Wurgler, J. (2009). The psychology of pricing in mergers and acquisitions. Working document, Harvard Business School, Boston.

Bammens, Y. and Collewaert, V. (2014). Trust between entrepreneurs and angel investors: Exploring positive and negative implications for venture performance assessments. *Journal of Management*, 40(7), 1980–2008.

Barber, B.M., Heath, C., Odean, T. (2003). Good reasons sell: Reason-based choice among group and individual investors in the stock market. *Management Science*, 49(12), 1636–1652.

Bargh, J.A. (1997). The automaticity of everyday life: Advances in social cognition. In *The Automaticity of Everyday Life: Advances in Social Cognition, Volume X*, Wyer Jr, R.S. (ed.). Psychology Press, Hove.

Bechara, A. and Damasio, A.R. (2005). The somatic marker hypothesis: A neural theory of economic decision. *Games and Economic Behavior*, 52(2), 336–372.

Bechara, A., Damasio, A.R., Damasio, H., Anderson, S.W. (1994). Insensitivity to future consequences following damage to human prefrontal cortex. *Cognition*, 50(1–3), 7–15.

Bechara, A., Damasio, H., Damasio, A.R., Lee, G.P. (1999). Different contributions of the human amygdala and ventromedial prefrontal cortex to decision-making. *Journal of Neuroscience*, 19(13), 5473–5481.

Bechter, C., Jentzsch, S., Frey, M. (2011). From wisdom of crowd to crowdfunding. *Journal of Communication and Computer*, 8(11), 951–957.

Becker, J.-M., Rai, A., Ringle, C.M., Völckner, F. (2013). Discovering unobserved heterogeneity in structural equation models to avert validity threats. *MIS Quarterly*, 37(3), 665–694.

Bell, D.E. (1985). Disappointment in decision making under uncertainty. *Operations Research*, 33(1), 1–27.

Belleflamme, P., Lambert, T., Schwienbacher, A. (2014). Crowdfunding: Tapping the right crowd. *Journal of Business Venturing*, 29(5), 585–609.

Bentham, J. (1789). An introduction to the principles of morals and legislation. In *The Collected Works of Jeremy Bentham: An Introduction to the Principles of Morals and Legislation*, Burns, J.H., Hart, H.L.A. (eds). Oxford University Press, Oxford.

Bentler, P.M. and Chou, C.-P. (1987). Practical issues in structural modeling. *Sociological Methods & Research*, 16(1), 78–117.

Bernoulli, D. (1954). Exposition of a new theory on the measurement of risk. *Econometrica*, 22(1), 22–36.

Bessière, V. and Stéphany, É. (2014). Le financement par crowdfunding. Quelles spécificités pour l'évaluation des entreprises ? *Revue française de gestion*, 40(242), 149–161.

Bessière, V. and Stéphany, É. (2015). Financement et gouvernance des start-ups en equity crowdfunding. *Finance Contrôle Stratégie*, 18(4).

Bessière, V. and Stéphany, É. (2017). *Le crowdfunding : fondements et pratiques, Business School*, 2nd ed. De Boeck University, Louvain-la-Neuve, Belgium.

Bhaskar, R. (1998). The logic of scientific discovery. In *Critical Realism: Essential Readings (Critical Realism: Interventions)*, Archer, M., Bhaskar, R., Collier, A., Lawson, T., Norrie, A. (eds). Routledge, London and New York.

Bickart, B.A. (1993). Carryover and backfire effects in marketing research. *Journal of Marketing Research*, 30(1), 52–62.

Billot, A.B. (1987). *Préférence et utilité floues*. Presses Universitaires de France, Paris.

Bleichrodt, H. and Wakker, P.P. (2015). Regret theory: A bold alternative to the alternatives. *The Economic Journal*, 125(583), 493–532.

Bonnet, C. (2005). La confiance entre capital-investisseurs et dirigeants : conséquences comportementales et influence sur la performance financière. *Finance Contrôle Stratégie*, 8(2), 99–132.

Bornstein, R.F. (1989). Exposure and affect: Overview and meta-analysis of research, 1968–1987. *Psychological Bulletin*, 106(2), 265–289.

Boudon, R. (1999). La “rationalité axiologique” : une notion essentielle pour l’analyse des phénomènes normatifs. *Sociologie et sociétés*, 31(1), 103.

Boudon, R. (2004). Théorie du choix rationnel ou individualisme méthodologique ? *Revue du MAUSS*, 24(2), 281–309.

Boudon, R. (2011). La théorie générale de la rationalité, base de la sociologie cognitive. In *La sociologie cognitive*, Kaufmann, L., Clément, F. (eds). Ophrys, Paris.

Boyle, G.J. (1989). Sex differences in reported mood states. *Personality and Individual Differences*, 10(11), 1179–1183.

Bretschneider, U., Knaub, K., Wieck, E. (2014). Motivations for crowdfunding: What drives the crowd to invest in start-ups? In *European Conference on Information Systems*. ECIS, Tel Aviv.

Brody, L. and Hall, J.A. (2008). Gender and emotion in context. *Handbook of Emotions*, 3rd ed. Guilford Press, New York.

Broihanne, M.-H., Merli, M., Roger, P. (2004). *Finance comportementale*. Economica, Paris.

Brown, B. and Perry, S. (1994). Removing the financial performance halo from fortune’s “most admired” companies. *Academy of Management Journal*, 37(5), 1347–1359.

Browne, M.W. (1984). Asymptotically distribution-free methods for the analysis of covariance structures. *British Journal of Mathematical and Statistical Psychology*, 37(1), 62–83.

Bryan, M. (2013). *Histoire illustrée de la philosophie*. Le Pré aux Clercs, Paris.

Bugg-Levine, A. and Emerson, J. (2011). Impact investing: Transforming how we make money while making a difference. *Innovations*, 6(3), 9–18.

Burke, L.A. and Miller, M.K. (1999). Taking the mystery out of intuitive decision making. *Academy of Management Executive*, 13(4), 91–99.

Burtch, G., Ghose, A., Wattal, S. (2014). Cultural differences and geography as determinants of online prosocial lending. *MIS Quarterly*, 38(3), 773–794.

Buttard, A. and Gadreau, M. (2008). D’une rationalité instrumentale à une rationalité interprétative de l’agent. Working document, University of de Bourgogne, Dijon.

Calvet, L., Campbell, J., Sodini, P. (2009). Measuring the financial sophistication of households. *American Economic Review*, 99(2), 393–398.

Camerer, C., Loewenstein, G., Prelec, D. (2005). Neuroeconomics: How neuro-science can inform economics. *Journal of Economic Literature*, 43(1), 9–64.

Cannon, W.B. (1927). The James-Lange theory of emotions: A critical examination and an alternative theory. *The American Journal of Psychology*, 39(1–4), 106.

Capelli, S., Guillot-Soulez, C., Sabadie, W. (2015). Engagement RSE et attractivité organisationnelle : la communication protège-t-elle en cas de crise ? *Revue de gestion des ressources humaines*, 96(2), 3–23.

Capraro, R.M. and Capraro, M.M. (2002). Myers-Briggs type indicator score reliability across: studies: A meta-analytic reliability generalization study. *Educational and Psychological Measurement*, 62(4), 590–602.

Carontini, E. (1990). Le rôle de l'abduction dans le processus d'interprétation. In *Technologies et symboliques de la communication*, Sfez, L., Coutlée, G. (eds). Presses Universitaires de Grenoble, Grenoble.

Cassel, C., Hackl, P., Westlund, A.H. (1999). Robustness of partial least-squares method for estimating latent variable quality structures. *Journal of Applied Statistics*, 26(4), 435–446.

Cattell, R.B. (1966). The scree test for the number of factors. *Multivariate Behavioral Research*, 1(2), 245–276.

Cauffman, E., Shulman, E.P., Steinberg, L., Claus, E., Banich, M.T., Graham, S. and Woolard, J. (2010). Age differences in affective decision making as indexed by performance on the Iowa Gambling Task. *Developmental Psychology*, 46(1), 193–207.

Chalmers, A.F. (1987). *Qu'est-ce que la science ? Popper, Kuhn, Lakatos, Feyrabend*. Livre de Poche, Paris.

Chamberlin, E.H. (1948). An experimental imperfect market. *Journal of Political Economy*, 56(2), 95–108.

Chapman, D.S., Uggerslev, K.L., Carroll, S.A., Piasentin, K.A., Jones, D.A. (2005). Applicant attraction to organizations and job choice: A meta-analytic review of the correlates of recruiting outcomes. *Journal of Applied Psychology*, 90(5), 928–944.

Charreaux, G. (1998). Le rôle de la confiance dans le système de gouvernance des entreprises. *Économie et societe, sciences de gestion*, 8–9, 47–65.

Charreaux, G. (2002). Au-delà de l'approche juridico-financière : le rôle cognitif des actionnaires et ses conséquences sur l'analyse de la structure de propriété et de la gouvernance. Document, University of Bourgogne, Dijon.

Charreaux, G. (2011). Quelle théorie pour la gouvernance ? De la gouvernance actionnariale à la gouvernance cognitive et comportementale. *Cahier du FARGO*, 1110402.

Chataigné, C. (2014). *Psychologie des valeurs*. De Boeck, Louvain-la-Neuve.

Chatman, J.A. (1989). Improving interactional organizational research: A model of personorganization fit. *Academy of Management Review*, 14(3), 333–349.

Chin, W.W. and Newsted, P.R. (1999). Structural equation modeling analysis with small samples using partial least squares. In *Statistical Strategies for Small Sample Research*, Hoyle, R. (ed). Sage Publication, London.

Chin, W.W., Marcolin, B.L., Newsted, P.R. (2003). A partial least squares latent variable modeling approach for measuring interaction effects: Results from a Monte Carlo simulation study and an electronic-mail emotion/adoption study. *Information Systems Research*, 14(2), 189–217.

Cholakova, M. and Clarysse, B. (2015). Does the possibility to make equity investments in crowdfunding projects crowd out reward-based investments? *Entrepreneurship: Theory & Practice*, 39(1), 145–172.

Churchill, J.J. (1979). A paradigm for developing better measures of marketing constructs. *Journal of Marketing Research*, 16(1), 64–73.

Cloren, G.L., Gasper, K., Garvin, E. (2001). Affect as information. In *Handbook of Affect and Social Cognition*, Forgas, J.P. (ed.). Lawrence Erlbaum Associates, Mahwah, New Jersey.

Coget, J.-F., Haag, C., Bonnefous, A.-M. (2009). Le rôle de l'émotion dans la prise de décision intuitive : zoom sur les réalisateurs-décideurs en période de tournage. *M@n@gement*, 12(2), 118–141.

Cohen, J. (1992). A power primer. *Psychological Bulletin*, 112(1), 155–159.

Cohen, J. (2009). *Statistical Power Analysis for the Behavioral Sciences*, 2nd ed. Psychology Press, New York.

Cohen, J.B., Pham, M.T., Andrade, E.B. (2008). The nature and role of affect in consumer behavior. In *Handbook of Consumer Psychology*, Haugtvedt, C.P., Herr, P., Kardes, F. (eds). Taylor & Francis, London.

Coley, A. and Burgess, B. (2003). Gender differences in cognitive and affective impulse buying. *Journal of Fashion Marketing and Management: An International Journal*, 7(3), 282–295.

Collins, L. and Pierrakis, Y. (2012). The venture crowd: Crowdfunding equity investment into business. Document, NESTA, London.

Connelly, B.L., Certo, S.T., Ireland, R.D., Reutzel, C.R. (2011). Signaling theory: A review and assessment. *Journal of Management*, 37(1), 39–67.

Cortina, J.M. (1993). What is coefficient alpha? An examination of theory and applications. *Journal of Applied Psychology*, 78(1), 98–104.

Cox, E.P. (1980). The optimal number of response alternatives for a scale: A review. *Journal of Marketing Research*, 17(4), 407–422.

Crié, D. (2005). De l'usage des modèles de mesure réflectifs ou formatifs dans les modèles d'équations structurelles. *Recherche et applications en marketing*, 20(2), 5–27.

Cronbach, L. (1951). Coefficient alpha and the internal structure of tests. *Psychometrika*, 16(3), 297–334.

Cuin, C.-H. (2001). Émotions et rationalité dans la sociologie classique : les cas de Weber et Durkheim. *European Journal of Social Sciences*, 39(120), 77–100.

Cumming, D. (2007). Government policy towards entrepreneurial finance: Innovation investment funds. *Journal of Business Venturing*, 22(2), 193–235.

Cummings, L. and Bromiley, P. (1996). The Organizational Trust Inventory (OTI): Development and validation. In *Trust in Organizations – Frontiers of Theory and Research*, Kramer, R., Tyler, T. (eds). Sage Publications, Thousand Oaks, California.

Damasio, A.R. (2006). *L'Erreur de Descartes*. Odile Jacob, Paris.

Damasio, A.R., Tranel, D., Hanna, D. (1990). Individuals with sociopathic behavior caused by frontal damage fail to respond autonomically to social stimuli. *Behavioural Brain Research*, 41(2), 81–94.

Dane, E. and Pratt, M.G. (2007). Exploring intuition and its role in managerial decision making. *Academy of Management Review*, 32(1), 33–54.

Dantzer, R. (2002). *Les émotions*, 3rd ed. Presses Universitaires de France, Paris.

Dantzer, R. (ed.) (2010). Introduction. In *Les émotions*. Presses Universitaires de France, Paris.

Darwin, C. (1872). *The Expression of the Emotions in Man and Animals*. John Murray, London.

Dasgupta, P. (2000). Trust as a commodity. In *Trust: Making and Breaking Cooperative Relations*, Gambetta, D. (ed.). University of Oxford, Oxford.

David, A. (1999). Logique, épistémologie et méthodologie en sciences de gestion. In *Conférence de l'AIMS*. AIMS, Chatenay-Malabry, Paris.

Davidson, R.J. (1998). Affective style and affective disorders: Perspectives from affective neuroscience. *Cognition & Emotion*, 12(3), 307–330.

Davis, B.C., Hmieleski, K.M., Webb, J.W., Coombs, J.E. (2017). Funders' positive affective reactions to entrepreneurs' crowdfunding pitches: The influence of perceived product creativity and entrepreneurial passion. *Journal of Business Venturing*, 32(1), 90–106.

Day, A.L. and Carroll, S.A. (2004). Using an ability-based measure of emotional intelligence to predict individual performance, group performance, and group citizenship behaviours. *Personality and Individual Differences*, 36(6), 1443–1458.

Deci, E.L. and Ryan, R.M. (1985). *Intrinsic Motivation and Self-determination in Human Behavior*. Plenum, New York.

Déjean, F. (2002). L'investissement socialement responsable : une revue de la littérature. Technologie et management de l'information : enjeux et impacts dans la comptabilité, le contrôle et l'audit [Online]. Available at: https://halshs.archives-ouvertes.fr/halshs-00584461/document [Accessed September 2016].

Derbaix, C. and Filser, M. (2011). *L'affectif dans les comportements d'achat et de consommation*. Economica, Paris.

Derbaix, C. and Pham, M.T. (1989). Pour un développement des mesures de l'affectif en marketing : synthèse des prérequis. *Recherche et applications en marketing*, 4(4), 71–87.

Derbaix, C. and Pham, M.T. (1991). Affective reactions to consumption situations: A pilot investigation. *Journal of Economic Psychology*, 12(2), 325–355.

Derbaix, C. and Poncin, I. (2005). La mesure des réactions affectives en marketing : évaluation des principaux outils. *Recherche et applications en marketing*, 20(2), 55–75.

Desbrières, P. (2001). Le capital-investissement. *Banque & marchés*, 51, 40–45.

Desbrières, P. and Broye, G. (2000). Critères d'évaluation des investisseurs en capital : le cas français. *Finance Contrôle Stratégie*.

Dhar, R. and Zhu, N. (2006). Up close and personal: Investor sophistication and the disposition effect. *Management Science*, 52(5), 726–740.

Diamantopoulos, A. (2006). The error term in formative measurement models: Interpretation and modeling implications. *Journal of Modelling in Management*, 1(1), 7–17.

Diamantopoulos, A. and Winklhofer, H.M. (2001). Index construction with formative indicators: An alternative to scale development. *Journal of Marketing Research*, 38(2), 269–277.

Diamantopoulos, A., Sarstedt, M., Fuchs, C., Wilczynski, P., Kaiser, S. (2012). Guidelines for choosing between multi-item and single-item scales for construct measurement: A predictive validity perspective. *Journal of the Academy of Marketing Science*, 40(3), 434–449.

Dorff, M.B. (2014). The siren call of equity crowdfunding. *Journal of Corporation Law*, 39(3), 493–524.

Dubocage, E. (2006). L'évaluation de la "start-up" par le capital-risqueur entre objectivité, jugement et mimétisme. *Vie & sciences de l'entreprise*, 173(4), 9–18.

Dumez, H. (2011). Faire une revue de littérature : pourquoi et comment ? *Le Libellio d'Aegis*, 7(2–summer), 15–27.

Dumez, H. (2012). Qu'est-ce que l'abduction, et en quoi peut-elle avoir un rapport avec la recherche qualitative ? *Le Libellio d'Aegis*, 8(3).

Eber, N. and Willinger, M. (2012). *L'économie expérimentale*. La Découverte, Paris.

Efron, B. (1987). Better bootstrap confidence intervals. *Journal of the American Statistical Association*, 82(397), 171.

Epstein, S. (1994). Integration of the cognitive and the psychodynamic unconscious. *American Psychologist*, 49(8), 709.

Ericsson, K.A. and Simon, H.A. (1980). Verbal reports as data. *Psychological Review*, 87(3), 215 251.

Feather, N.T. (1995). Values, valences, and choice: The influences of values on the perceived attractiveness and choice of alternatives. *Journal of Personality and Social Psychology*, 68(6), 1135–1151.

Fehle, F.R., Tsyplakov, S., Zdorovtsov, V.M. (2005). Can companies influence investor behavior through advertising? Super Bowl commercials and stock returns. *European Financial Management*, 11(5), 625–647.

Fenouillet, F. (2016). *Les théories de la motivation*, 2nd ed. Dunod, Paris.

Fernandes, V. (2012). En quoi l'approche PLS est-elle une méthode à (re)-découvrir pour les chercheurs en management ? *M@n@gement*, 15(1), 102–123.

Festinger, L. (1954). A theory of social comparison processes. *Human Relations*, 7(2), 117–140.

Festinger, L. (1957). *A Theory of Cognitive Dissonance.* Stanford University Press, Redwood City, California.

Filbeck, G. and Smith, L.L. (1997). Team building and conflict management: Strategies for family businesses. *Family Business Review*, 10(4), 339–352.

Filbeck, G., Hatfield, P., Horvath, P. (2005). Risk aversion and personality type. *The Journal of Behavioral Finance*, 6(4), 170–180.

Filser, M. (2015). Vers une consommation plus affective ? *Revue française de gestion*, 41(253), 173–187.

Finucane, M., Alhakami, A., Slovic, P., Johnson, S.M. (2000). The affect heuristic in judgments of risks and benefits. *Journal of Behavioral Decision Making*, 13(1), 17.

Fischhoff, B., Slovic, P., Lichtenstein, S., Read, S., Combs, B. (1978). How safe is safe enough? A psychometric study of attitudes towards technological risks and benefits. *Sciences*, 9, 127–152.

Fornell, C. and Larcker, D.F. (1981). Evaluating structural equation models with unobservable variables and measurement error. *Journal of Marketing Research*, 18(1), 39.

Frederick, S. (2002). Automated choice heuristics. In *Heuristics and Biases: The Psychology of Intuitive Judgment*, Gilovich, T., Griffin, D., Kahneman, D. (eds). Cambridge University Press, Cambridge.

Fredrickson, B.L. (2001). The role of positive emotions in positive psychology. *The American Psychologist*, 56(3), 218–226.

Freedman, S. and Jin, G.Z. (2014). The signaling value of online social networks: Lessons from peer-to-peer lending. Document, Indiana University, Indiana, and University of Maryland, Maryland.

Fried, V.H. and Hisrich, R.D. (1994). Toward a model of venture capital investment decision making. *Financial Management*, 23(3), 28.

Frieder, L. and Subrahmanyam, A. (2005). Brand perceptions and the market for common stock. *The Journal of Financial and Quantitative Analysis*, 40(1), 57–85.

Frijda, N.H. (1986). *The Emotions*. Cambridge University Press, Cambridge.

Frijda, N.H. (1988). The laws of emotion. *American Psychologist*, 43(5), 349–358.

Frijda, N.H. (2006). *The Laws of Emotion*. Lawrence Erlbaum Associates, Mahwah, New Jersey.

Füller, J. (2006). Why consumers engage in virtual new product developments initiated by producers. *ACR North American Advances, Association for Consumer Research*, 33, 639–646.

Ganesan, S. and Hess, R. (1997). Dimensions and levels of trust: Implications for commitment to a relationship. *Marketing Letters*, 8(4), 439–448.

Ganzach, Y. (2000). Judging risk and return of financial assets. *Organizational Behavior and Human Decision Processes*, 83(2), 353–370.

Garcia-Prieto, P., Tran, V., Wranik, T. (2005). Les théories de l'évaluation cognitive et de la différenciation des émotions : une clé pour comprendre le vécu émotionnel au travail. In *Comportement organisationnel (Vol. 1) – Contrat psychologique, émotions au travail, socialisation organisationnelle*, Delobbe, N., Herrbach, O., Lacaze, D., Migonac, K. (eds). De Boeck, Louvain-la-Neuve.

Gavard-Perret, M.-L., Gotteland, D., Haon, C., Jolibert, A. (2013). *Méthodologie de la recherche en sciences de gestion*. Pearson Education France, Paris.

Gayant, J.-P. (2017). *Risque et décision*. Vuibert, Paris.

Gefen, D. (2000). E-commerce: The role of familiarity and trust. *Omega*, 28(6), 725–737.

Geisser, S. (1974). A predictive approach to the random effect model. *Biometrika*, 61(1), 101.

Gerber, E.M. and Hui, J. (2013). Crowdfunding: Motivations and deterrents for participation. *ACM Transactions on Computer–Human Interaction (TOCHI)*, 20(6), 34.

Germon, R. and Maalaoui, A. (2014). Le crowdfunding, une nouvelle voie de financement pour les PME. In *Le grand livre de l'économie PME 2015*, Lecointre, G. (ed.). Gualino, Paris.

Gil, S. (2009). Comment étudier les émotions en laboratoire. *Revue électronique de psychologie sociale*, 4, 15–24.

Glaser, B.G. and Strauss, A.L. (1967). *The Discovery of Grounded Theory: Strategies for Qualitative Research*. Aldine Publishing Company, London.

Glöckner, A. and Witteman, C. (2010). Beyond dual-process models: A categorisation of processes underlying intuitive judgement and decision making. *Thinking & Reasoning*, 16(1), 1–25.

Goglin, C. (2020). *Emotions and Values in Equity Crowdfunding Investment Choices 1*. ISTE Ltd, London, and John Wiley & Sons, New York.

Gond, J.-P., El-Akremi, A., Igalens, J., Swaen, V. (2010). Corporate social responsibility influence on employees. ICCSR Research Paper Series, International Center for Corporate Social Responsibility, Nottingham University Business School, No. 54-2010 [Online], Available at: http://hdl.handle.net/2078.1/180416.

Graillot, L. (1996). Segmentation, choix de cibles et positionnement des produits touristiques : une approche méthodologique. PhD Thesis, University of Bourgogne, Dijon.

Grinblatt, M., Keloharju, M., Linnainmaa, J. (2011). IQ and stock market participation. *The Journal of Finance*, 66(6), 2121–2164.

Grullon, G., Kanatas, G., Weston, J.P. (2004). Advertising, breadth of ownership, and liquidity. *Review of Financial Studies*, 17(2), 439–461.

Gully, S.M., Phillips, J.M., Castellano, W.G., Han, K., Kim, A. (2013). A mediated moderation model of recruiting socially and environmentally responsible job applicants. *Personnel Psychology*, 66(4), 935–973.

Gurviez, P. and Korchia, M. (2002). Proposition d'une échelle de mesure multidimensionnelle de la confiance dans la marque. *Recherches et applications en marketing*, 17(3).

Gutman, J. (1982). A means-end chain model based on consumer categorization processes. *Journal of Marketing*, 46(2), 60–72.

Hackman, J. and Oldham, G. (1980). *Work Redesign*. Addison-Wesley, Reading.

Hadouni, L., Mesnildrey, L., Lesueur, M., Gouin, S. (2009). Étude des attentes des consommateurs de produits de la mer frais et de leurs produits de la mer frais et de leurs comportements selon les circuits de distribution distribution. *Analyse des dissonances cognitives*, 4.

Hahn, C., Johnson, M.D., Herrmann, A., Huber, F. (2002). Capturing customer heterogeneity using a finite mixture PLS approach. *Schmalenbach Business Review*, 54(3), 243–269.

Hair Jr, J.F., Black, W.C., Babin, B.J., Anderson, R.E. (2010). *Mutivariate Data Analysis*, 7th ed. Pearson, London.

Hair Jr, J.F., Ringle, C.M., Sarstedt, M. (2011). PLS-SEM: Indeed a silver bullet. *Journal of Marketing Theory and Practice*, 19(2), 139–152.

Hair Jr, J.F., Sarstedt, M., Pieper, T.M., Ringle, C.M. (2012). The use of partial least squares structural equation modeling in strategic management research: A review of past practices and recommendations for future applications. *Long Range Planning*, 45(5–6), 320–340.

Hair Jr, J.F., Hult, G.T.M., Ringle, C.M., Sarstedt, M. (2017). *A Primer on Partial Least Squares Structural Equation Modeling (PLS-SEM)*, 2nd ed. Sage Publications, Thousand Oaks, California.

Hall, J. and Hofer, C.W. (1993). Venture capitalists' decision criteria in new venture evaluation. *Journal of Business Venturing*, 8(1), 25–42.

Harrison, G.W. and List, J.A. (2004). Field experiments. *Journal of Economic Literature*, 42(4), 1009–1055.

Harrison, R.T., Dibben, M.R., Mason, C.M. (1997). The role of trust in the informal investor's investment decision: An exploratory analysis. *Entrepreneurship Theory and Practice*, 21(4), 63–81.

Hatfield, E., Cacioppo, J.T., Rapson, R.L. (1993). Emotional contagion. *Current Directions in Psychological Science*, 2(3), 96–99.

Heath, C. and Tversky, A. (1991). Preference and belief: Ambiguity and competence in choice under uncertainty. *Journal of Risk and Uncertainty*, 14(1), 5–28.

Heider, F. (1946). Attitudes and cognitive organization. *The Journal of Psychology*, 21, 107–112.

Heider, F. (1958). *The Psychology of Interpersonal Relations*. Wiley, New York.

Hemer, J. (2011). A snapshot on crowdfunding. Document, Fraunhofer ISI, Karlsruhe, Germany.

Henderson, J.C. and Nutt, P.C. (1980). The influence of decision style on decision making behavior. *Management Science*, 26(4), 371–386.

Hendrickx, M. (2014). Crowdfunding : mode d'emploi. Practical guide, EDI Pro 2.

Hendrickx, L., Vlek, C., Oppewal, H. (1989). Relative importance of scenario information and frequency information in the judgment of risk. *Acta Psychologica*, 72(1), 41–63.

Henseler, J. (2010). PLS-MGA: A non-parametric approach to partial least squares-based multi-group analysis. In *Challenges at the Interface of Data Analysis, Computer Science, and Optimization*, Gaul, W.A., Geyer-Schulz, A., Schmidt-Thieme, L., Kunze, J. (eds). Springer, Berlin.

Henseler, J., Ringle, C.M., Sarstedt, M. (2012). Using partial least squares path modeling in international advertising research: Basic concepts and recent issues. In *Handbook of Research on International Advertising*, Okazaki, S. (ed.). Edward Elgar, Cheltenham.

Henseler, J., Ringle, C.M., Sarstedt, M. (2015). A new criterion for assessing discriminant validity in variance-based structural equation modeling. *Journal of the Academy of Marketing Science*, 43(1), 115–135.

Henseler, J., Ringle, C.M., Sarstedt, M. (2016). Testing measurement invariance of composites using partial least squares. *International Marketing Review*, 33(3), 405–431.

Hervé, F., Manthé, E., Sannajust, A., Schwienbacher, A. (2016). Investor motivations in investment-based crowdfunding. *SSRN*, 2746398.

Hidi, S. (2000). An interest researcher's perspective: The effects of extrinsic and intrinsic factors on motivation. In *Intrinsic and Extrinsic Motivation*, Sansone, C., Hrackiewicz, J.M. (eds). Academic Press, San Diego.

Hidi, S. and Baird, W. (1986). Interestingness: A neglected variable in discourse processing. *Cognitive Science*, 10(2), 179–194.

Hidi, S. and Baird, W. (1988). Strategies for increasing text-based interest and students' recall of expository texts. *Reading Research Quarterly*, 23(4), 465.

Hidi, S. and Renninger, K.A. (2006). The four-phase model of interest development. *Educational Psychologist*, 41(2), 111–127.

Holbrook, M.B. (1986). Emotion in the consumption experience: Toward a new model of the human consumer. In *Consumer Behavior: Emerging Theories and Applications*, Peterson, R.A., Hoyer, W.D., Wilson, W.R. (eds). Lexington Books, Lanham, Maryland.

Holbrook, M.B. and O'Shaughnessy, J. (1984). The role of emotion in advertising. *Psychology & Marketing*, 1(2), 45–64.

Holland, J.L. (1985). *Making Vocational Choices: A Theory of Vocational Personalities and Work Environments*, 2nd ed. Prentice-Hall, Englewood Cliffs, New Jersey.

Hornuf, L. and Schwienbacher, A. (2015a). Portal design and funding dynamics in equity crowdfunding [Online]. Available at: http://ssrn.com/ abstract=2612998.

Hornuf, L. and Schwienbacher, A. (2015b). The emergence of crowdinvesting in Europe: With an in-depth analysis of the German market. Document n°. 2014-43, Department of Economics, University of Munich, Munich.

Hornuf, L. and Schwienbacher, A. (2016). Portal design and funding dynamics in equity crowdfunding [Online]. Available at: http://www. em-lyon. com/minisiteen/content/ download/169415/6656834/file/Hornuf.

Howard, R.A. (1988). Decision analysis: Practice and promise. *Management Science*, 34(6), 679–695.

Hu, L. and Bentler, P.M. (1998). Fit indices in covariance structure modeling: Sensitivity to underparameterized model misspecification. *Psychological Methods*, 3(4), 424–453.

Huang, L. and Pearce, J.L. (2015). Managing the unknowable: The effectiveness of earlystage investor gut feel in entrepreneurial investment decisions. *Administrative Science Quarterly*, 60(4), 634–670.

Huberman, G. (2001). Familiarity breeds investment. *Review of Financial Studies*, 14(3), 659–680.

Hull, C.L. (1943). *Principles of Behavior: An Introduction to Behavior Theory*. Appleton-Century-Crofts, New York.

Hutcheson, F. (1726). *An Inquiry into the Original of our Ideas of Beauty and Virtue*. Liberty Fund, Indianapolis.

Iizuka, M. (2014). *Le crowdfunding : les rouages du financement participatif.* Edubanque Editions.

Izard, C.E. (1977). *Human Emotions*. Kluwer Academic/Plenum Publishers, Amsterdam.

James, W. (1884). What is an emotion? *Mind*, 9(34), 188–205.

Jarvis, C.B., MacKenzie, S.B., Podsakoff, P.M. (2003). A critical review of construct indicators and measurement model misspecification in marketing and consumer research. *Journal of Consumer Research*, 30(2), 199–218.

Jevons, W.S. (1871). *The Theory of Political Economy*. Macmillan, London.

Jöreskog, K.G. (1971). Statistical analysis of sets of congeneric tests. *Psychometrika*, 36(2), 109–133.

Josue, R. and Bahm, C. (2016). Crowdfunding: Applying collective indexing of emotions to campaign videos. *ACM Conference on Computer Supported Cooperative Work and Social Computing*, 385–388.

Judge, T.A. and Cable, D.M. (1997). Applicant personality, organizational culture, and organization attraction. *Personnel Psychology*, 50(2), 359–394.

Jung, C.G. (1923). *Psychological Types*. Routledge Kegan Paul, London.

Junghans, P. (2016). Le Big Data pour construire une information d'anticipation. *I2D – Information, données & documents*, 53(4), 12–14.

Kahneman, D. (2003). A perspective on judgment and choice: Mapping bounded rationality. *American Psychologist*, 58(9), 697–720.

Kahneman, D. (2012). *Thinking, Fast and Slow*. Penguin, London.

Kahneman, D. and Frederick, S. (2002). Representativeness revisited: Attribute substitution in intuitive judgement. In *Heuristics and Biases: The Psychology of Intuitive Judgment*, Gilovich, T., Griffin, D., Kahneman, D. (eds). Cambridge University Press, Cambridge.

Kahneman, D. and Thaler, R. (2006). Anomalies: Utility maximization and experienced utility. *The Journal of Economic Perspectives*. 20(1), 221–234.

Kahneman, D. and Tversky, A. (1979). Prospect theory: An analysis of decision under risk. *Econometrica*, 47(2), 263–292.

Kaiser, H.F. (1960). The application of electronic computers to factor analysis. *Educational and Psychological Measurement*, 20(1), 141–151.

Kaiser, H.F. and Rice, J. (1974). Little jiffy, mark iv. *Educational and Psychological Measurement*, 34(1), 111–117.

Kast, R. (2002). *La théorie de la décision*. La Découverte, Paris.

Kenny, D.A. (2015). Moderator variables: Effect size and power [Online]. Available at: http://davidakenny.net/cm/moderation.htm.

Keynes, J.M. (1936). *The General Theory of Employment, Interest, and Money*. Palgrave Macmillan, London.

Kim, K. and Viswanathan, S. (2016). The experts in the crowd: The role of reputable investors in a crowdfunding market. In *The 41st Research Conference on Communication, Information and Internet Policy*, Mason, G. (ed.). University School of Law, Arlington, Virginia.

Kinder, P.D. (2005). *"Socially Responsible Investing": An Evolving Concept in a Changing World*. KLD Research & Analytics, Boston.

Kleemann, F., Voß, G.G., Rieder, K. (2008). Un(der)paid innovators: The commercial utilization of consumer work through crowdsourcing. *Science, Technology & Innovation Studies*, 4(1), 5–26.

Knight, F.H. (1921). *Risk, Uncertainty and Profit*. Houghton Mifflin, Boston.

Korchia, M. (2004). Connaissances de la marque : définition et mesures. In *Congrès de l'AFM*. AFM, Saint-Malo, Brittany.

Krapp, A. (2005). Basic needs and the development of interest and intrinsic motivational orientations. *Learning and Instruction*, 15, 381–395.

Kristof, A.L. (1996). Person-organization fit: An integrative review of its conceptualizations, measurement and implications. *Personnel Psychology*, 49(1), 1–49.

Kumar, A. (2009). Who gambles in the stock market? *The Journal of Finance*, 64(4), 1889–1933.

Kuppuswamy, V. and Bayus, B.L. (2015). Crowdfunding creative ideas: The dynamics of project backers in kickstarter. *SSRN Electronic Journal*, 5, 1–37.

La Porta, R., Lopez-de-Silanes, F., Shleifer, A. (1998). Law and finance. *Journal of Political Economy*, 106(6), 1113–1155.

Labreuche, J. (2010). Les principaux tests statistiques de l'analyse univariée : quand et comment les utiliser ? *Sang Thrombose Vaisseaux*, 22(10).

Laciana, C.E. and Weber, E.U. (2008). Correcting expected utility for comparisons between alternative outcomes: A unified parameterization of regret and disappointment. *Journal of Risk and Uncertainty*, 36(1), 1–17.

Lacroux, A. (2011). Les avantages et les limites de la méthode "Partial Least Square" (PLS) : une illustration empirique dans le domaine de la GRH. *Revue de gestion des ressources humaines*, 2, 45–64.

Lainé, M. (2016). Incertitude, probabilités et esprits animaux. Ontologie, épistémologie et théorie de la décision d'investissement productif chez Keynes. *Œconomia. History, Methodology, Philosophy*, 6–3, 403–439.

Lajante, M. (2013). Contribution des neurosciences à l'étude de l'émotion en persuasion publicitaire : concepts, méthodes et mesures. PhD Thesis, University of Rennes, Rennes.

Lambert, T. and Schwienbacher, A. (2010). An empirical analysis of crowdfunding [Online]. Available at: http://ssrn.com/abstract=1578175.

Lang, P.J. (1994). The motivational organization of emotions: Affect-reflex connections. In *Emotions: Essays on Emotion Theory*, van Goozen, S.H.M., Van de Poll, N.E., Sergeant, J.A. (eds). Psychology Press, Abingdon, Oxfordshire.

Lange, C. (1885). *Om Sinsbevaegelster : et psykofysiologiske studie.* Rasmussen, Copenhagen. Lavison, C. (2011). L'investissement socialement responsable. Report, École Polytechnique – Sciences Po Paris, Paris.

Lazarus, R.S. (1966). *Psychological Stress and the Coping Process.* McGraw-Hill Book Company, New York.

Lazarus, R.S. (1982). Thoughts on the relations between emotion and cognition. *American Psychologist*, 37(9), 1019–1024.

Lazarus, R.S. (1984). On the primacy of cognition. *American Psychologist*, 39(2), 124–129.

Lazarus, R.S. (2001). Relational meaning and discrete emotions. In *Appraisal Processes in Emotion: Theory, Methods, Research*, Scherer, K.R., Schorr, A., Johnstone, T. (eds). Oxford University Press, Oxford.

Le Heron, E. (2012). Formaliser la décision en incertitude radicale ? In *Conférence CEPN.* CEPN and Université Paris XIII, Paris.

Lebart, L. and Salem, A. (1994). *Statistique textuelle.* Dunod, Paris.

Lebraty, J. and Lobre-Lebraty, K. (2013). *Crowdsourcing: One Step Beyond.* ISTE Ltd, London, John Wiley & Sons, New York.

Lebrun, A.-M. (2002). Le rôle de la familiarité du contexte d'achat sur la tendance exploratoire et à la recherche de variété. *Revue française du marketing*, 186, 53.

Ledoux, J. (1998). *The Emotional Brain: The Mysterious Underpinnings of Emotional Life.* Simon and Schuster, New York.

Lefèvre, F. and Popescu, B.F. (2015). *Le Crowdfunding à la française.* Transvalor – Presses des Mines, Paris.

Lejeune, C. (2010). Montrer, calculer, explorer, analyser. Ce que l'informatique fait (faire) à l'analyse qualitative. *Logiciels pour l'analyse qualitative*, 9, 15–32.

Lelart, M. (2014). De la finance éthique à l'éthique dans la finance. Document, Laboratoire d'économie d'Orléans, Orléans.

Lemoine, J.-F. and Onnée, S. (2003). Vers une analyse des enjeux et des pratiques de la gestion de la relation avec l'actionnaire individuel. *Décisions marketing*, 31, 25–37.

Lemoine, J.-F. and Plichon, V. (2000). Le rôle des facteurs situationnels dans l'explication des réactions affectives du consommateur à l'intérieur d'un point de vente. *LEG – CERMAB/Centre de Recherche en Marketing de Bourgogne – Cahier de recherche*, Bourgogne.

Lesage, C. (2000). L'expérimentation de laboratoire en sciences de gestion. In *21ème congrès de l'AFC*. AFC, Angers.

Lesourne, J. (1965). *Technique économique et gestion industrielle*. Dunod, Paris.

Lewis, A. (2001). A focus group study of the motivation to invest: "Ethical/green" and "ordinary" investors compared. *The Journal of Socio-Economics*, 30(4), 331–341.

Li, J., Chen, X.-P., Kotha, S., Fisher, G. (2017). Catching fire and spreading it: A glimpse into displayed entrepreneurial passion in crowdfunding campaigns. *Journal of Applied Psychology*, 102(7), 1075–1090.

Lichtenstein, S., Slovic, P., Fischhoff, B., Layman, M., Combs, B. (1978). Judged frequency of lethal events. *Journal of Experimental Psychology: Human Learning and Memory*, 4(6), 551–578.

Lin, M. and Viswanathan, S. (2015). Home bias in online investments: An empirical study of an online crowdfunding market. *Management Science*, 62(5), 1393–1414.

Lin, M., Prabhala, N.R., Viswanathan, S. (2013). Judging borrowers by the company they keep: Friendship networks and information asymmetry in online peer-to-peer lending. *Management Science*, 59(1), 17–35.

Lin, Y., Boh, W.F., Goh, K.H. (2014). How different are crowdfunders? Examining archetypes of crowdfunders and their choice of projects. Submission 13309, Academy of Management Proceedings, Briarcliff Manor, New York.

Lindeman, M. and Verkasalo, M. (2005). Measuring values with the short Schwartz's value survey. *Journal of Personality Assessment*, 85(2), 170–178.

Linnenbrink-Garcia, L., Durik, A.M., Conley, A.M., Barron, K.E., Tauer, J.M., Karabenick, S.A., Harackiewicz, J.M. (2010). Measuring situational interest in academic domains. *Educational and Psychological Measurement*, 70(4), 647–671.

Lis, B. (2012). The relevance of corporate social responsibility for a sustainable human resource management: An analysis of organizational attractiveness as a determinant in employees' selection of a (potential) employer. *Management Revue*, 23, 279–295.

Lo, A.W. and Repin, D.V. (2002). The psychophysiology of real-time financial risk processing. *Journal of Cognitive Neuroscience*, 14(3), 323–339.

Loewenstein, G. (1987). Anticipation and the valuation of delayed consumption. *The Economic Journal*, 97(387), 666–684.

Loewenstein, G. (1999). Experimental economics from the vantage-point of behavioural economics. *The Economic Journal*, 109(453), 25–34.

Loewenstein, G.F., Weber, E.U., Hsee, C.K., Welch, N. (2001). Risk as feelings. *Psychological Bulletin*, 127(2), 267–286.

Loomes, G. and Sudgen, R. (1982). Regret theory: An alternative theory of rational choice under uncertainty. *The Economic Journal*, 92, 805–824.

Loomes, G. and Sudgen, R. (1987). Testing for regret and disappointment in choice under uncertainty. *The Economic Journal*, 97, 118–129.

Lopes, H. (2005). Utilité, normes et sentiments moraux. *Revue du MAUSS*, 25(1), 404–427.

Luhmann, N. (2001). Confiance et familiarité. *Réseaux*, 108(4), 15–35.

Lynn, D. (2012). The crowdfunding provisions of the JOBS Act. *Financial Executive*, 28(4), 42–44.

Lynn, D. and Sabbagh, H. (2012). The JOBS Act open door for crowdfunding offerings, *Morrison & Forrester Social Media Newsletter*, 4(11), 6–8.

Maalaoui, A. and Conreaux, P. (2014). *Crowdfunding : les clés du financement participatif.* Ellipses Marketing, Paris.

MacGregor, D.G., Slovic, P., Dreman, D., Berry, M. (2000). Imagery, affect, and financial judgment. *The Journal of Psychology and Financial Markets*, 1(2), 104–110.

Macmillan, I.C., Siegel, R., Narasimha, P.N.S. (1985). Criteria used by venture capitalists to evaluate new venture proposals. *Journal of Business Venturing*, 1(1), 119–128.

Macmillan, I.C., Kulow, D.M., Khoylian, R. (1989). Venture capitalists' involvement in their investments: Extent and performance. *Journal of Business Venturing*, 4(1), 27–47.

MacMullen, R. (2004). *Les émotions dans l'histoire, ancienne et moderne*. Les Belles Lettres, Paris.

Magron, C.-E. (2014). Approches comportementales de la gestion individuelle de portefeuille. Thesis, University of Strasbourg, Strasbourg.

Maio, G.R. and Olson, J.M. (1998). Values as truisms: Evidence and implications. *Journal of Personality and Social Psychology*, 74(2), 294–311.

Mangot, M. (2008). *Psychologie de l'investisseur et des marchés financiers*, 2nd ed. Dunod, Paris.

Mangot, M. (2013). 25 ans de finance comportementale ou l'émergence d'un nouveau paradigme. In *Grandeur et misère de la finance moderne*, Chambon, J.-L., Pluchart, J.-J. (eds). Eyrolles, Paris.

Manigart, S., Wright, M., Robbie, K., Desbrières, P., De Waele, K. (1997). Venture capitalists' appraisal of investment projects: An empirical European study. *Entrepreneurship: Theory & Practice*, 21(4), 29–43.

Marshall, A. (1890). *Principles of Economics*. Prometheus Books, Guilford.

Martinez, F. (2012). L'individu face au risque : l'apport de Kahneman et Tversky. *Idées économiques et sociales*, 161, 15–23.

Mason, C. and Stark, M. (2004). What do investors look for in a business plan? A comparison of the investment criteria of bankers, venture capitalists and business angels. *International Small Business Journal*, 22(3), 227–248.

Maxwell, A.L., Jeffrey, S.A., Lévesque, M. (2011). Business angel early stage decision making. *Journal of Business Venturing*, 26(2), 212–225.

Mayer, J.D., Caruso, D.R., Salovey, P. (1999). Emotional intelligence meets traditional standards for an intelligence. *Intelligence*, 27(4), 267–298.

McAllister, D.J. (1995). Affect- and cognition-based trust as foundations for interpersonal cooperation in organizations. *Academy of Management Journal*, 38(1), 24–59.

Mehrabian, A. and Russel, J.A. (1974). *An Approach to Environmental Psychology*. MIT Press, Cambridge.

Mellers, B.A. (2000). Choice and the relative pleasure of consequences. *Psychological Bulletin*, 126(6), 910–924.

Menger, C. (1871). *Principles of Economics*. Create Space Independent Publishing Platform, Scotts Valley, California.

Meyer, J.P. and Allen, N.J. (1991). A three-component conceptualization of organizational commitment. *Human Resource Management Review*, 1(1), 61–89.

Michinov, E. (2001). L'attraction interpersonnelle : un concept en évolution. *Les cahiers internationaux de psychologie sociale*, 50, 11–26.

Mill, J.S. (1882). *A System of Logic, Ratiocinative and Inductive*, 8th ed. Harper & Brothers, New York.

Miller, G.A. (1955). The magical number seven, plus or minus two some limits on our capacity for processing information. *Psychological Review*, 101(2), 343–352.

Millette, V. and Gagné, M. (2008). Designing volunteers' tasks to maximize motivation, satisfaction and performance: The impact of job characteristics on volunteer engagement. *Motivation and Emotion*, 32(1), 11–22.

Milovac, M., Sanchez-Burks, J., Baron, R.A. (2015). The psychology of crowdfunding: How mood, passion, and emotion make or break a pitch. *Academy of Management Annual Meeting Proceedings*, 1(1), 1.

Mollick, E. (2013). The dynamics of crowdfunding: An exploratory study. *Journal of Business Venturing*, 29(1), 1–16.

Mollick, E. and Nanda, R. (2015). Wisdom or madness? Comparing crowds with expert evaluation in funding the arts. Document, Harvard Business School, Boston.

Moorman, C., Zaltman, G., Deshpande, R. (1992). Relationships between providers and users of market research: The dynamics of trust within and between organizations. *Journal of Marketing Research*, 29(3), 314.

Morgan, R.M. and Hunt, S.D. (1994). The commitment-trust theory of relationship marketing. *Journal of Marketing*, 58(3), 20.

Mucchielli, A. (2005). Émotions, normes sociales, décisions et jugements. *Revue internationale de psychosociologie*, 11(25), 11–19.

Mucchielli, A. (2011). *Les motivations*. Presses Universitaires de France, Paris.

Murnieks, C.Y., Sudek, R., Wiltbank, R. (2015). The role of personality in angel investing. *The International Journal of Entrepreneurship and Innovation*, 16(1), 19–31.

Neumann, V.J. and Morgenstern, O. (1944). *Theory of Games and Economic Behavior*. Princeton University Press, Princeton.

Neveu, V. (2004). La confiance organisationnelle : définition et mesure. Document, Congrès de l'Association Française des Ressources Humaines, Paris.

Nisbett, R.E. and Wilson, T.D. (1977). The halo effect: Evidence for unconscious alteration of judgments. *Journal of Personality and Social Psychology*, 35(4), 250–256.

Nivoix, S. (2008). L'aversion au risque : pourquoi est-ce si difficile à mesurer ? *Management & Avenir*, 15, 65–78.

Nofsinger, J.R. (2001). *The Psychology of Investing*. Pearson Prentice Hall, Upper Saddle River, New Jersey.

Northcraft, G.B. and Neale, M.A. (1987). Experts, amateurs, and real estate: An anchoring-and-adjustment perspective on property pricing decisions. *Organizational Behavior and Human Decision Processes*, 39(1), 84–97.

Ochs, M. (2007). Modélisation, formalisation et mise en œuvre d'un agent rationnel dialoguant émotionnel empathique. PhD Thesis, Université Paris 8, Paris.

O'Keefe, D.J. (2002). *Persuasion: Theory and Research*. Sage Publications, Thousand Oaks, California.

Ola, A.M. (2016). L'identification des opportunités d'investissement en incertitude : le jugement intuitif des Business Angels dans le financement des firmes entrepreneuriales. PhD Thesis, University of Angers, Angers.

Olson, J. and Reynold, T. (1983). Understanding consumer's cognitive structures: Implications for advertising strategy, advertising and consumer psychology. In *Advertising and Consumer Psychology, Volume 1*, Percy, L., Woodside, A. (eds). Lexington Books, Lanham, Maryland.

Onnée, S. and Renault, S. (2014). Crowdfunding : vers une compréhension du rôle joué par la foule. *Management & Avenir*, 74, 117–133.

Ordanini, A., Miceli, L., Pizzetti, M., Parasuraman, A. (2011). Crowdfunding: Transforming customers into investors through innovative service platforms. *Journal of Service Management*, 22(4), 443–470.

Orléan, A. (2010). L'impossible évaluation du risque. *Prisme*, 18.

Ortony, A., Clore, G., Collins, A. (1988). *The Cognitive Structure of Emotions*. Cambridge University Press, Cambridge.

Osgood, C.E. and Tannenbaum, P.H. (1955). The principle of congruity in the prediction of attitude change. *Psychological Review*, 62(1), 42–55.

Osgood, C.E., Suci, G.J., Tannenbaum, P.H. (1957). *The Measurement of Meaning*. University of Illinois Press, Champaign, Illinois.

Overskeid, G. (2000). The slave of the passions: Experiencing problems and selecting solutions. *Review of General Psychology*, 4(3), 284–309.

Pare, J.L. and Rédis, J. (2011). Réorienter la recherche en finance entrepreneuriale. *Gestion 2000*, 28(4), 17–31.

Petit, E. (2013). *L'expérimentation en économie : méthode et principes fondateurs* [Online]. Available at: http://ressources.aunege.fr/nuxeo/site/esupversions/7d01faf2-0582-47bd-af37-a52852812398/co/RESS2-1_1.html.

Petty, R.E. and Cacioppo, J.T. (1984). Source factors and the elaboration likelihood model of persuasion. In *NA–Advances in Consumer Research Volume 11*, Thomas C. Kinnear, Provo (eds). UT: Association for Consumer Research, 668–672.

Petty, R.E. and Cacioppo, J.T. (1986). The elaboration likelihood model of persuasion. *Advances in Experimental Social Psychology*, 19, 123–205.

Pfister, H.-R. and Böhm, G. (2008). The multiplicity of emotions: A framework of emotional functions in decision making. *Judgement and Decision Making*, 3(1).

Pham, M.T. (1998). Representativeness, relevance, and the use of feelings in decision making. *Journal of Consumer Research*, 25(2), 144–159.

Piolat, A. and Bannour, R. (2008). Emotions et affects: Contribution de la psychologie cognitive. In *Le sujet des émotions au Moyen-Âge*, Nagy, P., Boquet, D. (eds). Beauchesne, Paris.

Plutchik, R. (1970). Emotions, evolution and adaptive processes. In *Feelings and Emotions: The Loyola Symposium*, Arnold, M. (ed.). Academic Press, New York.

Poggi, I. and Germani, M. (2003). Emotions at work. In *Conference on Human Aspects of Advanced Manufacturing: Agility and Hybrid Automation*. HAAMAHA, Rome.

Poissonnier, A. (2016). *Le financement participatif, un nouvel outil pour les entreprises*. Eyrolles, Paris.

Poncin, I. and Derbaix, C. (2009). Commercials as context for other commercials. *Journal of Advertising*, 38(3), 33–49.

Quenk, N.L. (2009). *Essentials of Myers-Briggs Type Indicator Assessment*, 2nd ed. John Wiley & Sons, Hoboken, New Jersey.

Quiggin, J. (1982). A theory of anticipated utility. *Journal of Economic Behavior & Organization*, 3(4), 323–343.

Ramsey, Y. (2012). What the heck is crowdfunding? *Business People*, 25(11), 54–57.

Reinert, A. (1983). Une méthode de classification descendante hiérarchique : application à l'analyse lexicale par contexte. *Les cahiers de l'analyse des données*, 8(2).

Rigdon, E.E. (2012). Rethinking partial least squares path modeling: In praise of simple methods. *Long Range Planning*, 45(5–6), 341–358.

Rigdon, E.E., Ringle, C.M., Sarstedt, M. (2010). Structural modeling of heterogeneous data with partial least squares. *Review of Marketing Research*, 7, 255–296.

Rimé, B. (2009). *Le partage social des émotions*. Presses Universitaires de France, Paris.

Rimé, B. (2016). L'émergence des émotions dans les sciences psychologiques. *Revue électronique du CRH*, 16.

Ringle, C.M., Wende, S., Becker, J.M. (2015). SmartPLS 3. *Boenningstedt: SmartPLS GmbH* [Online]. Available at: http://www.smartpls.com [Accessed November 2017].

Rokeach, M. (1973). *The Nature of Human Value*. Free Press, New York.

Roseman, I.J. (1991). Appraisal determinants of discrete emotions. *Cognition & Emotion*, 5(3), 161–200.

Roseman, I.J. (2001). A model of appraisal in the emotion system. In *Appraisal Processes in Emotion: Theory, Methods, Research*, Scherer, K.R., Schorr, A., Johnstone, T. (eds). Oxford University Press, Oxford.

Rosenberg, M.J. (1965). When dissonance fails: On eliminating evaluation apprehension from attitude measurement. *Journal of Personality and Social Psychology*, 1(1), 28–42.

Rosenzweig, P. (2007). Misunderstanding the nature of company performance: The halo effect and other business delusions. *California Management Review*, 49(4), 6–20.

Rousseau, D.M. (1977). Technological differences in job characteristics, employee satisfaction, and motivation: A synthesis of job design research and sociotechnical systems theory. *Organizational Behavior and Human Performance*, 19(1), 18–42.

Roy, B. (1985). *Méthodologie multicritère d'aide à la décision*. Economica, Paris.

Ruffieux, B., Rozan, A., Robin, S. (2008). Mesurer les préférences du consommateur pour orienter les décisions des pouvoirs publics : l'apport de la méthode expérimentale. *Économie & prévision*, 182(1), 113–127.

Russell, J.A. (1980). A circumplex model of affect. *Journal of Personality and Social Psychology*, 39(6), 1161–1178.

Russell, J.A. and Pratt, G. (1980). A description of the affective quality attributed to environments. *Journal of Personality and Social Psychology*, 38(2), 311–322.

Rynes, S.L. and Barber, A.E. (1990). Applicant attraction strategies: An organizational perspective. *Academy of Management Review*, 15(2), 286–310.

Ryu, S. and Kim, Y.-G. (2014). Dynamics of the crowdfunding platform: Crowdfunding participation model development and empirical analysis. *SSRN Electronic Journal*, 10.

Sadler-Smith, E. and Shefy, E. (2004). The intuitive executive: Understanding and applying "gut feel" in decision-making. *The Academy of Management Executive*, 18(4), 76–91.

Salem Khalifa, A. (2004). Customer value: A review of recent literature and an integrative configuration. *Management Decision*, 42(5), 645–666.

Salichs, M.A. and Malfaz, M. (2012). A new approach to modeling emotions and their use on a decision-making system for artificial agents. *IEEE Transactions on Affective Computing*, 3(1), 56–68.

Sander, D. and Scherer, K.R. (2014). *Traité de psychologie des émotions*. Dunod, Paris.

Sapienza, H.J. and Korsgaard, M.A. (1996). Procedural justice in entrepreneur-investor relations. *Academy of Management Journal*, 39(3), 544–574.

Sarstedt, M., Becker, J.-M., Ringle, C.M., Schwaiger, M. (2011a). Uncovering and treating unobserved heterogeneity with FIMIX-PLS: Which model selection criterion provides an appropriate number of segments? *Schmalenbach Business Review*, 63(1), 34–62.

Sarstedt, M., Henseler, J., Ringle, C.M. (2011b). Multigroup analysis in partial least squares (PLS) path modeling: Alternative methods and empirical results. In *Advances in International Marketing*, Sarstedt, M., Schwaiger, M., Taylor, C.R. (eds). Emerald Group Publishing Limited, Bingley, Bradford.

Sarstedt, M., Wilczynski, P., Melewar, T.C. (2013). Measuring reputation in global markets: A comparison of reputation measures' convergent and criterion validities. *Journal of World Business*, 48(3), 329–339.

Savage, L.J. (1951). The theory of statistical decision. *Journal of the American Statistical Association*, 46(253), 55–67.

Savage, L.J. (1954). *The Foundations of Statistics*. John Wiley and Sons, New York.

Scarbrough, H., Swan, J., Amaeshi, K., Briggs, T. (2013). Exploring the role of trust in the deal-making process for early-stage technology ventures. *Entrepreneurship Theory and Practice*, 37(5), 1203–1228.

Schachter, S. (1964). The interaction of cognitive and physiological determinants of emotional state. *Advances in Experimental Social Psychology*, 1, 49–80.

Scherer, K.R. (1993). Studying the emotion-antecedent appraisal process: An expert system approach. *Cognition & Emotion*, 7(3–4), 325–355.

Scherer, K.R. (2000). Emotion. In *Introduction to Social Psychology: A European Perspective*, Hewstone, M., Stroebe, W. (eds). Blackwell, Oxford.

Scherer, K.R. (2005). What are emotions? And how can they be measured? *Social Science Information*, 44(4), 695–729.

Schiefele, U. (1991). Interest, learning, and motivation. *Educational Psychologist*, 26(3–4), 299–323.

Schiefele, U. (2009). Situational and individual interest. In *Handbook of Motivation at School*, Wentzel, K., Wigfield, A. (eds). Routledge, New York.

Schiefele, U., Krapp, A., Wild, K.-P., Winteler, A. (1993). Der "Fragebogen zum Studieninteresse" (FSI). *Diagnostica*, 39(4), 335–351.

Schmidt, C. (2010). *Neuroéconomie*. Odile Jacob, Paris.

Schneider, B. (1987). The people make the place. *Personnel Psychology*, 40(3), 437–453.

Schram, A. (2005). Artificiality: The tension between internal and external validity in economic experiments. *Journal of Economic Methodology*, 12(2), 225–237.

Schwartz, S.H. (1992). Universals in the content and structure of values: Theoretical advances and empirical tests in 20 countries. *Advances in Experimental Social Psychology*, 25, 1–65.

Schwartz, S.H. (1994). Are there universal aspects in the structure and contents of human values? *Journal of Social Issues*, 50(4), 19–45.

Schwartz, S.H. (1996). Value priorities and behavior: Applying a theory of integrated value systems. In *The Psychology of Values: The Ontario Symposium*, Celigman, C., Olson, J.M., Zana, M.P. (eds). Psychology Press, Abingdon, Oxfordshire.

Schwartz, S.H. (2006). Les valeurs de base de la personne : théorie, mesures et applications. *Revue française de sociologie*, 47(4), 929–968.

Schwartz, S.H. (2007). Universalism values and the inclusiveness of our moral universe. *Journal of Cross-Cultural Psychology*, 38(6), 711–728.

Schwartz, N. and Clore, G.L. (2003). Mood as information: 20 years later. *Psychological Inquiry*, 14(3–4), 296–303.

Schwartz, S.H., Cieciuch, J., Vecchione, M., Davidov, E., Fischer, R., Beierlein, C., Ramos, A., Verkasalo, M., Lönnqvist, J.-E., Demirutku, K., Dirilen-Gumus, O., Konty, M. (2012). Refining the theory of basic individual values. *Journal of Personality and Social Psychology*, 103(4), 663–688.

Schwienbacher, A. (2015). Le Crowdinvesting : une nouvelle forme de finance entrepreneuriale. In *Le financement de l'innovation : nouvelles perspectives théoriques & pratiques*, Bessière, V., Stéphany, É. (eds). De Boeck, Paris.

Schwienbacher, A. and Larralde, B. (2010). Crowdfunding of small entrepreneurial ventures. In *The Oxford Handbook of Entrepreneurial Finance*, Cumming, D. (ed.). Oxford University Press, Oxford.

Shapiro, S. and Spence, M.T. (1997). Managerial intuition: A conceptual and operational framework. *Business Horizons*, 40(1), 63–68.

Sharma, D., Borna, S., Stearns, J.M. (2009). An investigation of the effects of corporate ethical values on employee commitment and performance: Examining the moderating role of perceived fairness. *Journal of Business Ethics*, 89(2), 251–260.

Shefrin, H. and Statman, M. (1985). The disposition to sell winners too early and ride losers too long: Theory and evidence. *The Journal of Finance*, 40(3), 777–790.

Shefrin, H. and Statman, M. (2000). Behavioral portfolio theory. *Journal of Financial and Quantitative Analysis*, 35(2), 127–151.

Shiller, R.J. (2000). *Irrational Exuberance*. Princeton University Press, Princeton.

Sigar, K. (2012). Fret no more: Inapplicability of crowdfunding concerns in the internet age and the JOBS Acts safeguards. *Administrative Law Review*, 2(64), 474–505.

Signol, A. (2011). La psychanalyse est-elle une science ? *Le Journal des psychologues*, 291, 54–58.

Signori, A. and Vismara, S. (2016). Returns on investments in equity crowdfunding. *SSRN* [Online], Available at: https://ssrn.com/abstract=2765488 or http://dx.doi.org/10.2139/ssrn.2765488.

Silvia, P.J. (2006). *Exploring the Psychology of Interest*. Oxford University Press, Oxford.

Simon, H.A. (1955). A behavioral model of rational choice. *The Quarterly Journal of Economics*, 69(1), 99.

Simon, H.A. (1956). Rational choice and the structure of the environment. *Psychological Review*, 63(2), 129–138.

Simon, H.A. (1987). Making management decisions: The role of intuition and emotion. *The Academy of Management Executive*, 1(1), 57–64.

Simon, É. (2007). La confiance dans tous ses états. *Revue française de gestion*, 175, 83–94.

Sinclair, M. and Ashkanasy, N. (2005). Intuition: Myth or a decision making tool? *Management Learning*, 36(3), 353–370.

Skoglund, E. and Stiernblad, M. (2013). The future of equity crowdfunding – Is "The Crowd" capable of good investment? [Online]. Available at: http://lup.lub.lu.se/luur/download?func=downloadFile&recordOId=3814918&fileOId=3814919/.

Slovic, P. (ed.) (2001). Cigarette smokers, rational actors or rational fools? In *Smoking: Risk, Perception, and Policy*. Sage Publications, Thousand Oaks, California.

Slovic, P., Layman, M., Kraus, N., Flynn, J., Chalmers, J., Gesell, G. (1991). Perceived risk, stigma, and potential economic impacts of a high-level nuclear waste repository in Nevada. *Risk Analysis*, 11(4), 683–696.

Slovic, P., Finucane, M., Peters, E., MacGregor, D.G. (2002). The affect heuristic. In *The Psychology of Intuitive Judgment*, Gilovich, T., Griffin, D., Kahneman, D. (eds). Cambridge University Press, New York.

Smith, A. (1822). *The Theory of Moral Sentiments*. J. Richardson, London.

Smith, V.L. (1962). An experimental study of competitive market behavior. *The Journal of Political Economy*, 70(2), 111–137.

Spence, M. (1973). Job market signaling. *The Quarterly Journal of Economics*, 87(3), 355–374.

Stanovich, K.E. and West, R.F. (2000). Individual differences in reasoning: Implications for the rationality debate? *Behavioral and Brain Sciences*, 23(5), 82.

Statman, M. (2002). Lottery players/stock traders. *Financial Analysts Journal*, 58(1), 14–21.

Stone, M. (1974). Cross-validatory choice and assessment of statistical predictions. *Journal of the Royal Statistical Society*, 36(2), 111–147.

Stucki, D. (2014). Financer une entreprise par le crowdfunding. *La Revue Banque*.

Sugden, R. (1991). Rational choice: A survey of contributions from economics and philosophy. *The Economic Journal*, 101(407), 751–785.

Sukiennik C. (2013). Plantin, Christian. 2011. Les bonnes raisons des émotions. Principes et méthode pour l'étude du discours émotionné (Berne : Peter Lang) ; Micheli, Raphaël. 2010. L'émotion argumentée. L'abolition de la peine de mort dans le débat parlementaire français (Paris : Le Cerf). *Argumentation et Analyse du Discours*, 11.

Taffler, R. (2014). Emotional finance: Theory and application. Document, Warwick Business School, Coventry.

Thaler, R. and Sustein, C. (2012). *Nudge*. Pocket, Paris.

Thorndike, E.L. (1920). A constant error in psychological ratings. *Journal of Applied Psychology*, 4(1), 25–29.

Thurstone, L.L. (1931). The indifference function. *The Journal of Social Psychology*, 2(2), 139–167.

Tieger, P., Barron, B., Tieger, K. (2014). *Do What You Are: Discover the Perfect Career For You through the Secrets of Personality Type*. Little, Brown Spark, New York.

Tirole, J. (2016). *Économie du bien commun*. Presses Universitaires de France, Paris.

Tom, V.R. (1971). The role of personality and organizational images in the recruiting process. *Organizational Behavior and Human Performance*, 6(5), 573–592.

Tomczak, A. and Brem, A. (2013). A conceptualized investment model of crowdfunding. *Venture Capital*, 15(4), 335–359.

Tomkins, S. (1962). *Affect Imagery Consciousness Volume I: The Positive Affects*. Springer Publishing Company, Berlin.

Trouilloud, D. and Sarrazin, P. (2003). Note de synthèse [Les connaissances actuelles sur l'effet Pygmalion : processus, poids et modulateurs]. *Revue française de pédagogie*, 145(1), 89–119.

Turban, D.B., Hendrickson, C., Forret, M.L. (1998). Applicant attraction to firms: Influences of organization reputation, job attributes, and recruiter behaviors. *Journal of Vocational Behavior*, 52(1), 24–44.

Tversky, A. and Kahneman, D. (1974). Judgment under uncertainty: Heuristics and biase. *Sciences*, 185(4157), 1124–1131.

Tversky, A. and Kahneman, D. (1992). Advances in prospect theory: Cumulative representation of uncertainty [Online]. Available at: http://cemi.ehess.fr/docannexe/file/2780/tversjy_kahneman_advances.pdf.

Tyebjee, T.T. and Bruno, A.V. (1984). A model of venture capitalist investment activity. *Management Science*, 30(9), 1051–1066.

Vaidis, D. and Halimi-Falkowicz, S. (2007). La théorie de la dissonance cognitive : une théorie âgée d'un demi-siècle. *Revue électronique de psychologie sociale*, 1, 9–18.

Valette-Florence, P. (1994). Introduction aux chaînages cognitifs. *Recherche et applications en marketing*, 9, 93–117.

Verplanken, B. and Holland, R.W. (2002). Motivated decision making: Effects of activation and self-centrality of values on choices and behavior. *Journal of Personality and Social Psychology*, 82(3), 434–447.

Vinzi, E.V., Chin, W.W., Henseler, J., Wang, H. (2010). *Handbook of Partial Least Squares: Concepts, Methods and Applications in Marketing and Related Fields*. Springer, Berlin.

Viviani, J.-L. (1994). Incertitude et rationalité. *Revue française d'économie*, 9(2), 105–146.

Voorbraak, K.J.P. (2011). Crowdfunding for financing new ventures consequences of the financial model on operational decisions. Document, Eindhoven University of Technology, Eindhoven.

Walrass, L. (1874). *Éléments d'économie politique pure : ou théorie de la richesse sociale*. Kessinger Publishing, Whitefish, Montana.

Wang, M., Keller, C., Siegrist, M. (2011). The less you know, the more you are afraid of – A survey on risk perceptions of investment products. *Journal of Behavioral Finance*, 12(1), 9–19.

Wash, R. (2013). The value of completing crowdfunding projects. In *Seventh International AAAI Conference on Weblogs and Social Media*. ICWSM, Cambridge.

Weber, M. (2003). *Économie et société, tome 1 : les catégories de la sociologie*. Pocket, Paris.

Weber, S.J. and Cook, T.D. (1972). Subject effects in laboratory research: An examination of subject roles, demand characteristics, and valid inference. *Psychological Bulletin*, 77(4), 273–295.

Wechsler, J. (2013). Know your crowd: The drivers of success in reward based crowdfunding. Document, University of Fribourg, Fribourg.

Weiner, B. and Graham, S. (1989). Understanding the motivational role of affect: Life-span research from an attributional perspective. *Cognition & Emotion*, 3(4), 401–419.

Wetzer, C. (2008). La finance comportementale, régulation des marchés financiers. Master's Thesis, Université Paris II Panthéon Assas, Paris.

Wheat, R.E., Wang, Y., Byrnes, J.E., Ranganathan, J. (2013). Raising money for scientific research through crowdfunding. *Trends in Ecology & Evolution*, 28(2), 71–72.

Wilkie, W.L. (ed.) (1990). Chapter 11. In *Consumer Behavior*. John Wiley & Sons, New York.

Wold, H. (1985). Partial least squares. In *Encyclopedia of Statistical Sciences, Volume 6*, Kotz, S., Johnson, N.L. (eds). John Wiley & Sons, New York.

Wright, P. (1975). Consumer choice strategies: Simplifying vs. optimizing. *Journal of Marketing Research*, 12(1), 60–67.

Wright, M. and Robbie, K. (1996). Venture capitalists, unquoted equity investment appraisal and the role of accounting information. *Accounting and Business Research*, 26(2), 153–168.

Wuillaume, A., Jacquemin, A., Janssen, F. (2016). L'influence du contenu émotionnel de la narration entrepreneuriale sur l'attitude et la prise de décision des contributeurs en crowdfunding. In *13ème Congrès International Francophone en Entrepreneuriat et PME*. CIFEPME, Trois-Rivières, Quebec.

Wuillaume, A., Jacquemin, A., Janssen, F. (2017). "Cher crowd, laisse-moi te raconter une histoire…" : l'influence du contenu émotionnel, du sentiment d'appartenance à la communauté et de l'authenticité de la narration entrepreneuriale sur le succès à lever des fonds via le crowdfunding. Document, Louvain Research Institute in Management and Organizations, Louvain.

Yennek, N. (2014). Contribution de l'intérêt situationnel à une reconsidération de la satisfaction dans la formation pour adultes. PhD Thesis, Université Paris Ouest Nanterre La Défense, Nanterre, Paris.

Yin, R.K. (2009). Case study research: Design and methods. *Applied Social Research Methods*, 4th ed. Sage Publications, Los Angeles.

Zajonc, R.B. (1968). Attitudinal effects of mere exposure. *Journal of Personality and Social Psychology*, 9(2), 1–27.

Zajonc, R.B. (1980). Feeling and thinking. *American Psychologist*, 1S1, 35(2), 151–175.

Zajonc, R.B. (2001). Mere exposure: A gateway to the subliminal. *Current Direction in Psychological Science*, 10(6), 224–228.

Zaleski, P.A. (2011). Start-ups and external equity: The role of entrepreneurial experience. *Business Economics*, 46(1), 43–50.

Zeelenberg, M. and Pieters, R. (1999). Comparing service delivery to what might have been. *Journal of Service Research*, 2(1), 86–99.

Zeelenberg, M., Nelissen, R.M., Breugelmans, S.M., Pieters, R. (2008). On emotion specificity in decision making: Why feeling is for doing. *Judgment and Decision Making*, 3(1), 18.

Zhao, X., Lynch, J.G., Chen, Q. (2010). Reconsidering Baron and Kenny: Myths and truths about mediation analysis. *Journal of Consumer Research*, 37(2), 197–206.

Zidi, A. (2009). Analyse de la fidélité des échelles mesurant la confiance entre le capital risqueur et l'entrepreneur et son impact dans la création de valeur : cas du contexte tunisien. Document, CERAM Business School et IAE d'Aix-en-Provence, Sophia-Antipolis.

Index

O, P

Q, R

S, T, U

V

Other titles from

iSTE

in

Innovation, Entrepreneurship and Management

2021

BOBILLIER CHAUMON Marc-Eric
Digital Transformations in the Challenge of Activity and Work: Understanding and Supporting Technological Changes (Technological Changes and Human Resources Set – Volume 3)

2020

ANDREOSSO-O'CALLAGHAN Bernadette, DZEVER Sam, JAUSSAUD Jacques, TAYLOR Robert
Sustainable Development and Energy Transition in Europe and Asia (Innovation and Technology Set – Volume 9)

BEN SLIMANE Sonia, M'HENNI Hatem
Entrepreneurship and Development: Realities and Future Prospects (Smart Innovation Set – Volume 30)

CHOUTEAU Marianne, FOREST Joëlle, NGUYEN Céline
Innovation for Society: The P.S.I. Approach (Smart Innovation Set – Volume 28)

CORON Clotilde
Quantifying Human Resources: Uses and Analysis
(Technological Changes and Human Resources Set – Volume 2)

CORON Clotilde, GILBERT Patrick
Technological Change
(Technological Changes and Human Resources Set – Volume 1)

CERDIN Jean-Luc, PERETTI Jean-Marie
The Success of Apprenticeships: Views of Stakeholders on Training and Learning
(Human Resources Management Set – Volume 3)

DELCHET-COCHET Karen
Circular Economy: From Waste Reduction to Value Creation
(Economic Growth Set – Volume 2)

DIDAY Edwin, GUAN Rong, SAPORTA Gilbert, WANG Huiwen
Advances in Data Science
(Big Data, Artificial Intelligence and Data Analysis Set – Volume 4)

DOS SANTOS PAULINO Victor
Innovation Trends in the Space Industry
(Smart Innovation Set – Volume 25)

GOGLIN Christian
Emotions and Values in Equity Crowdfunding Investment Choices 1: Transdisciplinary Theoretical Approach

GUILHON Bernard
Venture Capital and the Financing of Innovation
(Innovation Between Risk and Reward Set – Volume 6)

LATOUCHE Pascal
Open Innovation: Human Set-up
(Innovation and Technology Set – Volume 10)

MAKRIDES Andreas, KARAGRIGORIOU Alex, SKIADAS Christos H.
Data Analysis and Applications 3: Computational, Classification, Financial, Statistical and Stochastic Methods
(Big Data, Artificial Intelligence and Data Analysis Set – Volume 5)

Data Analysis and Applications 4: Financial Data Analysis and Methods (Big Data, Artificial Intelligence and Data Analysis Set – Volume 6)

MASSOTTE Pierre, CORSI Patrick
Complex Decision-Making in Economy and Finance

MEUNIER François-Xavier
Dual Innovation Systems : Concepts, Tools and Methods (Smart Innovation Set – Volume 31)

MICHAUD Thomas
Science Fiction and Innovation Design (Innovation in Engineering and Technology Set – Volume 6)

MONINO Jean-Louis
Data Control: Major Challenge for the Digital Society (Smart Innovation Set – Volume 29)

MORLAT Clément
Sustainable Productive System: Eco-development versus Sustainable Development (Smart Innovation Set – Volume 26)

SAULAIS Pierre, ERMINE Jean-Louis
Knowledge Management in Innovative Companies 2: Understanding and Deploying a KM Plan within a Learning Organization (Smart Innovation Set – Volume 27)

2019

AMENDOLA Mario, GAFFARD Jean-Luc
Disorder and Public Concern Around Globalization

BARBAROUX Pierre
Disruptive Technology and Defence Innovation Ecosystems (Innovation in Engineering and Technology Set – Volume 5)

DOU Henri, JUILLET Alain, CLERC Philippe
Strategic Intelligence for the Future 1: A New Strategic and Operational Approach
Strategic Intelligence for the Future 2: A New Information Function Approach

FRIKHA Azza
Measurement in Marketing: Operationalization of Latent Constructs

FRIMOUSSE Soufyane
Innovation and Agility in the Digital Age
(Human Resources Management Set – Volume 2)

GAY Claudine, SZOSTAK Bérangère L.
Innovation and Creativity in SMEs: Challenges, Evolutions and Prospects
(Smart Innovation Set – Volume 21)

GORIA Stéphane, HUMBERT Pierre, ROUSSEL Benoît
Information, Knowledge and Agile Creativity
(Smart Innovation Set – Volume 22)

HELLER David
Investment Decision-making Using Optional Models
(Economic Growth Set – Volume 2)

HELLER David, DE CHADIRAC Sylvain, HALAOUI Lana, JOUVET Camille
The Emergence of Start-ups
(Economic Growth Set – Volume 1)

HÉRAUD Jean-Alain, KERR Fiona, BURGER-HELMCHEN Thierry
Creative Management of Complex Systems
(Smart Innovation Set – Volume 19)

LATOUCHE Pascal
Open Innovation: Corporate Incubator
(Innovation and Technology Set – Volume 7)

LEHMANN Paul-Jacques
The Future of the Euro Currency

LEIGNEL Jean-Louis, MÉNAGER Emmanuel, YABLONSKY Serge
Sustainable Enterprise Performance: A Comprehensive Evaluation Method

LIÈVRE Pascal, AUBRY Monique, GAREL Gilles
Management of Extreme Situations: From Polar Expeditions to Exploration-Oriented Organizations

MILLOT Michel
Embarrassment of Product Choices 2: Towards a Society of Well-being

N'GOALA Gilles, PEZ-PÉRARD Virginie, PRIM-ALLAZ Isabelle
Augmented Customer Strategy: CRM in the Digital Age

NIKOLOVA Blagovesta
The RRI Challenge: Responsibilization in a State of Tension with Market Regulation
(Innovation and Responsibility Set – Volume 3)

PELLEGRIN-BOUCHER Estelle, ROY Pierre
Innovation in the Cultural and Creative Industries
(Innovation and Technology Set – Volume 8)

PRIOLON Joël
Financial Markets for Commodities

QUINIOU Matthieu
Blockchain: The Advent of Disintermediation

RAVIX Joël-Thomas, DESCHAMPS Marc
Innovation and Industrial Policies
(Innovation between Risk and Reward Set – Volume 5)

ROGER Alain, VINOT Didier
Skills Management: New Applications, New Questions
(Human Resources Management Set – Volume 1)

SAULAIS Pierre, ERMINE Jean-Louis
Knowledge Management in Innovative Companies 1: Understanding and Deploying a KM Plan within a Learning Organization
(Smart Innovation Set – Volume 23)

SERVAJEAN-HILST Romaric
Co-innovation Dynamics: The Management of Client-Supplier Interactions for Open Innovation
(Smart Innovation Set – Volume 20)

SKIADAS Christos H., BOZEMAN James R.
Data Analysis and Applications 1: Clustering and Regression, Modeling-estimating, Forecasting and Data Mining
(Big Data, Artificial Intelligence and Data Analysis Set – Volume 2)
Data Analysis and Applications 2: Utilization of Results in Europe and Other Topics
(Big Data, Artificial Intelligence and Data Analysis Set – Volume 3)

UZUNIDIS Dimitri
Systemic Innovation: Entrepreneurial Strategies and Market Dynamics

VIGEZZI Michel
World Industrialization: Shared Inventions, Competitive Innovations and Social Dynamics
(Smart Innovation Set – Volume 24)

2018

BURKHARDT Kirsten
Private Equity Firms: Their Role in the Formation of Strategic Alliances

CALLENS Stéphane
Creative Globalization
(Smart Innovation Set – Volume 16)

CASADELLA Vanessa
Innovation Systems in Emerging Economies: MINT – Mexico, Indonesia, Nigeria, Turkey
(Smart Innovation Set – Volume 18)

CHOUTEAU Marianne, FOREST Joëlle, NGUYEN Céline
Science, Technology and Innovation Culture
(Innovation in Engineering and Technology Set – Volume 3)

CORLOSQUET-HABART Marine, JANSSEN Jacques
Big Data for Insurance Companies
(Big Data, Artificial Intelligence and Data Analysis Set – Volume 1)

CROS Françoise
Innovation and Society
(Smart Innovation Set – Volume 15)

DEBREF Romain
Environmental Innovation and Ecodesign: Certainties and Controversies
(Smart Innovation Set – Volume 17)

DOMINGUEZ Noémie
SME Internationalization Strategies: Innovation to Conquer New Markets

ERMINE Jean-Louis
Knowledge Management: The Creative Loop
(Innovation and Technology Set – Volume 5)

GILBERT Patrick, BOBADILLA Natalia, GASTALDI Lise,
LE BOULAIRE Martine, LELEBINA Olga
Innovation, Research and Development Management

IBRAHIMI Mohammed
Mergers & Acquisitions: Theory, Strategy, Finance

LEMAÎTRE Denis
Training Engineers for Innovation

LÉVY Aldo, BEN BOUHENI Faten, AMMI Chantal
Financial Management: USGAAP and IFRS Standards
(Innovation and Technology Set – Volume 6)

MILLOT Michel
Embarrassment of Product Choices 1: How to Consume Differently

PANSERA Mario, OWEN Richard
Innovation and Development: The Politics at the Bottom of the Pyramid
(Innovation and Responsibility Set – Volume 2)

RICHEZ Yves
Corporate Talent Detection and Development

SACHETTI Philippe, ZUPPINGER Thibaud
New Technologies and Branding
(Innovation and Technology Set – Volume 4)

SAMIER Henri
Intuition, Creativity, Innovation

TEMPLE Ludovic, COMPAORÉ SAWADOGO Eveline M.F.W.
Innovation Processes in Agro-Ecological Transitions in Developing Countries
(Innovation in Engineering and Technology Set – Volume 2)

UZUNIDIS Dimitri
Collective Innovation Processes: Principles and Practices
(Innovation in Engineering and Technology Set – Volume 4)

VAN HOOREBEKE Delphine
The Management of Living Beings or Emo-management

2017

AÏT-EL-HADJ Smaïl
The Ongoing Technological System
(Smart Innovation Set – Volume 11)

BAUDRY Marc, DUMONT Béatrice
Patents: Prompting or Restricting Innovation?
(Smart Innovation Set – Volume 12)

BÉRARD Céline, TEYSSIER Christine
Risk Management: Lever for SME Development and Stakeholder Value Creation

CHALENÇON Ludivine
Location Strategies and Value Creation of International Mergers and Acquisitions

CHAUVEL Danièle, BORZILLO Stefano
The Innovative Company: An Ill-defined Object
(Innovation between Risk and Reward Set – Volume 1)

CORSI Patrick
Going Past Limits To Growth

D'ANDRIA Aude, GABARRET Inés
Building 21st Century Entrepreneurship
(Innovation and Technology Set – Volume 2)

DAIDJ Nabyla
Cooperation, Coopetition and Innovation
(Innovation and Technology Set – Volume 3)

FERNEZ-WALCH Sandrine
The Multiple Facets of Innovation Project Management
(Innovation between Risk and Reward Set – Volume 4)

FOREST Joëlle
Creative Rationality and Innovation
(Smart Innovation Set – Volume 14)

GUILHON Bernard
Innovation and Production Ecosystems
(Innovation between Risk and Reward Set – Volume 2)

HAMMOUDI Abdelhakim, DAIDJ Nabyla
Game Theory Approach to Managerial Strategies and Value Creation
(Diverse and Global Perspectives on Value Creation Set – Volume 3)

LALLEMENT Rémi
Intellectual Property and Innovation Protection: New Practices
and New Policy Issues
(Innovation between Risk and Reward Set – Volume 3)

LAPERCHE Blandine
Enterprise Knowledge Capital
(Smart Innovation Set – Volume 13)

LEBERT Didier, EL YOUNSI Hafida
International Specialization Dynamics
(Smart Innovation Set – Volume 9)

MAESSCHALCK Marc
Reflexive Governance for Research and Innovative Knowledge
(Responsible Research and Innovation Set – Volume 6)

MASSOTTE Pierre
Ethics in Social Networking and Business 1: Theory, Practice and Current Recommendations
Ethics in Social Networking and Business 2: The Future and Changing Paradigms

MASSOTTE Pierre, CORSI Patrick
Smart Decisions in Complex Systems

MEDINA Mercedes, HERRERO Mónica, URGELLÉS Alicia
Current and Emerging Issues in the Audiovisual Industry
(Diverse and Global Perspectives on Value Creation Set – Volume 1)

MICHAUD Thomas
Innovation, Between Science and Science Fiction
(Smart Innovation Set – Volume 10)

PELLÉ Sophie
Business, Innovation and Responsibility
(Responsible Research and Innovation Set – Volume 7)

SAVIGNAC Emmanuelle
The Gamification of Work: The Use of Games in the Workplace

SUGAHARA Satoshi, DAIDJ Nabyla, USHIO Sumitaka
Value Creation in Management Accounting and Strategic Management: An Integrated Approach
(Diverse and Global Perspectives on Value Creation Set –Volume 2)

UZUNIDIS Dimitri, SAULAIS Pierre
Innovation Engines: Entrepreneurs and Enterprises in a Turbulent World
(Innovation in Engineering and Technology Set – Volume 1)

2016

BARBAROUX Pierre, ATTOUR Amel, SCHENK Eric
Knowledge Management and Innovation
(Smart Innovation Set – Volume 6)

BEN BOUHENI Faten, AMMI Chantal, LEVY Aldo
Banking Governance, Performance And Risk-Taking: Conventional Banks Vs Islamic Banks

BOUTILLIER Sophie, CARRÉ Denis, LEVRATTO Nadine
Entrepreneurial Ecosystems (Smart Innovation Set – Volume 2)

BOUTILLIER Sophie, UZUNIDIS Dimitri
The Entrepreneur (Smart Innovation Set – Volume 8)

BOUVARD Patricia, SUZANNE Hervé
Collective Intelligence Development in Business

GALLAUD Delphine, LAPERCHE Blandine
Circular Economy, Industrial Ecology and Short Supply Chains
(Smart Innovation Set – Volume 4)

GUERRIER Claudine
Security and Privacy in the Digital Era
(Innovation and Technology Set – Volume 1)

MEGHOUAR Hicham
Corporate Takeover Targets

MONINO Jean-Louis, SEDKAOUI Soraya
Big Data, Open Data and Data Development
(Smart Innovation Set – Volume 3)

MOREL Laure, LE ROUX Serge
Fab Labs: Innovative User
(Smart Innovation Set – Volume 5)

PICARD Fabienne, TANGUY Corinne
Innovations and Techno-ecological Transition
(Smart Innovation Set – Volume 7)

2015

CASADELLA Vanessa, LIU Zeting, DIMITRI Uzunidis
Innovation Capabilities and Economic Development in Open Economies (Smart Innovation Set – Volume 1)

CORSI Patrick, MORIN Dominique
Sequencing Apple's DNA

CORSI Patrick, NEAU Erwan
Innovation Capability Maturity Model

FAIVRE-TAVIGNOT Bénédicte
Social Business and Base of the Pyramid

GODÉ Cécile
Team Coordination in Extreme Environments

MAILLARD Pierre
Competitive Quality and Innovation

MASSOTTE Pierre, CORSI Patrick
Operationalizing Sustainability

MASSOTTE Pierre, CORSI Patrick
Sustainability Calling

2014

DUBÉ Jean, LEGROS Diègo
Spatial Econometrics Using Microdata

LESCA Humbert, LESCA Nicolas
Strategic Decisions and Weak Signals

2013

HABART-CORLOSQUET Marine, JANSSEN Jacques, MANCA Raimondo
VaR Methodology for Non-Gaussian Finance

2012

DAL PONT Jean-Pierre
Process Engineering and Industrial Management

MAILLARD Pierre
Competitive Quality Strategies

POMEROL Jean-Charles
Decision-Making and Action

SZYLAR Christian
UCITS Handbook

2011

LESCA Nicolas
Environmental Scanning and Sustainable Development

LESCA Nicolas, LESCA Humbert
Weak Signals for Strategic Intelligence: Anticipation Tool for Managers

MERCIER-LAURENT Eunika
Innovation Ecosystems

2010

SZYLAR Christian
Risk Management under UCITS III/IV

2009

COHEN Corine
Business Intelligence

ZANINETTI Jean-Marc
Sustainable Development in the USA

2008

CORSI Patrick, DULIEU Mike
The Marketing of Technology Intensive Products and Services

DZEVER Sam, JAUSSAUD Jacques, ANDREOSSO Bernadette
Evolving Corporate Structures and Cultures in Asia: Impact of Globalization

2007

AMMI Chantal
Global Consumer Behavior

2006

BOUGHZALA Imed, ERMINE Jean-Louis
Trends in Enterprise Knowledge Management

CORSI Patrick *et al.*
Innovation Engineering: the Power of Intangible Networks